C. B. FRY'S MAGAZINE
OF SPORTS AND OUTDOOR LIFE

1904-1914

A History, Index and Bibliography

Chris Harte

This Book has been Published in a Limited Edition of One Hundred copies of which this is Number: **59**

[signature]

Sports History Publishing

APRIL 1904   **No 1**   SIXPENCE NET

C.B. FRY'S MAGAZINE

Coloured Cartoon: "ALFRED LYTTELTON."
By Tom Browne, R.I., R.B.A.

"PHYSICAL ENERGY" AND G. F. WATTS, R.A. By C. B. Fry.

THE BOATRACE FROM INSIDE.
1. By the Cambridge President.
2. By an Ex-President.
3. By an Ex-Cox.

ENGLAND v SCOTLAND. By J. J. Bentley.

THE GRAND NATIONAL By Alfred E. T. Watson.

DIET AND TRAINING. By G. H. R. Dabbs, M.D.

STORY. By K. and Hesketh Prichard.

EASTER AND APRIL FOR SPORTSMEN. By F. G. Aflalo.

RIGHTS AND WRONGS OF INTERNATIONAL CRICKET. By A. C. Maclaren.

MAN AND THE LIVE MOTOR. By Charles Jarrott.

"GREAT GOLFERS: THEIR METHODS AT A GLANCE."

SECRETS OF CATCH-AS-CATCH-CAN. By F. W. Ward.

EVERYDAY THINGS WE DO WRONG. By Fraulein Wilke.

SPECIAL FOOTBALL PORTRAITS.

FOR FULL LIST OF CONTENTS SEE PAGE XXIX.

LONDON: GEORGE NEWNES LTD

Sports History Publishing

First published in 2023

ISBN : 978-1-898010-17-3

Editor : Susan Lewis

Consultant Editor : Nicholas Harcourt-Hinds

Series Editor : Rupert Cavendish

Layout : Nick Beck

Contact : cavendishbibliographies@gmail.com

Sports History Publishing titles are distributed by Dodman Books from Morston Barn, The Street, Morston, Norfolk, NR25 7AA

No rights are reserved. Any part of this book may be reproduced or transmitted in any form or by any means, electronic or mechanical, including photocopying, recording or by any information storage and retrieval system without any need to get permission in writing, or other form, from the publisher.

Printed and bound in Wales

Recent Books by the Author include

Fores Sporting Notes & Sketches: A History, Index and Bibliography (2022)
Strange Stories of Sport (2021)
The Badminton Magazine: A History, Index and Bibliography (2021)
The Captain Magazine: A History, Index and Bibliography (2021)
The Sporting Mirror: A History, Index and Bibliography (2020)
Hunting in Carmarthenshire 1741-1975 (2019)
A History, Index and Bibliography of Baily's Magazine of Sports (2017)
A Season With the Carmarthenshire Hunt (2016)
Old Gold: Carmarthen Town Football Club (2013)
Watching Brief (2010)
Recollections of a Sportswriter (2009)
The History of Australian Cricket (2008)
Rugby Clubs and Grounds (2005)
English Rugby Clubs (2004)
Britain's Rugby Grounds (2003)
Australian Cricket History (2003)
Reminiscences of a Sportswriter (2002)
Menston Actually (2001)
Sports Books in Britain (2000)
Ramblings of a Sportswriter (1999)
A Year in the Sporting Pressbox (1998)
The Twickenham Papers (1997)
A Sportswriter's Year (1997)
Sporting Heritage (1996)
One Day in Leicester (1995)
A History of Australian Cricket (1993)
Cricket Indulgence (1991)
History of South Australian Cricket (1990)
South African International Cricket (1989)
Two Tours and Pollock (1988)
Seven Tests (1987)
Australians in South Africa (1987)
Cricket Safari (1986)
Australian Cricket Journal (1985)
Cricket Rebels (1985)
The History of the Sheffield Shield (1984)
The Fight for the Ashes (1983)
Cathedral End (1979)

In Preparation

A History and Bibliography
of Men Only Magazine
(to be published in 2024)

ACKNOWLEDGEMENTS

It is only right that I must thank those who have given me help and assistance in the compilation of this work. Without them I would have encountered major difficulties especially as important detail has needed to be unearthed.

Morwenna Broughton, senior librarian at the Bodleian Library in Oxford, has been a truly magnificent facilitator of information and without her support I would have struggled to get hold of the minutiae contained in the issues.

At the British Library, in London, I have been so grateful to Elias Mazzucio of the Rare Books section who cheerfully answered many of my questions and also made sure that when I visited all the documentation needed was readily available.

Mike Ashley, the noted author and bibliographer, welcomed me into his Medway home and let me examine material he had found in his vast collection of century-old periodicals. Then there has been Leeds based Phil Stephensen-Payne whose massive on-line index of authors, artists and magazines provided detail not available elsewhere.

Nearer to home Paul Morgan of Coch-y-Bonddu Books in Machynlleth has, as for my previous works, come up with information only a person of his considerable book knowledge would be aware.

* * * * *

The magazine had several names during its nearly eleven year life starting with *C.B.Fry's Magazine of Sports and Outdoor Life*. It then became *Fry's Magazine of Action and Outdoor Life; Fry's the Illustrated Magazine of Sport, Travel and Outdoor Life; Fry's Magazine of Sport; Fry's the Man's Magazine* and finally *Fry's the Outdoor Magazine*. When Fry's Magazine Limited purchased the title in 1911 it was renamed *The New Fry's Magazine* for just six issues before reverting to previously used names.

* * * * *

The publishers were George Newnes Ltd, 3-12 Southampton Street, Strand, London from issues dated April 1904 to March 1911, and printed by the London Printing Company, Exmoor Street, North Kensington. Then Fry's Magazine Ltd, Effingham House, Arundel Street, Strand, London from April 1911 until September 1912, followed by William Dawson & Sons Ltd, Cannon House, Breams Buildings, Covent Garden, London from October 1912 to October 1913. Fry's then moved to 188-189 Strand, London and took back publishing from November 1913 until the magazine's closure. The printers were Love & Malcomson Ltd, Dane Street, High Holborn.

Book Reviews Heading

Charles Fry

Walter Burton-Baldry

George Riddell

George Newnes

ISSUE INDEX

(Volumes 1 - 21, 125 issues)

Here it must be explained that the main page numbers only refer to the general text as found in the Newnes issued green binders. As was the habit with this magazine (from Issues 2 to 14) the mainly advertising pages at the beginning of each issue were given roman numerals and were not considered necessary to keep by the binders. However, there were always extra pages at the end of each issue which were, again, usually discarded. Alas, most had stories and articles in between the adverts. All of them had page numbering, which for succeeding issues would be ignored and the pages would revert back to the end of the previous issue. For example, an issue would have text from pages 1 to 96, then adverts and text to page 128. The next issue would then start at page 97. All of this extra material has been included as well as, on a few occasions, a note of the illustrator of a specifically designed advertisement. All this ceased when Fry's Magazine Limited took over control from the beginning of Volume 15 (New Series Volume One).

* * * * *

1	Issue 1 - April 1904	(p1-132)
	Issue 2 - May 1904	(p133-256)
	Issue 3 - June 1904	(p257-380)
	Issue 4 - July 1904	(p381-508)
	Issue 5 - August 1904	(p509-628)
	Issue 6 - September 1904	(p629-748)
2	Issue 7 - October 1904	(p1-120 + 4)
	Issue 8 - November 1904	(p121-232 + 12)
	Issue 9 - December 1904	(p233-352 + 16)
	Issue 10 - January 1905	(p353-468 + 20)
	Issue 11 - February 1905	(p469-572 + 24)
	Issue 12 - March 1905	(p573-668 + 32)
3	Issue 13 - April 1905	(p1-104 + 36)
	Issue 14 - May 1905	(p105-200 + 40)
	Issue 15 - June 1905	(p201-298 + 30)
	Issue 16 - July 1905	(p299-392 + 36)
	Issue 17 - August 1905	(p393-488 + 36)
	Issue 18 - September 1905	(p489-584 + 32)
4	Issue 19 - October 1905	(p1-96 + 36)
	Issue 20 - November 1905	(p97-192 + 36)
	Issue 21 - December 1905	(p193-288 + 48)
	Issue 22 - January 1906	(p289-388 + 44)
	Issue 23 - February 1906	(p389-484 + 40)
	Issue 24 - March 1906	(p485-580 + 48)
5	Issue 25 - April 1906	(p1-96 + 60)
	Issue 26 - May 1906	(p97-192 + 56)
	Issue 27 - June 1906	(p193-288 + 44)
	Issue 28 - July 1906	(p289-384 + 48)
	Issue 29 - August 1906	(p385-480 + 36)
	Issue 30 - September 1906	(p481-576 + 36)

Cecil Hughes

Ralph Hodgson

William Clarry

Wallis Myers

6	Issue 31 - October 1906	(p1-96 + 36)
	Issue 32 - November 1906	(p97-192 + 40)
	Issue 33 - December 1906	(p193-296 + 48)
	Issue 34 - January 1907	(p297-392 + 32)
	Issue 35 - February 1907	(p393-504 + 40)
	Issue 36 - March 1907	(p505-608 + 52)
7	Issue 37 - April 1907	(p1-112 + 48)
	Issue 38 - May 1907	(p113-208 + 48)
	Issue 39 - June 1907	(p209-304 + 44)
	Issue 40 - July 1907	(p305-400 + 44)
	Issue 41 - August 1907	(p401-496 + 48)
	Issue 42 - September 1907	(p497-592 + 32)
8	Issue 43 - October 1907	(p1-96 + 36)
	Issue 44 - November 1907	(p97-192 + 36)
	Issue 45 - December 1907	(p193-288 + 56)
	Issue 46 - January 1908	(p289-384 + 36)
	Issue 47 - February 1908	(p385-480 + 32)
	Issue 48 - March 1908	(p481-576 + 32)
9	Issue 49 - April 1908	(p1-96 + 44)
	Issue 50 - May 1908	(p97-192 + 44)
	Issue 51 - June 1908	(p193-288 + 40)
	Issue 52 - July 1908	(p289-384 + 48)
	Issue 53 - August 1908	(p385-480 + 36)
	Issue 54 - September 1908	(p481-576 + 40)
10	Issue 55 - October 1908	(p1-96 + 44)
	Issue 56 - November 1908	(p97-192 + 40)
	Issue 57 - December 1908	(p193-288 + 64)
	Issue 58 - January 1909	(p289-384 + 48)
	Issue 59 - February 1909	(p385-480 + 40)
	Issue 60 - March 1909	(p481-576 + 48)
11	Issue 61 - April 1909	(p1-96 + 60)
	Issue 62 - May 1909	(p97-192 + 76)
	Issue 63 - June 1909	(p193-288 + 72)
	Issue 64 - July 1909	(p289-384 + 68)
	Issue 65 - August 1909	(p385-480 + 64)
	Issue 66 - September 1909	(p481-576 + 48)
12	Issue 67 - October 1909	(p1-96 + 52)
	Issue 68 - November 1909	(p97-192 + 52)
	Issue 69 - December 1909	(p193-288 + 64)
	Issue 70 - January 1910	(p289-384 + 44)
	Issue 71 - February 1910	(p395-480 + 56)
	Issue 72 - March 1910	(p481-576 + 52)
13	Issue 73 - April 1910	(p1-96 + 64)
	Issue 74 - May 1910	(p97-192 + 64)

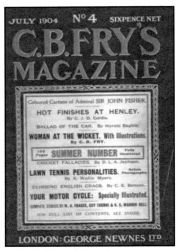
Issue 4

Issue 5

Issue 6

Issue 7

Issue 21

Issue 23

	Issue 75 - June 1910	(p193-288 + 64)
	Issue 76 - July 1910	(p289-384 + 56)
	Issue 77 - August 1910	(p385-480 + 48)
	Issue 78 - September 1910	(p481-576 + 52)
14	Issue 79 - October 1910	(p1-96 + 48)
	Issue 80 - November 1910	(p97-192 + 40)
	Issue 81 - December 1910	(p193-288 + 48)
	Issue 82 - January 1911	(p289-384 + 24)
	Issue 83 - February 1911	(p385-480 + 20)
	Issue 84 - March 1911	(p481-576 + 32)
15	Issue 85 - April 1911	(p1-120)
	Issue 86 - May 1911	(p121-240)
	Issue 87 - June 1911	(p241-368)
	Issue 88 - July 1911	(p369-488)
	Issue 89 - August 1911	(p489-600)
	Issue 90 - September 1911	(p601-720)
16	Issue 91 - October 1911	(p1-120)
	Issue 92 - November 1911	(p121-240)
	Issue 93 - December 1911	(p241-384)
	Issue 94 - January 1912	(p385-504)
	Issue 95 - February 1912	(p505-624)
	Issue 96 - March 1912	(p625-748)
17	Issue 97 - April 1912	(p1-136)
	Issue 98 - May 1912	(p137-280)
	Issue 99 - June 1912	(p281-416)
	Issue 100 - July 1912	(p417-552)
	Issue 101 - August 1912	(p553-688)
	Issue 102 - September 1912	(p689-820)
18	Issue 103 - October 1912	(p1-136)
	Issue 104 - November 1912	(p137-272)
	Issue 105 - December 1912	(p273-416)
	Issue 106 - January 1913	(p417-528)
	Issue 107 - February 1913	(p529-648)
	Issue 108 - March 1913	(p649-768)
19	Issue 109 - April 1913	(p1-120)
	Issue 110 - May 1913	(p121-240)
	Issue 111 - June 1913	(p241-368)
	Issue 112 - July 1913	(p369-504)
	Issue 113 - August 1913	(p505-640)
	Issue 114 - September 1913	(p641-776)
20	Issue 115 - October 1913	(p1-136)
	Issue 116 - November 1913	(p137-272)
	Issue 117 - December 1913	(p273-408)
	Issue 118 - January 1914	(p409-544)

Issue 25

Issue 26

Issue 27

Issue 28

Issue 29

Issue 30

Issue 32

Issue 33

Issue 34

Issue 119 - February 1914 (p545-672)
Issue 120 - March 1914 (p673-808)

21 Issue 121 - April 1914 (p1-136)
Issue 122 - May 1914 (p137-276)
Issue 123 - June 1914 (p277-412)
Issue 124 - July 1914 (p413-540)
Issue 125 - August 1914 (p541-668)

FRY'S THE OUTDOOR MAGAZINE.

EDITED BY C. B. FRY.

THE APRIL NUMBER OF FRY'S MAGAZINE NOW ON SALE HAS A MOST INSTRUCTIVE ARTICLE ON "CYCLING DANGERS AND HOW TO AVOID THEM," AND MANY OTHER FEATURES INTERESTING TO ALL OUTDOOR MEN AND WOMEN.

PRICE SIXPENCE NET.

Magazine Advertisement

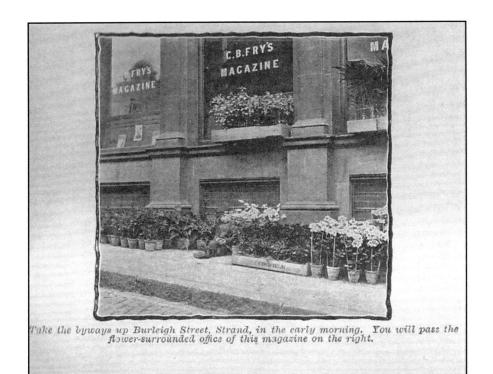

Take the byways up Burleigh Street, Strand, in the early morning. You will pass the flower-surrounded office of this magazine on the right.

Fry's Offices

A FALL IN THE PRODUCE MARKET
(Just outside our office, too.)

Outside the Office

INTRODUCTION

Charles Burgess Fry (1872-1956) was born in Croydon, the eldest son of a civil servant who was a clerk at New Scotland Yard. Following preparatory school in Chislehurst, during which time he played for both St.Mary Cray and West Kent Cricket Clubs, Fry won a Scholarship and started at Repton School in September 1885.

In his six years there his remarkable endowment of body, mind and personality dominated his generation. He spent four years in the first eleven cricket team, being captain in his last two; took charge of the football team and twice won the individual athletic prize. Before he left Repton he had been selected to play for the Casuals in the Football Association Cup and he also played cricket for Surrey a week after his schooldays were over.

Sport, however, did not monopolise his school interests: he enjoyed the classics; was an active member of the debating society, and was good enough to pass the Oxford scholarship examinations for both Trinity and Wadham Colleges. This success put paid to his idea of joining the Indian Civil Service.

Fry also travelled before arriving at University. He spent time in France (in the company of an American, Miss Sproull) where he found time for ice-skating; lectures at the Sorbonne and frequent visits to the Cafe St.Michel which was frequented by Georges Clemenceau, Claude Monet and Emile Zola.

The archaic past of Oxford's Colleges were being swept away when Fry arrived and he was fortunate to join Wadham, a place which provided more than enough elegance and intimacy. As a comparatively small college it had few cliques, a strong sense of community and a pressing need to find new players for its sports teams.

Fry more than fulfilled his promise. In his first term he won his blue for association football and that winter gained a full international cap for England. In April 1892 he won the long jump against Cambridge creating an English amateur record. In cricket he added a third blue with a century against Somerset. Only an injury prevented him from gaining a fourth blue as a wing three-quarter in rugby union.

After gaining his degree he spent two years on the staff at Charterhouse School but found sporting journalism a field in which he could enjoy writing and, at the same time, gave him more opportunity to play first-class cricket. He left teaching and by the summer of 1899 was picked to open the batting for England against the Australians.

Fry was not a novice at writing. He had written about sport while at Repton and did so more fully as an undergraduate using the pen-names of *Centurion, Spheroid* and *Pastor*. He provided *Isis* with articles on cricket, football and rugby as well as contributing the section on *Public School Cricket* for the 1894 edition of *Wisden Cricketers' Almanack*. He also became the main cricket columnist for *The Badminton Magazine of Sports & Pastimes* from its first issue in August 1895. Fry then started to receive commissions from the editors of other publications (particularly from John Corlett of *The Sporting Times*) such as the *New Review, Athletic News, Windsor Magazine, Lloyd's News, Daily Chronicle, Daily Express* and the *Westminster Gazette*.

However, it was Fry's close connection with George Newnes and his magazines which launched him into a thirteen year involvement with the companies' publications which only ended after the publisher's death. The association began when Newnes decided to launch 'A Magazine for Boys & Old Boys' which he called *The Captain*. The first issue stated quite firmly: "This magazine is crammed with stories, articles, pictures, photographs and funniments. It is ideal for boys at school and those who have left school. It has practical articles every month by C.B.Fry."

Newnes had conceived a magazine which would reflect the lives of 'respectable boys and old boys.' He decided to use new procedures of photographic reproduction throughout the publication all of which were copied extensively in the twentieth century. He added writers who were 'acknowledged authorities and real sporting heroes,' which was a completely new

Issue 36

Issue 37

Issue 38

Issue 40

Issue 47

Issue 48

Issue 55

Issue 56

Issue 58

technique in soliciting readers. Fry would continue this style in his own magazine.

Newnes knew who he wanted as editor. Warren Bell was poached from the *London Evening News* where he had been strongly influenced by Kennedy Jones, his first editor. Jones had adopted the style and concerns of the New Journalism. Short stories, puzzles, more illustrations, extended sports coverage and competitions, all of which made the newspaper extremely popular. Bell, and then Fry, would do the same with their magazines.

Fry had contributed to Newnes newspapers and magazines so was not unknown to the publisher. However, it was Warren Bell's brother John Keble Bell (who wrote under the pseudonym Keble Howard) who urged the appointment of Fry to *The Captain*. Bell, who had been at Worcester College in Oxford, was a great admirer of Fry at the time he was at Wadham College and knew he would be a success.

As the 'Athletics Editor,' Fry's first effort was titled *How to Train for Sports* and was accompanied by Fitzner Davey's engraving of Leslie Ward's caricature of Fry as an athlete. Warren Bell promoted his star recruit in glowing terms: 'Here is the finest athlete Oxford ever turned out showing the soundness of his brain-piece by writing for the first issue of *The Captain* as neat an article as you could wish to read. No padding, straightforward, nervous, clean English: Thinks out an idea, expresses his views on it and gets on to his next point in a way that all contributors to magazines should mark and digest.'

Before long, Fry's contributions became one of the cornerstones of the magazine and as a result his value to the Newnes organisation duly increased. Warren Bell paid him £10 for his first article later making it £20. Realising that other publishers could poach him Fry was offered, and accepted, a much more lucrative contract but on the condition he confined his magazine work to Newnes' publications. His £800 a year was an enormous sum by the standards of the time.

This did not, however, prevent him from writing for newspapers where editors and sub-editors did not appreciate much of his submitted copy. Jimmy Catton, when editor of the *Athletic News*, had a difficult relationship with Fry. He felt that Fry often scorned him, finding difficulty in appreciating that a professional and experienced newspaper man could actually disagree with the copy presented. After one lengthy article had been submitted by telegraph at huge cost (Fry having forgotten to ask for the discounted newspaper rate) the association was terminated. Catton recalled: "The article might as well have been written and posted the previous Christmas." Subsequently Fry moved to the newly created *Daily Express*.

Keble Bell realised after a time that *The Captain* needed to broaden its appeal to attract a wider audience. Sport was a popular item in some of the magazines but none were purely just on the subject. George Newnes, a man whose finger was always on the pulse of popular opinion, shared this view which Bell had been unable to convince his editor brother to follow. Newnes decided to launch another publication to fill this gap: he had a hugely successful track record and some highly experienced staff but needed someone who knew about sport.

Fry later wrote: 'Sir George sat me down in an office chair with an assistant editor and an office boy and left the whole thing entirely to me.' He had no experience of publishing and now had to plan, found, design and edit a new magazine.

By complete coincidence Newnes was visited the following day by Wallis Myers the amateur tennis player and journalist. His idea, put to Newnes, was that "of producing a sporting companion to the highly popular *Strand* magazine." The reply shook Myers: "You are a day behind the fair," Newnes told him. "I have already asked Charles Fry to be the chief of a new sports publication, but he is looking for an assistant."

Issue 61

Issue 69

Issue 72

Issue 73

Issue 82

Issue 83

Issue 84

Issue 85

Issue 86

Myers accepted the post of an Assistant Editor and remembered: "A while later I was present at a novel form of magazine conception. A dummy issue was mapped out on the wall. There were paper squares for the various branches of sport and these were changed and shifted about by an architect whose athletic agility did not require the use of a ladder." What Myers had witnessed was the layout concept Warren Bell was using for *The Captain* in the offices one floor below.

Fry was heavily involved in every aspect of the magazine's production; from designing its layout to dealing with printers; from planning its contents to writing many of the articles himself. Myers recalled: "He put almost superhuman energy into the new venture during the months before its launch."

Fry's high hopes of receiving a large number of unsolicited but perfectly useable articles from amateur writers did not come to pass, unlike at *The Captain* where such stories flooded in. He also had a problem when some of his early efforts at commissioning pieces met with little success. This meant that in the early days many articles were written in-house.

Some years later the then office boy, William Clarry, looked back on those early days. He had worked on the publication from the first issue to the last and had been considerably impressed by both the quality and quantity of Fry's contributions. Clarry said: "He was a brilliant writer who contributed hundreds of thousands of words a year."

The magazine buying public were impressed by Fry's first issue with Newnes praising the distinctiveness and originality of his work. Myers recalled: "The office was one of the liveliest places in London. Had we kept a visitor's book the juvenile autograph hunter would have been in clover. The burly form of Gilbert Grace occasionally filled the doorway. Ranji came once in a fur coat, and, though a big fire heated the room, wore it throughout his visit."

Leading up to the first issue Fry announced: "Our aim is to be the popular magazine of outdoor life. A publication of general interest, readable by everyone, carrying fresh air and the outdoor into the home; and yet one that deals expertly and with authority on all the various branches of sports, pastimes and recreative action."

At around the same time, in early 1904, another tennis player, Eustace Miles was discussing the possibility of a new magazine of sport with Eugen Sandow (real name Friedrich Muller) the noted bodybuilder. Sandow had produced a *Magazine of Physical Culture* since July 1898, along with editor Howard Spicer, but sales were declining and his publisher, Francis Game, was starting to lose money on the project. They decided to approach Fry, knowing of his connection with Newnes, and received a response from the latter: "We must not go in for the propaganda of a cult." The idea went no further.

Arthur Wallis Myers (1878-1939), the son of a missionary, had a background in sport but soon moved into journalism joining the *Westminster Gazette* before linking up with Fry. In 1909 he joined *The Daily Telegraph* but also had time to edit the *Ayers Lawn Tennis Almanack* and for twenty years was the lawn tennis editor of *The Field*.

Myers was followed as Fry's Assistant Editor by Cecil Eldred Hughes (1875-1941) an author and artist who contributed to *Punch* and, according to Fry, could produce admirable sketches. He, in turn, was followed by Bertram Atkey (1879-1952) who, in later years, became a popular fiction writer, using mainly the pseudonyms of J.Bird and Judson Bolt. Another Assistant, who became the Art Editor, was the poet Ralph Hodgson (1871-1962) who, at one time, confronted by a blank eighth of a page inserted a small half-tone block of a rabbit, more or less in the air, with a caption 'An Evening Nibble.' There was no evidence that the rabbit was eating or to be eaten, nor was there any hint of evening. Nevertheless this small item became repeated many times and was often spoken about.

The last Fry's Assistant-Editor was Walter Burton-Baldry (1888-1940) who eventually had a successful career on the Stock Exchange in the City of London. He took over the Editor's post from Fry in April 1911 and was also a Director of Fry's company. Another who was in the office was George Henry Roque Dabbs (1846-1913) a medical man who had left his practice on the Isle of Wight in 1903 to become the editor and proprietor of *My Journal*. After disposing of his publication

MR. C. B. FRY ON TOUR

Fry's Sketch

he became a magazine writer and worked part-time at Newnes' but never held a high opinion of Fry. In 1912 he wrote: "I fear that CB will always be a plougher of the lonely furrow. He lacks the art of hiding his disdain of that incomplete preparation which makes all his cricket so solemn and profoundly dutiful a thing. He was a sort of Kitchener of the crease."

As mentioned, the office boy was William Clarry who eventually rose to an editorial position on *Strand* magazine. A further sub-editor was Aubrey Gentry who went on to become the business director of *Cassell's*. The Sales Manager was William Beadle while William Irving-Hamilton became the Advertisement Manager, and after the closure in August 1914 founded a successful advertising agency in New York.

One of the contributors to the first issue, Lancing schoolmaster and Tottenham Hotspur footballer, Alan Haig-Brown, observed that the magazine's novelty lay in the manner in which it combined the practical and idealistic dimensions of sport. He wrote: "One saw at once that the periodical struck a new note in regard to matters of sport. It was to stand side by side with sport in the sphere of thought." This opinion proved correct for in no time circulation had passed the one-hundred thousand mark and was enjoying some enthusiastic support.

Moreover, Fry's Magazine started to attract quite a number of advertisements and, intriguingly, many of them featured the editor. His name, signature and image advertised a wide range of products which included cocoa and horsehair friction gloves. In addition to carrying advertisements the pages promoted the merits of numerous items in its columns; particularly those written by Fry.

As well as making money from advertising, Fry was being paid for writing about the football and cricket matches in which he played. He had soon firmly established himself as the most prolific cricketer-journalist in Britain. In addition he both edited and contributed to various sporting books and manuals.

After a quiet start issue eight appeared with a section entitled *Straight Talk* in which Fry made comment on whatever appeared to be on his mind at the time. He started by remarking about the number of lady readers who had taken out subscriptions then wrote about a letter he had received from one of them in France.

Then came his thoughts on newspapers. "Perhaps the amount of space devoted to sport and games in the daily press creates an impression that the public has a bloated interest in these subjects. The truth is that a morning journal which devotes a page to football, and a paragraph to a naval battle, does so because it has heaps of information about the clubs and next to nothing about the battle. Moreover, sporting events take place during the day and are over before dark so the news which comes in about them arrives in good time and is very easy to handle."

In issue nine he stated: "We are always very keen to hear from our readers. A magazine is not thrown aside like a newspaper: it stays on the table for a month and is read by others than its original purchaser." Readers were then invited to comment on anything they had read.

It was in this issue (page 247) that Fry gave away the fact that there were extra pages at the end of each issue which were not available in the Newnes produced bound volumes. At the conclusion of a general news feature he wrote: "The attention of our readers is specially directed to *Expert Opinion* on various branches of outdoor life, which will be found at the end of each number. Also, *Latest From Headquarters*, a new feature of immediate concern to members of organisations governing popular games." However, neither the volume's Index nor the issue itself carried these, or any other, articles.

Right at the finish of his *Straight Talk* section (page 352), Fry hints at a reason for this strange turn of events. With a heading which read *Our New Features*' he wrote: "The new features, included last month, '*Expert Opinion* and *The Referee's Room*, have turned out very popular with our readers."

"We find it a great advantage to print these features with the end pages, because these go to press nearly three weeks later than the main body of the magazine; we gain three weeks, so to speak, in up-to-dateness. Indeed, we are contemplating extending this convenient arrangement."

For reasons which were never explained the Newnes organisation had made a decision to make

Issue 87

Issue 88

Issue 89

Issue 90

Issue 111

Issue 112

Issue 113

Issue 114

Issue 115

the numbering of the pages of each month's issue notionally ninety-six and multiples thereafter. Some month's pagination ran to a further seventy-six pages but these were discarded (sometimes in mid-article) to allow for a common size when the half-yearly volumes were bound in cases supplied by the company.

To give an example: Volume Five has 576 pages in any bound volume. The six magazines concerned had a total of 856 pages of which 280 were discarded. The type-setters were instructed to start the pagination of each issue as 1, 97, 193, 289, 385 and 481 to make a total of 576 pages per volume.

This meant, as Fry correctly said, that each magazine could be set and printed with any additional pages added at the last minute. This method lasted until 1911 and changed to normal binding once Fry's financial backers had purchased the magazine from Newnes and became their own publishers.

However, this method of binding had attracted complaints as soon as the second volume was received by readers who had sent their issues to be bound by Newnes-approved binders. The July 1905 issue contained a number of criticisms with a Devon subscriber stating: "I see that you wish your readers to offer any suggestions they may have. 'From Headquarters,' 'Expert Opinion' and other articles are very good but when we have our volumes bound we have to lose all these pages."

"Now I think this is a pity because the pages are full of useful information, especially those of Dr Dabbs. Could you not put all the advertisements at the end of the magazine?"

In reply Cecil Hughes went off at a complete tangent, not replying to the question but moaning about the cost of the magazine's production. He talked about the price of "producing a magazine like Fry's with its picture cover, its profusion of illustrations, most of which have to be exclusively obtained, and its expert articles by leading men in their line: not to mention the heavy expenditure on paper, the price of printing so many extra thousand copies per month and binding them up."

Twisting the Devonian's words, Hughes added: "If he wants no advertisements at all then he must be prepared to see on the bookstall a magazine very inferior from both the production and literary point of view to that which he now so zealously supports."

The question about losing many rear pages each issue was left unanswered. This meant a shoal of further letters of complaint to the office which were noted in the following month's issue, without any reasonable explanation being given. The matter was then ignored.

The seemingly chaotic way the magazine was being run was made clear just before Christmas 1905 when the New Year issue was published. The previous month the Newnes produced *Strand* had carried detail of a *Fry's* competition regarding finding out the real name of the author of a forthcoming serial. In the *Strand* blurb, Fry himself had written about the author.

Fry's own magazine, the January 1906 issue, contained a virtual full-page block, in large type, headed "An Apology." The final two paragraphs read: "Mr C.B.Fry is sorry to say that owing to the name of the author becoming public in an unforeseen way, the competition must be withdrawn." It concluded with: "Mr Fry hopes that anyone who buys his magazine on account of this advertised competition will forgive his mistake."

In later life Fry's mental health would deteriorate. However, the signs of these problems were being laid bare in the page after page ranting in his end of issue columns. They started showing in mid-1905 with his views about training, fitness and the need for every man to be able to shoot. He made some astonishing comments about "the rural brain" and how "countrymen and women" were "utterly unconscious of their surroundings."

He went on to talk about "the insanity of oversanity," adding: "I know that insanity is proved to be on the increase among us. It's another lamentable fact." He finished with "I believe that kissing has been said to be an unhealthy custom and a hotbed of engendered disease," concluding with "civil war rages over the merits and demerits of porridge."

Two months later he devoted nearly four pages in giving his readers instructions as to how to train for going on holiday suggesting that the month of July should be used as training time. "The July evenings are light," he wrote. "The July half-holidays are long. Think of the swimming, boating and walking that might be got through, in gradually increasing spells until, by the end of

Issue 116

Issue 117

Issue 118

Issue 119

Issue 120

Issue 121

Issue 122

Issue 123

Issue 124

four weeks, we are hard and keen, and ready for an ordinarily athletic good time."

"We need schools to teach us how to enjoy ourselves. Half of us are hopeless dunces in the art and deserve stools of repentance and fool's caps. Let us start an *Academy of Enjoyment*. Society would flock to it until it was firmly established."

As each month progressed so Fry's diatribes varied from the obscure to being plainly ridiculous. By late 1905 he was suggesting that boots should not be worn and that "one would then need to take such steps in the natural and original way of walking to get the full and unchafed enjoyment out of it." In the same article he ridiculed the wearing of gloves and hats!

His views became more and more extreme especially in a three-issue series titled *The Blot on English Games*. The articles had little to do with games and contained suggestions such as the rounding up of inner-city male youths to be shipped off to Canada to work on farms; natural mobilisation and the suggestion of creating 'baby farms.' It was then only the start of the cricket season, which saw him infrequently in the office, which saw his writings diminish.

The one thing Warren Bell had taught Fry was that American magazines, their writers and illustrators in particular, were streets ahead of the staid productions coming from other British publishers. Wallis Myers, on his tennis travels, had brought back numerous examples of the lively titles which now adorned American bookstalls. Fry then made contact with some North American writers and illustrators and their contributions started to make an impact by the beginning of the third volume.

Artists such as Michael Bracker, Walter Enright, Urquhart Wilcox and Harry Williamson were added to the other transatlantic names of Louis Berneker, Charles Bull, Thomas Fogarty, Philip Goodwin, William King, Henry Raleigh, Charles Sarka, Frederick Strothmann and Allen True. All were new to British readers and their impact was such that by the end of 1905 circulation had risen to over two-hundred thousand copies per issue.

Fry tried to take some of the glory in a puff section hidden among the advertisements. Titled *Talk Of The Office*, he eulogised the fact that his idea of having cover pictures: "... which are not mere pictorial devices for attracting attention but have proved a success and have increased our circulation." He went on: "Have you noticed that the panel-design of our covers enable you to cut off the magazine title and have the lower panel mounted and framed and so secure a first-rate coloured picture printed on expensive art paper?" What the illustrator, Thomas Browne, thought of this is not recorded.

Fry continued: Our Portrait Gallery has developed astonishingly. In fact it has overflowed outside the windows of our office causing quite a number of passers-by to cease passing by in order to examine our window display."

The fresh writing also played its part in attracting new readers. The humour of Joseph Cone; the sports writing of Arthur Duffey; the Canadian adventures stories of William Fraser and the contributions of Ladbroke Black, Cyrus Brady, George Fitch, Ruth Havens, Charles Roberts and Herman Viele plus the war correspondent reports by Frederick Palmer added to the spice.

Fry did not let up in his trans-Atlantic push and wrote a piece titled *Read The Advertisement Pages*. "An editor of an American magazine declares his advertisement pages are a monthly liberal education. It is a mistake not to study your advertisement pages carefully, because they are useful in telling you up-to-date news of the latest developments in the interesting paraphernalia of outdoor life, as well as much else besides."

By the beginning of 1906, with no readers letters worth printing, Fry started stepping up his various thoughts and opinions in *Straight Talk*. He seemed to have little understanding of those who were not as athletic or educated as he considered himself to be and could not understand why the government did not introduce conscription for the working classes.

He had previously wondered why these type of people had never had rifle training (ignoring the fact that the cost would have been prohibitive) stating how "it would give them a chance of a journey out of Gutterland." Fry also encouraged the poor "to consider juvenile emigration in order

FREE. To the Readers of C. B. Fry's Magazine.

A Presentation Photograph of
Mr. C. B. FRY.

This is the latest photograph of Mr. C. B. Fry, and has been taken specially for this presentation. It is **Cabinet size**, on plate-sunk mount, and with Mr. Fry's facsimile signature. Mr. C. B. Fry has kindly consented to allow us to make this offer to our customers and the readers of Fry's Magazine.

One of these beautiful photographs will be given to every purchaser of our

Personal Greeting Christmas Cards.

These Cards are the most fashionable, the most popular, and most convenient form of Christmas Greeting. Beautifully printed and embossed with the Senders' Name, Address and Monogram, from 2/- per dozen, post free. Readers of C. B. Fry's Magazine are requested to fill up the following form, and send to us as soon as possible.

To Messrs. SHARP WALKER & Co., Holborn Bars, London, E.C.

In accordance with your announcement in C. B. Fry's Magazine, please send me your Sample Book of Personal Greeting Christmas Cards (post free), which I will return in due course.

Name..

Address..

....

....

Address to **Messrs. SHARP WALKER & Co.,**
HOLBORN BARS, LONDON, E.C.

to give rising generations of the cities a fair glimpse of what lies beyond."

To back up these convictions, he quoted at length from: "A London head teacher who had declared that two generations of London life means deterioration." Fry then added: "See him smoking and playing in the streets, full of suppressed insolence and taking his ideas upon the subject of manliness from men whose language, habits and points of view have been fixed in the mould of the undesirable by a boyhood spent in town in their own turn." On and on he droned before turning to the subject of 'The English-Speaking Alien.' This was followed by a number of paragraphs on 'Natural Mobilisation,' followed two months later by 'The Dignity of Natural Selection.'

This came to a head in February 1906 when the revered Frederick Roberts (Earl Roberts of Kandahar), who was probably one of Britain's finest ever military leaders, came out in support of Fry. In an article, 'British Bushido,' Roberts stated about "a call to patriotic duty" and how "it is vitally important that skill in the use of the rifle be made a national habit."

The racism and class distinction perpetuated by Fry would be totally abhorrent in our modern times yet his views found solid support around the country. For the rest of the life of the magazine these undercurrents were never too far away with supporting stories and articles printed on a regular basis.

The magazine began to lose direction towards the latter part of 1906. Each issue had more photographs and a black and white inside cover picture came between the advertisements and articles. Some of the stories reflected the humour of the times and have worn badly. In particular the serials titled Cobbeldick of Wam-Wam and Diary of a Honeymoon, the latter of which ran on under different headings.

In the November 1906 issue Fry, in an piece headed *The Editor Says*, wanted, yet again, to stamp his views quite firmly on the readership. He commented: "One aim of an Outdoor and Sporting Magazine should, I think you will agree, be the acquistion and maintenance of authority. That is to say, its contributors on special subjects should be, as far as possible, men and women who have done things and not writers whose knowledge is collected at second or third hand."

"At any rate, that is the ideal which this magazine holds in view and does its best to achieve. We in the office are rather stern critics of our results and have often been disappointed with numbers which our readers have been kind enough to approve of. We are rather hopeful that we shall not be disappointed with future issues."

However, the circulation of the magazine was still acceptable to the Newnes organisation while Fry's income, from articles and advertisements, and added to his salary made him quite prosperous. Not only did he and his wife have a twenty-five room mansion in Hampshire but it was staffed by a number of servants.

Always simmering under the surface of Fry's writings was his self-belief in his own opinions and the fact that his fame and fortune would not create any criticism or disagreement of any kind. Therefore his complete shock and horror at being criticised in the *Sporting Life* resulted in a long-winded and self-justifying editorial in his January 1907 issue.

He wrote: "A few weeks ago at the request of the Warden of the Browning Settlement in Walworth, I went and gave an address on *The Value of Sport*. The main point I made was how mistaken is the idea that field sports and games are in any way incompatible with success in business, a high standard of conduct, or the best kind of religion. Stress was laid upon the value of popular games. Finally, I pointed out that some people erroneously condemn sport as a bad influence, simply because they mistake the parasites of sport for sport itself. The evils of excessive drinking and of systematic gambling, especially when they occur in connection with popular sport, were explained."

"But how was I to know that the *Sporting Life* was present at a Sunday gathering of young men in Walworth? It was, though. The column it devoted next morning to the address represented me as a virulent opponent of football who told how football is honeycombed with drink and undermined by gambling with suitable sensational headlines. I fact, I was represented as having talked unmitigated

July 1904

Magazine Publicity

nonsense."

"Of course, letters poured in upon the *Sporting Life* from all the usual crew and were duly published. Most of them were concerned with criticising me for something I never went near saying: they were nearly all quite irrelevant. Indeed, the *Sporting Life*, after receiving and publishing my denial admitted the correspondence was irrelevant."

The *Sporting Life* editor, William Will, who had been appointed to the position in order to 'tidy up' the poor reporting and sensationalism which had crept into the paper under his predecessor had obviously failed to control his sub-editors. Fry continued his comments with: "I wish, moreover, that the representative had been an Irishman. Irishmen have humour. For the *Sporting Life*, in the final stages of its gallop, said that in any case Mr Fry had brought this trouble on his own head, for evidently he is too nervous to be able to control his tongue. He actually, in all seriousness, made the ridiculous statement that the position of President of the Football Association is the most important in the country. Argument curdles; speech is frozen; the pen splutters."

Fry then appeared to calm down somewhat, adding: "I fancy the *Sporting Life*, which is an excellent and authoritative paper, was doing a little leg-pulling. But the provincial press was pleased to copy and I was bombarded with letters telling me of the hypocrisy of conducting a magazine which upholds sport of the right kind as a fine pursuit, and of misconducting my speech at Walworth by decrying all sport. No man is safe against headlines." He concluded by reprinting an American newspaper headline which read: 'C.B.Fry Murders a Referee.'

By now it was becoming apparent that Fry was spending more time on matters other than his magazine. Articles from him decreased in number and editorials, under various guises, seemed to be rushed with little attention paid to detail. He was still advertising various products with his smiling countenance glowing from the pages. Also creeping in were, what are now called, advertorials where what seems to be a story turns out to be nothing more than a paid advertisement. Prominent were those for insurance and tobacco.

The magazine was now publishing many more stories from Canada and America, some of which were being illustrated by prominent artists. Whether these were being lifted from overseas publications or were commissioned is unknown, yet some of them can be found by research although in some cases the title heading has been changed.

With Wallis Myers also away for the summer months playing tennis, a laziness appears to creep into the makeup of each issue. As had happened with some declining publications the serialisation of book extracts filled pages where there were no fresh articles to use. In early 1910, Robert Surtees' character Mr Jorrocks occupied pages in a number of issues having previously first seen the light of day in 1838 and 1843.

With George Newnes still in control of the company, Fry must have felt secure in his fiefdom. He had business matters, other than cricket, to take much of his time even more so his naval training ship in Hampshire. It seems he was unaware of the growing influence of George Riddell around the boardroom table.

Newnes had invited Riddell to become a director of his company in 1903 having been impressed by the former solicitor's move into newspaper ownership. He had turned *The News of the World* from near bankruptcy into a profitable weekly publication and had been advising Newnes accordingly. By 1906, Riddell was virtual head of the firm adding both *Country Life* and *John O'London's Weekly* to its stable

He kept a close eye on the company's various magazines and was privately expressing concern about Fry, his views, and his lack of attendance at the office. A Liberal, by political persuasion, Riddell found the opinions being championed to be excessive and continual, but while Newnes was chairman there was little he could do about the problem.

Vanity was something Fry had in many forms. In between his cricket and editing the magazine he, and his formidable wife Beatrice, wrote a novel titled *A Mother's Son*. Newnes book department declined to publish so Fry eventually got Algernon Methuen to add it to his list of titles. As Methuen

 Charles Adair-Dighton
 Edwin Arnold
 Frederick Aflalo

 George Abraham
 James Atlay
 Mary Amherst

 Reginald Arkell
 Algernon Blackwood
 Armiger Barclay

later said: "I used to publish the mediocre in order to be able to publish the things which I valued such as the facsimile reprints of the Connoisseur's Library."

Fry did not see his novel in this light and took half a page in his issue of December 1907 to state: "So many of our readers have expressed disappointment that the novel was not to be serialised in this magazine that we have ventured to include an episode from it."

Therefore a story appeared with the title *In the Shadow of Buskett Steeple* and concerned a horse running in a Hunt Cup event. The following month another extract *The Gordon Cup* appeared with the sub-heading of 'Another Incident from *A Mother's Son*. By now the publishing house of Methuen were losing patience with Fry as his contract with them contained the serialisation rights, a fact he had blatantly ignored. It took a strong word from his friend Edward Lucas on behalf of the firm which rather cooled Fry's enthusiasm.

Another incident which reared up in early 1908 concerned an article written in the *Badminton Magazine* by Sir Home Gordon. Titled *The Past Cricket Season*, in it Gordon had expressed his views over a number of things particularly the refusal of fifteen players to tour Australia as well as the fitness of older county cricketers.

Home Seaton Charles Montagu Gordon (1871-1956) had an impeccable pedigree. As well as being a journalist and author, he was chairman of the publishing firm of Williams & Norgate; he had numerous cricket books to his name; was President of both the London Club Cricketers' Conference and Sussex County Cricket Club; wrote many articles for *Encyclopedia Britannia* and was in high demand for contributions from magazine editors especially *The Cricketer* where he had a monthly column.

Fry (who was one of the fifteen) took immediate umbrage with the points of view stated and let off steam in his *Sportsman's View Point* columns. He did not agree with Gordon that the best England team manager would have been Lord Martin Hawke; he found it abhorrent that a formerly versatile aging bowler could be said to "lack perseverance;" that a fast bowler "had an unsound leg;" that an all-rounder had been "ordered" to stand down from a Test match and that fourth choice captain Reginald Foster "was deficient in handling the bowling."

Fry then received a detailed reply from Gordon which he printed in the March 1908 issue along with his own comments which spread over thirteen pages! Gordon's opening paragraph stated: "In a signed editorial in *Fry's Magazine* the editor made an attack, as undignified as it was inaccurate, upon me as the writer of an article upon cricket. I am replying in the earliest available issue in order to show the correctness of all my statements. I shall address myself mainly to the question of fact. The unquestionably bad taste of the tone of the article can be left to the judgment of readers after perusing some of the extracts cited."

To each of Gordon's points Fry replied, but the main point of the spat was Fry's sensitivity to being criticised. As Gordon wrote: "Eminence in batting can make no man an autocrat of criticism on cricket, nor does it give the right to dictate opinions either to other judges or to the public. My reply is to an onslaught made not with the rapier of argument, but with the bludgeon of reckless virulence."

The crunch points came in Gordon's article when he wrote about Fry's low scores for England; "spectator's being rude to Fry at Canterbury;" and stating "nothing can derogate from the fame of Mr C.B.Fry yet on each of the four occasions I saw a display of feebleness with the bat that would not have given a colt a further trial." Gordon then commented that Fry and Walter Brearley had been selected to play for England to fulfil the (unwritten) quota of amateur players in the representative team.

One could imagine Fry foaming at the mouth at this comment. His reply was: "If this is a reflection upon the Marylebone Cricket Club Committee, I should like to know what right has Home Gordon to criticise their procedure?" He added: "I should like to point out the bad taste of publishing the order of selection which is a private matter assumed to be known only to the selectors. He should regard such matters as private."

Arthur Bettinson

Bernard Bosanquet

Claude Benson

Cyrus Brady

Ellis Butler

Francis Burrow

George Beldam

George Brann

Harold Begbie

Gordon concluded his defence by quoting all of the newspapers, journals, books and magazines in which he had written about the game. He listed his editorial work and finished with: "What an enormous amount of ignorance I must have disseminated if Mr Fry is to be believed."

By the Spring of 1909, Charles Fry was spending most of his time on his training ship *Mercury* and giving little attention to his editorial duties. His ranting had ceased with the March issue and Cecil Hughes took the reins. Within a short time, however, the vigour and energy sapped from the pages and articles and stories were being reprinted from other publications. One story appeared the same month in another English magazine (with no change to the title) while the pages of the American *Cosmopolitan* were culled for snippets. In October 1910 a story about Morocco, written by Lawrence Harris was reprinted exactly as it had appeared two months previously in New York.

Advertorials were increasing in number with Eugen Sandow taking eight pages in the October 1910 issue which also contained text on health foods, cigarettes and insurance, a total of fifteen pages out of one hundred and forty-four.

However, Fry's position still looked secure so long as he had the support of George Newnes. On 9 June 1910, Newnes died and George Riddell took charge of the company. Fry was asked to attend a meeting with the new board of directors with Riddell stating that it was their view that Fry should pay more attention to the magazine which bore his name. In addition Fry's editorial control would be limited and no further opinionated paragraphs would be allowed unless he had received approval.

By Christmas of 1910 things had got to a head with Riddell presenting Fry with an ultimatum: the *Mercury* or the magazine. Financially Fry might have chosen to stay but with his wife's considerable income being used to support the ship, and to the directors' surprise, Fry resigned from the editor's position. This meant that for the first time since its launch the magazine was Fry's in name only.

It was arranged that the March 1911 issue would be his last in charge. What was completely unexpected was a black-boxed, heavy type announcement on the final main text page of that month's issue. It read: *Notice To Our Readers*. "Owing to the termination of the agreement between Messrs George Newnes Limited, the publishers of this magazine, and Mr C.B.Fry, the publication will cease with this issue." It would be solicitor Cuthbert Frederick Corbould-Ellis along with Walter Burton-Baldry, a former editor of *Ouseley's Magazine*, who had strong connections to the London Stock Exchange, who would come to the rescue.

The New Fry's Magazine was on the bookstalls exactly six weeks after the final Newnes produced edition. Considerable work had been done to get new advertisers; a few of the former backroom staff had moved to the new venture, while Charles Fry had obtained articles from some of his influential friends. The page numbering reverted to a normal magazine format and although the issue and volume numbering started again it was not long until it was changed back to reflect the old style.

Lord Birkenhead (Frederick Smith, Fry's Oxford University contemporary) had the lead story, with others from Sir Edward Grey, Desmond Shaw and Robert Blatchford, none of whom had written before for Fry. Alas, Fry himself wrote a eulogising piece on politician Horatio Bottomley without accepting that he had already been charged with fraud and would later serve a lengthy prison sentence.

Strangely the Editorial was placed on the inside back cover. Titled, *Of More Than Passing Interest*, it lauded the new production. "With this issue of *Fry's Magazine* commences a new series, and the journalism of out-of-doors meaning a new era. We believe that every reader of this number will recognise and welcome the new spirit of enterprise which animates its pages; forthcoming numbers will prove that their interest was not vainly extended."

"Entirely unique essays into the literature of sport and the open-air world will be made by men and women who have achieved wide name and fame in other walks of life. Earnest of this will be found in the arresting article which opens these pages. On the other hand, names entirely new

 Hilaire Belloc
 James Bazley
 James Braid

 Ladbroke Black
 Lilian Bland
 Mattias Bodkin

 Ray Baker
 Raymond Blathwayt
 Rex Beach

but worthy of wide recognition among our readers will compete for celebrity with a large staff of already well known writers in every branch of honourable sport."

After a few more paragraphs of puffery the article concludes: "With regard to illustrations, no pains will be spared to make our pages the Mecca of all who seek the first, freshest and best from the camera and the artist."

Naturally, the Editorial for the following month (May 1911) was full of praise about letters sent in by readers. "It is an often repeated saying in Fleet Street that each person who troubles to put a pen to enthusiasm aroused by any new enterprise in journalism represents a solid thousand others."

"If there is any truth in the axiom then, indeed, if we judge from the pile of letters we have received from far and wide, each and all expressing content and pleasure in the first number of the new issue, we may well feel that our future is laid out along an ever lengthening path of roses."

With the next issue the title had been changed. *To Our Readers* started with: "We sometimes wonder whether anyone would guess at all near the mark if we offered a prize for the nearest shot at the number of letters we receive in any one month. These letters mount up a number which would be scarcely credited."

"Lately we have had more letters than ever of a kind we are very glad of. Letters expressing satisfaction and pleasure at the contents of recent numbers of the magazine. There seems a pleasant unanimity that the magazine is more interesting than ever before."

At the end of the fourth issue of the new series (July 1911) the editorial had been replaced with *Special Note to our Readers* in which it became plainly obvious that there had been very few defections from the Newnes organisation to the new magazine. Illustrators were, in the main, freelance but it was the shortage of writers which was hitting home. The previous issues had seen two stories lifted from the *Journal of the Royal Society of Arts* and another from *The Captain*.

The plea stated: "Our attention has over and over again been drawn to the fact that there are numberless men and women amongst our readers who, while not being professed authorities upon sports and games, are yet possessed of mines of specific information which could with advantage to themselves and us be opened to the general body of our readers."

"Many a time we have met amateurs of sailing craft, trout streams, setters and a score of like interests who, thanks to a special eye of observation coupled with the power of expressing what they see, held one spellbound for an hour with matter often enough outside the ken of the professed expert."

"It occurs to us, then, to extend a general invitation to such of our readers to offer contributions from the stores of their knowledge to the editorial pages of this magazine."

Things ran fairly smoothly for the next few numbers although it was quite apparent that illustrators were not of the previous variety. In issue nine (ninety-three of the correct numbering) the artist Oscar Larum produced a montage titled *Some Well-Known Hunting Men*. It was an innocent page of sketches of people from a selection of hunts. However, those from the Belvoir Hunt took exception and in the next issue a note appeared, in strong bold type, which read: *A Regret:* Walter Burton-Baldry wrote: "We are much disturbed to learn that the drawing of Sir Gilbert Greenall in our December number has given pain to Sir Gilbert's family. We wish to give publicity to our sincere regret that the drawing has appeared in our pages. The Editor."

This, of course, had no effect on the editorial staff who decided to prepare a self-praise article for the end of the January 1912 issue. With the heading *As Others See Us* the introduction, in capital letters, ran: "Nothing has afforded the Proprietorship of *Frys Magazine* more genuine pleasure and satisfaction than the knowledge that the leading London and Provincial Press have so generally and lengthily quoted and reviewed the articles which have appeared in the magazine during the last few months. Not only have many hundreds of press notices and scores of individual columns appeared but we have in many instances been favoured by leading articles. From our readers, too, in all parts of the world."

This lead to an extract from a reader's letter which said: "I have six or seven different magazines each month but *Fry's* is the only one I keep and have bound. The sporting illustrations are good and

Stacey Blake

Thomas Bridges

Walter Buckmaster

Warren Bell

William Beach-Thomas

Arthur Croome

Hall Caine

Charles Chetwynd-Talbot

Ernest Coussell

the reading matter is most interesting. Especially I like the new *Fry's*."

Following this letter came quotes from other publications. *The Times* had: "In Fry's magazine the articles are well informed and sensible, and make for the right objects; further papers are wisely written in this well-conducted magazine." *The Sportsman* noted: "A very entertaining number," while *The Field* said: "An unusually interesting number." *The Shooting Times* commented: "It contains several articles of far more than ordinary interest," with the *Review of Reviews* noting: "It brings with it not a whiff but a breeze of open air pleasures."

Provincial newspapers added their views. The *Leicester Mercury* had: "All kinds of sport are dealt with by competent writers and the illustrations leave nothing to be desired," with the *Edinburgh Evening News* agreeing: "It contains articles on a fine variety of sporting subjects." The *Cromer Post* wrote: "It takes us on tour over the world of sport," with the *Leeds Mercury* saying: "A breezy and altogether delightful number." In the *Glasgow Evening Times* the reviewer said: "This popular sporting miscellany makes a wide appeal," while the *Western Daily Press* had: "It contains, as usual, a number of well written articles on various phases of sport."

The article was now picking up steam with quotes coming from the *Midlands County Chronicle* which said: "Votaries of sports are all catered for in the well written pages of this magazine," with the *Bournemouth Directory* adding: "It contains a number of articles of more than ordinary interest; all tastes are catered for, and all are finely illustrated." The *Belfast Newsletter* said: "It is, again, an excellent number," with the *Manchester City News* adding: "Copious illustrations and topical articles place this magazine in a unique place among the many monthlies on the market." The *Glasgow News* had: "It maintains the high level of interest readers have come to look for in this monthly," with the *Lowestoft Weekly Standard* adding: "It is exceedingly good."

But it was the *Midland Counties Herald* which summed things up. It printed: "There is not a page in this sporting monthly which does not bear evidence of careful editorial supervision. The illustrations which embellish nearly every page are of general excellence and no sporting library can be regarded as complete without *Fry's Magazine* being included among its periodicals."

Had those who researched and prepared this self-laudatory piece seen the reviews in newspapers in New Zealand (particularly), Australia, India and South Africa then it would have run to many more pages.

Nine months later the editorial staff were at it again. This time it was an article headed: *The Editor's Chair*. In it, Walter Burton-Baldry waffled about "looking to the public for support through the written and illustrated pages." He added: "Even an editor is not without his susceptibilities and it is a matter of keen personal interest to him as the representative of his magazine to know what the public think concerning the journal which he presents to them from time to time."

"Almost the only means he has of keeping his finger on the pulse of his readers is by carefully watching what their representatives, the general Press, say concerning it. If we, of Fry's, may judge by the almost universal chorus of approval bestowed upon us by the vast body of Metropolitan and Provincial journals, which review our pages from month to month, we may modestly but confidentially hope that we are well on the way towards producing an ideal Magazine of Sport, Travel and Outdoor Life."

"For instance here are a few extracts from long reviews selected at random. *The Shooting Times*: 'It is impossible to mention even by name half the attractive contents of this well illustrated magazine.' *The Glasgow Daily Herald*: 'Fry's has the customary wide variety of subjects. In addition there are all the usual odds and ends that go to make Fry's a most interesting magazine for readers.' *The Observer*: 'The magazine contains a series of exceptionally interesting contributions.' *The Glasgow Evening Times*: 'All branches of sport and outdoor life are generously catered for in Fry's, the excellent all-the-sports monthly.' *The Mid-Counties Express*: 'Excellent reading for the sportsman is provided in Fry's with a great variety of subjects receiving expert treatment.' *The Sporting Life*: 'This issue of Fry's is a particularly strong number with an admirable array of informative articles covering a remarkably wide range of sport.'"

Ernest Crawley

Eugene Corri

Harding Cox

Hylton Cleaver

Jean Conneau

John Corlett

Joseph Cone

Laurence Cade

Lucia Chamberlain

All this praise did not stop Burton-Baldry from adding a boxed, bold-type statement at the end of this issue. Encouraged by his new publishers William Dawson and Sons, who were expanding the publishing side of their business, it read: "We wish to make it known to our readers and also to our contributors that we are always prepared to consider any manuscripts with a view to separate publication. We have unique facilities for publishing any books or pamphlets on sport of any kind and should be pleased to report on any work submitted to us; or to afford an interview to any of our readers desiring to publish any work coming within our scope."

By late 1912, the balance of the magazine had changed considerably from that of its early days. Gone were regular articles on popular sports such as rugby, football, racing and cricket. In their place came contributions on cats, dogs, rabbits, donkeys and ponies. It must be presumed that the editor was both an angler and a golfing person for these subjects started to dominate the pages of each issue. Therefore it was no surprise to see a boxed advertisement placed in the early pages of the magazine which had the heading: *To Our Readers*: It read: "In this number of the magazine we have several specially illustrated articles. Out of our many thousands of readers there will be a great number who may wish to draw the attention of a friend or friends to the contributions on sport, games, animals and fish. For this purpose we are inserting at the end of the magazine two postcards which we hope out readers will make use of."

The cards, coloured with a red background, were little more than subscription offers. There appeared to be a slight panic in this approach as the magazine was widely known but since Charles Fry had been side-lined it had certainly lost its zest and ability to be controversial. In fact, some of the issues had become routine and somewhat predictable. Something had to change otherwise readership would dwindle and costs would overtake income.

The first few numbers of 1913 indicated that the editor and his assistants had lost the direction the magazine originally had taken. Regular articles were trimmed to a single column and placed on the final pages of each issue. Golf was the only sport which seemed to gain extra pages while the concentration of stories on pets and seemingly irrelevant full-page photographs would have left a reader somewhat confused. As the Fry's office was on the same floor as *Universe*, a Catholic newspaper ("articles from non-Catholics not accepted"), it might be wondered if its editor Dunbar McConnell was supplying some of this 'wholesome' photographic copy.

The appeal for stories from the public resulted in three-hundred word pieces with ludicrous pseudonyms given in place of proper names. Some were easily identified as coming from writers attached to other magazines but others saw the light of day in just a single number. The lifting of stories from American periodicals had virtually ceased as had the paid-for advertorials. As the rumours of potential war in Europe gained momentum so Fry's magazine was slowly grinding its way to its finale. By the issue of May 1913, no illustrators were being used; animal stories were proliferating, and Charles Fry's animus, Home Gordon, was providing articles.

However, this did not stop Burton-Baldry carrying on with his aim to create a golf tournament based on the counties in and around London. He had used previous issues to put forward the idea under the heading of *The Social Side of Golf*, and had in tow Endersly Howard, the well-known golf writer. Thirty-nine year old Robert Endersly Mansfield Howard had a good pedigree: he had a golf column in the *Daily Mail*; wrote regularly for *The Sportsman* and *Golf Illustrated*; was the editor of *World of Golf*; had golf books published, and was based nearby at 151 Fleet Street.

The place chosen for the meeting was the historic Anderton's Hotel six doors along from Howard's office. It was held on the evening of 9 April 1913 with delegates attending from far and wide. Twenty-one County Golf Associations were represented and they listened as Burton-Baldry put forward a proposal for the institution of a tournament open to the Counties. After some discussion the matter met with unanimous favour and then rules were framed from a draft which was circulated.

Naturally the competition would be called 'The Fry's Challenge Trophy' with the cup and twenty-five guineas going to the victors. Pulling the rabbit out of the hat, Burton-Baldry then announced to

Ludovick Cameron

Roy Cohen

Thomas Carruthers

William Cadby

Albert Dorrington

Arthur Duffey

Bernard Darwin

Bonnycastle Dale

Frederick Duquesne

acclaim that the Schweppes company had presented a one-hundred guinea Gold Challenge Cup for the winners who, if they won it three years in succession, would keep the trophy.

The match play event would be played on Home Counties courses by amateur players with other rules being those generally accepted for such events. A committee was formed with Edward Leman (better known for the sport of rifle shooting) in the chair and eight county representatives. Endersly Howard was elected as secretary having also offered the use of his office for any future committee meetings.

The first meeting of the Executive Committee took place in early May where some of the rules were amended and preliminary round venues decided. In his notes Howard commented: "There have been inquiries as to whether ladies should be allowed to be represented. It would be admirable to see the fair sex but as the event is to be decided under handicap, and the standard of handicapping is so different in men's clubs from that which obtains in ladies clubs, such a pleasure is impossible. But why should not the gentler sex have a similar tournament all to themselves?"

The June 1913 issue appeared with a striking multi-coloured front cover illustrated by Alfred Leete. Gone was the dull purple border with a sketch in the centre of Diana, the virginal Roman goddess of the hunt which had been used for over two years. Although golf still dominated, the subjects of the main articles were more varied and written by experienced people. Near to the end of the number came two pages titled *Editorial*: Walter Burton-Baldry wrote: "For some considerable time we have been considering the advisability of a monthly editorial in the magazine. The present issue is an opportune moment for the innovation as we have somewhat revised our policy. We shall have a different pictorial cover every month. Fry's will, as always, be a magazine of sport. We shall use our best endeavour to appeal to sportsmen and women, and we shall be grateful for information and suggestions from our readers in any and every part of the world."

He continued by running through the sports and writers to be featured in future issues. There were also quotes used from newspapers and other journals referring to their "unconscious advertising of Fry's." Quietly slipped in was the fact that Charles Fry would now be returning to contribute regularly and that "no one in this country is more qualified to speak on subjects as Mr Fry. His views will gain attention all over the world, besides which, such straightforward statements of opinion cannot fail to gain the admiration of the public."

The editorial concluded with the news that one of the *Fry's Magazine Cups* [presumably for golf, but left unsaid] had been won by the Aldwych Club, with another presented to Melvill Jamieson, a journalist on the staff of *The Montreal Star* newspaper.

This news would have come as a surprise to virtually every reader for nowhere in any past issues had any mention been made of any trophies of any kind; what they might be for; what competition needed to be entered and for what sport or sports.

Shortly afterwards, in the issue for September 1913, it was announced that "Fry's Magazine Limited will shortly be publishing *Success at Golf* with an introduction by Endersly Howard; over one-hundred action photographs from Humphrey Joel; and hints for the player of moderate ability by Harry Vardon, George Duncan, Alexander Herd, Wilfrid Reid, Lawrence Ayton, Jack White and Thomas Ball."

The blurb went on to describe the various chapters of the book, finishing: "With a copy you can perfect your game at home at a cost of just one shilling. We are printing a huge first edition [it was a print run of 10,000 copies] but it is certain to be sold out. Therefore, if you are wise, you will send us a postal order for one shilling and twopence to our office and we will send you a copy post free directly the book comes from the press."

George Dabbs

Henry Dudeney

James Dwyer

Maud Drummond

Desmond Shaw

Thomas Dale

Walter de la Mare

Nicholas Everitt

Selwyn Edge

The start of the final year of the life of the magazine began with yet another puff from Walter Burton-Baldry about the quality of the contents and what other people thought of them. No other periodicals of the time have been noted as being so insecure of themselves that they had to devote editorial space to self-praise and qualification of their contents. Admittedly Fry's had drifted quite a considerable way from its impressive start of being a magazine devoted to all sports with the early excellent essays being replaced by somewhat dull stories many of which would have had little interest, except to those absorbed with golf.

Issue 114, for September 1913, devoted appreciable space to the Editor's comments. It was headlined *Concerning Fry's Magazine* and read: "You, good reader, buy your Fry's month by month. You read it, I hope, with interest, and then you lay it aside with, perhaps, a word of commendation for the excellence of the contents. Does it ever occur to you that there is a vast amount of energy expended, and trouble taken, month by month, to produce this magazine."

"Fry's is vastly different to the ordinary fiction monthly, which can be prepared a long time ahead with comparatively little trouble. Fry's is essentially topical; each month's issue must deal with the sports of the month and they must be penned by those who are in a position to speak with authority. Have you considered this fact and its relation to this magazine?"

"The point is that I only hear from about 2% of my readers; the average sportsman hates writing letters; and so I have to take for granted the approbation of the vast majority by the fact that they continue to purchase the magazine monthly. It is, therefore, with a feeling of gratification, that I append herewith a few extracts from the Press concerning our last issue."

"They are but a few of the hundreds of tributes we received from our contemporaries throughout the country. And with it, is it necessary for me to add that my services are always at your disposal?"

The article then goes on to quote from fourteen publications many of which give the impression of the writers having read just the Table of Contents or, at most, having glanced through the pages. *The Observer* said: "The number is an exceedingly good one," with *The Scotsman* noting: "It is an especially bright and readable issue." *The Westminster Gazette* commented on the single fiction story with the *Aberdeen Free Press* mentioning the need to study the diagrams of cycle-car defects. The others picked up on the single, or half-page, pieces on the popular sports but said nothing on the main features of climbing, camping, motor-polo, canine ailments, men's clothing, poems or of two writers reminiscing about their recent holidays.

A month later came the news that the offices in Effingham House, Arundel Street had been vacated and that new premises had been leased on the first floor of 188-189 Strand, a building about fifty yards away. Announced in the magazine with a blazing headline reading *Just A Moment*, the news was given in capital letters.

"Owing to the recent rapid increase in the sales of Fry's Magazine, and the growth of our advertisement and publicity departments, we have found ourselves compelled to obtain much larger premises. We have, therefore, removed the whole business of Fry's Magazine of Sport to the Strand (next to W.H.Smith & Son). All communications for the editorial, advertisement and publicity departments should therefore be sent to our new address."

Much of this should be taken with a pinch of salt as Cuthbert Corbould-Ellis and Walter Burton-Baldry had been discussing with Charles Fry the possibility of raising finance through various possible methods. Admittedly advertising in the magazine had shown a slight increase but the main publicity had been either through reviews in other publications or posters situated mainly on railway station concourses. None of the autobiographies of the main people involved with the magazine refer to any large rise in circulation at this time. The move was probably connected with the publishers, William Dawson & Sons, giving notice that they did not wish to continue in their role. Therefore, new publishers had to be found with those situated in Bream's Building [a London street housing many publishing companies] showing no interest.

The next issue contained a full page blurb headed *Two Points of View*. There were sections which were marked Editorial and Advertising: the first being a comment piece in the *Belfast Evening Telegraph*, written by Thomas Moles, the leader writer, which detailed the contents of

George Fitch

Jack Fairfax-Blakeborough

John Freeman

Mary Fair

Raoul de Frechencourt

William Fraser

Arthur Guiterman

Claude Grahame-White

Edward Grey

the September number concluding with: "It is surely a bill of fare sufficient to satisfy the most exacting in the matter of sporting pabulum. In addition to these, there are several excellent stories and pictures galore."

The second was a letter sent in by Claude Harper who wrote: "About seven months ago I inserted an advertisement in your magazine about my new system of physical education. The result being that I have received enquiries not only from all parts of the world but even as lately as this week they are still coming in from that same advertisement." Harper concluded by stating that he would advertise again.

The issue for Christmas 1913 had an article in the preliminary pages with the heading: *To the Readers of Fry's Magazine*. It was written by William Beadle, the Sales Manager, and took up a whole page. In it he was discussing the subject of food beverages and it can only be presumed it was an advertorial paid for by certain importers and manufacturers.

There are some very strange references in the text. The second paragraph read: "Cream costs more than skimmed milk; oysters cost more than cockles; skilled labour costs more than unskilled. But the lowest price does not often mean the cheapest. A manufacturer is very much like a workman. He gets the lowest price he can. If his article isn't worth more he must be content with a lower price. Your draper doesn't give you a yard of silk with every twenty yards of calico you buy because he sells his calico at its intrinsic value. I don't think I need say more on that point."

He makes reference to food which "is so much more popular among the industrial classes; those that have to work hardest for a living." The penultimate paragraph of this most strange piece continues in the same vein. "Among the great industrial classes of this country - the miners, the railroaders, the weavers and spinners, the ironworkers, the potters - those who must make the weekly earnings go furthest, who must keep fit and strong and able to work, then a place of honour is held among the food beverages."

What relevance this has in a sporting magazine produced for a completely different type of person, basically the clerical, business, military and landed classes, is a matter of conjecture. Has it anything to do with getting the masses fitter for the war that seemed inevitable? Certainly Charles Fry had been calling for some years for his countrymen to become fitter and more skilled in matters such as rifle shooting and physical training. Whatever the answer, it was an article completely out of place and unexpected in a magazine such as Fry's.

In the same number Walter Burton-Baldry wrote an editorial, dated 12 November 1913, which had the title *To Our Readers*. It said: "With the issue of this number, and the closing of 1913, we are saying goodbye to the tenth year of our existence. We are not saying goodbye to these ten years with any feeling of regret, for we can look back at our record with the feeling that we have made a little corner for ourselves, and one that we can call our own, in the world of sport."

"The position we have attained, and this recognition of our standing, has not been due to our efforts alone. We have done our best to provide good material for our readers. So many editors forget the debt of gratitude they owe to their readers but we have not forgotten this fact. The great sporting public has supported Fry's in increasing numbers and we wish to thank you for your support."

"When, nearly three years ago, Fry's became an independent publication, forsaking the support and the organisation of the huge concern that had hitherto controlled its destinies, we took a step that Fleet Street, in its wisdom, told us courted failure. But Fleet Street did not count on us obtaining the continued support of the sporting public that we knew so well, and we have won through, in spite of everything."

"We are an independent magazine. Our opinions are not controlled or dictated by the politics or tastes of any proprietary concern or publishing house. We owe allegiance to no trade business or sporting organisation. The opinions we set forth are honest and unbiased; our sole concern is the welfare of sport."

Burton-Baldry carried on by praising his contributors and, yet again, mentioning the large amount

Gilbert Grace

Harry Graham

Sidney Galtrey

Strickland Gillilan

Walter Gallichan

William Goldston

Zona Gale

Alan Haig-Brown

Arthur Hales

of correspondence received in the office. "We are seriously considering the advisability of forming an Advisory Board," he said, "with their opinions being at the disposal of our readers through the medium of these editorial pages."

What he did not mention was the increasing number of stories being taken, unacknowledged, from American journals. For example, issues 117 and 118 contained fiction written by the Californian based novelist Peter Kyne, each of which had been published three months previously in *The Red Book Magazine* (with their comment that they 'will appeal mainly to women'). In order to expand the stories the editor had commissioned John Woolrich to illustrate the pages to give more effect.

For all of his bluff and bluster Burton-Baldry knew that the finances of the company were not in good shape. With the sudden departure of Dawsons, Fry's Magazine Limited were now organising publishing and distribution by themselves, which must have added extra worry and inconvenient time to all concerned.

The next few months saw the front advertising pages filled with self-glorification and virtually begging subscribers to get friends to buy copies of the magazine. Full-page pleas were titled *Fry's Magazine and the Purchasing Public* with the text essentially imploring readers to purchase goods and services from advertisers.

The pages of reviews of the company's first book, *Success at Golf*, bordered on the embarrassing. After letting readers know that "the enormous first print run" had sold out and "the huge second edition is nearly exhausted," the magazine then quoted as many comments as it could find.

World of Golf said: "It is undoubtedly one of the best instructive works that has yet appeared." *Winning Post* remarked: "A Wonderful little shilling's worth." *Vanity Fair* wrote: "Instructive Articles," with *The Sportsman* saying: "You Cannot Fail to Profit From the Instructions." These were followed by quotes from *The Leicester Mail, Oxford Journal, Manchester Evening Chronicle, Sunday Times, Glasgow Daily Herald* and many other newspapers. The book's financial success had saved the magazine for the present.

Issue 120 contained a number of surprising changes. Many regular columns and columnists had been discarded and in their places came writers, many of whom had not before been in print. A couple of discarded old-faithfuls from the past were resurrected but the tone of the issue seemed to be getting more to that of advising sportsmen where to travel. Something had changed behind the scenes.

Although it had not yet been announced, Charles Fry had returned to take over the editor's chair and this was his first issue. Discussions and negotiations had been going on for some while with Walter Burton-Baldry dropping down to become Office Editor and chief writer. This was soon noted by his various articles on golf, new cars, sporting events and football.

He also had another half-page *To Our Readers* article in which it was announced that the magazine covers were going to be reproduced on fine art paper for readers to purchase. "This is not an advertising dodge," he wrote, having previously referred to the huge number of requests received in the office asking if reproductions would be allowed.

Volume 21 started with the official news that Fry had rejoined the magazine which carried his name. The public reasons given were published in a full-page Editorial (see opposite page). What had happened was that the Fry's Magazine Limited financial backer, Cuthbert Corbould-Ellis, had been deeply concerned about the direction the publication had been taking although mollified by the profits the golf book was bringing in to the Company.

He had been to Hamble to discuss matters with Fry and his wife with Beatrice agreeing to take over more of the running of their training ship. It was agreed that Corbould-Ellis would initially put more money into the periodical while they went about raising up to £15,000 by issuing new Shares (see next pages). However, this did not meet with the approval of the partner of his solicitor's practice, Horace Mitchell.

Based at 14 Clement's Lane, by Lombard Street, the practice had grown larger as it had become more successful. Corbould-Ellis (1866-1936) had become very influential in the City of London and was chairman of the Corporation's Art Gallery. He had a large house in Stevenage where his

Anthony Hope

Charles Holder

Clive Holland

Eleanor Helme

Harold Hilton

Herbert de Hamel

Horace Hutchinson

Jack Hobbs

John Horsley

wife, Eveline, had her artists studio. She created miniatures which were very popular and brought in a considerable income.

Knowing that money had been promised from the firm without his knowledge, Mitchell then moved for a dissolution of the practice which was granted two months later. This caused a financial vacuum which meant that any publicity and promotion for the Share Issue had to be increased fairly promptly.

The return of Fry as editor had an immediate impact. Suddenly the magazine sprang to life again. The contents were balanced; the writers knew their subject and best of all opinionated and critical points of view were aired. He published reader's letters which complained bitterly about the amount of the magazine devoted to golf with one, calling himself 'Fed Up With Golf Piffle,' saying that a quarter of the previous issue had been golf related and "it would be interesting to know if the editorial staff have heard of any of the following sports; boat-racing, swimming, rifle shooting, lawn tennis, walking tours and others."

Fortunately Fry had seen the problem. His return number had articles on hunting, services rugby, fishing, boating, baseball, lawn tennis and sport in Australia. His Editorial did not hold back citing at length, with quotes from the *Natal Witness*, about the behaviour and rudeness of captain Johnny Douglas and the English cricket tourists. The contretemps created by the refusal of captain and players to attend official functions, or by arriving very late and staying for only a short time, had raised ire amongst the South African cricket and establishment communities. He then dealt with the board of enquiry which looked into members' complaints against the All England Lawn Tennis & Croquet Club Committee. Fry noted that the complaints had been dismissed but sympathised with those who had argued against the committee by suggesting that they should change their rules about voting on matters in which they had a pecuniary interest.

Fry's next issue, May 1914, carried on the discussion about the boorish behaviour of the England cricketers with a lengthy article from a South African correspondent with attaching stories from the *Bloemfontein Friend*, *Natal Advertiser* and *Transvaal Leader* newspapers. He also reversed the policy of not acknowledging the taking of stories and extracts from American magazines by mentioning those from *Outing*, *Red Book*, *Collier's*, *Life* and *Rod & Gun* which he had used.

However, the real criticism came in his *Straight Talk* section of the Editorial when, after praising the late William Stead for his opinions and investigative journalism, rather pulled his predecessor to pieces. Fry wrote: "In its earlier days this magazine was more topical and free-spoken than later on. Some of us went away attending to affairs which at the time seemed more important than the world of sport, travel and outdoor life embodied in a magazine. We are back again now and our main object here is to reproduce the old *Fry's Magazine* in all its essentials. We do not expect to do this off the reel in a single month but we are on the job."

Fry then made an appeal for former readers to once again purchase the magazine, hinting that circulation had dropped badly in recent times. He finished with a bold statement. "We used generally to have a fight on; sometimes several; never in a case unworthy of a fight. We feel brewing up for one or two that need decision just now. But of them, anon."

In the June number Fry had two places to make his views known. On the first page he wrote: "Fry's is getting back on to the rails it left nearly three years ago. Have you noticed the change? The results are already making us feel more cheerful in the office. Our circulation went up last month; the advance orders tell us it is going up much more for this issue. We are aiming for that one-hundred thousand mark we reached some years ago."

He also made sure that the public knew about the potential share issue: "We wish to thank all our readers who have applied for shares in our new undertaking. We have arranged for as wide a distribution of the shares as possible in order that all those readers who have applied may have an interest in the magazine and our coming publications."

 Linton Hope
 Martin Hawke
 Mary Howarth

 Maud Haviland
 May Hezlet
 Montague Holbein

 Robert Hichens
 Stanley Hyatt
 Thomas Hammond

The confident feeling sent out to potential purchasers can be traced to the Prospectus where Cuthbert Corbould-Ellis had written: "Mr C.B.Fry will renew his active connection with the management, both in writing for the magazine and carrying on the business of the Company, and his unique experience and wide knowledge will be at the disposal of the Company."

Then, in bold black type: "The Company has entered into an agreement with Mr C.B.Fry whereby they secure his services as Advisory Editor, both for the magazine and for the Book Department, for a period of five years." There must have been moves not recorded as Fry returned immediately as Editor and, as stated, made an immediate impact.

In July 1914 a whole page was given over to William Irving-Hamilton, the Advertising Manager, for him to extol the fact that things were far better and that potential advertisers should take note. Headed *A Few Truths About Fry's Magazine*, he noted that newspapers and weekly publications "are read and thrown away." He added: "But if you wish to reach a specialised public there is only one medium to use, and that is Fry's. It is read - and kept. It is under the editorial control of Mr C.B.Fry who knows his public."

Irving-Hamilton eventually got to the main point. He wanted more advertisers for the magazine. He made some rash statements about how it would pay to show products and services then added: "I know the class of people who read Fry's; and they are the class of people who will buy your goods. I say it is going to pay you because I have proof that it has paid other people. If I was not sure of this fact I would not be filling this valuable page. Think it over."

What was to be the magazine's final issue, although it was not known at the time, contained three pages of matters relevant to the publication and current plans in hand. These were all situated with the adverting section at the front and before the Table of Contents. The first was titled *Golf Talk* and written by Charles Fry. In it he wrote about the golf book the magazine had published and with the second edition now sold out (with total sales of twenty-thousand copies) how another print run was taking place "to fulfil the large trade order we have in hand." He added: "We underestimated the demand and our printers have been unable to get a new edition out quickly enough. It's sad, but it's true." The point he was making to readers was to order a copy now before it was too late.

Two pages later came a most extraordinary announcement, especially from a publishing house. What passes as mail-order on-line trading of today was being suggested in 1914. The column was headed *Captain Armstrong's Department*: An Innovation for Readers of Fry's, with sub-headings of: *An Expert to Buy Your Goods* - Free to Fry's Readers.

It started: "For some time past Captain Armstrong, who conducts the Clothes Department of Fry's Magazine, has been receiving letters from readers in all parts of the world asking his advice and help on matters connected with dress and kindred matters pertaining thereto. We have therefore decided, with the co-operation of Fry's experts in branches of sport and outdoor life, to start a purchasing bureau. It is intended to help all readers in the purchasing of articles and goods. This may sound a very simple matter but, in point of fact, it is really most difficult if carried out properly."

"The idea is this. Supposing a reader living in some out-of-the-way place desires to purchase a fly rod or a gun, and he is a little doubtful about entrusting his order to the post. Then all he need to do is to mail the money for the goods he desires to us, sending sufficient to cover the cost of transmitting the goods, and one of our experts will visit the stores or the manufacturers and select the rod or gun required. We shall make no charge for this. We shall add nothing to the advertised price for expenses. Our sole desire is to help our readers and in this matter we feel we are helping them in a practical way. If you want advice about anything, or you want to purchase anything, send a line to us."

Naturally, with war declared a few days after publication the concept never got off the ground.

A page later William Irving-Hamilton was at it again: this time haranguing readers to read the advertisements. He explained: "In the first place we cater for the man, and the sportsman, with our advertising pages directed to the same end. There is a definite advertising policy pursued in the pages of this magazine. Our advertisers are the best; they sell the best goods; they tell the truth; and

FRY'S MAGAZINE OF SPORT

Vol. XXI. APRIL, 1914. No. 1.

IMPORTANT.
TO OUR READERS.

On pages i., ii. and iii of this issue of the Magazine will be found some particulars of a new Company which has been formed in order to extend the scope of FRY'S MAGAZINE considerably, and further, to enable us to utilise to the full the unrivalled opportunities we possess for publishing sporting books. It is also proposed to start a sister Magazine to FRY'S, to be called the THE SPORTSWOMAN, in order that we may be able to meet the increasing demands of our lady readers, which we find it impossible to gratify in this Magazine.

As all our readers know, this Magazine was founded eleven years ago by Mr. C. B. Fry, whose position and standing is unique in the annals of sport. His knowledge of sporting matters is unrivalled, and the benefit of his practical experience is an asset possessed by no other sporting magazine or weekly in the world.

Some three years ago Mr. Fry was compelled, for private reasons, to relinquish any executive control in this Magazine, but arrangements have now been completed whereby he will be enabled to renew his immediate connection with the Magazine that bears his name, and to supervise the entire editorial policy, as well as to write regularly. The Magazine, therefore, in future will bear the imprint of his personality, and readers will obtain the benefit of his opinions on matters covering the whole field of sport.

With the extension of the business of the Magazine, and the flattering reception that has been accorded the publication of our first book, "Success at Golf," it has been found necessary to introduce fresh capital. We are, therefore, giving our readers an opportunity to become shareholders in FRY'S MAGAZINE and THE SPORTSWOMAN and their book publishing department. We want the interest of all our readers and friends to take a practical form, because we would rather have our shares divided among a number of readers in order that they should participate in our projected wide development than allow the moneyed man to step in and purchase the majority of the shares.

There are only 14,000 £1 shares offered for subscription, and this will not allow of half our readers being allotted one share each. We shall, therefore, deal with applications and allot shares in strict rotation, but please do not think that small holdings will be unwelcome, rather the contrary.

We shall be pleased to see any of our readers at any time, and advise them on matters connected with sport. At the same time, we shall be equally pleased if any readers will call on us, in order to afford us an opportunity of making their personal acquaintance, and to offer them any information as to our present plans.

A copy of the full prospectus regarding the new Company will be supplied at once on application, personal or written, to

THE EDITOR

THERE ARE NO PROMOTION OR UNDERWRITING PROFITS AND THE WHOLE OF THE CAPITAL WILL BE USED FOR THE PURPOSES OF THE COMPANY.

Notice of a Prospectus which is being issued by

FRY'S PUBLISHING COMPANY,
LIMITED.

(Incorporated under the Companies Acts, 1908 and 1913.)

CAPITAL - - £15,000
DIVIDED INTO

14,000 Participating Cumulative Preference Shares of £1 each	£14,000
20,000 Ordinary Shares of 1s. each	1,000
	£15,000

ISSUE OF 14,000 7% PARTICIPATING CUMULATIVE PREFERENCE SHARES OF £1 EACH

which are now offered for Subscription at par, payable as follows:—

On Application	2/6
On Allotment	5/-
One Month after Allotment	12/6

The Preference Shares carry a fixed Cumulative Preferential Dividend of 7 per cent. per annum and rank as to such 7 per cent. Dividend and Capital in priority to the Ordinary Shares. The remaining profits are distributable as 25 per cent. to the holders of the Preference Shares and the balance to the holders of the Ordinary Shares.

Directors.

C. F. CORBOULD-ELLIS, J.P.,
  Cromwell Lodge, Stevenage, Herts.
W. BURTON BALDRY,
  Sunningdale, East Molesey, Surrey.
C. B. FRY,
  Hamble, Hants.

} Directors of Fry's Magazine, Limited, 188, Strand, London, W.C.

Bankers.
THE LONDON COUNTY & WESTMINSTER BANK,
Law Courts Branch, 263, Strand, W.C.

Solicitor.
HORACE C. MITCHELL, 14, Clement's Lane, E.C.

Secretary and Offices.
L. R. ANDREWS, 188, Strand, London, W.C.

PROSPECTUS.

This Company has been formed with the objects set out in the Memorandum of Association and primarily to:—
1. Acquire the publication known as "Fry's Magazine."
2. To carry on a monthly illustrated Sporting Magazine for Ladies to be known as "The Sportswoman."
3. To carry on the publication of Books on Sport and Outdoor Life.

FRY'S MAGAZINE

was founded some years ago by Mr. C. B. Fry, and at once secured its position. It is undoubtedly regarded as the Magazine of authority in the world of sport, travel and outdoor life, and no magazine has ever maintained a stronger set of contributors who are the leading experts and authorities on their subjects.

It is a powerful Magazine with a wide circle of the best class of readers and a first-class advertising connection, both capable of large developments. It has an established reputation, and is now in its eleventh year of publication.

It has always afforded the management of "Fry's Magazine" satisfaction that the leading London and Provincial Press quote and review its articles more generally and extensively than those appearing in any other magazine. Every year many hundreds of such Press notices and scores of individual columns have appeared. In many instances accompanied by leading articles.

From readers in all parts of the world appreciative letters are continually received.

A FEW EXTRACTS FROM SOME RECENT PRESS NOTICES :—

THE TIMES.
"In 'Fry's Magazine' the articles containing suggestions as to the government of golf and criticisms on the morals of county cricket are well informed and sensible, and make for the right objects; the further paper on the standardisation of golf balls is also wisely written."

THE SPORTSMAN.
"A very entertaining number."

THE FIELD.
"An unusually interesting number."

SHOOTING TIMES.
". . . contains several articles of far more than ordinary interest. It is impossible to mention, even by name, half the attractive contents of this well-illustrated magazine."

MANCHESTER TIMES.
"The contents of 'Fry's Magazine' for August should appeal to a wide circle of sportsmen. Tennis and golf enthusiasts anxious to improve their game will read with interest the helpful articles on these subjects by Mr. A. F. Wilding and Harry Vardon. . . . The illustrations all maintain the unique standard which 'Fry's' has always set, and this issue should make an ideal companion for the moors or the seaside."

EDINBURGH EVENING NEWS.
"As a purveyor of sporting literature obtainable within the limits of the popular purse, 'Fry's Magazine' stands alone without a compeer. It is replete with splendid contributions of varied interest . . . all combining to make a number of superlative value."

DEVON AND EXETER GAZETTE.
"'Fry's Magazine' continues to increase in popularity, a circumstance not to be wondered at considering that the articles on all branches of sport, of which each issue is brimful, are penned by authorities on the subjects they treat . . . in fact 'Fry's' is full of good things."

MIDLAND DAILY TELEGRAPH.
"This issue is again fully up to the high standard of its predecessors, the articles being most informing, while the illustrations add considerably to the attractiveness of this very popular magazine."

MIDLAND COUNTIES HERALD.
"There is not a page in this sporting monthly which does not bear evidence of careful editorial supervision. The illustrations which embellish nearly every page are of general excellence, and no sporting library can be regarded as complete without 'Fry's Magazine' being included among its periodicals."

THE "SPORTSWOMAN."

With regard to the proposed Magazine for Ladies, there has in recent years been an extraordinary increase in the feminine interest in Sport and Outdoor pursuits. Large and increasing numbers devote themselves actively to suitable field-sports and field-games.

It is considered that, as there is at present no Magazine dealing with Outdoor subjects for Ladies in the same way that "Fry's Magazine" does for men, the projected Magazine will achieve its expected success.

"The Sportswoman," which will be published at Sixpence, will aim at producing contributions from writers of the highest standing with the necessary experience to write with authority on the particular subjects dealt with. The Magazine will also contain the best class of fiction and articles on Dress, which in fact will be made an important feature. Gardening and other outdoor pursuits will be given particular attention.

Ladies are great buyers of magazines, and the Directors confidently anticipate a good circulation, and they have the support already of well-known ladies interested in the new magazine. It is an accepted fact in the publishing world that the right kind of publication for ladies commands an exceptional advertising revenue.

Two further points should be noted. First, that two magazines working together, in the way "Fry's Magazine" and "The Sportswoman" will be conducted, command a larger proportionate advertising revenue than two equally good separate magazines, while production expenses are proportionately reduced in a marked degree. Secondly, the possession by the Company of the new Magazine will give a leverage for the sale of books and subsidiary publications for ladies, such as is already attached to "Fry's Magazine" in the case of men.

BOOKS ON SPORT AND OUTDOOR LIFE.

With regard to the publication of these books, there is an increasing demand for such as are written by authors of authority and sold at a popular price. Success in such publications depends essentially on expert knowledge, which is already commanded by this Company.

A publishing business possessing an established magazine such as "Fry's Magazine" is in a strong position for earning profits from subsidiary publications in its own line.

The Company proposes to develop this side of their undertaking, as they are convinced that a successful and profitable business can be carried on. They propose to proceed on the lines adopted by "Fry's Magazine," Limited, who recently published at a shilling "Success at Golf." The first edition of 10,000 copies was sold out within six weeks of publication, and a second edition has been printed, and a substantial profit has been made from the first edition of this book alone, exclusive of the American rights, which have been disposed of on satisfactory terms. Many successful publishing houses, especially in America, publish magazines primarily as a main means of securing sales for their books.

Mr. C. B. Fry will renew his active connection with the management, both in writing for the Magazine and carrying on the business of the Company, and his unique experience and wide knowledge will be at the disposal of the Company.

The Company has entered into an agreement with Mr. C. B. Fry whereby they secure his services as Advisory Editor, both for the Magazines and for the Book Department, for a period of five years. The Company will take over the present very advantageous offices in the Strand, and the Staff of "Fry's Magazine," Limited, and will, therefore, commence business with the benefit of an existing organisation and a proved and expert staff necessary to carry on the business of magazine proprietors and book publishers. The present existence of this organisation will effect a considerable saving in starting the "Sportswoman," as much of the expense usually entailed in commencing a new magazine will be unnecessary.

Unlike most magazines other than those published by large general publishing firms, "Fry's Magazine," Limited, has its own publishing department, which has during the past year been specially organised with a view to the developments now proposed, and also with a view to being in a position, if advisable, to publish on commission other magazines and periodicals, a form of business which is very profitable and entails practically no additional outlay to a company with an efficient publishing department of its own.

The Directors have carefully considered the question of profits that may be expected from the combination of "Fry's Magazine" and the "Sportswoman" and the publication of books of the kind as already tried, and they are of opinion that at least £3,000 a year should be made. This figure has been estimated on a conservative basis, and the profits should be considerably more. The Directors, as outlined above, have in main view the building up of an extensive publishing business from the present position, but they do not consider it proper at this stage to propose an estimate of consequent additional profits.

The profits of the Company will be applied first in paying the fixed Cumulative Preference Dividend of 7% per annum, and the balance will be distributed as to 25% to the Preference Shareholders and the balance to the holders of the Ordinary Shares.

No Debentures can be issued without the consent of three-fourths of the holders of the Preference Shares.

Copies of the Prospectus, on which application for Shares alone can be received, can be obtained at the Offices of the Company.

Frederick Jane

Gilbert Jessop

Harvey Jarvis

Owen Jones

Albert Knight

Bart Kennedy

George Kelson

Herbert Knight-Horsfield

Lees Knowles

therefore we give them our endorsement."

"The editorial has articles of interest to you, otherwise you would not buy this magazine. The advertiser has articles of interest to you, otherwise he would not use this magazine. It's only logic."

Once the war started many of the printing and office staff rushed off to enlist to fight a skirmish, which they were told, "would be over by Christmas." No one said which Christmas. Many of the regular contributors were killed, one a day after arriving in France.

The issue for September 1914 was in its final stages of preparation before the directors decided to suspend publication. The idea was to resume when the war was over, but by mid-1915 it was obvious this was never going to happen and the magazine formally closed. Many years later Fry tried to revive the idea of a sporting magazine but nothing came of his hopes.

The share issue had seen just over two-thirds taken up by the public. The money paid for shares was held in trust but by the time the Frys company was wound up, in 1917, inflation had reduced its purchasing power to very little. Investors were contacted and requested to reclaim their money but only few did, the rest never replied.

Walter Burton-Baldry wrote to his readers: "In such a crisis as the present we must consider our country and its needs rather than our individual ambitions and aspirations. This is not a good time for sport. National endeavour is diverted to other and more important channels. The matters that come within our scope must take a back place, even though in allocating them this back place we are depriving ourselves of our livelihood."

"There is work to be done, and even though the sword cannot edit *Fry's Magazine*, we lay down our pen with the assurance that it can be used to better advantage after the war is done." He then joined the Oxford and Bucks Light Infantry, eventually rising to the rank of Captain and being mentioned twice in despatches. Later in the war he was given a desk job as Secretary to the Ministry of National Service, East Anglian Region. After leaving the army he became a Director of Public Companies and a Member of the London Stock Exchange.

Burton-Baldry did not give up writing. He wrote a Weekly Review which dealt with world financial happenings and economic trends. This proved to be of wide interest and he continued with it until illness forced him to cease. He died at the young age of fifty-one.

Cuthbert Corbould-Ellis was forty-eight years old when war broke out and was too old for military service. He continued in his solicitor's practice and in 1915 was appointed a Magistrate for the county of Oxfordshire. His home in Stevenage was large enough for his wife's studio to expand and her artistic success is well recorded. He died in 1936 having had no further involvement in any other publication.

Charles Fry had a far more cosy and comfortable war than many, if not most, of his contemporaries. It was one which was entirely devoid of danger. In 1914 he was given the honorary rank of Lieutenant in the Royal Naval Reserve and two years later promoted to Commander in spite of his wife running their Naval training ship and he spending most of his time in the office.

Looking back, *Fry's Magazine* was of its time and would probably have had a longer life had George Newnes not died at the age of fifty-nine. His entrepreneurial spirit had seen his publishing empire grow and his appointment of a sporting icon to edit a journal was the first of its kind. The contents in early issues are, nowadays, of huge benefit to sports historians as they contain reflections and eye-witness accounts of events recorded very differently by newspapers at the time.

The magazine started to lose its way when Fry got distracted by his training ship on the River Hamble, leaving a lot of the editorial decisions to Wallis Myers and Cecil Hughes. When the board of directors started interfering after Newnes death in trying to control both Fry, and the contents, the end seemed nigh. However, a new company was formed and the name survived although the articles became dull, repetitive and golf heavy.

Charles Fry's return as editor, albeit for far too brief a time, saw the pages come back to life again. Old contributors reappeared and fiction stories were plundered from American magazines. The issues for 1914 were as good as those from 1904. Alas, war intervened.

Peter Kyne

Arnold Lunn

Bohun Lynch

Dick Luckman

Dorothy Levitt

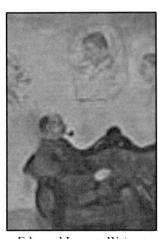
Edmund Lacon- Watson

Edward Lucas

Henry Leach

Jack London

EXTRACTED FROM OTHER PUBLICATIONS

During the period 1880 to 1914, many British publications reprinted articles, stories, poems and illustrations from American newspapers and periodicals. Most of these acknowledged the name of the author but hardly ever the name of the source. In a number of instances the title was changed which has made modern day comparisons and checking somewhat difficult.

Below are noted some of those which appeared in Fry's Magazine but they are only ones which could be cross-checked against other titles. Many, which are not mentioned here, can be seen by reference to this book as having been created by Americans whose work never, officially, was published outside of their country.

Issue 1

The Sa'-Zada Tales (1): Of White, Yellow and Black Leopards by William Fraser in *Metropolitan*, October 1903

Issue 2

The Sa'-Zada Tales (2): Of Hathi Ganesh the White-Eared Elephant by William Fraser in *Metropolitan*, November 1903

Mah Little by Maurice Smiley in *Collier's*, March 1904

Issue 3

The Sa'-Zada Tales (3): Of Gidar the Jackal and Coyote the Prairie Wolf by William Fraser in *Metropolitan*, December 1903

A Straight Tip by Harry Greene in *Leslie's*, February 1904

The Foreman by Stewart White in *McClure's*, August 1903

Issue 4

The Sa'-Zada Tales (4): Of Raj Bagh the King Tiger by William Fraser in *Metropolitan*, January 1904

Issue 5

The Alien of the Wild by Charles Roberts in *McClure's*, March 1904

The Sa'-Zada Tales (5): Of the Tribe of King Cobra by William Fraser in *Metropolitan*, February 1904

Issue 6

The Riverman by Stewart White in *McClure's*, April 1903

The Sa'-Zada Tales (6): The Night of the Monkeys by William Fraser in *Metropolitan*, March 1904

John Lewis

Percy Longhurst

Rudi Lehmann

Archibald Maclaren

Arthur Mills

Charles Matson

Charles McEvoy

Cora Matson-Dolson

Eustace Miles

Issue 7

The Sa'-Zada Tales (7): Birds of a Feather by William Fraser in *Metropolitan*, April 1904

Issue 8

A Modern Adam by Frederic Stimson in *McClure's*, April 1904

Theodore Roosevelt by Harry Graham in *Metropolitan*, July 1904

The Sa'-Zada Tales (8): The Narrative of Buffalo and Bison by William Fraser in *Metropolitan*, May 1904

[* There were four further stories in this series which Fry's did not use]

Issue 9

The Big Brother by Frederick Palmer in *Collier's*, May 1904

Issue 12

The Crowning of Dolly by Ridley Beal in *Leslie's*, December 1904

Issue 16

The Faithful Brady by Larrey Bowman in *McClure's*, April 1905

Issue 17

The Battle to the Strong by John Whitson in *Delineator*, May 1904

Out in the Country by Cora Matson-Dolson in *National*, May 1905

Issue 19

The Song of the Bass by Alice Calhoun-Haines in *Metropolitan*, May 1905

The Black Roan of 265 by Winifried Rolker in *McClure's*, November 1904

A Tale of a Cinnamon Bear by Perry Robinson in *Bellman*, September 1904

Issue 20

Mr MG From Sanford by Lue Hall in *Leslie's*, February 1905

Issue 22

The Story of Keesh by Jack London in *Holiday*, January 1904

Issue 23

Lotteridge by Ray Stannard Baker in *Collier's*, May 1905

 Frederick MacKenzie

 Harold Macfarlane

 Henry Moncrieff-Tennent

 Hiram Maxim

 John Mackie

 Lucy Montgomery

 Preston Muddock

 Richard Mecredy

 Scipio Mussabini

Issue 31

The Doing by Ruth Havers in *Metropolitan*, November 1905

Issue 32

The True Wisdom by Ruth Havers in *Metropolitan*, December 1905

Issue 37

Chickens by Eugene Wood in *McClure's*, January 1907

Issue 47

The Vindication by Arthur Pier in *Collier's*, November 1907

Issue 48

In Arizona by Cyrus Brady in *Cosmopolitan*, January 1905

Untrodden Ways by Archibald Sullivan in *Smart Set*, January 1907

Issue 49

The Kinship of Ages by James Barr in *Popular*, July 1907

Issue 55

The Man With the Dingo by Albert Dorrington in *Popular*, December 1907

Issue 60

The Black Brant by Bonnycastle Dale in *Outing*, December 1908

Issue 63

The Taking of a Sunfish by Charles Holder in *Metropolitan*, June 1906

Issue 65

Convincing Mr Whipple by Frederick Brown in *Metropolitan*, November 1908

Issue 66

The Dignity of Justice by Frank Symons in *Saturday Evening Post*, September 1908

Issue 69

On the Floe by Archibald Sullivan in *Sievier's*, July 1909

Issue 71

A Four Cylinder White Elephant by George Fitch in *Hampton's*, October 1909

William McNutt

Alfred Nossig

Guy Nickalls

Elliott O'Donnell

William Ogilvie

William Osborne

Arthur Pier

Carter Platts

Edwin Pugh

Issue 72

Trapping Big Game in the Heart of Africa by Fritz Duquesne in *Hampton's*, August 1909

Issue 73

Ole Skjarsen's First Touchdown by George Fitch in *Saturday Evening Post*, November 1909

Issue 77

The Man Who Knew by Bertram Atkey in *Outing*, October 1909

Issue 79

An Experiment in Gyro Hats by Ellis Butler in *Hampton's*, June 1910

Issue 84

Just Like a Cat by Ellis Butler in *Cosmopolitan*, February 1909

Adventure by Jack London in *Popular*, November 1910

Issue 95

The Rhode Island Red by Arthur Wheeler in *Outing*, January 1912

Issue 97

Caring for the Clutch by Harold Whiting in *Outing*, March 1912

Issue 101

The Scottie and Irish Terrier by William Haynes in *Outing*, March 1912

Issue 105

The Opportunities of Timoleon Brass by Bertram Atkey in *Red*, October 1912

   [* Only the First Story of the Series republished in Fry's]

Issue 108

The Fight by Rex Beach in *Collier's*, January 1910

Issue 113

All's Fair by Ralph Stock in *All-Story*, February 1908

Issue 117

Corncob Kelly's Benefit by Peter Kyne in *Red*, September 1913

Ernest Phillips

Ernest Punshon

Frederick Palmer

George Pollock-Hodsoll

Hesketh Prichard

Kate Prichard

Ralph Paine

Roger Pocock

Charles Roberts

Issue 118

Hassayampa Jim by Peter Kyne in *Red*, August 1913

Issue 119

Bill Heenan Kidnapper by William McNutt in *Ainslee's*, October 1913

Issue 120

The Lure of the Links by Alfred Swoyer in *American*, December 1913

Issue 121

Joy Ranching by Jesse Williams in *Metropolitan*, October 1913

Issue 122

A Fisherman's Petition, uncredited, in *Rod & Gun*, January 1914

Issue 123

The Lure of Little Voices by Grantland Rice in *Collier's*, August 1913

The Champion by Charles Gibson in *Collier's*, December 1912

Issue 124

The Heart of the Shadow by Roy Cohen in *Red*, May 1914

Issue 125

What Money Can't Buy by Pip van Buren in *Life*, December 1913

Difficulties With Golf by William Wright in *Life*, January 1914

Alderson's Easy Job by Frederick Bechdolt in *Red*, June 1914

Editorial Heading

Fletcher Ransom

John Robertson-Scott

Kumar Ranjitsinhji

Perry Robinson

Pett Ridge

Theodore Roberts

William Roberts

Edith Somerville

Edward Sewell

BIBLIOGRAPHY

Series, Stories, Articles and Illustrations

Volume 1

Issue 1 : April 1904 (p1-132)

Cover Design; Illustrated by William Robinson
Navy Mixture; Illustrated by Victor Beveridge
The Progress of Sport [inc. Spring Sport in Scotland; Association Football; Rugby; Lincolnshire Handicap; Grand National; Inter-Varsity Sports; Boat Race; England Cricketers in Australia]
Outdoor Men: Alfred Lyttelton by Wallis Myers; Illustrated by Thomas Browne
Physical Energy and George Watts by Charles Fry
The Leg Hit; Illustrated by George Watts
Strength [verses] by Harold Begbie
The Sa'-zada Tales (1): First Night - Tales of White, Yellow and Black Lepoards by WilliamFraser; Illustrated by Arthur Heming
The Retriever [verses] by Alan Haig-Brown
The Blue in the Making by John Edwards-Moss
A Cox and His Course by Frederick Begg
The Day and the Race by Claude Goldie
Out of Harness [Decima Moore; Francis Jeune; Frederic Gorell-Barnes, Cora Brown-Potter; Max Pemberton; Frances Greville; Kennerley Rumford; Evie Greene; Michael Foster and Forbes Robertson]
The American Reporter by Gilbert Jessop; Illustrated by William Christie
England versus Scotland by John Bentley
Games in Season [Winter Lawn Tennis; Baseball in England; Progress in Lacrosse; Badminton Championships; Hockey Advances]
The Fight at Out Camp (1) by Katherine Prichard & Hesketh Prichard; Illustrated by Stanley Wood
The Grand National by Alfred Watson
Secrets of Catch-as-Catch-Can by Frederick Ward & James Bolton with Ferdinand Gruhn
Where for Easter and April Holidays by Frederick Aflalo
Review of: *Great Golfers: Their Methods at a Glance* by George Beldam
Our Noah's Ark [A Sick Elephant; Falconry; Polar Bears; Zebra Training; Reindeer; Armadillo; Lions in Mid-Air]
The Rights and Wrongs of International Cricket by Archibald Maclaren
Training and Diet: The Headlands by George Dabbs
Everyday Things We Do Wrong: Dorette Wilke by Cecil Hughes
Man and the Live Motor by Charles Jarrott
Under the Sky [Rabbit Hunting With Ferrets in Germany; Lessons in Golf; First Varsity Athletics Meeting; Cyclist Soldiers; Ostrich Feathers; Ranjitsinhji Fishing]
Jiu-Jitsu by Wallis Myers
Topical Trophies [Boat Race, Steeplechasing, Football]; Illustrated by Percy Gossop
Photographs of Footballers [Jack Robertson, Vivian Woodward, William Brawn, Alfred Common, Albert Buick]

Edward Sorenson

Edward Step

Eugen Sandow

Evelyn Sharp

Frances Simpson

Frederic Stimson

Frederick Selous

Frederick Shaw

Frederick Smith

I've Got to Come In; Illustrated by Hall Thorpe
Always First; Illustrated by Ernest Thomson
Who's Catchin' Fish?; Illustrated by Frederick Buchanan
Big Manicuring Contracts; Illustrated by Hall Thorpe
Bang Goes Saxpence; Illustrated by Dudley Hardy

Issue 2 : May 1904 (p133-256)

Cover Design; Illustrated by William Robinson

Outdoor Men: Arthur Winnington-Ingram by Wallis Myers; Illustrated by Thomas Browne

The Progress of Sport [inc. County Cricket; Corinthians Football; Field Trials; Stamford Bridge Ground; Covered Court Championships; The Guineas Horse Races; Inter-Varsity Golf; Alfred Shrubb; Fencing; Hesketh Prichard; George Dabbs; William Fraser; Hurdling in Germany; Illustration of Pelham Warner by Edgar Fischer]

The War God [verses] by Harold Begbie

The Ethics of Athletics: Edmond Warre by Raymond Blathwayt

The Sa'-zada Tales (2): The Tale of Hathi Ganesh the White-Eared Elephant by William Fraser; Illustrated by Arthur Heming

Riding a Racehorse by Mornington Cannon & James Bolton

Small Bore Rifles by Frederick Selous

Mr Watch, Pawnbroker: The Pearl of Great Price by George Dabbs; Illustrated by Percy Hickling

On Buying a Motor Car by Francis Armstrong

Where to Catch Trout in April and Early May by Robert Marston

The Amateur Golf Championship by George Beldam

The Fight at Out Camp (2) by Katherine Prichard & Hesketh Prichard; Illustrated by Stanley Wood

Horse versus Motor by Charles Chetwynd-Talbot; Illustrated by Henry Lucas

Mah Littles [verses] by Maurice Smiley

Belinda in Search of a Body by Evelyn Sharp; Illustrated by Percy Hickling

Out of Harness [Albert Saxe-Coburg; George Cambridge; Wilhelm Hohenzollern; Thomas Cannon; Olga Nethersole; George Sims; Charlotte Wiehe]

Postcards and Photography by Archibald Williams

The Alphabet of Boxing by Thomas Henry Browne

Off Finisterre [verses] by Herman Viele

Training and Diet: Hints by George Dabbs

Sun Song [verses] by Zona Gale

Our Noah's Ark [Samoyede Sledge Dogs; Acclimatising Tropical Animals; Fox Terrier; Five Hundred Year Old Tortoise; Ostriches]

Review of *The Dog Up-to-Date* by Herbert Compton; reviewed by Walter Burton-Baldry

The New and The Old in Cricket [Review of *Cricket* by Horace Hutchinson] by Charles Fry

Under the Sky [New Locks at Teddington; Motorcycle Record; A Floating Nest; Seven Stages of an Oar]

Cup Final Fancies by Charles Fry; Illustrated by Roland Hill

Topical Trophies [Football, Golf, Tennis]

Photographs of Footballers [Bolton Wanderers team; Manchester City team; Thomas Crawshaw; Jack Sharp; Thomas Baddeley; Jack Cox; Alec Leake; Joseph Bache; James McEwan]

Henry Seton-Karr

Hugh Sheringham

Jack Sharp

John Stead

Nihal Singh

Ralph Stock

Reeves Shaw

William Stead

William Stepney-Rawson

A Bit of Wire; Illustrated by Hall Thorpe
I Want to Get Off; Illustrated by Rex Osborne

Issue 3 : June 1904 (p257-380)

Cover Design; Illustrated by William Robinson
Outdoor Men: Martin Hawke by Wallis Myers; Illustrated by Thomas Browne
The Progress of Sport [The Derby; South African Cricket; Poetry of Bones; Call of the Road; Old Breeks; Motor Tracks; Camille Jenatzy; The Scholar-Fisherman; Scottish Angling; Thames Salmon; Metropolitan Lawn Tennis; Constance Wilson; Clyde Yachting; Royal Military Tournament; Illustration of George Gunn senior by Edgar Fischer]
The Proud Cricketer [verses] by Harold Begbie
Derby Horses at Kingsclere by John Porter; Illustrated by William Sextie
Joseph Hawley; Illustrated by Alfred Thompson
The Sa'-zada Tales (3): The Tale of Gidar the Jackal and Coyote the Prairie Wolf by William Fraser; Illustrated by Arthur Heming
Hamburg for the Modest Man by Wallis Myers
The Gordon-Bennett Race by Selwyn Edge
A Demi-God as Sportsman by Philip Bussy; Illustrated by himself
The Secret of Yorkshire's Success by Martin Hawke
A Straight Tip by Harry Greene; Illustrated by William King
The Mind of a Horse by Henry Merwin
Training and Diet: Concerning Fluids by George Dabbs
Rights and Wrongs of Cycling by Archibald Williams
The Soul of the Hooligan by Edwin Pugh; Illustrated by Rex Osborne
The Open Golf Championship by George Beldam
The Wee White Ball [verses] by Cyril Mullett
The Foreman by Stewart White; Illustrated by Power O'Malley
The Question of Polo by Walter Buckmaster
Flower Friends of June by Edward Step
Out of Harness [Hugh Grosvenor; Charles Stanhope at Polo; Alberto Santos-Dumont; Madge Crichton at Sculling; Rough-Rider Archibald Roosevelt; Crown Equerry Henry Ewart]
The Motoring of Hiawatha [verses]; by Archibald Williams; Illustrated by Wallis Mills
Our Noah's Ark [Theodore Roosevelt's Dogs; A Crocodile over Niagara Falls; Chicken; Zoo Operations; Lhassa Terrier]
Off the Beaten Track: Review of *Highways and Byways in Sussex* by Edward Lucas; Illustrated by Frederick Griggs
Under the Sky [Sport in Austria; Hugo Windischgratz; War Pigeons; Cattle School; Scottish Trout; India's Natives at Play; English School in Egypt; Wrestling in Germany; Shooting; Trotting Records]
Photographs of Cricketers [Gregor MacGregor; Frederick Fane; Harold Garnett; Samuel Hargreave; Ernest Hayes; Joseph Vine]
And in the Bright Moonlight; Illustrated by Rex Osborne
Rap It Out; Illustrated by Frederick Buchanan

Alfred Tennyson

Basil Tozer

Ethel Talbot

Guy Thorne

John Turner

Leo Trevor

Philip Trevor

Herman Vielé

Philip Vaile

Issue 4 : July 1904 (p381-508)

Cover Design; Illustrated by William Robinson
The Duffer; Illustrated by Gordon Browne
Outdoor Men: John Fisher by Wallis Myers; Illustrated by Edward Skinner
The Progress of Sport [Bisley Shooting; Inter Varsity Cricket; Cricket Scoreboards; Open-Space Cricket; Motorboats; Amateur Athletics Championships; Croquet; Lily Gower; Thames Sailing; Bowls; Royal Academy; Northern Dog Racing; Henley Regatta; John Guille Millais; Illustration of Gilbert Jessop by Edgar Fischer]
Ballad of the Car [verses] by Harold Begbie
The Last Trek by John Guille Millais; Illustrated by John Everett Millais
Woman at the Wicket by Charles Fry
The Wine Throwers by Guy Thorne; Illustrated by Paul Hardy
The Birds and Fishes of Japanese Artists by Frederick Aflalo
Hot Finishes at Henley by Claude Goldie
Belinda and the Far East by Evelyn Sharp; Illustrated by Percy Hickling
Climbing English Crags by Claude Benson
Some Cricket Fallacies by Digby Jephson; Illustrated by Rex Osborne
Lawn Tennis Personalities by Wallis Myers
For the Old County by Warren Bell; Illustrated by Henry Brock
Out of Harness [Arthur Balfour and Gerald Balfour at Golf; Seymour Hicks; Ellaline Terriss; Henry Hawkins; Henry Esmond; Armyne Gordon]
The Sa'-zada Tales (4): The Story of Raj Bagh the King Tiger by William Fraser; Illustrated by Arthur Heming
The Infant Cricket [verses] by Cecil Hughes
Your Motorcycle by Archibald Williams
Problems in the Open (1) by Henry Dudeney; Illustrated by Paul Hardy
The Real and Unreal [verses] by Joseph Cone
Our Noah's Ark [Monkeys; The Cat of Siam; Elephants' Bath; Tall and Tiny Horses; Burslem Park Birds; Foxhound 'Bluecap']
Tent Pegging [verses] by Constance Farmar; Illustrated by Elisabeth Butler
In Tidal Waters by Hamish Stuart
Under the Sky [Moose Hunting; Long-Eared Owl; Earth Houses; Lizards; Alexander Webbe Silver Shield; South African Snake; Motor Monocycle; Rat Trap; Elephant Rock; Froggery; Sport in Japan; Ladies Parasol]
Photographs of Cricketers [Samuel Day; George Wilson; William Lockwood; Thomas Richardson; Jack Hearne; Harry Butt]
Our Revolving Bookcase [Reviews of *By Thames and Cotswold* by William Hutton; Illustrated by Henry Alken; *Big Game Shooting and Travel in South-East Africa* by Frederick Findlay; *Three Years in the Klondike* by Jeremiah Lynch; *Poultry Keeping on Farms and Small Holdings* by Walter Gilbey; *Summer and Fall in Western Alaska* by Claude Cane; *Thomas' Hunting Diary* by Walter May; *Motoring Annual* by John Scott-Montagu]
Motoring; Illustrated by Victor Beveridge
A Stimulant: Illustrated by Dudley Cleaver

Robert Vernede

Alfred Watson

Archibald Williams

Edgar Wallace

Eugene Wood

Francis Walbran

Frederick Ward

Frederick Webster

Frederick White

Issue 5 : August 1904 (p509-628)

Cover Design; Illustrated by William Robinson
The Tired Chauffeur; Illustrated by Rossi Ashton
Outdoor Men: Frederick Roberts by Wallis Myers; Illustrated by Thomas Browne
The Progress of Sport [Cricket; Gilbert Grace; George Hirst; Albert Craig; Cowes Yachting; Outline Club; Goodwood Races; Grouse; Archery; Bisley Shooting; Camping; Army Athletics; John Stivens]
The Clerk [verses] by Harold Begbie; Illustrated by Anthony Helmer
Is Hodge a Fool? by John Robertson-Scott
The Alien of the Wild by Charles Roberts; Illustrated by Philip Goodwin
Once Upon a Time [verses] by Clifford Chase
Swimming and Diving for Girls by Clive Holland
My Indian Lion Hunt by Kumar Ranjitsinhji and James Bolton
The Oval on Bank Holiday [verses] by Digby Jephson; Illustrated by Rex Osborne
The Art of Catching by Edward Sewell
Problems in the Open (2) by Henry Dudeney
The Swimmers by Percy White; Illustrated by Edward Skinner
The Call of the Gulls by Frederick Aflalo
First Rate Otter Hunting by William Abrey
Out of Harness [Hall Caine; Walter Rothschild; Thomas Macnamara; Carl Stefan; Adelina Vay; William Senior]
The Sa'-zada Tales (5): Of the Tribe of King Cobra by William Fraser; Illustrated by Arthur Heming
The Kent Nursery at Tonbridge by Thomas Pawley
Golf Cricket by George Brann; Illustrated by Alfred Smith
Our Noah's Ark [Leopard from Manchuria; A Pig Cart; Eland Meat; Goat Chaise; Monkey Collar]
Week Ending on the Broads by Newton Scott
Under the Sky [Ballboys; A Chamonix Guide; Sculling for Girls; Sand Antics; Chamois Shooting; A Barnes Common Tramp]
Photographs of Cricketers [Maynard Ashcroft; Charles McGahey; Robert Abel; Colin Blythe]
Our Revolving Bookcase [Reviews of *How we Recovered the Ashes* by Pelham Warner; *Wayside and Woodland Trees* by Edward Step; *Ladies Golf* by May Hezlet; *The Racing World and Its Inhabitants* by Alfred Watson] by Charles Fry

Issue 6 : September 1904 (p629-748)

Cover Design; Illustrated by William Robinson
On the Links; Illustrated by Bertram Smale
Outdoor Men: Oliver Lodge by Wallis Myers; Illustrated by Thomas Browne
The Progress of Sport [Grouse Moors; Horseracing in America; Brooklyn Racecourse; St.Leger Meeting; Heredity in Golf; Harrogate Cricket; London Parks; Ladies Cricket; Grasmere Athletics; Scottish Fishing; Ralph Rose; Walking; Army Boxing; Illustration of Arthur Jones by Edgar Fischer]
The London Curate [verses] by Harold Begbie

Horace Wyndham

Jesse Williams

Pelham Warner

Frederick Wall

Sammy Woods

Stewart White

Walter Winans

Cyril Austin

George Armstrong

The Best Room in the House by Eustace Miles; Illustrated by Edward Gillett
The League System in Club Cricket by John Bentley
The Disc Maker by Guy Thorne; Illustrated by Paul Hardy
The Racing Pigeon in the Making by Alfred Osman
Games of the Pavement by Pett Ridge; Illustrated by Anthony Helmer
A Fall Hunting Trip in Newfoundland (1) by Hesketh Prichard
The Toadstool Hunter by Edward Step
The Riverman by Stewart White; Illustrated by Thomas Fogarty
The Game [verses] by Digby Jephson
Fitting an American University Eight by Earl Mayo
Out of Harness [George Grossmith; Olga de Meyer; Gustaf Adolph; John Shakespeare; Allen Upward; George Alexander]
The Whole Art of Caravanning by Bertram Smith
The Sa'-zada Tales (6): The Night of the Monkeys by William Fraser; Illustrated by Arthur Heming
Our Noah's Ark [Dog as a Caddy; Tame Fox; Texas Dog; Mammoth Pumpkin; Japanese Cat]
A Human Paradox by Philip Stevenson; Illustrated by Alfred Pearse
A First Class Nightmare by Charles Townsend
Under the Sky [Shetland Whales; Edward Sewell, Davy Stephens; Lawn Tennis at St.Moritz; Seals; Pigeon Farm; Rooms at Oxford; Edinburgh Botanic Gardens; Lumley Shield]
Photographs of Cricketers [Cloudesley Marsham; David Denton; Joseph Humphries; Edward Arnold; Jack Board]
Our Revolving Bookcase [Reviews of *Shooting* by Horace Hutchinson; *The Twentieth Century Dog* by Herbert Compton; *History of Yorkshire County Cricket 1833-1903* by Robert Holmes; *Five Years Adventures in the Far Interior of South Africa* by Roualeyn Cumming; *Modern Lawn Tennis* by Philip Vaile; *The Automobile Industry* by Geoffrey Stone; *American Yachting* by William Stephens]

Harry Alexander

William Applegarth

Aldred Barker

Alfred Beamish

Keble Bell

Dermot Bourke

Frederick Begg

Frederick Buckley

Frederick Burlingham

Volume 2

Issue 7 : October 1904 (p1-120 + 4)

Cover Design; Illustrated by William Robinson
Strength; Illustrated by Richard Clarke
A Hero in Wolfskin; Illustrated by Joseph Finnemore
Outdoor Men: Edward Grey by Wallis Myers; Illustrated by Thomas Browne
The Progress of Sport [Association Football; Rugby, Cricket; Obituary of William Renshaw; Motoring; Basketball; Athletics; Sport in Argyllshire]
The Philosopher on a Cycling Tour by Archibald Williams; Illustrated by Thomas Whitwell
Byways to Business by May Doney
The Sa'-zada Tales (7): Birds of a Feather by William Fraser; Illustrated by Arthur Heming
The Telephone Girl [verses] by Harold Begbie
Aston Villa by William McGregor
The Art of Fencing by Thomas Henry Browne
An Attack of Buck Fever by Perry Robinson; Illustrated by Colbron Pearse
A Fall Hunting Trip in Newfoundland (2) by Hesketh Prichard; Illustrated by himself
The Mysteries of a Duck Decoy Pool by Andrews Loring
Belinda in Heroic Mood by Evelyn Sharp; Illustrated by Percy Hickling
Lest We Forget: Some Cricket Souvenirs by Harold Macfarlane
Out of Harness [Charles Dilke; Ladapo Ademola; Victor Cavendish; Vera Nicholl; Edward Sewell; William Smith]
London to Hampton Court by Horace Wyndham
Fights With a Salmon and a Peal by Alfred Burden
Our Test Matches and Other Things by George Best
Our Noah's Ark [Dog Colony; Tame Hares; Pack Oxen; Equine Tresses; Beach Donkeys; Llamas]
Hints on the Purchase of a Motor by Francis Armstrong; Illustrated by Frederick Bennett
Under the Sky [Bicycle Polo; Living Chess; Battleship Cricket; Sparrows Nests; Buffalo Horns]
Photographs of Athletes [Claude Jupp; Kinahan Cornwallis; William Workman; Alfred Shrubb; George Larner
Our Revolving Bookcase [Reviews of *Swimming* by Ralph Thomas; *Billiards Expounded* by John Mannock; *Rowing* by William East; *At Scotland Yard* by John Sweeney; *Confessions of a Journalist* by Christopher Healy]
Answers to Correspondents
The Most Wonderful Telegraphic System in the World by Eugen Sandow; Illustrated by Percy Thomson

Issue 8 : November 1904 (p121-232 + 12)

Cover Design; Illustrated by William Robinson
Outdoor Men: George Meredith by Wallis Myers
Progress in the Outdoor World [Motoring; Australian Rules Football; Pigeon Post; Photography; Steeplechasing; Horse Racing in India; Bangalore Cup; Western India Turf Club; Sporting Appliances; Canadian Amateur Athletic Team; Rink Hockey]
The City Postman [verses] by Harold Begbie; Illustrated by Anthony Helmer

George Beldam

Harry Blake

John Bentley

Robert Batho

Tommy Burns

Alexander Campbell

Alfred Cooper

Alice Calhoun-Haines

Charles Coventry

My Touring Reminiscences by Charles Rolls
Hunting on a Small Income by Archibald Hamilton
A Modern Adam by Frederic Stimson; Illustrated by Charles Bull and Adam Horne
The Government of Our Winter Game by John Bentley
Theodore Roosevelt [verses] by Harry Graham; Illustrated by Frederick Strothmann
The Rise and Progress of Sea Angling by Frederick Aflalo
The Race by Bart Kennedy; Illustrated by Louis Berneker
Among the High Alps by Frank Ormiston-Smith
The Spurs in Mufti by Cecil Hughes
The Dead Thrush [verses] by Gwendoline Johnes
The Sa'-Zada Tales (8): The Narrative of Buffalo and Bison by William Fraser; Illustrated by Arthur Heming
The Art of Handling a Crosse by William Stepney-Rawson
What It Costs to Keep a Motorboat by Charles Matson
An Aerial Episode by Stephen Hallett; Illustrated by Matthew Hewerdine
Out of Harness [Sandringham Shooting Parties; Sarah Bernhardt; Cecil Aldin]
The Alphabet of Hawking by Edward Michell
To George Meredith [verses] by Jonathan Dwight
A Man Manufactory by Harold Begbie
Our Revolving Bookcase [Reviews of *The Trotting and the Pacing Horse in America* by Hamilton Busbey; *The Master of Hounds* by George Underhill]
Our Noah's Ark [Puppies; Rat Fanciers; Freak Sheep; Lizards]
Straight Talk [Editorial Misunderstanding; Cruelty to Animals; Sportsmen; Professional Sport; Football Spectators; Newspaper Influence] by Charles Fry; Illustrated by George Thorp
The Motor Afield and Afloat [Bartlett Patent; Review of *The Complete Motorist* by Filson Young; *L'Auto* Transatlantic Race] by Francis Armstrong
The Cycle and the Motorcycle [Tricycles; Road Mending] by Archibald Williams
Outdoor Dress [Sporting Clothes and Fashions] by Leo Trevor
Diet and Training [Mutton Fat; Jockey Weights] by George Dabbs
The Referee's Room [The Corinthians Football Team; Winter Lawn Tennis] by Charles Fry
An Ideal Food; Illustrated by Cecil Thomas

Issue 9 : December 1904 (p233-352 + 16)

Cover Design; Illustrated by Thomas Browne
Outdoor Men: Charles Dickens by Ernest Coussell; Illustrated by Thomas Browne
Progress in the Outdoor World [Winter Sports; New Zealand Rugby; London Omnibus; Above the Alps; Cycle Racing; Foxhounds in Portugal; Hockey in Holland; Scottish Salmon Fishing; Walnut Women; Shop Assistants]
To See Him Triumph by Guy Thorne; Illustrated by Paul Hardy
The Story of the Corinthians by Charles Fry
King of the Kerb by May Doney
The Big Brother by Frederick Palmer; Illustrated by George Soper
How to Handle a Revolver by Walter Winans
Christmas on the Coach by Alfred Cooper; Illustrated by Joseph Shayer, Hugh Thompson, Charles Henderson and James Pollard

Cyril Corbally

Dorothy Campbell

Frank Croft

Harry Colt

Horace Cheshire

Humphry Cobb

James Carruthers

John Campbell

Leo Cheney

The Man-Tracker in Training by Stanhope Sprigg
Manisty's Island by Archibald Demain-Grange; Illustrated by Edward Hodgson
One of the Old School [verses] by Bertram Atkey; Illustrated by Anthony Helmer
The Wind by Bart Kennedy; Illustrated by Louis Berneker
Out of Harness [Nicholas Romanov, Dom Carlos, Lees Knowles, Jerome Jerome, Alexander Bruce and Cyril Maude]
Pretty Polly: Queen of the Turf by Dick Luckman
Is the Farmer a Fool? by John Robertson-Scott
Our Noah's Ark [Snapping Turtle; A Young Lion; Glen Island Zoo; Pet Pony; Chinese Chow-Dog; Horned Toad; Pet Lamb; Musk Calf]
Straight Talk [Pictorial Front Covers; London Playing Fields Society; Arabella Kenealy, Arthur Brodrick; Football Referees; Four-in-Hands] by Charles Fry
From Headquarters [Hockey Match Expenses; Middlesex Badminton Championships] by Wallis Myers
The Motor Afield and Afloat [Carriage Varnish; Reliability Trials] by Francis Armstrong
The Cycle and the Motorcycle [Motor Shows; Compression] by Archibald Williams
Outdoor Dress [Gentlemen's Clothing; The Cricketer's Moustache] by Leo Trevor
The Outdoor Girl; Illustrated by Charles Dawson
Diet and Training [Sound Teeth; Fitness Training] by George Dabbs
The Referee's Room [Lawn Tennis Twins; Crystalate Billiard Balls] by Charles Fry
The Prize Winner; Illustrated by Charles Pears

Issue 10 : January 1905 (p353-468 + 20)

Cover Design; Illustrated by Thomas Browne
Outdoor Men: Charles Beresford by Ernest Coussell
Progress in the Outdoor World [Fitness; Sailors; Horse Racing; Presidents of Sporting Bodies; *Wisden's Cricketers' Almanack*; Gipsy Quarters; Discus Throwing; Percy Coles Rugby Football Union Secretary]
His Majesty the Groom [verses] by Bertram Atkey; Illustrated by Thomas Browne
Glasgow: The City of Football by Robert Livingstone
The Charioteer by Guy Thorne; Illustrated by Paul Hardy
Golf Faults Illustrated (1): The Drive by John Taylor & George Beldam
The History of Billiards in Pictures by Cecil Hughes
Tally-Ho! [verses] by May Doney; Illustrated by Edward Skinner
Saturday Night With the Pugs by George Edgar; Illustrated by Henry Bacon
The Caesar of Cumberland: Hugh Lowther by Harold Begbie
In the Prophet's Treasury by Edwin Arnold; Illustrated by Thornton Oakley
For England and Rugby Football by Philip Trevor
The Freeman Shod With Steel by Vance Thompson
Out of Harness [Reginald Campbell; Henrietta Stannard; William Montagu; Charles Axel; Christian Axel; Arthur Bourchier; William Treloar]
The New Service Rifle by Charles Fry
Our Noah's Ark [Cats and Rats; German Ketch; Lemur; Polar Bears]
The Modern Hockey Stick by Eustace White

Mornington Cannon

Rufus Carter

William Curtis

Bargrave Deane

Charles Dixon

Dorothy Dickinson

Frank Day

George Duncan

Jonathan Dwight

Our Revolving Bookcase [Reviews of *Fifty Leaders of Sport* by Frederick Aflalo; *Avoiding the Sunset in the South* by Eustace Reynolds-Ball; *Rowing & Sculling* by Guy Rixon; *National Physical Training* by John Atkins]
Straight Talk [Marie Corelli; Motorcar Accidents; Oxford College Scholarships; Bearing-Reins; Professional Football; Australian Cricketers; Theodore Roosevelt; Lionel Ford; Frank Wethered; William Hodgson; Women and Exercise] by Charles Fry
From Headquarters [Sunderland Football Suspensions; Dublin Badminton Championships] by Wallis Myers
The Motor Afield and Afloat [Air Vents; Speed Records] by Francis Armstrong
The Cycle and the Motorcycle [Stanley Show; Tricars] by Archibald Williams
Outdoor Dress [Greatcoats; Inverness Capes] by Leo Trevor
Diet and Training [Toast Water; Plumbism; Barley] by George Dabbs
The Referee's Room [Acetylene Lamps; Model Motor Cars] by Charles Fry

Issue 11 : February 1905 (p469-572 + 24)

Cover Design; Illustrated by Thomas Browne
Outdoor Men: Alfred Tennyson by Ernest Coussell; Illustrated by George Thorp
Progress in the Outdoor World [Winter Holidays; The Northern Games; John Raphael Rugby Three-Quarters; James MacDonald; Leon Meredith; George Lohmann; Athletic Policemen; Hubert Ramsey Lacrosse; Canadian Farms; Alpine Views; Scottish Salmon Fishing]
The Song of the Winter Road [verses] by May Doney; Illustrated by Joseph Skelton
The Captures of Carington (1) by Philip Trevor; Illustrated by Stanley Wood
How to Drive a Trotter by Walter Winans
Golf Faults Illustrated (2): The Mashie by John Taylor & George Beldam
Woolwich Arsenal in Training by Cecil Hughes
The Shadow by Owen Oliver
Nature Under the Snow by Edward Step
Points in Rugby Play (1): The Knack of Kicking a Rugby Ball by Harry Alexander
The Ocean by Bart Kennedy; Illustrated by Louis Berneker
Tips for Road Riders by George Olley
Illegalities of Hockey by Henry Moncrieff-Tennent
Out of Harness [Constance Stewart-Richardson; William Barker; Robert Horton]
The Coach from Wales by Arthur Ranger-Gull; Illustrated by Edward Skinner
Our Noah's Ark [Mice; Dog Collection; Bears; Italian Greyhounds; Rome Cats]
Straight Talk [Test Cricket; Walking; Outdoor Socialism; Bus Horses; *Les Sports* and *La Vie au Grand Air* French Newspapers; Army Veterinary Department; Belfast Women] by Charles Fry
From Headquarters [Football Association Cup Final Venue; George Harnett Rugby Referee; Lancashire Cricket] by Wallis Myers
The Motor Afield and Afloat [Paris Exhibition; Paris to Madrid Race Disasters] by Francis Armstrong
The Cycle and the Motorcycle [Motorcycle Journals; Cycling Clubdom] by Archibald Williams
Outdoor Dress [Leather Gaiters; Stage Costumes] by Leo Trevor
Diet and Training [Lead Poisoning; Glazed Windows] by George Dabbs
Our Revolving Bookcase [Reviews of *Hints on Revolver Shooting* by Walter Winans; *Nature and*

Stanley Duncan

Charles Eldred

John Edwards-Moss

Joseph Elwell

Anthony Fane

Herbert Fowler

Leonard Flemming

Miss Beatrice Fry

Reginald Foster

Sport in Britain by Henry Bryden; *Curly* by Roger Pocock; *The Sportsman's Book for India* by Montague Gerard; *Angling Observations of a Coarse Fisherman* by Charles Marson; *Animal Autobiographies* by Geraldine Mitton; *William Tell Told Again* by Pelham Wodehouse]
The Referee's Room [Rim Brakes; Eyas Hawks; Army Coaching] by Charles Fry

Issue 12 : March 1905 (p573-668 + 32)

Cover Design; Illustrated by Thomas Browne
The Talk of the Office by Bertram Atkey
Outdoor Men: Charles Kingsley by Ernest Coussell
Progress in the Outdoor World [Cricket Captains; Calcio; United Hospitals Rugby; Ardennes Motor Circuit; Hampstead Hockey Club; John Kerr Scottish Amateur Athletic Association; Shooting; Boxing; Cycling in Scotland]
The Lurcher [verses] by Bertram Atkey; Illustrated by Charles Tresidder
Shall We Beat Australia by Reginald Foster
The Captures of Carington (2) by Philip Trevor; Illustrated by Stanley Wood
The Romance of the Motorcycle by Cecil Hughes
The Best Team in Lancashire by John Bentley
The Crowning of Dolly by Ridley Beal; Illustrated by Allen True
What Makes the Sprinter by Arthur Duffey
The Art of Starting by Charles Fry
How to Handle a Frightened Horse by Charles Fry
Golf Faults Illustrated (3): Mashie Play by John Taylor & George Beldam
The Zoo of the East End by Bertram Atkey
Out of Harness [John Williams-Benn; Dom Alfonso; Alexander Macduff]
Our Noah's Ark [Havier Deer; Paris Ratodrome; Sleighs; Small Horses]
Straight Talk [Test Cricket; Weather; Dartmoor Foxes; Animal Training; Playgrounds] by Charles Fry
From Headquarters [Lowestoft Town Football Club Suspension; Public Schools Rugby; Jockey Club Reform] by Wallis Myers
The Motor Afield and Afloat [Automobile Club of France; Society of Motor Manufacturers and Traders] by Francis Armstrong
The Cycle and Motorcycle [Revolving Cylinders; Charging Cells] by Archibald Williams
Outdoor Dress [Tailors] by Leo Trevor
Diet and Training [Ambidexterity; Review of *The Commonsense Diet for Training* by Alexander Haig] by George Dabbs
Our Revolving Bookcase [Reviews of *Photography for the Sportsman Naturalist* by Leverett Brownell; *Lawn Tennis* by Jahial Parmly-Paret; *Physical Educator* by Eustace Miles; *Mr Watch* by George Dabbs; *Picturesque Middlesex* by Frederick Robinson]
The Referee's Room [Sewer Gas; Antwerp Cycling Championships; Review of *The Sportsman's Yearbook* by Wallis Myers] by Charles Fry

Volume 3

Issue 13 : April 1905 (p1-104 + 36)

Cover Design; Illustrated by Thomas Browne
Talk of the Office by Bertram Atkey
Outdoor Men: Richard Webster by Ernest Coussell
In the Outdoor World [Indoor Cricket Pitches; First Boat Race; Thomas Dewar; Frederick McKenzie; Staines Hockey Team]
Famous Old Rowing Blues: James Hornby, Albert de Rutzen, Edward Macnaghten, Edmond Warre, John Edwards-Moss, Arthur Russell, William Grenfell, Reginald McKenna
John Roberts [Billiards] by Sydenham Dixon
The Man Behind the Horn [verses] by Bertram Atkey; Illustrated by Thomas Browne
Golf Faults Illustrated (4): More Mashie Play by John Taylor & George Beldam
The Captures of Carington (3) by Philip Trevor; Illustrated by Stanley Wood
The Nation's Ball [verses] by May Doney
Football in Sheffield by Cecil Hughes
Realities of Baseball by Earl Mayo
Walter Gilbey [Elsenham Stud] by Harold Begbie
Internationals on Internationals [Tinsley Lindley, John Tait Robertson, George Brann, Frederick Spiksley, Ernest Needham, Alexander McMahon, Walter Arnott] by Wallis Myers
The Secret of the Japanese Army by Frederick McKenzie
The Barrister, The Blue and The Lady by Percy White; Illustrated by Henry Brock
Football From the Pressbox by Archibald De Bear
Out of Harness [Sydney Holland; Silvester Horne; Vera Ponsonby, Susan Muir-Mackenzie, Francis Campbell]
Our Noah's Ark [The Weka; London Seagulls; Crabs]
Straight Talk [Athletics; Professional Football; Betting; The Rural Brain; Clothing; Fitness; George Butler] by Charles Fry
From Headquarters [Cambridge University Cross-Country Race; Football Association Cup Attendances and Gate Money; Irish Football Referee's Association; Davis Cup Tennis] by Wallis Myers
Golfer's Gear; Illustrated by William Robinson
The Motor Afield and Afloat [Olympia Exhibition; Ten Miles an Hour Speed Limit Refusal] by Francis Armstrong
The Cycle and the Motorcycle [Cyclists' Touring Club; Police Traps] by Archibald Williams
Outdoor Dress [Military Tailors; Army Clothing Manufactory] by Leo Trevor
Diet and Training [Athletic Association Surgeons; Review of *Book of Health* by Malcolm Morris; Indian Club Swinging] by George Dabbs
Our Revolving Bookcase [Reviews of *Great Lawn Tennis Players* by George Beldham; *A Boy's Control* by Eustace Miles; *Cycle and Camp* by Thomas Holding; *Jim Mortimer, Surgeon* by Warren Bell; *Scientific Weight-Lifting* by Thomas Inch; *Inexpensive Holiday Homes* by Douglas Allport]
The Referee's Room [London Athletic Club; Cricket Pitch Maintenance] by Charles Fry
See The King; Illustrated by Victor Beveridge
Pedestrianism; Illustrated by Dudley Cleaver

Archibald Hamilton

Basil Hill

Cecil Hutchison

Eyre Hussey

Frederic Harrison

Henry Hughes

John Hutcheon

Leonard Hill

Reginald Hands

Issue 14 : May 1905 (p105-200 + 40)

Cover Design; Illustrated by Thomas Browne
Pelham Warner; Illustrated by Roland Hill
Outdoor Men: Arthur Balfour by Ernest Coussell
In the Outdoor World [Continental Sport; Ernest Shipton Cyclists' Touring Club; County Cricket; County Captains Illustrated; Gunnery; Motorboats; Scottish Athletics; Highland Cattle]
Joseph Nicholas - Umpire [verses] by Bertram Atkey; Illustrated by Thomas Browne
How Steve Mackerley Got Even by William Osborne; Illustrated by Harry Williamson
The Cricket Ball in the Making by Cecil Hughes
Variable Speed Gears by Richard Mecredy
The Knack of Jumping by Charles Fry
America on the English Turf by Dick Luckman
To the River Between Barnes and Kew Bridges [verses] by Cyril Austin
Golf Faults Illustrated (5): Golfing Swing by John Taylor & George Beldam
Strength and Grace by Macdonald Smith
The Captures of Carington (4) by Philip Trevor; Illustrated by Stanley Wood
The Garden God [verses] by Cecil Hughes
The People of the Water Lanes by May Doney
Out of Harness [Leslie Stuart; Frances Wolseley; Thomas Dewar; Edward Grace; Emmanuel Grecia; Arthur Balfour]
The Symbol of the Cestus by Guy Thorne; Illustrated by Paul Hardy
Our Noah's Ark [Otters; The Kea; Brazilian Toads]
Straight Talk [Laziness, Fishing; Otter Hunting; Clothing; Hackney Horse Show; Nebraska; Trans-Atlantic Cattle Trade] by Charles Fry
From Headquarters [Athletic Trophies; Highgate Harriers; Club Cricket; Belfast Charity Football Cup; Fettes College Rugby; Middlesex Walking Club] by Charles Fry
The Motor Afield and Afloat [Motorcycle Side-Slip; Islington Exhibition] by Francis Armstrong
The Cycle and Motorcycle [Cheap Bicycles; Grinding Valves] by Richard Mecredy
Outdoor Dress [Straw Hats; Flannel Clothing] by Leo Trevor
Diet and Training [Foul Air; Sanitary Surroundings] by George Dabbs
Our Revolving Bookcase [Reviews of *The Charms of Driving in Motors* by David Salomons; *The Roedeer* by Ernest Harwar; *Trout Fishing* by Earl Hodgson; *The Outdoor Handy Book* by Daniel Beard; *Miss Lavinia Badsworth MFH* by Eyre Hussey]
The Referee's Room [Cricket Scoring Books; Queen's Club Tennis; Swiss Milk] by Charles Fry

Issue 15 : June 1905 (p201-298 + 30)

Cover Design; Illustrated by Thomas Browne
The Talk of the Office by Bertram Atkey
Outdoor Men: Edward Lyttelton by Ernest Coussell
In the Outdoor World [Amateur Golf Championship; Jack White; Mid-Surrey Golf Club; Grace Brothers; Alfred Shaw; Charles Herbert; Ernest Vogler; The Derby; Josiah Ritchie; Alexander Stevenson Scottish Football Association President; Henry Stevenson; Herbert Beerbohm-Tree]
The Australian Batsman in the Making by Victor Trumper and James Bolton
Athletes Without Knowing It by Cecil Hughes

 Stanley Harris
 Thomas Holding
 William Houghton

 Williams Haynes
 Gordon Inglis
 Thomas Inch

 Alfred Jardine
 Charles Jarrott
 Claude Scudamore-Jarvis

If Menchikoff had not Called for Coffee by Dorothea Conyers; Illustrated by Alfred Pearse
Golf Faults Illustrated (6): Difficulties Through the Green by John Taylor & George Beldam
How to Make Records on the Road by George Olley
The Furze Folk (1) by Bertram Atkey; Illustrated by Harry Rountree
Ode to a Pig [verses] by Litchfield Woods
Points in Batsmanship (1) by Charles Fry
Our Noah's Ark [Predatory Cat; Swan versus Fox; Canaries; Fox-Terrier]
The Captures of Carington (5) by Philip Trevor; Illustrated by Stanley Wood
My Lord the Gardener [verses] by Bertram Atkey; Illustrated by Thomas Browne
Out of Harness [Francis Carruthers-Gould; Kumar Ranjitsinhji; Archibald Maclaren]
Straight Talk [Games; Gardens; Living in Flats; Garden Cities] by Charles Fry
From Headquarters [Amateur Athletic Championships; Scottish Amateur Athletic Association; Polo; Scottish Lawn Tennis; Amateur Swimming Association; West of Scotland Cricket Club] by Charles Fry
The Motor and The Cycle [Tyre Repair; Royal Marines Artillery Chauffeurs; Motor Car Traffic] by Richard Mecredy
Outdoor Dress [I Zingari Blazers; Green Jackets] by Leo Trevor
Diet and Training [Japanese Soldiers' Rations; American Episcopate] by George Dabbs
Our Revolving Bookcase [Reviews of *The Sea Fishing of England and Wales* by Frederick Aflalo; *Wild Flowers* by Edward Step; *Flowering Plants* by Anne Pratt; *Fergy the Guide* by Henry Canfield; *An Angler's Hours* by Hugh Sheringham; *Tracks of a Rolling Stone* by Henry Coke]
The Referee's Room [Croquet Records; Arthur Dunn Cup; Midland Tennis Club] by Charles Fry

Issue 16 : July 1905 (p299-392 + 36)

Cover Design; Illustrated by Thomas Browne
The Talk of the Office [The Question of Binding] by Bernard Atkey
Outdoor Men: Walter Long by Ernest Coussell
In the Outdoor World [Australian Cricketers; Frank Laver; County Cricketers; Lady Swimmers in Queensland; Lawn Tennis Championships; Polo; Kensington Gardens; Sailors Ashore]
Is Golf An Old Man's Game? [Arthur Balfour, Alfred Lyttelton, John Laidlay, Marshall Hall, Max Pemberton, Leslie Balfour-Melville, James Braid, May Hezlet] by Wallis Myers; Illustrated by Thomas Browne
Cricket in Kensington Gardens by James Barrie
Points in Batsmanship (2) by Charles Fry
The Faithful Brady by Larrey Bowman; Illustrated by Urquhart Wilcox
The American Service: A Lawn Tennis Paradox by Edgar Timmis
The Furze Folk (2) by Bertram Atkey; Illustrated by Harry Rountree
The Story of Leander by Rudolf Lehmann
The Captures of Carington (6) by Philip Trevor; Illustrated by Stanley Wood
The Wars of England [verses] by Arthur Lodge
The Freeman of the Moor by May Doney
Village Sports: A Proposal by William Beach-Thomas; Illustrated by Rex Osborne
The Bowler and His Art by Hugh Trumble and James Bolton
Our Noah's Ark [Theatre Dogs; Dingo Puppies; Colin Campbell; Bactrian Camel]

Digby Jephson

Gwendoline Johnes

John Jackett

Richard Jeffries

Walter Jerrold

Leopold Katscher

William Knowles

Charles Lane

Clifford Leigh

Don'ts For Polo Players by Richard Carlisle

Country Cricket in South Africa by Leonard Flemming; Illustrated by Rex Osborne

Straight Talk [Holiday Training; River Maniacs; Outdoor Artists] by Charles Fry

From Headquarters [Hammer-Throwing; Blackheath Harriers; University Polo; Romford Croquet Club; New Boat Racing Laws] by Charles Fry

The Motor and The Cycle [Anfield Bicycle Club; Irish Motorcycle Union; Cyclometers] by Richard Mecredy

Outdoor Dress [Suits; Boots; Borrowed Clothing] by Leo Trevor

Health, Diet and Training [Indian Food; Siberian Fish-Bread; Review of *Food in Health and Disease* by Burney Yeo] by George Dabbs

Our Revolving Bookcase [Reviews of *Wild Ducks* by Coape Oates; *Herbert Asquith* by John Alderson; *Rifle and Romance in the Indian Jungle* by Alexander Glasfurd]

The Referee's Room [More Criticism of the Magazine's Bound Volumes; Poultry Farming] by Charles Fry

Issue 17 : August 1905 (p393-488 + 36)

Cover Design; Illustrated by Thomas Browne

Talk of the Office by Bertram Atkey

Outdoor Men: Winston Churchill by Ernest Coussell

In the Outdoor World [Stanley Jackson; Harry Butt; Lawn Tennis; Ciceley Foster; Nina Coote; Bernard Keiran; David Lloyd-George; Joseph Chandler; Stanley Noble]

The Battle to the Strong by John Whitson; Illustrated by Stanley Wood

Success in Bowling by Frederick Spofforth and James Bolton

Greenway's Training System by Philip Arp; Illustrated by Rex Osborne

The Music That Carries [verses] by Strickland Gillilan

When Priscilla Holds the Wheel [verses] by Mabel Richards; Illustrated by Frederick Buchanan

The Four-Ball Break in Croquet by Frank Croft

The Tyranny of Golf by McDonnell Bodkin; Illustrated by Thomas Browne

The Polo Pony at School by May Doney

Out in the Country [verses] by Cora Matson-Dolson

Linnet-Singing as an East London Diversion by Ralph Paine

Marigolds: A Fisherman's Idyll by Lucy Montgomery; Illustrated by Wallis Mills

Points in Batsmanship (3) by Charles Fry

The Quick Change Remorqueur by Arthur Ranger-Gull; Illustrated by Joseph Skelton

Our Noah's Ark [Dog Breeding; Tibetan Wild Ass]

What is a Foot-Fault by Harry Scrivener

Straight Talk [Simple Life; Paris Motoring; Holiday Photography; Alphabet; Game Shooting; Piscatorial Trophies] by Charles Fry

From the Willow to the Wicket by Timothy Gradidge

Review Essay: *Polo, Past and Present* by Thomas Dale

From Headquarters [Ranelagh Harriers; Glasgow Police Sports; Ostend Polo Tournament; Obituary of Harold Mahony, Irish Lawn Tennis Player] by Charles Fry

A Cricketer's Grave [Percy McDonnell] from the *Brisbane Saturday Observer*

The Motor and The Cycle [Cycle Camping; Irish Motor Union] by Richard Mecredy

 Ethel Larcombe
 Freeman Lloyd
 Henry Lock

 Lorin Lathop
 Robert Lattimer
 Alan Marshal

 Alexander Macdonald
 Aymer Maxwell
 Edward Michell

Outdoor Dress [Top-Hats; Soda Water; Umbrellas] by Leo Trevor
Health, Diet and Training [Holidays; Mountain Climbing] by George Dabbs
Our Revolving Bookcase [Reviews of *From Tokyo to Tiflis* by Frederick McKenzie; *Guns, Ammunition and Tackle* by Albert Money; *The Physical Culture Life* by Irving Hancock; *Oxford and Cambridge Scores and Biographies* by John Betham; *Carthusian Memories* by William Haig-Brown]
The Referee's Room [Havelock Cycle Club; Old Westminsters Football Club] by Charles Fry

Issue 18 : September 1905 (p489-584 + 32)

Cover Design; Illustrated by Thomas Browne
Talk of the Office by Bertram Atkey
Outdoor Men: Stanley Jackson by Charles Fry
In the Outdoor World [Cricket; Lawn Tennis; Coaching; Henley Regatta; Road Racing; Polo in New Zealand; London Bathing; San Remo Golf Club]
Allelooyer Joe by Warren Bell; Illustrated by Stanley Wood
The Pilgrim of the Links [verses] by Bertram Atkey; Illustrated by Thomas Browne
Points in Batsmanship (4) by Charles Fry
The Furze Folk (3) by Bertram Atkey; Illustrated by Harry Rountree
Life on the Busy Beach by Frederick Aflalo
Pilli-Pang-Wang by Frederick Walworth; Illustrated by Walter Enright
Why Golf is Good for Girls by Bertha Thompson
Sailing: The Real Thing by George Hopcroft
Leg-Before-Wicket on Paper by Edward Sewell; Illustrated by Frederick Leist
The Groundsmen of Europe by Frank Ormiston-Smith
Our Noah's Ark [The Opossum; Mice on Submarines; Indian Hornbills]
Scouting in England by Roger Pocock
A Man's Risk by Owen Oliver; Illustrated by Caton Woodville
A French School of Arms by Charles Fry
A Garden at Lausanne [verses] by Cecil Hughes
Straight Talk [Sport; Cooking; Gardens; Children; Boots; Ball Games; Yachting] by Charles Fry
Citizen Soldiers in Camp: Out of Doors With the Volunteers
From Headquarters [Golf Ball Court Case; Indian Polo Association; Clydesdale Harriers] by Charles Fry
The Motor and The Cycle [Irish Cycling; New Era Extinguisher] by Richard Mecredy
Outdoor Dress [Luggage; Review of *Dress Outfits for Abroad* by Ardern Holt] by Leo Trevor
Health, Diet and Training [Family Health; Cholera] by George Dabbs
The Referee's Room [Kent Cricket; Hockey Clubs; Car Air Valves] by Charles Fry
A New Inter-County Cricket Competition by Charles Fry
Navy Mixture; Illustrated by Victor Beveridge

George Meagher

George Miller

Henry Merwin

Howard Marks

Robert Marston

Stewart Massey

William McGregor

Edward Newitt

Raymond Needham

Volume 4

Issue 19 : October 1905 (p1-96 + 36)

Cover Design; Illustrated by Thomas Browne
Talk of the Office by Bertram Atkey
Outdoor Men: Andrew Carnegie by William Stead
In the Outdoor World [New Zealand Rugby Tourists; David Bedell-Sivwright; Football League Teams; Cricket; Lawn Tennis; London Heroes; Robert Perks, Chairman of London Underground]
The Song of the Bass [verses] by Alice Calhoun-Haines; Illustrated by Louis Rhead
The Black Roan of 265 by Winfried Rolker; Illustrated by Power O'Malley
A Lament [verses] by Mabel Richards
Machine-Made Marksmen by Robert Barson
Forest Football by Bertram Atkey; Illustrated by John Hassall
The Bag-Punchers by Arthur Ranger-Gull; Illustrated by Henry Bacon
The Alpine Ice-Axe by Frank Ormiston-Smith
The Gipsy of England by Ralph Paine
The Furze Folk (4) by Bertram Atkey; Illustrated by Harry Rountree
A College Education by Theodore Roosevelt
The Lost Heritage [verses] by Bertram Atkey
The Art of Peter Latham by Eustace Miles
A Tale of a Cinnamon Bear by Perry Robinson; Illustrated by Rex Osborne
Modern Sport in Sculpture by Alfred Nossig
Our Noah's Ark [Mole Traps]
Rod Fishing on the South African Coast by Benjamin Bennion
The Transformation of the Bulldog by James Watson
Straight Talk [Sporting Stomach; Walking; Baby Farming; Bigotry; Society Dancing; Indoor Animals] by Charles Fry
Our Photo Prize Competition by Charles Fry
From Headquarters [Golf Rules; Athletic Handicapping; Billy Meredith Bribery Case; Amateur Football; Robert Kyle, Sunderland Secretary; Edinburgh University Rugby] by Charles Fry
The Motor and The Cycle [Lubrication; Touring] by Richard Mecredy
Outdoor Dress [Gloves; Shooting; Railway Ticket Inspectors] by Leo Trevor
Health, Diet and Training [Skin Grazing; Channel Swimming; Hobbies] by George Dabbs
Our Revolving Bookcase [Reviews of *The Evolution of the Trotter* by Hamilton Busbey; *Cricket Poems* by George Wilson]
The Referee's Room [Camberwell Indoor Cricket; Ladies' Golf Clubs] by Charles Fry
The Motor Smoker; Illustrated by Charles Harrison

Issue 20 : November 1905 (p97-192 + 36)

Cover Design; Illustrated by Thomas Browne
Talk of the Office by Bertram Atkey
Outdoor Men: Horatio Nelson by Ernest Coussell
In the Outdoor World [Football; John Lewis; Referees; John McDowall, Scottish Football

Stanley Noble

Frank Ormiston-Smith

George Olley

Henrik Pontoppidan

Issette Pearson

James Parke

John Porter

Sidney Phipps

Charles Rolls

Association Secretary; Arthur Lilley; Fettes College; John McGough; Irish Hockey; London Open Spaces; New York Recreation Grounds; Cyclist Newsboys; English Ladies Golf Championship; Wild Duck; Cats; Hermit's Derby; Plymouth Reservoir]
The River Bandit [verses] by Bertram Atkey; Illustrated by Thomas Browne
Tuck-of-Drum by Alfred Sheppard; Illustrated by Caton Woodville
The Leader [verses] by George Raymond
The Horse and the Way by Edith Somerville
Points in Rugby Play (2): Catching and Saving by Harry Alexander
The New Schoolmaster by Norman Innes; Illustrated by Alfred Pearse
Essentials for the Wrestler and the Boxer by Ernest Coll
The Tobacco Plantation by Bart Kennedy; Illustrated by Rex Osborne
City Fathers of Football by John Bentley
Dick's Drive by Arthur Guiterman; Illustrated by Rex Osborne
The Points of a Racehorse by Frederic Inskip-Harrison
A Golf Stick in the Making by Wallis Myers
How a Turtle Builds its Nest by Ray Baker
Where School Football Teams Fail by Alan Haig-Brown
The Furze Folk (5) by Bertram Atkey; Illustrated by Harry Rountree
The Art of Heading by John Robertson and James Bolton
Mr MG From Sanford by Lue Hall; Illustrated by Alexander Svoboda
Advice to a Young Man by Martin Steenson
Straight Talk [The Human Boy; *The National League for Physical Education and Improvement*; The Alien Question; Courtesies of Sport; Natural Mobilisation; Playing Fields] by Charles Fry
From Headquarters [Sandwich Golf Club; Athletics Official Starters; Football Maximum Wage] by Charles Fry
The Motor and The Cycle [Cost of Motoring; Goggles; Auto Cycle Club] by Richard Mecredy
Outdoor Dress [Tropical Clothing; Fishing Outfits; Oilskin Apron] by Leo Trevor
Health, Diet and Training [Modern Fireplaces; Ventilation; Theatre Drainage Systems] by George Dabbs
Our Revolving Bookcase [Reviews of *Country Cottages* by John Robertson-Scott; *The Practical Angler* by William Stewart; *The Hundred Days* by Max Pemberton; *Golf Faults* by George Beldam & John Taylor; *Lifting the Veil* by Frederick Payn]
The Outdoor Girl [Women's Hobbies; Ladies' Golf] by Esther Meynell
The Referee's Room [Dublin University Cricket Club; Walking Boots; Regent Street Polytechnic] by Charles Fry

Issue 21 : December 1905 (p193-288 + 48)

Cover Design; Illustrated by Thomas Browne
Beautifully Mild; Illustrated by Frank Reynolds
The King of Mazy May; Illustrated by Caton Woodville
Talk of the Office by Bertram Atkey
Outdoor Men: Albert Saxe-Coburg by Ernest Coussell
In the Outdoor World [*Punch* Magazine; Berlin Ice Switchback; Grindelwald; Outdoor London; Motor Omnibuses; Rugby; Argentina Football Association; James Braid; Thomas Pethick; Western Counties Hockey Association; William Johnstone; Edward Salvesen; James Burns]

George Raymond

George Robertson

John Raphael

John Robertson

Mabel Richards

Bertram Smith

Edgar Syers

Frederick Spofforth

Gilbert Smith

On the Banks of the Sacramento by Jack London; Illustrated by Caton Woodville
Kicking Commandments Illustrated by Charles Fry
The Furze Folk (6) by Bertram Atkey; Illustrated by Harry Rountree
With the Korps-Students in Germany by Lees Knowles
How to Score Goals at Hockey by Eustace White
The Auctioneer [verses] by Bertram Atkey; Illustrated by Thomas Browne
Some Curious Golf Lies by Alexander Robertson; Illustrated by Rex Osborne
An Old International by Edgar Barnes-Austin; Illustrated by Alfred Pearse
The Soul of Saturday [verses] by May Doney
The Parliament of Cycling by Stanley Noble
Points in Rugby Play (3): Collaring by Harry Alexander
How the Major Lost His Arm by Perry Robinson; Illustrated by Rex Osborne
Friends by George Edgar; Illustrated by Caton Woodville
Time in a Village by Robert Stevenson
Our Noah's Ark [Cats; Collie Dogs; Apes]
Straight Talk [Presents; Firesides; Open-Top Bus; Animal Physiognomy; Clothes; Swimming] by Charles Fry
Holiday Photograph Competition
From Headquarters [Amateur Athletics; Steve Bloomer Testimonial; Scottish Football; Irish Army Football Cup; Amateur Football Clubs; Scottish Rugby Union; Hockey; Badminton] by Charles Fry
By Jove!; Illustrated by Charles Pears
The Motor and The Cycle [Wire Wheels; Lighter Bicycles; Length of Wheelbase; Back Wheel Hub Brakes] by Richard Mecredy
The Best of Things; Illustrated by Charles Harrison
Outdoor Dress [Hairy Car Coats; Breeches & Gaiters; Leather Clothing] by Leo Trevor; Illustrated by Thomas Browne
Health, Diet and Training [Chilblains; Rugby Training; Amateur Theatricals; Debating Societies] by George Dabbs; Illustrated by Rex Osborne
Our Revolving Bookcase [Reviews of *The Car Road Book* by John Scott-Montagu; *Model Sailing Yachts* by Percival Marshall; *Horse Breaking* by Alma Campbell; *Life of Dan Leno* by Hickory Wood; *Pictures From Punch* by Francis Burnand, Illustrated by George Jalland & Doris Hatt; *Brains and Ink* by Eleanor Abbott]
The Outdoor Girl [Clubbing; Basketball, Cycling] by Esther Meynell
The Referee's Room [British Guiana Motorcycles; Indoor Cricket Pitches; Queen's Club Lawn Tennis; Pair-Oared Rowing; Western Australian Farms] by Charles Fry
So Near Yet So Far; Illustrated by Thomas Browne

Issue 22 : January 1906 (p289-388 + 44)

Cover Design; Illustrated by Charles Crombie
Outdoor Men: George Saxe-Coburg by Ernest Coussell
In the Outdoor World [New Zealand Rugby Tour; Miniature Rifle Range; Bournemouth Golf Course; Steeplejacks; Sheep in Regents Park]
Cobbeldick of Wam-Wam (1) by Harold Begbie; Illustrated by Harry Rountree

Harry Stevenson

Madeline Syers

Maud Stuart

Newton Scott

Philip Squire

Robert Surtees

Stanley Shoveller

Willy Sulzbacher

Bertha Thompson

The Explorers by Bertram Atkey
The Weather Test in Golf (1) by John Taylor & George Beldam
Roper's Ride by Peter Rowley; Illustrated by Thomas Browne
Old Pipe of Mine [verses] by Elizabeth Payne
The Goalkeeper's Art by Charles Fry
Sergeant Ruggles by Christopher Scrope; Illustrated by John Stewart
Hockey Strokes and How to Play Them by Eustace White
National Character in Figure Skating by Edgar Syers
Points in Rugby Play (4): The Scrum by Harry Alexander
The Football Candidate by Philip Trevor; Illustrated by Alfred Pearse
The Blot on British Games (1) by Charles Fry
The Story of Keesh by Jack London; Illustrated by Caton Woodville
A Private View of the Pressbox by Philip Bussy; Illustrated by himself
Opportunity [verses] by Jeanette Carey
How to Use a Rifle by Robert Pearson
Straight Talk [German Cookery Classes; Bulldogs; Slum Babies; *The Keepers' Benefit Society*]
    by Charles Fry
Our Noah's Ark [Cats; Siding Horses; Dog Outfitters]
The New Zealanders' Football Song by Edward Secker
From Headquarters [Bertha Thompson, Ladies Golfer; London Caledonian Football Club;
    Cambridge University Rugby] by Charles Fry
As We See Ourselves; Illustrated by Guy Thorne
The Outdoor Girl [Business Girls; Clothing; Sporting Attire] by Esther Meynell
Health, Diet and Training [Debating Societies; Elocution; Literary Tests] by George Dabbs
Outdoor Dress [Motoring Headgear; Ready-Made Clothes] by Leo Trevor
The Referee's Room [Lawn Tennis Club Management; Winter Cricket; Portable Rifle Range]
    by Charles Fry
An Apology: Withdrawl of Competition [Charles Fry 'error']
The Motor and The Cycle [Engine Filters; Bicycle Frames; Spring Forks] by Richard Mecredy
Possibilities by Edward Anton
Our Book Corner [Reviews of *Poultry Farming* by John Robertson-Scott; *Retrievers and
    Retrieving* by William Eley; *The Ladder of Pain* by George Dabbs; *Physical Culture Exercise*
    by Frederick Stevens; *Strength for All* by John Melville; *Wildfowl* by Lewis Shaw; *Big Game
    Shooting* by Horace Hutchinson]

Issue 23 : February 1906 (p389-484 + 40)

Cover Design; Illustrated by Charles Crombie
Frontispiece: Frederick Roberts; Illustrated by George Thorp
British Bushido by Charles Fry
The Maily Face [verses] by Bertram Atkey
The Ashes of English Rugby by Samuel Woods and James Bolton
Ministerial Sportsmen [Henry Campbell-Bannerman, Edward Grey, Rupert Carington, Winston
    Churchill, Herbert Asquith, John Burns, Robert Reid, Herbert Gladstone,
    Robert Crewe-Milnes, James Bryce] by Wallis Myers

Charles Townsend

Edgar Timmis

Frederick Thomas

George Thompson

Hugh Trumble

Jesse Taylor

John Taylor

Richard Turner

Victor Trumper

Mine Host [verses] by Bertram Atkey; Illustrated by Thomas Browne
Cobbeldick of Wam-Wam (2) by Harold Begbie; Illustrated by Harry Rountree
The Weather Test in Golf (2) by John Taylor & George Beldam
How Curling Stones Are Made by Peat Miller
To a Pigeon [verses] by Bertram Atkey
How the Squire Ratted by Peter Rowley; Illustrated by Thomas Browne
On Glittering Blades by George Meagher
Never Travel Alone by Jack London; Illustrated by Caton Woodville
Examples of Back Play by Charles Fry
Lottridge by Ray Baker; Illustrated by George Gibbs
Bobby the Half-Back by Kathleen Barrow; Illustrated by William Dewar
The Blot on British Games (2) by Charles Fry
Points in Rugby Play (5): Passing by Harry Alexander
The Rubaiyat of the Rugby Football Union [verses] by Archibald Demain-Grange
Straight Talk [Motoring; Clothing; Children's Food] by Charles Fry; Illustrated by George Thorp
    & Frederick Buchanan
The Try [verses] by Bertram Atkey
Our Noah's Ark [Humming-Bird; Gibbets; Cormorants]
From Headquarters [Athletics; Football, Rugby, Hockey, Lacrosse; Wimbledon Badminton Club]
Our Book Corner [Reviews of *Highways and Byways in Oxford and the Cotswolds* by Herbert
    Evans; *Billiards for Everybody* by Charles Roberts; *The Badminton Annual Register* by
    Edward Dyer; *The Fighting Man of Japan* by Francis Norman; *Gale's Almanac*; *The Pig Book*
    by Leslie Brooke]
The Outdoor Girl [Ladies Hockey] by Esther Meynell
The Motor & The Cycle [Carburettors; Tachometers; First-Aid Medical Case; Zenith Bicar]
    by Richard Mecredy
Health and Happiness [Temperament; Horse's Teeth; City Meals] by George Dabbs; Illustrated
    by Frederick Buchanan
Told in the Clubroom [Golf; Cricket]
Outdoor Dress [Waistcoats; Cricket Trousers] by John May
The Camera in the Field [Nature Photography; Coastal Views] by Edward Step
Guns, Gunners and Game by Charles Lancaster
The Referee's Room [Model Engines; Hockey Rules; Review of *Model Sailing Yachts*
    by James Walton; Wincycle Roadster Bicycle] by Charles Fry
The Thrill of the Hunt; Illustrated by John Sturgess

Issue 24 : March 1906 (p485-580 + 48)

Cover Design; Illustrated by Charles Crombie
Civilian Rifle Clubs and the Volunteers by Charles Fry; Illustrated by George Thorp
In the Outdoor World [American Football; Pelota; Duck Shooting; Scottish Salmon; Golf Clubs]
The New Zealanders [verses] by Alfred Cooper; Illustrated by Stephen Dadd
Cobbeldick of Wam-Wam (3) by Harold Begbie; Illustrated by Harry Rountree
Lines to a Dandy [verses] by Bertram Atkey
How to Buy Your New Cycle by Stanley Noble

 Courtney Vernon

 Melvin Vaniman

 Anthony Wilding

 Arthur Wheeler

 Dorette Wilke

 Elizabeth Wolstenholme-Elmy

 Frederic Weiss

 Frederick Ward

 George Warner

The Carthorse Soliloquises [verses] by Bertram Atkey; Illustrated by Thomas Browne
Miniature Rifles by Howard Marks
The Lighthouse Keepers by Bertram Atkey
The Lost Poacher by Jack London; Illustrated by Caton Woodville
Where John Bull Fails by Philip Vaile; Illustrated by John Hassall & Frederick Buchanan
The Fireman [verses] by Cecil Hughes
The Half-Back: His Art by Charles Fry
In the Time of Flowers by Edgar Cook
The Blot on British Games (3) by Charles Fry
Drowning to Order by Peter Rowley; Illustrated by Thomas Brown
How to Save Goals at Hockey by Eustace White
The Art of Green-Keeping by Peter Lees & John Taylor
The Case of Scotland versus New Zealand by Philip Vaile
Did New Zealand Score Against Wales? by Philip Vaile
From Headquarters [Richmond Golf; South London Harriers; London Charity Football Cup; Jack Reid, Irish Football Association Secretary] by Charles Fry
The Outdoor Girl [Outdoor Recreations] by Esther Meynell
Over-Training in Daily Life by Eugen Sandow
The Motor and The Cycle [Blow-Back; Single Cylinder Car; Wheels] by Richard Mecredy
Health, Diet and Training [Japanese Skin Care; Exercise; C.B.Fry Interfering With This Column] by George Dabbs
Outdoor Dress [Waterproof Boots; Cycling Shoes; Garters] by Leo Trevor
Out of Town [Austria; Touring Switzerland] by Alfred Cooper
Our Revolving Bookcase [Reviews of *Red Fox* by Charles Roberts; *Rugby Football Hints* by William Moss; *Jules of the Great Heart* by Lawrence Mott; *Northern Trails* by William Long]
Miniature Rifle Shooting by Edward Leman
The Camera in the Field [Woods and Hedgerows; Colour Screens; Photographing Daffodils; Riversides] by Edward Step
In the Clubroom [Riflemen; Boston Blacking Company; Lawn Tennis; Fives]

Gerald Weigall

James Watson

John Whitson

Lechmere Worrall

Rendell Wilson

Thomas Walls

Cecil Aldin

Denholm Armour

George Ashton

Volume 5

Issue 25 : April 1906 (p1-96 + 60)

Cover Design; Illustrated by Charles Crombie
Talk of the Office by Bertram Atkey
A Nation of Marksmen by Charles Fry; Illustrated by Ernst Wuthrich
In the Outdoor World [Ranjitsinhji's Correct Title; Joseph McCormick; American Athletics; Polytechnic Boxing Club]
No Luck [verses] by Bertram Atkey; Illustrated by Thomas Browne
The Diary of a Honeymoon (1) by Blundell Barrett; Illustrated by Wallis Mills
Danger Moments in Cycling by Pollock Castors
Mr Denham's Nephew by Peter Rowley; Illustrated by Thomas Browne
Sampan Idyl [verses] by Constance Farmar
The Open Stance by John Taylor & George Beldam
Cobbeldick of Wam-Wam (4) by Harold Begbie; Illustrated by Harry Rountree
The Blot on British Games (4) by Charles Fry
A Lesson in Billiards by Warren Bell; Illustrated by Henry Brock
Things John Bull May Learn From His Sons by Philip Vaile; Illustrated by Frederick Buchanan
With the Wind by Philip Vaile
The Forward: His Art by Charles Fry
The Sporting Possibilities of Rifle Shooting by Edward Newitt
Borders Beautiful by Edward Step
Straight Talk [Holidays; Free Railway Tickets; The Muscular Mind] by Charles Fry
From Headquarters [University Golf; London Athletic Club; London Football Association; Midlands Hockey; Thames Amateur Rowing Council]
Our Book Corner [Reviews of *A Girl's Garden* by Margaret Rankin; *The Salt of My Life* by Frederick Aflalo; *The Game of Ju-Jitsu* by Taro Miyake; *Association Football and the Men Who Made It* (2) by Alfred Caxton & William Pickford; *The Unlucky Number* by Eden Phillpotts]; Illustrated by George Thorp
The Outdoor Girl [Side and Cross-Saddle] by Esther Meynell
The Motor and The Cycle [Multi-Cylinder Engines; Variable Speed Gears; Sunbeam Motorbikes] by Richard Mecredy
The History of the Motor-Car: Review Essay of *The Book of the Motorcar* by Robert Sloss
Maxims for Motormen: Review of *Hints and Tips* by Herbert Staner
Health and Happiness [Labour Party Success; Spiritualism; Female Athletes] by George Dabbs; Illustrated by Frederick Buchanan
Out of Town [Great Eastern Railway; Reviews of *The Cornish Riviera* by Sidney Heath and *Summer Holidays* by Percy Lindley] by Alfred Cooper
The German; Illustrated by Charles Harrison
Outdoor Dress [Umbrellas; Oilskin Mackintosh] by Henry Gage
Craven is Arcadia; Illustrated by Charles Pears
Miniature Rifle Shooting [National Rifle Association; Society of Miniature Rifle Clubs; South Wales Rifle League; *The Rifleman* Journal] by Robert Pearson; Illustrated by George Thorp
The Camera in the Field [Photographing Plants] by Edward Step
In the Clubroom [Cycling; Running; Bell Tent; Cricket Outfitters; Golf Putters]

Charles Bull

Frederick Buchanan

Gordon Browne

Henry Bateman

Henry Brock

John Burns

Leone Bracker

Louis Berneker

Raeburn van Buren

Cavalry Riding; Illustrated by John Sturgess

Issue 26 : May 1906 (p97-192 + 56)

Cover Design; Illustrated by Charles Crombie
Talk of the Office by Bertram Atkey
Official Sanction by Charles Fry
In the Outdoor World [Olympian Games; Racehorse Eclipse; Horse Doping; Cricket]
The Tipster's Monologue [verses] by Bertram Atkey; Illustrated by Thomas Browne
The Highwayman by Peter Rowley; Illustrated by Thomas Browne
A Great Sporting Trial by James Atlay
The Blot on British Games (5) by Charles Fry
Cobbeldick of Wam-Wam (5) by Harold Begbie; Illustrated by Harry Rountree
The Race by Bertram Atkey
A Word for League Cricket by Charles Townsend
To a Football [verses] by Alan Haig-Brown
A French Sportswoman: Camille du Gast by Willy Sulzbacher
How to Make a Tee by Francis Burrow
The Diary of a Honeymoon (2) by Blundell Barrett; Illustrated by Wallis Mills
Lines to a Cheerful Busman [verses] by Bertram Atkey; Illustrated by Thomas Browne
The Cyclist's Small Worries by Pollock Castors; Illustrated by George Thorp
John Bull's Nerves by Philip Vaile; Illustrated by Frederick Buchanan
Pine and Oak [verses] by Arthur Horspool
How to Take Corners in a Motor by Richard Mecredy
The Air-Gun as a Serious Weapon by Howard Marks
Two Rifles by Howard Marks
Straight Talk [Ellen Terry; Isaac Newton; House of Commons] by Charles Fry
From Headquarters [Inter-County Golf; Tottenham House Cricket Club; Charles Alcock
    Presentation; London Scottish Rugby Club]
Outdoor Dress [Flannels; Cricket Shirts; Boots] by Henry Gage
The Outdoor Girl [Straw Hats; Flat Heels; Blouses] by Esther Meynell
The Motor and The Cycle [High Tension Magneto Systems; Motorcycle Belts; Irish Tenden Tour]
    by Richard Mecredy
She: A Motor Fancy by Eugene Shelley; Illustrated by Frederick Buchanan
The Anerley Bicycle Club by George Olley
The Camera in the Field [Butterflies; Beetles; Entomologists] by Edward Step
Camera Notes [View Finders; Drying Prints] by Archibald Williams
The Stockjobber; Illustrated by William Owen
Health and Happiness [Medical Books; Bottled Cider] by George Dabbs; Illustrated
    by Frederick Buchanan
The Elusive Egg by Bertram Atkey
Out of Town [Norway; Great Central Railway; New Palace Steamers; The Mediterranean]
    by Alfred Cooper; Illustrated by Percy Gossop
Rifle Shooting [Club Rifles; Cleansing Rod] by Robert Pearson
In the Clubroom [Badminton; Coaster Brakes; Cricket; Golf Balls]

Thomas Browne

Victor Beveridge

Charles Crombie

Christopher Clark

Cyrus Cuneo

Dudley Cleaver

George Cowell

Horace Crowther-Smith

John Charlton

Issue 27 : June 1906 (p193-288 + 44)

Cover Design; Illustrated by Charles Crombie
Sport and Drink by Guy Thorne
In the Outdoor World [County Cricketers' Golf Tournament; Frank Farrands Cricket; Water Polo; Dady Golwalla; Framroze Golwalla; Channel Swimming; Cab-Drivers; Reigate Rifle Range]; Illustrated by Stephen de la Bere
The Diary of a Honeymoon (3) by Blundell Barrett; Illustrated by Wallis Mills
The Holiday Car [verses] by Bertram Atkey
Resignation [verses] by Bertram Atkey; Illustrated by Thomas Browne
Bowls: The North Country Game by James Carruthers
The Cycle as a Carrier by Pollock Castors
Mr Prodgers' Century by Sackville Martin; Illustrated by Thomas Browne
A Worker's Song [verses] by Margaret Ross
The Backhand Drive at Lawn Tennis by Philip Vaile
Cobbeldick of Wam-Wam (6) by Harold Begbie; Illustrated by Harry Rountree
The Storm [verses] by May Doney
The French Turf of Today by Dick Luckman
The Art of Punting by Philip Squire
A Question of Omens by Stuart Wishing; Illustrated by Thomas Whitwell
Some Real Little Problems in Golf by George Brann & Charles Finlason
The Secret of the Googlie by Bernard Bosanquet & James Bolton
Straight Talk [Railway Fares; Book Reading] by Charles Fry
Our Book Corner [Reviews of *Performing Animals and Their Treatment* by Annie Bradshaw; *Practical Rifle Shooting* by Walter Winans; *Thunder and Lightning* by Camille Flammarion; *Rambles in Normandy* by Francis Miltoun; *Atlas of the World's Commerce* by John Bartholomew; *Early Lessons in Gardening* by Albert Kerridge]
Out of Town [Review of *Picturesque Normandy* by Samuel Bensusan, Illustrated by Archibald Forrest; The South Coast; Belle Steamers] by Alfred Cooper
Health and Happiness [Food and Sleep; Pasteurisation] by George Dabbs
Jarrott's Ride to Monte Carlo by Charles Jarrott
The Outdoor Girl [Paintings; French Cycling Knickerbockers; Boating Sweaters; Hockey Boots] by Esther Meynell
Outdoor Dress [Blazers; Cholera Belts] by Henry Gage
The Motor and The Cycle [Autoloc; Water-Jacket; Irish Chauffeurs; Cycling Tourists] by Richard Mecredy
Camera Notes [Clouds; South Downs] by Archibald Williams
Rifle Shooting [County Council Rifle Clubs; Liverpool Military Rifle Tournament] by Robert Pearson
In the Club Room [Hockey; Athletics; Rowing; Petrol Mowers; Lawn Tennis]

Issue 28 : July 1906 (p289-384 + 48)

Cover Design; Illustrated by Charles Crombie
William Grenfell by Charles Fry

Frederick Dickinson

Horace Davis

Maynard Dixon

Stephen Dadd

Arthur Elsley

Keppie Elcock

Lionel Edwards

Maud Earl

Walter Enright

In the Outdoor World [School and University Cricket; Matting Pitches; Ascot Racing; National Rifle Association; Real Tennis; Croquet]
The Letter of the Law by Philip Arp; Illustrated by Thomas Browne
The Scarecrow [verses] by Bertram Atkey; Illustrated by Thomas Browne
The Olympian Games by Arthur Johnson
Company for George by Warren Bell; Illustrated by Henry Brock
Persicos Odi [verses] by Bertram Atkey
The American Service at Lawn Tennis by Philip Vaile
Why Pay Rent or Hotel Bills by Richard Mecredy
The Diary of a Honeymoon (4) by Blundell Barrett; Illustrated by Wallis Mills
The Knack of Throwing by Gilbert Jessop and James Bolton
John Nyren: The Man and His Book by Edward Lucas
Diving: Simple and Otherwise by Charles Hammond
Cobbeldick of Wam-Wam (7) by Harold Begbie; Illustrated by Harry Rountree
Straight Talk [Manhood; Clothes] by Charles Fry
Out of Town [Reviews of *Sea Angling Twixt Humber and Tweed* by Frederick Aflalo and *Golf in North-Eastern England* by Alexander Robertson; Picnic Tours; Jersey; Steamers] by Alfred Cooper
Our Book Corner [Reviews of *A Tramp Camp* by Bart Kennedy; *Let Youth But Know* by William Archer; *Physical Efficiency* by James Cantlie; *Petrol Peter* by Archibald Williams; *Great Japan* by Alfred Stead]
Health and Happiness [Infected Milk; Dangers of Smoking] by George Dabbs
The Motor and The Cycle [Brakes; Secondhand Cars; Shoes for Cycling] by Richard Mecredy
The Outdoor Girl [Books; Motor Veils; Golfing Dress] by Esther Meynell; Illustrated by Beatrice Spiller
Outdoor Dress [Jodhpur Breeches; Indian Shoes; Motor Caps] by Henry Gage
The Force; Illustrated by William Owen
Camera Notes [Dark Room Lamps; Exposure Meters] by Archibald Williams
Rifle Shooting [Birmingham Rifle Meeting; Musketry Regulations] by Robert Pearson
A New [Lebel] Rifle by Robert Pearson
In the Club Room [Gun License Act; Review of *Great Lawn Tennis Players* by Philip Vaile; Air-Guns; Golf Balls]

Issue 29 : August 1906 (p385-480 + 36)

Cover Design; Illustrated by Charles Crombie
In the Outdoor World [Goodwood Meeting; Canterbury Cricket Week; Cowes Yachting; Lawn Tennis; John Tyldesley; Tom Hayward]
The Life of Pretty Polly by Bernard Parsons
The Capt'n [verses] by Bertram Atkey; Illustrated by Thomas Browne
Feats in Fielding by Charles Fry
How to Choose and Use a Hand Camera by Archibald Williams
The Travelling Companion [verses] by Cecil Hughes; Illustrated by himself
Billy the Mug by Edgar Barnes-Austin; Illustrated by Henry Brock
The Forehand Drive in Lawn Tennis by Philip Vaile

Charles Folkard　　　Clement Flower　　　Clifford Fleming-Williams

Joseph Finnemore　　　Percy Fearon　　　Thomas Fogarty

Francis Carruthers-Gould　　　Charles Gibson　　　Frederick Griggs

To a Cricket Bat [verses] by Alan Haig-Brown
By Favour of the White Mist by Bertram Atkey; Illustrated by Edward Wigfull
Sculling for Girls by Charles Thomas
The Diary of a Honeymoon (5) by Blundell Barrett; Illustrated by Wallis Mills
Baseball by Jack Sharp
Cobbeldick of Wam-Wam (8) by Harold Begbie; Illustrated by Harry Rountree
A Unique Canoe Trip (1) by Richard Burt
Straight Talk [Germs; Cricket] by Charles Fry
Rifle Shooting [Ham & Petersham Range; War Office Cadet Rifle] by Robert Pearson
Our Book Corner [Reviews of *The Car Road Book and Guide* by John Scott-Montagu; *Fisherman's Luck* by Henry van Dyke; *The Jungle* by Upton Sinclair; *The Encyclopedia of Motoring* by Richard Mecredy; *Butterflies of the British Isles* by Richard South; *Outdoor Pastimes of An American Hunter* by Theodore Roosevelt; *Mr Baxter Sportsman* by Charles Marsh
Magazine Binding: *The Strand* by Charles Fry
The Outdoor Girl [Luggage, Coats] by Esther Meynell; Illustrated by Beatrice Spiller
Outdoor Dress [Braces, Cricket Gloves] by Henry Gage
Out of Town [The Rhine; Clyde Shipping Company; The Thames Valley; Brittany; Isle of Man; Scottish and Belgian Railways] by Alfred Cooper
The Motor Cars of 1906 (1) by Richard Mecredy
Health and Happiness [Sea Sickness; Sporting Accidents] by George Dabbs
The Clubman; Illustrated by William Owen
Camera Notes [Bromide Paper; Platinum Printing] by Archibald Williams
Taking Guard; Illustrated by Thomas Whitwell
In the Club Room [Golf Balls; Boxing; Cricket; Rowing]

Issue 30 : September 1906 (p481-576 + 36)

Cover Design; Illustrated by Charles Crombie
Betting and Sport by Guy Thorne
On the Downs [verses] by Eugene Shelley
Three Cricketers of the Year [Thomas Hayward; George Hirst; Jack Crawford] by Charles Fry
The Circus [verses] by Bertram Atkey; Illustrated by Thomas Browne
The Trembling Brave by Lucia Chamberlain; Illustrated by Charles Taffs
Hills, Wind, Dust and the Cyclist by Pollock Castors
Tom: An Epic [verses] by Cecil Hughes; Illustrated by himself
River Emergencies by Charles Thomas
How to Climb the Matterhorn by John Freeman
The Outlaw by Bernard Atkey; Illustrated by Harry Rountree
A Unique Canoe Trip (2) by Richard Burt
The Man Who Kept On by Jack London; Illustrated by Caton Woodville
The Peril of the Wires: Pheasants by Bertram Atkey
Boxing for Amateurs by Bohun Lynch
A Horse Deal by Nicholas Everitt; Illustrated by Alfred Munnings
The Diary of a Honeymoon (6) by Blundell Barrett; Illustrated by Wallis Mills
Degrees of Comparison [verses] by Alfred Cooper

George Gibbs

Percy Gossop

Philip Goodwin

Warwick Goble

Arthur Heming

David Hutchison

Dorothy Hardy

Dudley Hardy

Edgar Holloway

A Few Words on Swimming by Richard Sandon
Street Cricket by Edwin Pugh; Illustrated by Alfred Leete
The New Stance Indicator by Charles Fry
Straight Talk [Cricket Bats; Baths; Walking] by Charles Fry
Out of Town [South Eastern & Chatham Railway; Belgium] by Alfred Cooper
Our Book Corner [Reviews of *In the Heart of the Country* by Ford Hueffer; *From a Cornish Window* by Arthur Quiller-Couch; *Salted Almonds* by Thomas Anstey; *Manchester Boys* by Charles Russell; *Cricket Guide* by Kumar Ranjisinhji; *The Balkan Trail* by Frederick Moore; *The Romance of the South Seas* by Clement Wragge; *Cricket* by Archibald Maclaren; *The British Motor Tourist* by Gertrude Campbell; *The Lawn Tennis Handbook* by Evan Noel; *Recreations of a Naturalist* by James Harting]
Health and Happiness [Sprains; Gunshot Wounds; Cheap Brandy] by George Dabbs
The Motor Cars of 1906 (2) by Richard Mecredy
Outdoor Dress [Ventilated Shoes; Storm Cuffs] by Henry Gage
The Brighter Side [verses] by Bertram Atkey
The Outdoor Girl [Gardening Dress; Travelling Bath; Bathing Shoes; Suffragettes] by Esther Meynell
Camera Notes [Fixation; Intensification] by Archibald Williams
Golfers; Illustrated by Thomas Whitwell
Rifle Shooting [Bisley Meeting; International Shooting Match] by Robert Pearson
The River Man; Illustrated by William Owen
In the Club Room [Lawn Tennis; Golf Scorebooks; Punting; Model Yachting; Motor Spirit] Illustrated by George Thorp

Competition

Edward Hodgson

John Hassall

Paul Hardy

Reginald Higgins

Roland Hill

Garth Jones

Humphrey Joel

Charles Keene

Rollin Kirby

Volume 6

Issue 31 : October 1906 (p1-96 + 36)

Cover Design; Illustrated by Lawson Wood
In the Rough; Illustrated by Harry Rountree
Heronhaye (1) by Katherine Prichard & Hesketh Prichard; Illustrated by Lawson Wood
The Doing [verses] by Ruth Havens
Facial Expression and Physical Effort by Charles Fry
Messengers of Death by Paul Flemming
The Dust Problem by Edison Jones; Illustrated by George Studdy
The Incorrigible by Miriam Alexander; Illustrated by George Soper
To Paint the Lily [verses] by Bertram Atkey
Round the Clock With a Jockey by Bernard Parsons
The Gentleman With the Pick [verses] by Bertram Atkey; Illustrated by Thomas Browne
The Diary of a Honeymoon (7) by Blundell Barrett; Illustrated by Wallis Mills
How the Viper Sought Revenge by Bertram Atkey; Illustrated by Harry Rountree
What Really Happened [verses] by Cecil Hughes; Illustrated by himself
The Wayward Wooden Club by Charles Finlason & George Brann
A Health Tip by Richard Jeffries
The Legion of Frontiersmen by Hill Rowan
Is the Motorcycle a Failure? by Pollock Castors
Harbouring a Stag by Archibald Hamilton
Behind the Scenes of the [County Cricket] Championship (1) by Charles Fry
Railway Flower Gardens by May Doney
The Little Brown Water Lord by Ludovick Cameron
Football: Amateur and Professional by George Pollock-Hodsoll
Young Man [verses] by Cecil Hughes; Illustrated by himself
The Wisdom of Belinda's Mother by Evelyn Sharp; Illustrated by Percy Hickling
Straight Talk [T.P's Magazine; Boxing; Betting; Rifle Ranges] by Charles Fry
Rifle Shooting [Erith Rifle Club Range] by Robert Pearson
Our Book Corner [Reviews of *Animal Heroes* by Ernest Thompson-Seton; *The Gamekeeper at Home* by Richard Jeffries; *Market Gardening* by Lewis Castle; *Miniature Road Book* and *The Portsmouth Road* both by Charles Harper; *Henry Northcote* by John Snaith; *A Girl of Resources* by Eyre Hussey]
The Outdoor Girl [Roman Cloak; Pliable Leather Belts; Currant Bread] by Esther Meynell
Outdoor Dress [Motor Sweater; Golf Suit] by Henry Gage
The Motor and The Cycle [Cross Roads; James Percy, Irish Cyclist] by Richard Mecredy
Motoring; Illustrated by Thomas Whitwell
Health and Happiness [Quillaia Bark; Food Experiments] by George Dabbs
Out of Town [Brixham; Review of *Through England and Scotland* by George Eyre-Todd] by Alfred Cooper
Camera Notes [Goerz Anschutz Camera; Telephoto Lens] by Archibald Williams
In the Clubroom [Outdoor Structural Improvements; Growing Tomatoes]

Ada Lehaney

Alfred Leete

Frederick Leist

George Lodge

Alfred Munnings

Arthur Michael

George Morrow

Howard McCormick

John Mellor

Issue 32 : November 1906 (p97-192 + 40)

Cover Design; Illustrated by Charles Crombie
An Imaginative Man by Robert Hichens
The Editor Says [Magazine Aims; Golf, Motoring; Rugby; Cricket; Cycling; Hockey; Sea-Fishing; Lacrosse; Football; Gardening] by Charles Fry
The Stage and Athletics by Reginald Bacchus; Illustrated by Harold Hogg
National Style in Rugby by Arthur Gould & James Bolton
Walking: The How and The Why by Montague Holbein
The True Wisdom [verses] by Ruth Havens
The Wooing of the Widow by Walter Grogan; Illustrated by William Dewar
Ladies: Improve Your Hockey by Eustace White
Heronhaye (2) by Katherine Prichard & Hesketh Prichard; Illustrated by Lawson Wood
The Song of an Eight [verses] by John Dickinson
Scrambles in Yorkshire by Claude Benson
Move On [verses] by Bart Kennedy; Illustrated by Charles Crombie
The Diary of a Honeymoon (8) by Blundell Barrett; Illustrated by Wallis Mills
The Optics of Rifle Shooting by Edward Newitt
Learning Golf by Charles Finlason; Illustrated by Harold Hogg
The Origin of Hunting by William Somervile
The Garden in Autumn by Edgar Cook
Do Professional Footballers Play Only for Money by John Bentley
An Ice-Boat Elopement by Stacey Blake; Illustrated by John Hassall
Ratting and Ratters by Owen Jones
Settlers' Cricket [verses] by Leonard Flemming; Illustrated by Ralph Hodgson
Straight Talk [Cricketer Journalists; Croquet Manners; Off-Hand Questions] by Charles Fry
The Outdoor Girl [Goloshes; Golf Coats; Hockey Boots] by Esther Meynell
Out of Town [Skating & Tobogganing; Switzerland; Lake District] by Alfred Cooper
In the Clubroom [Swimming; Hockey Ruling; Distemper]
The Motor and The Cycle [Hill Climbing Competitions; Long Cranks; Palmer Tyres] by Richard Mecredy
A Hockey Match; Illustrated by Thomas Whitwell
A Choice of Football Boots by Charles Fry
The Handy Man; Illustrated by William Owen
Rifle Shooting [Rifling Cleaner; Liverpool City Police] by Robert Pearson
Outdoor Dress [Motor Coats; Goggles; Hunting Boots] by Henry Gage
Health and Happiness [Bathing; Turkish Baths; Schoolmasters] by George Dabbs
Kicks and Falls [Advertorial] by William Connell
Our Book Corner [Reviews of *From a Dartmoor Cot* by William Crossing; *Short Holidays in Small Open Boats* by William Macpherson; *Silas Strong* by Irving Bacheller; *A Pixy in Petticoats* by Ernest Henham; *Drink* by Hall Caine; *Yearbook of Photography* by Francis Mortimer; *The Fox* by Thomas Dale; *Lyra Venatica* by John Reeve; *Handbook of British Inland Birds* by Anthony Collett; *The Rhine From Cleve to Mainz* by Sabine Baring-Gould; *My Garden* by Eden Phillpotts; *Connemara and the Neighbouring Spots of Beauty and Interest* by Harris Stone]

Richard Mathews

Wallace Morgan

Power O'Malley

Thornton Oakley

Alfred Pearse

Charles Pears

Colbron Pearse

Frederick Pegram

Malcolm Patterson

Issue 33 : December 1906 (p193-296 + 48)

Cover Design; Illustrated by Lawson Wood
Mehalah by Sabine Baring-Gould
The Worries of the Age; Illustrated by William Owen
A Bird's Eye View: Charles Rolls by Harold Begbie
The South African Rugby Team by Charles Fry
The Bogey of the Barstham Links by Perry Robinson; Illustrated by Henry Brook
Mr Jorrocks Speaks by Robert Surtees
That Reminds Me by Bertram Atkey; Illustrated by Harry Rountree
Heronhaye (3) by Katherine Prichard & Hesketh Prichard; Illustrated by Lawson Wood
Dress for Golf by Mary Hezlet; Illustrated by Harold Hogg
Mixed Fields [Animal Racing]
Beautiful English Gardening by Edgar Cook
Character Sketch and Real Conversation: John Scott-Montagu by Charles Fry; Illustrated by George Thorp
Advanced Golf (1): The Selection and Effect of Wooden Clubs by James Braid & Henry Leach
Behind the Scenes of the [County Cricket] Championship (2) by Charles Fry
The League Idea: Amateur Football by John Lewis; Illustrated by Lawson Wood
Winter Cycling and How to Enjoy It by Stanley Noble
Lacrosse Progress by Hubert Ramsey
The Sea for Sport by Frederick Aflalo
Tactics in Hockey by Stanley Shoveller
The Olympia Motor Show by Pollock Castors; Illustrated by Harry Rountree
The Best Dog Friend by Horace Hutchinson
The Sportsman's View Point [Cricket; Football; Athletic Ability; London Bus Routes; Golf; Poetry; Leander Club; University Boxing] by Charles Fry
Motorcycles of 1907 by Richard Mecredy
A Football Match; Illustrated by Thomas Whitwell
Specifications of the Best Motorcycles by Richard Mecredy
Specification of the Coventry Humber Light Car by Richard Mecredy
Out of Town [Egypt; Canary Islands; Fishing in Worcestershire] by Alfred Cooper
Outdoor Dress [Leather Oil; Knitted Silk; Hunting Hats] by Henry Gage; Illustrated by John Hassall
The Outdoor Girl [Sydney Smith; *The Saturday Review*; Covent Garden Market] by Esther Meynell; Illustrated by John Hassall
Health and Happiness [Antiseptics; Water Supply; Alcoholic Inebriety; Cocoa] by George Dabbs; Illustrated by John Hassall
First Aid for Athletes [Advertorial]
Maori Stoicism by Philip Vaile
Our Book Corner [Reviews of *In Green Fields* by Oswald Crawfurd; *The Other Side of the Lantern* by Frederick Treves; *In Constable's Country* by Herbert Tompkins; *How It Works* by Archibald Williams; *Some Irish Yesterdays* by Edith Somerville; *The Guarded Flame* by William Maxwell; *Association Football and the Men who Made It (4)* by Alfred Gibson & William Pickford; *Puck of Pook's Hill* by Rudyard Kipling; *Boy and Girl* by Vivian Grey; *The Poacher's Wife* by Eden Phillpotts]; Illustrated by John Hassall

Alick Ritchie

Edward Reed

Frank Reynolds

George Rankin

George Roller

Harold Read

Harry Rountree

Henry Raleigh

Leonard Raven-Hill

The Longshoreman; Illustrated by William Owen

Rifle Shooting [Maori Rifle Shield; Safety Bullet Catcher; Clive Morrison-Bell] by Robert Pearson; Illustrated by John Hassall

Our Friends Say [Hungarian Partridges; Ladies Golf in Scotland; Poaching Alarm Gun; Skating in Friesland]

Issue 34 : January 1907 (p297-392 + 32)

Cover Design; Illustrated by Lawson Wood

The Last Hope by Henry Merriman

What is a Sportsman: Robert Sievier by Harold Begbie

Heronhaye (4) by Katherine Prichard & Hesketh Prichard; Illustrated by Lawson Wood

The Motor Hooligan [verses] by May Doney; Illustrated by Harry Rountree

Swimming the Channel by Montague Holbein

Euphemia's Lucy (1) by Blundell Barrett; Illustrated by Gordon Browne

The Emigrant [verses] by Bertram Atkey

The Modest Man's Motor Up-to-Date (1) by Charles Matson; Illustrated by George Morrow

Steam Engine and Petrol Motor Compared by Charles Matson; Illustrated by Percy Home

The Romance of Ranjitsinhji's Princedom by Charles Fry; Illustrated by George Thorp

Advanced Golf (2): The Selection and Effect of Iron Clubs by James Braid & Henry Leach

Tom Hayward's Bat by Charles Fry

Varsity Rugby Pictures by Edward Sewell; Illustrated by Charles Ambrose

Over the White Snows by Stacey Blake; Illustrated by George Soper

That Reminds Me by Bertram Atkey; Illustrated by Edgar Holloway

The Great Question in County Cricket by Gilbert Grace & James Bolton

Some Don'ts for Association Football by Gilbert Smith

Dress for Lady Golfers by Dorothy Campbell, Issette Pearson, Maud Stuart & Julia Aungier

Success of Wales in Rugby Football by Robert Lattimer

Cycling as a Moral Force by Stanley Noble

Our Friend the Horse by Thomas Dale

The Sportsman's View Point [*Sporting Life* Report; Football Referees; Public School Football Clubs; Kumar Ranjitsinhji] by Charles Fry; Illustrated by George Thorp

The Motor and The Cycle [Small Cars; Erratic Cyclists] by Richard Mecredy; Illustrated by John Hassall

Health and Happiness [Buttermilk; Green Tea; The Colonial Horizon; Eyes] by George Dabbs; Illustrated by John Hassall

In the Clubroom [Photographic Lenses; Queen's Club; Wood Carving]

Outdoor Dress [Francis Thompson; Red Slippers; Dancing] by Henry Gage

Our Friends Say [Fijian Mlili-Mlili; A Duel; Hockey; A Stumping; Pigeon Jar; Shooting]

Our Book Corner [Reviews of *The Priest* by Harold Begbie; *With Knapsack and Notebook* by Arthur Cooper; *The Citizen Rifleman* by Edward Newitt; *The Romance of Animal Arts & Crafts* by Henri Coupin]

Rifle Shooting [Hendon & Cricklewood Rifle Club; War Office Rifle] by Robert Pearson

Out of Town [Nile River; Travel Exhibition; Hotel Cecil] by Alfred Cooper

Louis Rhead

William Heath Robinson

William Robinson

Alexander Svoboda

Byam Shaw

Charles Sarka

Edmund Sullivan

Edward Skinner

Edwin Shrader

Issue 35 : February 1907 (p393-504 + 40)

Cover Design; Illustrated by Lawson Wood
The Comedy of Climbing; Illustrated by Thomas Browne
The Conquest of the Air: Alberto Santos-Dumont by Charles Fry
Angels in Waiting by Warren Bell; Illustrated by Henry Brock
The Training of the Eye by Eustace Miles
The Golfer and His Millions by Henry Leach
Maori Stoicism: Another Instance by Philip Vaile
Tales of the Turf: Dan Dawson by Ladbroke Black
The Modest Man's Motor Up-to-Date (2) by Charles Matson; Illustrated by George Morrow
Heronhaye (5) by Katherine Prichard & Hesketh Prichard; Illustrated by Lawson Wood
The Early Year in the Garden by Edgar Cook
The Art of Skiing by Frank Ormiston-Smith
Curling at Carsebreck by Daniel McDonald
A Bitter School [An Ardent Golfer]
With the Rugby Internationals by Edward Sewell; Illustrated by Charles Ambrose
With the Foot Beagles by Alexander Campbell
Euphemia's Lucy (2) by Blundell Barrett; Illustrated by Gordon Browne
Advanced Golf (3): Long Driving by James Braid & Henry Leach
Indoor Cricket: Its Possibilities by Kumar Ranjitsinhji & James Bolton
Skating for Ladies by Madeline Syers
Packing and Attacking in New Zealand [Rugby] Football by John Stead
The Making of a Modern Football Ground by Unite Jones
[Football] Forward Play by Stanley Harris & Bertie Corbett
That Reminds Me by Bertram Atkey; Illustrated by Frederick Buchanan
The Sportsman's View Point [Aero Club of France; Gwyn Nicholls; Edward Morgan, Arthur Harding; Adrian Stoop; Frederick Brooks; Rugby Reminiscences; County Cricket Qualifaction] by Charles Fry
Out of Town [Winter Sports in Sweden and Switzerland] by Alfred Cooper
Our Friends Say [Alpine Climbers; Physical Culture for Women; Mont Blanc; *The Ladies' Field*; Cartridges]
Health and Happiness [Bread; Oysters; Fresh Meat; Hygiene; Betting; Gymnastics] by George Dabbs; Illustrated by John Hassall
The Motor and The Cycle [Stanley Cycle Show] by Richard Mecredy; Illustrated by John Hassall
Country Cycling; Illustrated by Thomas Whitwell
Outdoor Dress [Shooting Jackets; Detachable Cuffs] by Henry Gage
Rifle Shooting [Hyposcope; Army Council] by Robert Pearson; Illustrated by John Hassall

Issue 36 : March 1907 (p505-608 + 52)

Cover Design; Illustrated by Henry Brock
The Blue Ribbon of the Leash: Waterloo Cup by Henry Leach
Heronhaye (6) by Katherine Prichard & Hesketh Prichard
Refereeing in the Rugby Game by Edward Sewell; Illustrated by Charles Ambrose
The Mysterious Wright Brothers by Andre de Masfrand

Frank Southgate

George Soper

George Stampa

George Studdy

Henry Saÿen

Henry Stannard

John Sturgess

Joseph Simpson

Septimus Scott

National Training: Reginald Brabazon
The Modest Man's Motor Up-to-Date (3) by Charles Matson; Illustrated by George Morrow
Advanced Golf (4): Intentional Pulling and Slicing by James Braid & Henry Leach
A Famous Turf Duel by Ladbroke Black
Sprinting in the Fifties: John Astley
Gwyn Nicholls: Character Sketch by Wallis Myers
Mistakes Made at Billiards by Harry Stevenson
That Reminds Me by Bertram Atkey; Illustrated by Frederick Buchanan
The Devil of Golf by Henry Leach
The Devil Game: Diabolo by Charles Fry
Euphemia's Lucy (3) by Blundell Barrett; Illustrated by Gordon Browne
The Polytechnic by Charles Fry
Cricket Grounds by Gilbert Grace & James Bolton
Badminton: The Game by Ethel Larcombe
Should An English Crew Visit America by Guy Nickalls
The Blackheath Experiment by Basil Hill
How to Make a Rifle Club a Success by Edward Newitt
King and Countrymen [verses] by Harold Begbie & Kate Lester
The Sportsman's View Point [Indian Princes (letter sent from solicitors stating that Ranjitsinhji is not a Prince); Rugby] by Charles Fry
Our Friends Say [Sportswoman Constance Stewart-Richardson; Fishery Commissioner of New Brunswick; Basque Sport]
In the Clubroom [Physical Culture; Council Planning Applications]
Outdoor Dress [Welsh Flannels; Tam-o'-Shanters] by Henry Gage
Bulls-Eye; Illustrated by George Guston
The Motor and The Cycle [Contact Makers; Silent Cars; Grease] by Richard Mecredy
Health and Happiness [Betting; Russian Women; Beef Powders; Review of *How to Keep Well* by Stanford Read] by George Dabbs
The Rower; Illustrated by Thomas Whitwell
Out of Town [River Blackwater; Switzerland; Cornwall] by Alfred Cooper
Our Book Corner [Reviews of *Listener's Lure* by Edward Lucas; *Mister Bill* by Albert Lyons; *In the Days of the Comet* by Herbert Wells]
Rifle Shooting [Welsh Miniature Rifle Association] by Robert Pearson; Illustrated by John Hassall

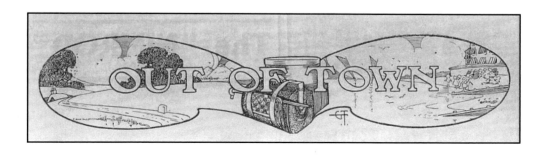

William Stott

Allen True

Archibald Thorburn

Charles Taffs

Fletcher Thomas

Frank Taylor

Hall Thorpe

George Varian

Arthur Watts

Volume 7

Issue 37 : April 1907 (p1-112 + 48)

Cover Design; Illustrated by Henry Brock
Falls: The Steeplechase Rider's Risks by Sidney Phipps
Out of the Race [verses] by William Ogilvie
A Case of Circumstantial Evidence by Herbert Hamel; Illustrated by Henry Brock
L'Entente Cordiale Sportive by Edward Sewell; Illustrated by Charles Ambrose
Heronhaye (7) by Katherine Prichard & Hesketh Prichard; Illustrated by Lawson Wood
To a Trout Rod [verses] by Alan Haig-Brown
How I Won That Car by Perry Robinson; Illustrated by Frederick Buchanan
The Fate of the Blue by Bernard Carter; Illustrated by George Soper
Advanced Golf (5): Straight Winds and Wet Weather by James Braid & Henry Leach
Chickens by Eugene Wood; Illustrated by Joseph Conde
That Reminds Me by Bertram Atkey; Illustrated by Frederick Buchanan
Do Golf and Hockey Clash by Eleanor Helme; Illustrated by George Thorp
Town and Field [verses] by Ethel Talbot
Quoits by John Campbell
Science and the Golf Ball by Henry Leach
The South Africans by Pelham Warner; Illustrated by George Thorp
An Afternoon with the Varsity Crews by Guy Nickalls
Points to Study in Ordering a Motorcar Body by Alexander Wallis-Tayler
The County Captain: An Ideal by Albert Knight
Hints on Housing a Cycle by Pollock Castors
Euphemia's Lucy (4) by Blundell Barrett; Illustrated by Gordon Browne
The Sportsman's View Point [American Sport, Amateur Football, Scottish Football, Mechanical Bowling Machine] by Charles Fry
Out of Town [Fish & Eels Hotel in Hoddesdon; Southampton Yacht and Boat Agency] by Alfred Cooper
Field and Covert [Old Cartridges; Pheasant Eggs] by Owen Jones
The Motor and The Cycle [Physical Development; Mountain Cycling] by Richard Mecredy
Premier; Illustrated by Patten Wilson
On the Scientific Increase of Income [Advertorial]
Health and Happiness [Nervous System; Over-Population; Review of *Nature and Health* by Edward Curtis] by George Dabbs
In the Clubroom [Japanese Jujitsu; Wire-Wove Roofing]
Outdoor Dress [Old Dresses; Neck Wraps; Brown Boots] by Henry Gage
Gardening for the Month by Edgar Cook
Camera Notes [Plates and Film Wastage; Daylight Loading; Eclipse Stereoscopic] by Archibald Williams
Rifle Shooting [Arthur Morrison-Bell; Maldon & Coombe Rifle Club] by Robert Pearson
Our Friends Say [Indian Law; Girls' Swimming; Walrus Hunting]
Our Book Corner [Reviews of *My Dog* by Maurice Maeterlinck; *Potato Growing* by Walter Wright & Edward Castle; *With Flashlight and Rifle* by Carl Schillings;

Caton Woodville

David Wilcox

Dyke White

Edward Wigfull

Frederic Whiting

Harry Williamson

John de Walton

Lawson Wood

Stanley Wood

The Duffer by Warren Bell; *Charles Dickens* by Gilbert Chesterton; *The Complete Photographer* by Roger Child-Bayley]

Issue 38 : May 1907 (p113-208 + 48)

Cover Design; Illustrated by Henry Brock
W.G. Goes Beagling; Illustrated by Charles Ambrose
Ranelagh [Club] by Sidney Galtrey; Illustrated by George Thorp
Heronhaye (8) by Katherine Prichard & Hesketh Prichard; Illustrated by Lawson Wood
Personalities in Golf by Arthur Croome; Illustrated by Charles Ambrose
Sunshine and Rain by Bernard Carter; Illustrated William Mein
The Wiles of Delilah by Allan Lambourne; Illustrated by Thomas Browne
The Motor in Relation to Agriculture by Alexander Wallis-Tayler
The Bruce Lowe Theories by Thomas Henry Browne
Advanced Golf (6): Abnormal Stances by James Braid & Henry Leach
The Truth About Weightlifting by Thomas Inch & James Bolton
My Twenty-First Consecutive Final by John Bentley
Dry Fly Fishing by Frederick Aflalo [Review of *The Science of Dry Fly Fishing* by Frederick Shaw]
How the Brindled Whelp Hunted Alone by Bertram Atkey; Illustrated by Harry Rountree
A Cricket Duel: Nicholas Wanostrocht & Alfred Mynn
The Flight of the Golf Ball by Henry Leach
Euphemia's Lucy (5) by Blundell Barrett; Illustrated by Gordon Browne
The Sportsman's View Point [South African Cricket Tourists; County and University Cricket] by Charles Fry
The Starting Gate by Charles Fry
Field and Covert [Fox Cubs; Rookery Rents] by Owen Jones
Out of Town [Walking Tours; London Restaurants; Review of *Southern Ireland: Its Lakes and Landscapes* by Arthur White] by Alfred Cooper
Our Friends Say [Hare Breeding; Tacoma Cycle Bridge; Women Mountaineers
The Motor and The Cycle [Coil Troubles; Defective Brakes; War Office; La Motosacoche] by Richard Mecredy
International [Rugby] Football by Robert Lattimer
Health and Happiness [Obesity; Typhoid; Writers' Cramp; Edible Fungi] by George Dabbs
The Cricketer; Illustrated by Thomas Whitwell
Outdoor Dress [Cycling Gloves; Review of *The Gentleman's Dress Manual* by Adern Holt; Serge; Long Coats] by Henry Gage
Camera Notes [Catalogues] by Archibald Williams
Rifle Shooting [Ian Hamilton; War Office Miniature Rifle] by Robert Pearson
Gardening for the Month by Edgar Cook
In the Clubroom [Cricket Queries; Club Badges]
Our Book Corner [Reviews of *The Romance of Polar Exploration* by George Firth-Scott & Robert Rudmose-Brown; *The Diary of a Working Farmer* by Primrose McConnell; *How to Choose a Dog* by Vero Shaw; *Epitaphs* by Frederick Unger]

Thomas Whitwell

Thomas Wilkinson

Baden Baden-Powell

Bertie Corbett

Douglas Clinch

Hugh Chisholm

Olive Allen

Ralph Blumenfeld

Samuel Bensusan

Issue 39 : June 1907 (p209-304 + 44)

Cover Design; Illustrated by Henry Brock
Jay Gould; Illustrated by Charles Ambrose
The Derby Wonderful by Bernard Carter; Illustrated by George Soper
Did Captain Matthew Webb Swim the Channel by Montague Holbein
Heronhaye (9) by Katherine Prichard & Hesketh Prichard; Illustrated by Lawson Wood
Terriers [Review of *Dogs* by Harding Cox] by Horace Hutchinson
The Southbound Car (1): The Road to Spain by Owen Llewellyn; Illustrated by Leonard Raven-Hill
The Ways of Wild Animals by Frederick Aflalo [Review of *Hunting and Shooting in Ceylon* by Harry Storey]
Cricket and the Pyramids by Edmund Christian
Going Foreign by Charles Pears
The Vanderbilt Horses by Wallis Myers
Advanced Golf (7): Difficulties Through the Green by James Braid & Henry Leach
Euphemia's Lucy (6) by Blundell Barrett; Illustrated by Gordon Browne
That Reminds Me by Bertram Atkey; Illustrated by Frederick Buchanan
Wrist Work by Charles Fry
This Year's Championship Links by Henry Leach
The Sportsman's View Point [Channel Swimming; Cricket; Action Photographs; Amateurism; John Astley; Thunderstorm Baths; Dust; Roads in France] by Charles Fry
Boating [The Thames; Skiffs; Monkey Island; Rose Inn at Shifford] by Charles Thomas; Illustrated by George Thorp
Our Friends Say [Grampian Bird Life; Joseph Ward; Bushido]
Gardening for the Month by Edgar Cook
The Knowing Dogs; Illustrated by Frank Swaine
Health and Happiness [Disinfectants; Parquet Flooring; Arsenic Coloured Wallpaper] by George Dabbs
The Motor and The Cycle [Women Car Drivers; Cord Tyres; *Athletic News*] by Richard Mecredy
Outdoor Dress [Waistcoats; Woollen Hats; Fashion Changes] by Henry Gage
An Overcoat; Illustrated by Beatrice Spiller
Out of Town [Kiel Regatta; Paris Trip; Pyrenees] by Alfred Cooper
Field and Covert [Partridges; Pheasant Shooting] by Owen Jones
Terriers; Illustrated by Rubens Moore
Camera Notes [Self-Developing Plates; Reflex Camera; Dark Room Aprons] by Archibald Williams
Rifle Shooting [Rifle Ranges] by Robert Pearson
In the Clubroom [Tennis Racket Grips; Sporting Equipment; Cycle Touring]

Issue 40 : July 1907 (p305-400 + 44)

Cover Design; Illustrated by Henry Brock
Percy Sherwell; Illustrated by Charles Ambrose
The Story of Hurlingham by Sidney Galtrey; Illustrated by George Thorp

The Southbound Car: Towards the Pyrenees (2) by Owen Llewellyn; Illustrated by Leonard Raven-Hill
Lawn Tennis Past and Present by Wallis Myers; Illustrated by Charles Ambrose
The Boy at Dusk [verses] by Bertram Atkey
The Problem of the Channel Swim (1) by Montague Holbein; Illustrated by Frederic Whiting
Heronhaye (10) by Katherine Prichard & Hesketh Prichard; Illustrated by Lawson Wood
Colonials and County Cricket by Alan Marshal; Illustrated by himself
Advanced Golf (8): Variations in the Short Game by James Braid & Henry Leach
Surface Lures for Bottom Fish by Walter Gallichan
The Secrets of Long Driving (1) by Henry Leach
Footwork in Batting by Charles Fry
A Record Lightweight: George Thompson by George Finch-Mason
Euphemia's Lucy (7) by Blundell Barrett; Illustrated by Gordon Browne
The Sportsman's View Point [Cricket in South Africa; Rudyard Kipling; Royal Naval School; Kent Cricket; Walter Griggs; Review of *Ballooning as a Sport* by Robert Baden-Powell; Swimming] by Charles Fry
Rifle Shooting [Midland Railway Rifle Club] by Robert Pearson
Our Friends Say [Bee-Keeping; Beira (Mozambique) Tram System; Boulogne Fishing]
Field and Covert [Hedgehog Nurseries; River Test Trout] by Owen Jones
Gardening for the Month by Edgar Cook
Boating [Walton Regatta; Bourne End Sailing; Henley Season] by Charles Thomas; Illustrated by George Thorp
Out of Town [Mannheim Jubilee Exhibition; Isle of Man; *The Vegetarian Messenger*] by Alfred Cooper
The Motor and The Cycle [Contact Breakers; Lamps; Luggage Grid; Inflating Tyres] by Richard Mecredy
Health and Happiness [Ox-Tongues; Vacuum Cleaners; Maize; Dried Vegetables] by George Dabbs
In the Clubhouse [Punctures; Cricket Bats]
Outdoor Dress [Weekend Umbrella; River Clothes; Silk Garments] by Henry Gage
Camera Notes [Early Morning Photography; Mounting Prints] by Archibald Williams
Our Book Corner [Reviews of *New Chronicles of Don Q* by Katherine Prichard & Hesketh Prichard; *Nature and Health* by Edward Curtis]

Issue 41 : August 1907 (p401-496 + 48)

Cover Design; Illustrated by Henry Brock
The Southbound Car: The Road to Barcelona (3) by Owen Llewellyn; Illustrated by Leonard Raven-Hill
The Rook [verses] by Bertram Atkey
The Oolta-Poolta Team by Edward Sewell; Illustrated by Charles Ambrose
The Running of Sprint Races by Charles Fry
Some Intricacies of Croquet by Maud Drummond
Advanced Golf (9): Putting Strokes by James Braid & Henry Leach
The Last Over by Digby Jephson; Illustrated by William Moony

The Problem of the Channel Swim (2) by Montague Holbein; Illustrated by Frederic Whiting
Heronhaye (11) by Katherine Prichard & Hesketh Prichard; Illustrated by Lawson Wood
Golfing Holidays by Henry Leach
The Favourite Strokes of Leading Lawn Tennis Players by Eustace White
Euphemia's Lucy (8) by Blundell Barrett; Illustrated by Gordon Browne
The Secrets of Long Driving (2) by Henry Leach
That Reminds Me by Bertram Atkey
The Sportsman's View Point [American Olympic Funding; Amateur Football Association; Reviews of *Our Gardens* by Reynolds Hole and *The Horse's Mind* by Noel Birch; *The Cavalry Journal*; Holy Island Golf Course; Road Dust] by Charles Fry
Our Friends Say [Pigeon Cotes; French Cow-Baiting; Millicent Hall, Fencing Champion]
Health and Happiness [Cheese; Icilma Cream; Wine] by George Dabbs
In the Clubroom [Golf Balls; Cricket Spikes]
Outdoor Dress [Seaside Fishing; Hot Weather Cycling; Accessories; Review of *The Well Dressed Woman* by Lilian Joy] by Henry Gage
The Motor and The Cycle [Motor Racing; Horns and Whistles; Japanese Road Racers; Derrynane Cycling Camp] by Richard Mecredy
Always Interesting; Illustrated by Anutot Pickford
Out of Town [East Coast Golf Links; Carriers, Montana] by Alfred Cooper
Cruises; Illustrated by Robert Nisbet
Boating [Putney Regatta; Thames Punting Club; Hampton Court Skiff Racing] by Charles Thomas
Cabby; Illustrated by William Owen
Field and Covert [Cats as Foster Mothers; Partridges; Rabbits] by Owen Jones
Gardening for the Month by Edgar Cook
Camera Notes [Shutter Speed Tests; Calculating Exposures; Chemicals] by Archibald Williams
Rifle Shooting [Surbiton Urban District Rifle Club; War Office Opticians] by Robert Pearson
Our Book Corner [Reviews of *The Fair Hills of Ireland* by Stephen Gwynn; *Engines of Social Progress* by Walter George; *Great Golfers* by Henry Leach]

Issue 42 : September 1907 (p497-592 + 32)

Cover Design; Illustrated by Henry Brock
Flor-de-Dindigul; Illustrated by Fletcher Ransom
The Race for the Motoring Grand Prix: Felice Nazzaro
The Grouse Migration by Bernard Carter; Illustrated by George Thorp & Archibald Thorburn
The Southbound Car: Among the Bull Fighters (4) by Owen Llewellyn; Illustrated by Leonard Raven-Hill
A Good Sportsman by Sackville Martin; Illustrated by Thomas Browne
Rhymes on the Rhymester [verses] by John Horsley
Fishes of the Sea (1) by Frederick Aflalo
Our Friend Humpty Dumpty by Edward Sewell; Illustrated by Charles Ambrose
The Interval [verses] by John Horsley
Advanced Golf (10): Problems on the Putting Green by James Braid & Henry Leach
Deer Stalking in Arran by John Astley

Water Polo: The Game and Its Tactics by George Brodribb
The Relieving Officer by Cecil Hughes; Illustrated by himself
Heronhaye (12) by Katherine Prichard & Hesketh Prichard; Illustrated by Lawson Wood
Man Over Timber by Charles Fry
The St.Leger: The Great Race at Doncaster by Norman Wentworth; Illustrated by George Thorp
Maori Fieldcraft by Philip Vaile
The Open Air Life by Richard Mecredy
A Short Story by Bertram Atkey
Jelf's Transformation Car [verses] by Mabel Gifford; Illustrated by Frederick Bennett
The Sportsman's View Point [Cricket Selectors; Caspar Whitney; American Golf; Brooklands Motor Racing; Yachting; George Fordham] by Charles Fry
Our Friends Say [Across America by Motorcycle; Wigton Rifle Butts; Poultry Farming]
Field and Covert [Good Cartridges; Partridge Shooting; Sporting Holidays] by Owen Jones
Motorcycle Notes by George Barnes
Gardening for the Month by Edgar Cook
Health and Happiness [Hallucinations; Poisonous Flesh; Spanish Goats; Chocolate Manufacturers] by George Dabbs
In the Clubroom [First Aid; Physical Culture]
The Motor and The Cycle [Misfires and Explosions; Control on Hills; Sparklet Inflator] by Richard Mecredy
Outdoor Dress [Sweaters; Panama Hats] by Henry Gage
The Boating Man; Illustrated by William Owen
Boating [Boat Builders; Wargrave; Sunbury Lock; Teddington Reach] by Charles Thomas
Rifle Shooting [Bisley Meeting] by Robert Pearson
Camera Notes [Double Toning; Aluminium Fittings] by Archibald Williams
Out of Town [Belgian Coast Golf Links; Channel Islands Sea Bathing; Cruden Bay Tennis and Croquet] by Alfred Cooper

STRAIGHT TALK BY THE EDITOR

Volume 8

Issue 43 : October 1907 (p1-96 + 36)

Cover Design; Illustrated by Henry Brock
The Red Deer; Illustrated by George Rankin
A Group of Famous Jockeys; Illustrated by George Thorp
Jockey Club Romance by Sidney Galtrey; Illustrated by George Thorp
Cricket From the Pressbox by Edward Sewell; Illustrated by Charles Ambrose
A Strange Happening by Edgar Barnes-Austin; Illustrated by Harry Rountree
The Perfect Fluke in Golf by Leslie Carne; Illustrated by Thomas Browne
The Southbound Car (5): Motoring Through Spain by Owen Llewellyn; Illustrated by Leonard Raven-Hill
The Bat by Bertram Atkey; Illustrated by George Soper
How the Golden Eagle Lost His Mate by Bertram Atkey; Illustrated by Harry Rountree
The Olympic Games by Bernard Carter
Heronhaye (13) by Katherine Prichard & Hesketh Prichard; Illustrated by Lawson Wood
Flight Netting by Thomas Henry Browne
The Latest Version [verses] by Frederick Buckley
In the Engine Room by Herbert Shaw; Illustrated by Edward Hodgson
Fishes of the Sea (2) by Frederick Aflalo
How to Manage Your Dog by Owen Jones
The Sportsman's View Point [Channel Swimming; Hidden Names; Cricket; Rugby League] by Charles Fry
Out of Town [Arnhem; Continental Guides; Hampton Court; Cruden Bay Golf Course; Llandudno] by Alfred Cooper
In the Clubroom [Football Lists; Tennis Photography]
Health and Happiness [Climate Changes; American Civil War] by George Dabbs
Outdoor Dress [Football Clothes; Yachting Caps; Cycling Ankle Clips; Golfing Boot] by Henry Gage
Our Friends Say [Extracts From Newnes magazines *Country Life, Woman's Life, Strand, Ladies' Field, Tit-Bits, Wide World*]
Boating [London Rowing Club Regatta; Thames Sailing Club; Angler's Inns; Oxford Steamers] by Charles Thomas
Gardening for the Month by Edgar Cook
The Motor and The Cycle [Dry Batteries; Car Trunks; Triplex Hub] by Richard Mecredy
Field and Covert [Pheasants and Water; Dormice; Gun Dogs] by Owen Jones
Rifle Shooting [Queen's Cup for Miniature Rifle Shooting; Alfred Banks] by Robert Pearson
Camera Notes [Dark Room Illuminant; Review of *The Complete Photographer* by Roger Child-Bayley; The Oil Process] by Archibald Williams
O'Midg; Illustrated by Harry Williamson
Review of *The Touring Atlas of the British Isles* by John Bartholomew

Issue 44 : November 1907 (p97-192 + 36)

Cover Design; Illustrated by Thomas Browne

Review of *History of the English People* by John Green
Hard Pressed; Illustrated by Arthur Elsley
Heard at a Check; Illustrated by Lionel Edwards
The Romance of Tattersall's by Norman Wentworth
Out Cubbing by Rina Ramsay; Illustrated by Arthur Gough
The Southbound Car (6): From Valencia to Madrid by Owen Llewellyn; Illustrated by Leonard Raven-Hill
Big Fishing Matches by James Bazley
The Deceivers by Eugene Shelley
A Real Good Thing by George Collins; Illustrated by Thomas Somerfield
The Royal and Ancient Golf Club by Henry Leach
The Perfect Sporting Gun by Archibald Williams
Confessions of a Poacher by John Bristow-Noble
The Solitary Spectator by David Bevington; Illustrated by Frederick Bennett
Lord [Harry] Dalmeny; Illustrated by Charles Ambrose
Surrey County Cricket Club 1905-07 by Charles Fry
Among the Cracks by Arthur Croome; Illustrated by Charles Ambrose
The Plunger by Bertram Crisp; Illustrated by Henry Brock
Firmin by Bertram Atkey; Illustrated by Frederic Whiting
Kicking in the Rugby Game by Edward Sewell
The Problem of Fitness by Charles Fry
The Sportsman's View Point [Football Politics; Amateur Football Association; *The Cape Times*; Frank Iredale; The Turf; Reviews of *Sport and Anecdotes* by Charles Birch-Reynardson and *Reminiscences of the Wensleydale Hounds* by Frederick Chapman; Big Trout; Angling] by Charles Fry
Gardening for the Month by Edgar Cook
Field and Covert [Judicious Bird Driving; Sloe Gin] by Owen Jones
Health and Happiness [Cavalry Horses; Gipsy Medical Lore; [Benjamin] Disraeli's Sonnet; Review of *Himalayan Mountains* by Joseph Hooker] by George Dabbs
Outdoor Dress [Straw Hats; Waistcoats; Moths] by Henry Gage
Out of Town [Finland Fishing; Western Highlands of Scotland] by Alfred Cooper
The Motor and The Cycle [Ignition Trouble; Wicklow Camping; Tandem Riding] by Richard Mecredy
In the Clubroom [South British Trading Company; Home Billiards; Central Railway Foxhunt Stations]
Our Friends Say [Extracts From Newnes Magazines]
Our Book Corner [Reviews of *The Problems of Cricket* by Philip Trevor; *How and Where to Fish in Ireland* by John Dunne; *The Horse* by Frank Barton; *The Swiss Family Robinson* illustrated by Harry Rountree; *Club Swinging* by Thomas Burrows; *The Australian Golfer* by Daniel Soutar]
Rifle Shooting [Post Matches; The Palma Trophy] by Robert Pearson

Issue 45 : December 1907 (p193-288 + 56)

Cover Design; Illustrated by Charles Crombie

Sport in the Antarctic by Bernard Carter
The Bird by Daniel Wheeler; Illustrated by Frederick Bennett
The Southbound Car (7): Through Toledo and Madrid by Owen Llewellyn; Illustrated by Leonard Raven-Hill
Parkinson's Aunt by Rina Ramsay; Illustrated by Frederic Whiting
The Whitest Game [verses] by Charles Fry
A Land of Golf: Eastern Kent by Henry Leach
In the Shadow of Buskett Steeple by Beatrice Fry & Charles Fry; Illustrated by Arthur Gough
Arthur Jones; Illustrated by Charles Ambrose
Jonah [England Cricket Captain] by Charles Fry
The Sporting Tenants by Bertram Atkey; Illustrated by Frederick Buchanan
The Art of Buying a Hunter by Archibald Hamilton; Illustrated by Frederic Whiting
The Modern Game of Diabolo by Charles Fry
The Greater Game by Herbert de Hamel; Illustrated by George Soper
The New Zealand [Rugby League] Professionals by Edward Sewell; Illustrated by William Robinson
A Rub on the Green by Philip Arp; Illustrated by Henry Brock
The New Billiards by Frederic Weiss
The Public Schools Winter Sports Club by Dora Jones; Illustrated by George Soper
The Sportsman's View Point [George Fordham; Jockeys; Harry Custance; Hunting; Maud Wynter; Cricket; Home Gordon; Henry Hawkins, Brooklands, Motor Racing, Prize Fighting; Dirigible; Balloon Accident; Diabolo; John Porter; Golf; Shooting; Cycling; Bowls] by Charles Fry
Ladies' Golfer; Illustrated by Felix Sharp
Our Book Corner [Reviews of *Big Game Shooting on the Equator* by Francis Dickinson; *Jock of the Bushveld* by Percy Fitzpatrick; *Two Dianas in Somaliland* by Agnes Herbert; *The Haunters of the Silence* by Charles Roberts; *Folk of the Wild* by Bertram Atkey; *The Man-Eaters of Tsavo* by John Patterson]
Health and Happiness [Scholastic Houses; Modern Languages; Rail Travel; Dog Shoplifter; Japanese Doctors] by George Dabbs
In the Clubroom [Dry Cleaning; Golf Clothing; Model Railways]
Our Friends Say [Extracts From Newnes Magazines]

Issue 46 : January 1908 (p289-384 + 36)

Cover Design; Illustrated by Charles Crombie
No Game Laws for Me; Illustrated by George Lodge
The Romance of the Road by Mervyn Tregaskis; Illustrated by William Robinson
The Black Beast in the Pool by John Dodington; Illustrated by Thomas Browne
Last Rounds and Knockout Blows by Norman Wentworth
A Sporting Chance by Archibald Demain-Grange; Illustrated by Gordon Browne
The Boy Encounters a Problem [verses] by Bertram Atkey
Newbury [Racecourse] by John Porter
John Porter [Racehorse Trainer] by Charles Fry
The Gordon Cup by Beatrice Fry & Charles Fry; Illustrated by Arthur Gough

Holiday [verses] by Eugene Shelley
A Convenient Bunker by Alfred Cooper; Illustrated by Henry Brock
Marylebone Cricket Club Team by Edward Sewell; Illustrated by Charles Ambrose
A Stolen Run by Rina Ramsay; Illustrated by Lionel Edwards
A Ghostly Tip by Richard Meysey-Thompson
Duellists and Duelling by Henry Bagge
Basil Maclear [Rugby] by Edward Sewell; Illustrated by Charles Ambrose
A September Pheasant by Marmaduke Athorpe; Illustrated by Harry Rountree
Still a Chance by Bertram Atkey
Problems of Winter Golf by Henry Leach; Illustrated by Edward Mitchell
The Gospel of Little Mary by George Dabbs
The Sportsman's View Point [Diary of a Dog; Etienne Boileau; The Motorcycling Club; Australian Rules Football; Hunting; America's Cup; Football; Motor Shows; Billiards; Shoots; Jockeys; Betting; Cricket] by Charles Fry
Our Book Corner [Reviews of *Wild Life on a Norfolk Estuary* by Arthur Patterson; *Adventures on the Roof of the World* by Elizabeth Leblond; *In the Land of Pearl and Gold* by Alexander MacDonald; *Nimrod's Wife* by Grace Seton; *The Prodigal Nephew* by Bertram Atkey]
Health and Happiness [Alaska; Thomas Arnold; Hereditary Hygiene; Meteorites] by George Dabbs
In the Clubroom [School Guides; Monople Cycles; Nairobi Shooting; Skittles]

Issue 47 : February 1908 (p385-480 + 32)

Cover Design; Illustrated by Lionel Edwards
In the Marshes in Winter; Illustrated by Henry Stannard
Tragedies of the Air by Leonard Hampol; Illustrated by George Thorp
The Steerswoman by David Brandon; Illustrated by George Soper
La Savate by Henry Bagge
Plungers and Plunging by Norman Wentworth; Illustrated by George Thorp
A Sporting Comedian: George Robey by Edward Sewell
Philopena by Marmaduke Athorpe; Illustrated by Henry Brock
Cue Tips by Cecil Hughes
A Blue Checker by Wilson Slaney; Illustrated by Frederick Bennett
The Choice of a Gun by Archibald Williams
Kings at the Game by Henry Leach; Illustrated by George Thorp
The Old Hunter [verses] by Christopher Scrope
Bloodhound Tracking by Francis Craven
The Vindication by Arthur Pier; Illustrated by Arthur Gough
The Reformation of Passon Puddephatt by Walter Gallichan; Illustrated by Thomas Browne
A Little Oversight [Golf]
The Great Universal Cattle Cure by Bertram Atkey; Illustrated by Frederick Buchanan
The Pageant of the Year [Review of *Memories of the Months* by Herbert Maxwell] by Frederick Aflalo
The Sportsman's View Point [Proposed Matterhorn Railway; Reviews of *The Matterhorn* by Guido Rey and *Leaves From the Notebooks of Dorothy Nevill* by Ralph Nevill;

John Sholto-Douglas; Price of Petrol; Tar-Spraying; Ladies Hockey; Women's Cricket; Riflewomen; Swordswomen; Cycling; Fox Hunting; Brooklands; Kilts] by Charles Fry

Our Book Corner [Reviews of *Five Years' Adventures in the Far Interior of South Africa* by Gordon Cummings; *Kate Meredith* by Cutcliffe Hyne; *The Throwback* by Alfred Lewis; *The City of Pleasure* by Arnold Bennett; *Wild Life Stories* by Samuel Bensusan; *The Moon of Bath* by Beth Ellis; *The White Darkness* by Lawrence Mott; *The Progress of Hugh Rendal* by Lionel Partman]

Health and Happiness [Animal Sales; Favourite Horses] by George Dabbs

Throw It Sixty Feet; Illustrated by Ernest Blaikley

In the Clubroom [Napier Cars; Lacrosse Boots; Billiard Table Makers]

Our Friends Say [Extracts From Newnes Magazines]

I Find Them; Illustrated by Frank Reynolds

Issue 48 : March 1908 (p481-576 + 32)

Cover Design; Illustrated by Henry Brock

John Chaworth-Musters; Illustrated by Samuel Carter

Thomas Assheton-Smith; Illustrated by William Thomas

Traditions of the Hunts by Norman Wentworth; Illustrated by George Thorp

In Arizona by Cyrus Brady; Illustrated by George Gibbs

The Imperial Cricket Triangle by Charles Fry; Illustrated by Charles Folkard

A Chip of the Old Block by Arthur Hales; Illustrated by Henry Brock

In Defence of Wagers by Frederick Aflalo; Illustrated by Ada Lehany

The Hireling by Rina Ramsay; Illustrated by George Jalland

The Treasure Finders by Bertram Atkey; Illustrated by Frederick Bennett

Lawn Tennis Under Cover by Wallis Myers

A Song of Soccer [verses] by Cyril Austin

The Truth About Fielding by Gilbert Jessop & James Bolton; Illustrated by Thomas Browne

Obituary: The Late Edward Hanlan by Guy Nickalls

Untrodden Ways by Archibald Sullivan; Illustrated by Harry Rountree

The Golf Temperament by Henry Leach; Illustrated by William Robinson

Sampson's Salmon by Clifford Cordley; Illustrated by George Soper

A Golf Retrospect by Bertram Atkey

The Eye in Sport by Charles Fry

The Problem of Fitness by Guy Nickalls; Illustrated by George Thorp

The Sportsman's View Point [Ideal Motorcar; Airships; Wrestling; Pedestrianism; Cigarettes; Henry Colville; Highway Obstructions; Home Gordon; Cycling; Men's Fashions] by Charles Fry; Illustrated by George Thorp

Cycling at Easter; Illustrated by Henry Walker

Our Book Corner [Review of *The Recollections of a Journalist* by Frank Scudamore]

Health and Happiness [Treasure Hunting; William Phipps; A Magnetic Island; Evolution of the Omnibus; Grenoble Restaurants] by George Dabbs

Rifle Shooting [Review of *The Citizen Rifleman* by Edward Newitt; Air-Rifles; Sporting Guns] by Edward Leman

In the Clubroom [Squirrel Brand Wool; Poker Dominoes]

Volume 9

Issue 49 : April 1908 (p1-96 + 44)

Cover Design; Illustrated by Charles Crombie
Frederick Roberts; Illustrated by Charles Folkard
Arms and the Sportsman by Frederick Roberts
The Waterloo Cup by Ludovick Cameron; Illustrated by Stephen Dadd
Physical Culture for Thoroughbreds by William Allison
The Kinship of Ages by James Barr; Illustrated by Harry Rountree
Who's Who on the Olympic Council [Howard Vincent, John Scott-Montagu, Lees Knowles, Theodore Cook, William Henry, Thomas Britten, Andrew Stoddart, Herbert Eaton, Charles Newton-Robinson, Frederick Wall, Henry Montcreiff-Tennent, Ryder Richardson] by Wallis Myers
The Man Behind the Olympic Games [William Grenfell] by Wallis Myers
The Luck by Bertram Crisp; Illustrated by Henry Brock
Rowing Methods of the Past by Guy Nickalls
Golf at £10 a Year by Henry Sabine; Illustrated by George Thorp
The Unfurnished Caravan by Bertram Atkey; Illustrated by Frederick Bennett
The Lincolnshire Handicap by Norman Wentworth
The River House by Owen Llewellyn; Illustrated by Gordon Browne
An Extraordinary Dead Heat
Sportsmen of the Stock Exchange by Roland Belfort; Illustrated by Charles Ambrose
The Grand National by Arthur Nightingall; Illustrated by George Thorp
Finnzha: The Seven Starred by Frederick Graves; Illustrated by Arthur Gough
The Colonel by Patrick Maxwell; Illustrated by Frederic Whiting
Philippa by Maud Stawell; Illustrated by Charles Bull
The Sportsman's View Point [Olympic Games; Canadian Marathon; Cricket; Physical Fitness; Bridges, Design of Twickenham; Rugby Tour of New Zealand; Prices of Racehorses; Tattersall's Sales, Mauser Pistols; Charles Absolon; Bacon's Country Maps; *The Cycling Gazette* by Abraham Rumney; Nickel Plating Fraud; Photography; Mudguards] by Charles Fry
Our Book Corner [Reviews of *That Little* by Eyre Hussey; *The Diary of Master William Silence* by Dodgson Madden; *The Sorcery Shop* by Robert Blatchford]
Cabby; Illustrated by William Owen
Health and Happiness [Landladies; Young Rats; Old Fashioned Boot Drier; Horse Purchase; London Milk] by George Dabbs
Rifle Shooting [National Rifle Association; The Astor Trust] by Edward Leman
Camping in Woods by Thomas Holding
Our Friends Say [Extracts From Newnes Magazines]

Issue 50 : May 1908 (p96-192 + 44)

Cover Design; Illustrated by Charles Crombie
Diamond Jubilee; Illustrated by George Thorp
The Best Horse I Ever Rode by George Chesterton; Illustrated by George Thorp
The Spur by Philip Arp; Illustrated by Henry Brock

The Humour of the Caddie by Harold Hilton; Illustrated by Charles Crombie
Among the Hockey Cracks by Eustace White; Illustrated by Charles Ambrose
Trout Fishing in Reservoirs by Paul Taylor; Illustrated by George Thorp & William Robinson
The City and Suburban Handicap by Bernard Carter; Illustrated by George Thorp
The Taunt by Robert Tarnacre; Illustrated by Gordon Browne
The Hurdle Race by Cyril Ffrench; Illustrated by Harry Rountree
A Sportsman's Paradise by Philip Vaile
Jack Mytton by Digby Jephson; Illustrated by George Soper
The Blackheath Golfing Tercentenary by Henry Leach
Matie by Paul Elgood; Illustrated by Henry Brock
The Compensation Case by Bertram Atkey; Illustrated by Frederick Bennett
The Catch of the Season by Archibald Demain-Grange; Illustrated by Frederic Whiting
A Losing Game by Sackville Martin; Illustrated by Arthur Mills
The Sportsman's View Point [Golf Expenses; Golf Links; Harry de Windt; Car Rally; Football Transfers; International Cricket; Walking; Thomas Cribb; Steeplechasing; Railway Charges; Bicycles; Camping; Cameras; Men's Fashions; *The Fishing Gazette*] by Charles Fry
Motorcycle Notes [Paris Racing Tracks; Stanley Show; Motosacoche] by George Barnes
Health and Happiness [Youthful Depravity; Daily Bath; London Publishers; Cholera Epidemic; Abraham Lincoln] by George Dabbs
Rifle Shooting [Rifle Clubs; Rifle Committees] by Edward Leman
In the Clubroom [Bicycle Saddles; Porcelain Postcards; Road Maps]

Issue 51 : June 1908 (p193-288 + 40)

Cover Design; Illustrated by Charles Crombie
The Elixir of Pace; Illustrated by Cecil Brown
The Evolution of Polo by Sidney Galtrey; Illustrated by Leonard Raven-Hill
Modern Polo; Illustrated by Cecil Brown
An Amateur Championship Week by Bernard Darwin; Illustrated by Edward Mitchell
Jimmy Logan by Achibald Demain-Grange; Illustrated by Gordon Browne
Queer Fishing by Thomas Bridges; Illustrated by George Soper
Weatherby's by Norman Wentworth; Illustrated by George Thorp
Secrets of Success in Boxing by Tommy Burns & James Bolton
Miss Blake of Ballygarret by Claremont Clare; Illustrated by Henry Brock
The Billiard Sharp by Bertram Atkey; Illustrated by Frederick Bennett
Sandwich and Prestwick Golf Links by Henry Leach
Rabbiting With Ferrets and Gun by Owen Jones
Peelin's by Archibald Sullivan; Illustrated by Harry Rountree
The Cricket Champions by Charles Fry; Illustrated by Charles Ambrose
Spitfire by Bertram Crisp; Illustrated by George Jalland
The Case for the Motor Bicycle (1) by Pollock Castors; Illustrated by George Thorp
The Sportsman's View Point [George Robertson; Olympic Games; American Athletics; George Washington; Boxing; Nathaniel Gould; Cycling; Humber Cars; Tyres; Print Trimmers; Cricket Shoes] by Charles Fry
Our Book Corner [Review of *The Physical Side of Rowing* by Raymond Etherington-Smith]

Health and Happiness [Pure Milk Association; Fraudulent Nursing Homes; Collectors and Collections; Review of *Glimpses of the French Revolution* by John Alger] by George Dabbs

Rifle Shooting [Rifle Club Memberships; Erection of Butts; Review of *Miniature Rifle Shooting* by William Greener] by Edward Leman

In the Clubhouse [Tennis Rackets; Cycle Vibration; Amateur Photographers]

Issue 52 : July 1908 (p289-384 + 48)

Cover Design; Illustrated by Harry Rountree

The National Art Union by George Godwin

The Yearling Gamble by Sidney Galtrey

The Truth About the Tests by Charles Fry

The New Dianas by Edwin Pugh; Illustrated by Henry Brock

High Diving by William Webb; Illustrated by George Thorp

The Ancient Olympic Games by George Robertson; Illustrated by George Thorp

Golfing Schools and Styles by Bernard Darwin; Illustrated by Edward Mitchell

He Who Steals Wot Isn't His'n by Edgar Barnes-Austin; Illustrated by George Stampa

The Case for the Motor Bicycle (2) by Pollock Castors

Court Favourites by Eustace White; Illustrated by Charles Ambrose

A Beautiful Idea by Bertram Atkey; Illustrated by Frederick Bennett

The Problem of Fitness by Eugen Sandow; Illustrated by George Thorp

How to Preserve Golf Balls by William Knowles

A Lost Ball by Francis Barnett; Illustrated by Gordon Browne

Ascot and Goodwood Race Meetings by Norman Wentworth

The Sportsman's View Point [Olympic Games; Football; Inner Tubes; Magneto; Timothy Gradidge; Jack Johnson; Photography Exhibition; Golf Balls] by Charles Fry

Health and Happiness [Quacker Doctors; City-Fed Cows; Bankruptcy; Kashmir; Courage] by George Dabbs

Rifle Shooting [Rifle Sights; Society of Miniature Rifle Clubs; Francis Roberts editor of *The Rifleman*] by Edward Leman

Motor Fact and Opinion [Misuse of Cars; Taxation of Vehicles; Pullman Omnibuses; New Police Speed-Traps] by Arthur Padley

Travel Supplement [Includes Reviews of *Sea-Fishing for Amateurs* by Frank Hudson; *The Golfers Guide to the Great Northern Railway* by William Butler; *Camp Herald* by John Cunningham] by Alfred Cooper

Issue 53 : August 1908 (p385-480 + 36)

Cover Design; Illustrated by Edwin Noble

Cowes Tales by George Hopcroft; Illustrated by George Thorp

Golf Lies: Good and Bad (1) by Arthur Croome; Illustrated by Charles Crombie

The Kilbride Races by Florence Maguire; Illustrated by Frederic Whiting

A Baited Bunker by Gilbert Jessop; Illustrated by Frederic Whiting

How to See the Broads by Harold Josling

Behind the Scenes at a Lawn Tennis Tournament by Wallis Myers

The Lost Trail by Archibald Sullivan; Illustrated by Harry Rountree

The Gunner's Song [verses] by Alan Haig-Brown
Putting and Putters by Bernard Darwin; Illustrated by Edward Mitchell
The Grouse Festival by Owen Jones; Illustrated by George Soper
Lady Golfers by Eustace White; Illustrated by Charles Ambrose
Walking a Puppy by Rina Ramsay; Illustrated by Frederic Whiting
The Goat That Baker Bought by Bertram Atkey; Illustrated by Frederic Whiting
The Land of the Wet Fly by James Bazley
Kent Cricket by Edward Sewell
Theodore Roosevelt by Frederick McKenzie; Illustrated by Frederick Strothmann
A Point of Honour by Bohun Lynch; Illustrated by Graham Hoggarth
On Tour With a Tent [Review of *The Camper's Handbook* by Thomas Holding] by Alfred Cooper; Illustrated by Frederick Bennett
The Sportsman's View Point [Flying Machines; Orville Wright; Wilbur Wright; Car Camping; Reflex Cameras] by Charles Fry
Our Book Corner [Review of *The Royal Yacht Squadron* by Montague Guest & William Boulton
Health and Happiness [Dried Figs; Russian Timber; Child Mortality] by George Dabbs
Rifle Shooting [Inter-Club Matches; Rifleman's Certificates] by Edward Leman
Motor Fact and Opinion [Automobile Association Inspectors; Provincial Exhibitions; Motor Works Schools] by Arthur Padley
In the Clubroom [Orange Golf Balls; The Unity Cycle Club; New Dunlop Tyre Factory]

Issue 54 : September 1908 (p480-576 + 40)

Cover Design; Illustrated by Charles Crombie
Chevalier Ginistrelli; Illustrated by George Thorp
Eduardo Ginisrrelli at Home by Bernard Parsons; Illustrated by George Thorp
Fishing by Archibald Sullivan; Illustrated by George Soper
Golf Lies: Good and Bad (2) by Arthur Croome; Illustrated by Charles Crombie
The Traitor by Bertram Smith; Illustrated by Frederic Whiting
The Great Days and Cricket Wagering by Bernard Carter
The Deciding Game by Perry Robinson; Illustrated by Henry Brock
The Red Deer: His Domain by Norman Wentworth; Illustrated by George Soper
The Song of the Hunting Man [verses] by Alan Haig-Brown
The Sporting Maloneys by Owen Oliver; Illustrated by George Stampa
Golfing Politics and Politicians by Bernard Darwin; Illustrated by Edward Mitchell
In the Quantocks with a Caravan by Alfred Cooper; Illustrated by George Stampa
A Bold Stroke by George Surrey; Illustrated by Arthur Gough
The Old Pugilist [verses] by Bertram Atkey
Partridge Shooting by Owen Jones; Illustrated by Harry Rountree
Concerning Systems by George Chesterton; Illustrated by Frederic Whiting
Hush by Bertram Atkey; Illustrated by Frederick Bennett
Falcons and Falconry by John Bristow-Noble
Lochaber no More by John Dodington; Illustrated by William Robinson
The Sportsman's View Point [Eduardo Ginistrelli; Brighton Coaching; Review of *The Complete Lawn Tennis Player* by Wallis Myers; French Bicycles; Shooting Schools; William Taft; White City Exhibition; Norfolk Broads] by Charles Fry

The Admiral; Illustrated by Bertram Smale

Insurance Ideas (1) [Advertorial] by John MacLennan; Illustrated by George Thorp

Ballade of the Butts [verses] by Edward Shepherd

Health and Happiness [Review of *Wastage of Child Life* by John Johnston; Doctors in Court; Redvers Buller] by George Dabbs

Rifle Shooting [Donegall Bronze Badge; Skilled Shots Certificates; National Roll of Marksmen] by Edward Leman

Motor Fact and Opinion [Marcus Samuel; Consumption of Motor Spirits; Brooklands Track Contests; Country Motorbus Services] by Arthur Padley

In the Clubroom [Thames Sea Trips; Harley Hill Climb]

 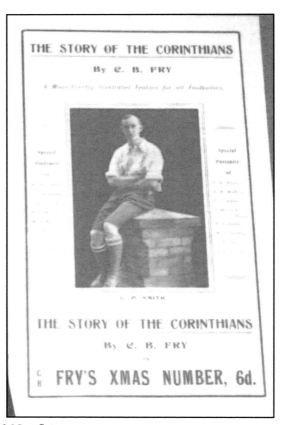

Christmas 1906 Leaflets

Volume 10

Issue 55 : October 1908 (p1-96 + 44)

Cover Design; Illustrated by Harry Rountree
The Rogue's Badge; Illustrated by George Thorp
Rogues Among Racehorses by Sidney Galtrey
On Going Foreign in a Motorcar by Owen Llewellyn; Illustrated by Thomas Browne
The Shot in the Cavern by James Barr; Illustrated by Harry Rountree
Golf Lies: Good and Bad (3) by Arthur Croome; Illustrated by Charles Crombie
The Lady in the Black Habit by John Dodington; Illustrated by William Robinson
Foxes at Work and Play by Owen Jones
The Country Client by Bertram Atkey; Illustrated by George Stampa
Some Dog Champions by Charles Alford; Illustrated by Maud Earl
A Last Year's Tennis Ball [verses] by William Ogilvie
The Sea Angler on the Yorkshire Scars by Carter Platts; Illustrated by William Robinson
The Man with the Dingo by Albert Dorrington; Illustrated by Harry Rountree
The Olympic Games by Charles Fry; Illustrated by George Thorp
First Miss Out by Herbert Knight-Horsfield; Illustrated by George Soper
The Cheerful Pedestrian [verses] by Christopher Scrope
The Professionals at Work by Bernard Darwin; Illustrated by Edward Mitchell
Brainless Bobby by Edward Lebreton-Martin; Illustrated by Arthur Mills
The Schooling of a Hunter by Lilian Bland
The Sportsman's View Point [Athletic Oxygen; Pan-Britannic Games; Triangular Cricket; Football Politics; Golf; Household Brigade Steeplechase; Thomas Lipton; Dog Training; Motorcycles; Photography] by Charles Fry; Illustrated by William Robinson
Health and Happiness [Nursing Qualifications; Squeaking Boots; Socialism; Commerce] by George Dabbs
William George [Athlete]; Illustrated by David Cottington-Taylor
Insurance Ideas (2) [Advertorial] by John MacLennan
Rifle Shooting [Indoor Ranges; National Air Rifle Association; The Greener Ladies Challenge Trophy] by Edward Leman
Motor Fact and Opinion [Motor Schools; Car Labour; Steering Gears] by Arthur Padley
In the Clubroom [Meat Tablets; Field Glasses; Sports Outfitters]
Good Business by Perry Robinson

Issue 56 : November 1908 (p97-192 + 40)

Cover Design; Illustrated by Harry Rountree
The Gnarled Head; Illustrated by Harry Rountree
Footsteps on the Sea by James Barr; Illustrated by Harry Rountree
The Past Cricket Season by Edward Sewell; Illustrated by Frank Gillett
The Amazing Match by George Riddell & Bernard Darwin; Illustrated by Henry Brock
Pike and Pike Fishing by Alfred Jardine; Illustrated by George Thorp
That Robin [verses] by Bertram Atkey
The Trials of a First Day's Hunting by Dorothea Conyers; Illustrated by Frederic Whiting

A Wild Cat Scheme by Bertram Atkey; Illustrated by Frederick Bennett
The Father of Shooting [Peter Hawker] by Basil Tozer
The Last Four Punctures by Cecil Hughes; Illustrated by Gordon Browne
Afoot in Normandy [verses] by Ralph Chafy
The No Bar Billiard Table by Sydenham Dixon
Golf Lies: Good and Bad (4) by Arthur Croome; Illustrated by Charles Crombie
Missed by Perry Robinson; Illustrated by Henry Brock
The Crux of Association Football by Charles Fry
The Black Sheep by Peter Rowley; Illustrated by Thomas Browne
Poker Patience by William Dalton
How to Buy a Secondhand Gun by Basil Tozer
The Sportsman's View Point [County Cricket; Hambledon Match; Football Association; Game Guns; Hunting Counties; Queensland Athletics; Fashions; Hydroplanes; Motorcar Prices; Pigmenting; Colour Photography; Puttees] by Charles Fry
Our Book Corner [Reviews of *Who's Who of Golf* by Henry Leach; *Whirlwind's Year* by Nathaniel Gould]
Reaping; Illustrated by Garth Jones
Insurance Ideas (3) [Advertorial] by John MacLennan
Health and Happiness [Military Training; Stadium Sports; Tipping; Metric System; Reviews of *Cooking Up-To-Date* by May Little and *An Author in The Territorials* by Coulson Kernahan] by George Dabbs
Rifle Shooting [Average Shots; Club Slackness] by Edward Leman
In the Clubroom [Pitman's School; Philatelic Congress; Wool Underwear]

Issue 57 : December 1908 (p193-288 + 64)

Cover Design; Illustrated by Harry Rountree
Golf Front Covers by Charles Fry
Look After Yourselves; Illustrated by Caton Woodville
A Great Turf Fraud (1) by James Muddock; Illustrated by Caton Woodville
Thieves Hollow by John Dodington; Illustrated by Edward Wigfull
To a Foxhound Pup [verses] by Edgar Newgass; Illustrated by Frederick Bennett
Providence in the Saddle by Rina Ramsay; Illustrated by Arthur Gough
A Big Game Expedition by Albert Dorrington; Illustrated by Stanley Wood
A Lost Elixir by George Riddell & Bernard Darwin; Illustrated by Charles Crombie
My First Pheasant [verses] by Ralph Chafy
Sport in a Nutshell (1) by Bertram Atkey; Illustrated by Frederick Buchanan
The Test by David Brandon; Illustrated by George Soper
The Ensnaring of Doreen by Reeves Shaw; Illustrated by Henry Brock
The Count's New Cue by Cecil Hughes; Illustrated by Sigurd Schou
Concerning Catchpole by Harold Begbie; Illustrated by George Stampa
An Artic Reformer by Bertram Atkey; Illustrated by Harry Rountree
The Twelfth Rat by Bertram Atkey; Illustrated by Frederick Bennett
The Peaceful Golfer by Henry Leach
The Sportsman's View Point [Amateur Athletics Association; Tweed Salmon; Angling; Puttees; Athletic Clubs; Amateur Football] by Charles Fry

Canoeing and Sport on the Upper Ottawa [River] by Charles Stokes
An Infallible System [Advertorial]
Well Away; Illustrated by Garth Jones
The Earliest Fox by Perry Robinson
Among the Golfers [Edward Lassen; New Rules; Oxford University Golf Team] by Henry Harley
A Good Retriever by Alan Haig-Brown
Smoker of Experience; Illustrated by William Owen
The Threatened Extinction of Shore Shooting by Stanley Duncan
Auction Bridge by William Dalton
Hare Tracing in the Snow by Edward Caswall
A True Story of Interest by Joseph Fry
Health and Happiness [Donkey-Cart; Cucumber; Church Atmosphere; The Agricultural College of Ontario] by George Dabbs
Hold All the Honours; Illustrated by James Halpin
Rifle Shooting [Surrey Rifle Club] by Edward Leman
Insanitary Telephones by Francis Allan
In the Clubroom [White City Souvenirs; Photographic Cards]
Hold All the Honours; Illustrated by James Halpin

Issue 58 : January 1909 (p288-384 + 48)

Cover Design; Illustrated by Henry Brock
At the Fair; Illustrated by Denholm Armour
The Poor Man's Hunter by Denholm Armour; Illustrated by himself
Pike and the Sportswoman by Carter Platts
Winter Cruising in Small Yachts by Linton Hope; Illustrated by Edward Wigfull
A Neglected Force in Rugby Football by Edward Sewell
Mr Longman's Hounds (1): The Pack by George Collins; Illustrated by Frederic Whiting
Sport in a Nutshell (2) by Bertram Atkey; Illustrated by Frederick Buchanan
The Secret of the Golf Swing (1) by Thomas Carruthers & George Beldam
A Great Turf Fraud (2) by James Muddock; Illustrated by Caton Woodville
The Ladies Purse by Rina Ramsay; Illustrated by Frederic Whiting
Pigeon Shooting in Winter by Owen Jones; Illustrated by George Soper
An Automatic Moneymaker by John MacLennan; Illustrated by Louis Sargent
A Woman in Camp: Mabel Long by John Bristow-Noble
Style in Boxing by Frederick Shaw
Uncle Miser by Bertram Atkey; Illustrated by Frederick Bennett
The Conversion of Bertie by Perry Robinson; Illustrated by Arthur Mills
The Sportsman's View Point [American Sport; Olympic Council; Wrestling; Motorcar Speed; Moroccan Camels; Aerial Sport; International Cricket; County Cricket Membership] by Charles Fry
Foxhunting in the Highlands by Alexander Inkson-McConnochie; Illustrated by George Soper
A Wilderness Ordeal by Edward Rydall; Illustrated by Warwick Goble
That Bird Among Birds by Owen Jones; Illustrated by Dyke White
After Ibex in Baltistan by Ethel Tweddell; Illustrated by Ada Lehaney

Business Losses After Fire [Advertorial] by John MacLennan; Illustrated by George Thorp
Rifle Shooting [Aid From Public Funds; The Astor Fund; War Office Rifles] by Edward Leman
Health and Happiness [Dutch Courage; Rain in Peru; Illegal Reading Rooms; Piccadilly; Canning Industry] by George Dabbs
Percy Bush [Rugby]; Illustrated by David Cottington-Taylor
The Garden and The Gardner by Edward Lebreton-Martin
In the Clubroom [Rudge-Whitworth Motorcycles; Lacrosse Boots; The Boomerang; Dumb-Bells]

Issue 59 : February 1909 (p385-480 + 40)

Cover Design; Illustrated by Harry Rountree
The Tully Stud Farm by Sidney Galtrey; Illustrated by George Thorp
Sportsmen on Lloyd's by Wallis Myers; Illustrated by Charles Ambrose
The Jack Snipe by McDonnell Bodkin; Illustrated by Henry Brock
Tactics in Welsh [Rugby] Football by Edward Sewell; Illustrated by Charles Ambrose
The Revolver Flourish by Walter Winans
Colonel Buckley's Diplomacy by Gilbert Jessop; Illustrated by George Soper
After the Kill by Agnes Herbert
Oxygen: A New Factor in Physical Efficiency by Leonard Hill; Illustrated by Charles Ambrose
Sport in a Nutshell (3) by Bertram Atkey; Illustrated by Frederick Buchanan
The Bus by Bertram Atkey; Illustrated by Frederick Bennett
The Secret of the Golf Swing (2) by Thomas Carruthers & George Beldam
Mr Longman's Hounds (2): The Honorary Whippers-In by George Collins; Illustrated by Frederic Whiting
The Capricious Barbel by Hugh Sheringham
The Lady of the Streams by Francis Walbran
The Chances of Steeplechasing by Charles Coventry
A Battle of Kings by Lloyd Roberts; Illustrated by Harry Rountree
A Bride for the Desert by Courtenay Lacey; Illustrated by Caton Woodville
The Sportsman's View Point [County Cricket Captains' Meeting; Cricket Board of Control] by Charles Fry
Dawn on the Saltings by Arthur Conway; Illustrated by Caton Woodville
Golf in Midwinter by Bernard Darwin; Illustrated by Edward Mitchell
Rifle Shooting [Lady Rifle Shots; Musketry] by Edward Leman
Starting Your Son in Business [Advertorial] by John MacLennan
Health and Happiness [National League for Physical Education; Overcrowded Dwellings; Water Supplies] by George Dabbs
A New Rowing Exerciser by Charles Fry
The Garden and The Gardener by Edward Lebreton-Martin
The Loud Voiced Otter Hunter by Ludovick Cameron
In the Clubroom [Review of *The Swastika* by Powell Rees; American Boots; Riding Breeches]
Rugby Tackles; Illustrated by Cecil Thomas

Issue 60 : March 1909 (p481-576 + 48)

Cover Design; Illustrated by Harry Rountree

The Secret of the Golf Swing (3) by Thomas Carruthers & George Beldam
My Brother Keepers by Owen Jones; Illustrated by Ada Lehany
Wet Fly Wisdom by Ewen Tod
The Art of Hurdling by Arthur Croome; Illustrated by Charles Ambrose
The Corinthians and the Colonies by Bertie Corbett
Cuthbert's Coup by Charles Greswell; Illustrated by Arthur Gough
Sport in a Nutshell (4) by Bertram Atkey; Illustrated by Frederick Buchanan
Mr Longman's Hounds (3): The Farmers' Dinner by George Collins; Illustrated by Frederic Whiting
The Amateur Mechanic by John Knight
The Black Brant: Wild Goose Shooting by Bonnycastle Dale
The Compleat Greyhound [verses]
The New Self Defence by Bernard Parsons
The Racing Pigeon by Alfred Osman; Illustrated by George Thorp
The Philosophic Wildfowler by Walter Fallon
The Royal Pig by James Muddock; Illustrated by Harry Rountree
Welsh Moonrakers by Owen Llewellyn; Illustrated by Alfred Smith
The Last of the Cockfighters by Unite Jones
Golf in 2009 by Bernard Darwin; Illustrated by Edward Mitchell
The Unsportsmanlike Jack by Grace Seton
Hares and Hare Driving by Frank Bonnett; Illustrated by Harry Rountree
The Old Brandy Hunt by Stephen Moore; Illustrated by Harry Rountree
The Ideal Hockey Team by Harry Moncreiff-Tennent
The Sportsman's View Point [Scottish Rugby Football Union; Rugby Union Publicity; New Zealand Rugby] by Charles Fry; Illustrated by Thomas Somerfield
Motor Engineering by Mervyn O'Gorman
Genille Cave-Browne-Cave [Horse Trainer]; Illustrated by David Cottington-Taylor
Health and Happiness [Voltaire (Francois Arouet), City Populations; Palmistry] by George Dabbs
Rifle Shooting [Hythe School of Musketry; Granville Egerton] by Edward Leman
Points Worth Knowing About Death Duties [Advertorial] by John MacLennan; Illustrated by Percy Gossop
The Troublesome Motor by Harry Harby
Among the Golfers [Wooden Clubs; Knickerbockers; Shetland Waistcoats] by Bernard Darwin
The Premier Rugby Referee [Arthur Jones] by Edward Sewell
A Weekend on a Motorcycle by Bernard Parsons; Illustrated by John de Walton
Mountaineering Disasters by Frederic Harrison
The Garden and The Gardener by Edward Lebreton-Martin
In the Clubroom [Scotch Tweeds; Sporting Suspenders]

Volume 11

Issue 61 : April 1909 (p1-96 + 60)

Cover Design; Illustrated by Harry Rountree
African Antelope Heads; Illustrated by George Thorp
America's Heads and Horns by Cyrus Brady; Illustrated by George Thorp
A Stalking Model by Alfred Carey
Hare Splitting by Henry Alexander; Illustrated by Charles Crombie
An Inferior Crittur by Robert Surtees
The Grand National by Sidney Galtrey; Illustrated by Charles Ambrose
The Twins by George Riddell; Illustrated by Henry Brock
The Cooking of a Trout by John Dunne
The Sailing Canoe by Linton Hope; Illustrated by himself
Who Goes Trottin? by Herbert Shaw; Illustrated by George Soper
Twixt Devil and Deep Sea by James Barr; Illustrated by Harry Rountree
The Whippet and His Work by Frank Barton
The Heritage of the Marshmen by Francis Atkins; Illustrated by Harry Rountree
Sport Among the Destroyers by Horace Davis; Illustrated by himself
The Working of Ferrets by William Carnegie
Mr Longman's Hounds (4): The Hunt Ball by George Collins; Illustrated by Frederic Whiting
The Life History of a Salmon Fly by George Kelson; Illustrated by Louis Sargent & Reginald Higgins
The Great Brown Bear of Alaska by Charles Lane; Illustrated by Ada Lehany
In Nature's Disguise by Arthur Patterson
The Secret of the Golf Swing (4) by Thomas Carruthers and George Beldam; Illustrated by George Thorp
Lines [verses] by Ralph Hodgson
The Calcutta Cup by Edward Sewell
Camping in Uganda by Cyrus Brady
The Sportsman's View Point [Scottish Rugby Union] by Edward Sewell
The Perfect Physique by Bart Kennedy
Five Days in Shropshire and North Wales by Pollock Castors
Catching Wild Horses by Harold Shepstone
With Rod and Gun [Pike Fishing; Pigeon Shooting] by George Kelson
Among the Golfers [Over-Golfing; Golfing Tours; Golf Diaries; Fashion in Clubs] by Bernard Darwin; Illustrated by Thomas Browne
The Ensuring of Educations [Advertorial]; Illustrated by Percy Gossop
The Charm of Mountaineering by Frederic Harrison
The Motorcycle of Today by William McMinnies
Schooling Young Horses for the Hunting Field by Harry Harby
Health and Happiness [Bathing; Turkish Baths] by George Dabbs
Having No Spade, Partner? by William Dalton
The Pace of Hounds by Jack Fairfax-Blakeborough; Illustrated by George Soper
Rifle Shooting [National Rifle Association Annual Report; All-England Rifle Meeting] by Edward Leman

In the Clubroom [Trustees; Sauces; Cricket Bats; Sports & Games Association; Carbis Bay; Bloodstock Booklet]
The Perfect Nail for Golf Shoes by Alan Hebert

Issue 62 : May 1909 (p97-192 + 76)

Cover Design; Illustrated by Harry Rountree
Across the Atlantic by Aeroplane [Henry de la Vauix, Leon Delagrange, Percival Spender, Baden Baden-Powell, Charles Rolls, Walter Windham, Hiram Maxim, Frank Hedges-Butler, Selwyn Edge] by Wallis Myers
The Breath that Failed by Horace Hutchinson & George Riddell; Illustrated by Henry Brock
The Pleasures of the Long Line by Frank Hudson
Rooks and Rook Shooting by Frank Bonnett; Illustrated by George Soper
Playing to the Gallery by Bohun Lynch; Illustrated by Graham Hoggarth
The Secret of the Golf Swing (5) by Thomas Carruthers & George Beldam; Illustrated by George Thorp
The Scientist's Game by Edmund Lacon-Watson
When Greek Meets Greek by Stephen Moore; Illustrated by Ada Lehany
Man Behind the Marques [Etienne de Zuyler, Albert Malfiance, Alexandre Darracq, Henri Brasier, Louis Renault, Adolphe Clement, Ferdinand Charron, Jelineck Mercedes] by George Black; Illustrated by George Roller
The Convalescence of Solomon by Bertram Atkey; Illustrated by George Stampa
The Healthy Woods by Edward Thomas
The Luck of the N'hlatu by Stanley Hyatt; Illustrated by Harry Rountree
The Australian Cricket Tour; Illustrated by George Thorp
Roulette Systems by Hiram Maxim
In the Billiard Room by Sidney Fry; Illustrated by Frederick Buchanan
Mr Longman's Hounds (5): The Run of the Season by George Collins; Illustrated by Frederic Whiting
Soldiers' Polo by Sidney Galtrey; Illustrated by Cecil Brown & Charles Ambrose
Polo Notes by Francis Egerton-Green
The Sportsman's View Point [Australian Cricket Team] by Charles Fry
The World's Health by Mervyn Lang
Trying a Racehorse by Archibald Hamilton
My Record Ride by Pollock Castors; Illustrated by John de Walton
Among the Golfers [Muirfield Championship; Jerome Travers; International Match] by Bernard Darwin
The Judging of a Greyhound by Hugh Dalziel
With Rod and Gun [Gun-Dogs; Kennel Club; William Pape] by George Kelson
Health and Happiness [Railway Advertisements; Atmospheric Density; Sea-Sickness] by George Dabbs
The Art of Investing [Advertorial] by John MacLennan; Illustrated by George Thorp
A Sporting Bag by Charles St.John
The Motorcycle of Tomorrow by William McMinnies
Rifle Shooting [Royal Agricultural Hall Rifle Tournament; National Rifle Clubs' Dinner] by Edward Leman

Riding on an Avalanche by Maurice Steinmann; Illustrated by Ada Lehany
Men versus Animal by Frederick Aflalo
A New Tennis Racket by Cecil Hughes
The Intelligence of Horses by Charles O'Sullivan
In the Clubroom [Clean Footwear; Leg Guards; Review of *Who's Who in Golf* by Henry Leach]

Issue 63 : June 1909 (p193-288 + 72)

Cover Design; Illustrated by Frederic Whiting
Alec Taylor; Illustrated by Charles Ambrose
Racehorse and Trainer at Home: Alec Taylor (1) by Sidney Galtrey; Illustrated by George Thorp
Vermin and Game Preserving by Frank Bonnett
A Bond of Union by Horace Hutchinson & George Riddell; Illustrated by Henry Brock
A Sporting Parson by Wallis Myers; Illustrated by George Soper
The Mayfly Trout by Frank Bonnett
My Reminiscences by Danny Maher & James Bolton; Illustrated by George Soper
A Game of Croquet by Justus Williams; Illustrated by George Soper
Sport in the Rockies by Henry Seton-Karr; Illustrated by Stanley Wood
The Decoyman's Epitaph by Ralph Payne-Gallwey
The Taking of a Sunfish by Charles Holder
The Great Dane by George Chesterton
Mr Longman's Hounds (6): The Point-to-Point Steeplechases by George Collins; Illustrated by Frederic Whiting
Rubs on the Green by Bernard Darwin; Illustrated by Charles Ambrose
The Fox Terrar
A Bargain in Castles by Cecil Hughes; Illustrated by Malcolm Patterson
The Secret of the Golf Swing (6) by Thomas Carruthers & George Beldam; Illustrated by George Thorp
False Economy [Fishing Tackle] by Charles Cook
A Forced Decision by Archibald Sullivan; Illustrated by Henry Brock
The Sportsman's View Point [Indian Cricket] by Charles Fry
The Marauding Rat by John Bristow-Noble; Illustrated by Caton Woodville
There and Back by Pollock Castors
The Companionable Dog by John Maxtee
Among the Golfers [Deal Golf Course; Wetbobs versus Drybobs Match] by Bernard Darwin
The Amateur International Golf Team
Tennis Topics [Frederick Alexander; Continental Tennis; South African Tour] by Eustace White
Lawn Tennis in India by Wallis Myers
Health and Happiness [Lowestoft; Review of *Cromer Past and Present* by Walter Rye] by George Dabbs
The Passenger Motorcycle by William McMinnies
Motorcycle Notes by George Barnes
The Ideal Motorist's Workshop by John Knight
Rifle Shooting [Tournaments; Territorial Army] by Edward Leman
Everyday Risks [Advertorial] by John MacLennan; Illustrated by Percy Gossop

With Rod and Gun [Spring Salmon Fishing; River Itchen Trout; New Spinning Reel; Partridge Shooting] by George Kelson
The Lighter Side by Bertram Atkey; Illustrated by Louis Sargent
Breaking it Gently by Thomas Henry Browne
In the Clubroom [Adams Cars; Game Preserves; Yachting Cruises; Model Aeroplanes]
Tennis Server; Illustrated by Cecil Thomas

Issue 64 : July 1909 (p289-384 + 68)

Cover Design; Illustrated by Charles Crombie
Contented Angler; Illustrated by William Owen
Sam Darling; Illustrated by George Thorp
Racehorse and Trainer at Home: Sam Darling (2) by Sidney Galtrey
Two Up and One to Play by Kenneth Henderson; Illustrated by Henry Brock
The Somnambulist; Illustrated by Ralph Hodgson
Memorable Matches at Wimbledon by Wallis Myers
The One Meal a Day Diet by Joshua Duke
The White Boar of the Nhodas by Hilton Brown; Illustrated by George Soper
The Strongest Man of his Time [Frederick Burnaby] by Thomas Wright
Good Wickets: The Art of Samuel Apted by Charles Fry; Illustrated by Charles Ambrose
Wagers at White's by Annesley Bazett; Illustrated by Joseph Skelton
Bicycle Polo for Ladies by Mabel Richards
The Big Game Hunter's Menu by William Hornaday
Mr Blackstone's Broncho by Bertram Atkey; Illustrated by George Stampa
The Making of Henley by Bernard Carter
A Horse Deal by Evelyn Grogan; Illustrated by Frederic Whiting
Summer Camps on the Danube by Algernon Blackwood
After Bream in the Lincoln Fens by James Bazley
Croquet: Retrospective and Otherwise by Cyril Corbally
The Road to Como by Roy Trevor
The Secret of the Golf Swing (7) by Thomas Carruthers & George Beldam; Illustrated by George Thorp
The Gipsy Holiday by Charles McEvoy
Sportsman's Land [Canada] by Frederick Aflalo
The Mountain Lion by Lincoln Wilbar
Among the Golfers [Holiday Golf; Sea Breezes; Grips; Newmarket Golf Course] by Bernard Darwin
A First Night by Pollock Castors
Health and Happiness [Great Northern Railway; Coastal Visits; Lakeland] by George Dabbs
Tennis Topics [Early Training; The English Grip; Harry Parker; Queen's Club] by Eustace White
The Holiday Burglar [Advertorial] by John MacLennan; Illustrated by Percy Gossop
Lightweight Motorcycles (1) by William McMinnies
Rifle Shooting [Report on National Rifle Clubs' Dinner and Speeches] by Edward Leman
The Lighter Side by Bertram Atkey; Illustrated by Louis Sargent
Things as They Are; Illustrated by Ralph Hodgson

With Rod and Gun [Trout Disease; Herring-Skin Bait; Gun-Makers' Schools] by George Kelson
Sport With the Mackerel by Paul Fleming; Illustrated by Frederick Bennett
In the Clubroom [Golf Club Rust; Historic Houses; Marylebone Cricket Club Specialities; Lawn Mowers]

Issue 65 : August 1909 (p384-480 + 64)

Cover Design; Illustrated by Charles Pears
The Home of the Moose; Illustrated by William Denslow
The Sporting Estates of England: Highclere by Frank Bonnett; Illustrated by George Thorp
All Right! Clear Off!; Illustrated by Frederick Buchanan
A Shameless Minx by Bernard Darwin; Illustrated by Henry Brock
The Thirteenth Australian Team by Edward Sewell; Illustrated by Charles Ambrose
The Genesis of the Motorcar by Douglas Leechman
A Single Handed Cruise by Charles Pears; Illustrated by himself
The Man and the Apparel: Cecil Rhodes by Harry Woon
Needs Must When by Gilbert Jessop; Illustrated by George Soper
A Camp on the Beach by Frederick Innes
The Best [Bridge] Player by Archibald Dunn
Convincing Mr Whipple by Frederick Brown; Illustrated by Frances Wirgman
A Night with the Bustard by Carter Platts
Andrew Joyner; Illustrated by George Thorp
Racehorse and Trainer at Home: Andrew Joyner (3) by Sidney Galtrey
Wood Pigeon Practice by Owen Jones
The Sportsman's Equipment Guide by Cecil Hughes; Illustrated by Frederick Buchanan
Still Hunting Moose in New Brunswick by Douglas Clinch; Illustrated by George Soper
Freak Golf Matches by Horace Hutchinson; Illustrated by Frederick Buchanan
A Letter to His Father by Bertram Atkey
Exercise That Cures Illness by Eugen Sandow
The Coming of Netball by John Norris
Among the Golfers [*News of the World* Tournament; Golf and the Artist; Ball Testing] by Bernard Darwin
Nothing to Crow About by Ralph Hodgson
The Turf [Epsom Meeting; Manchester Cup; Northumberland Plate] by Norman Wentworth
No Darkroom Needed; Illustrated by Thomas Whitwell
The Ethics of Lending by George Riddell
Out of Town [North Wales; Killarney; Lorraine] by Alfred Cooper
The Borrowed Bicycle by Pollock Castors
Holiday Accidents [Advertorial] by John MacLennan
Two Good Cricket Books [Reviews of *Twenty-Five Cricket Stories* by Pelham Wodehouse; *WG's Little Book* by Gilbert Grace]
Game and Game Preserving (1): The Up-To-Date Game Farm by George Malcolm
Tennis Topics [Tennis Literature; Poverty of Class Among Lady Players; Harry Parker] by Eustace White
Lightweight Motorcycles (2) by William McMinnies

Rifle Shooting [Government Grant of Free Ammunition] by Edward Leman; Illustrated by George Thorp
With Rod and Gun [Grouse Disease; Shooting Etiquette; Slip-Knots] by George Kelson
In the Clubroom [Quorn Belt; Bicycle Distance Records]
Saluting the Flag; Illustrated by Stanley Wood

Issue 66 : September 1909 (p481-576 + 48)

Cover Design; Illustrated by Harry Rountree
Racehorse and Trainer at Home: Richard Marsh (4) by Sidney Galtrey; Illustrated by George Thorp
My Reminiscences by Sam Langford & James Bolton; Illustrated by George Soper
L'Abbesse de Jouarre by Jeanette Cornwallis-West
From Hammersmith to Burnham in a Half Decked Yacht by Charles Pears; illustrated by himself
Great Men and Golf (1) by Bertram Atkey; Illustrated by Charles Crombie
To My First Rod [verses] by Edward Lebreton-Martin
The Education of Big Game [Review of *Hunting Trips in North America* by Frederick Selous] by Frederick Aflalo; Illustrated by George Soper
My Lady's Glove [verses] by Leslie Oyler
The Failure of Chudsey's Mayor by Reeves Shaw; Illustrated by George Stampa
The Down Stream Fly Fisher by Carter Platts
The Poacher at Work by William Carnegie
A Simple Mistake by Dorothea Conyers; Illustrated by Frederic Whiting
Decoys and Decoymen by Frank Bonnett; Illustrated from *The Book of Duck Decoys* by Ralph Payne-Gallwey
The Art of Landscape Photography by James Eaton-Fearn
The Dignity of Justice by Frank Symons; Illustrated by Arthur Gough
[Ladies] Golf Championship Reminiscences by May Hezlet
The National Sporting Club by Arthur Bettinson
August [verses] by Warren Bell
The Sporting Estates of England: Stratfield Saye by Frank Bonnett; Illustrated by George Thorp
The Red Grouse of the North by George Malcolm; Illustrated by George Soper
More Celebrities in Court by Wallis Myers; Illustrated by Charles Ambrose
Food Fads and Physical Fitness by Bart Kennedy
The Turf [Ascot Gold Cup; Royal Hunt Cup; Liverpool Cup] by Norman Wentworth
Game and Game Preserving (2): Partridge Protection and Encouragment by George Malcolm
Early Uppingham Cricket by William Patterson
Among the Golfers [Water Jumps; Four-Ball Exhibition Matches; Mallets versus Putters] by Bernard Darwin
Kennel Companions [Show Dogs] by George Chesterton
The Sporting Side of Motorcycling (1) by William McMinnies
Out of Town [East Coast Golf Links; Guernsey; Irish Coast at Parknasilla] by Alfred Cooper
An Adequate Income for Old Age [Advertorial] by John MacLennan
The Eternal Tragedy; Illustrated by Frederick Buchanan
An Ideal Holiday for a Cycling Townsman by Frederick Welham

Rifle Shooting [British Fleet in the Thames; National Service Act] by Edward Leman
With Rod and Gun [Lock Leven Fishing; Grouse Breeding; Norway Problems] by George Kelson
In the Clubhouse [Puttee Breeches; Spring-Grip Shoe Soles; Haskell Golf Ball; Racehorse Insurance]
Ice-Bound Desert; Illustrated by Stanley Wood
In All Weathers; Illustrated by Cecil Thomas

Francis Egerton-Green

Granville Egerton

Herbert Dicksee

Jack Crawford

James Catton

Stanley Doust

Volume 12

Issue 67 : October 1909 (p1-96 + 52)

Cover Design; Illustrated by Frederic Whiting

The Lonely Golfer; Illustrated by Russell Westover

Racehorse and Trainer at Home: George Lambton (5) by Sidney Galtrey; Illustrated by George Thorp

The Lady and the Motor by Dorothy Levitt

Great Men and Golf (2) by Bertram Atkey; Illustrated by Charles Crombie

The Jackeen by Miriam Alexander; Illustrated by Frederic Whiting

Best Games of Patience by Charles Diehl; Illustrated by George Soper

The Partridge by Owen Jones

Incidents in Tuna Fishing by Charles Holder

The Sporting Estates of England: The Grange at Alresford by Frank Bonnett; Illustrated by George Thorp

The Wellman Airship by Melvin Vaniman

Golf for Duffers by McDonnell Bodkin; Illustrated by Edward Mitchell

The Invincible Trout by Louis Rhead; Illustrated by himself

The Delicate Sport by Frederick Shaw

The Middleman Between Grouse and Gun by Frederick McKenzie; Illustrated by George Soper

Cailean Gorach by John Dodington; Illustrated by Edward Wigfull

When the Sun Shines by George Chetwynd

Caribou Shooting in New Brunswick by Douglas Clinch

One Point of View by Henry Donovan

A Winning Hazard Machine by William Robbins

The Harvest Rabbit by Owen Jones

Health Without Medicine by Eugen Sandow

Game and Game Preserving (3): Partridge Protection and Encouragement by George Malcolm; Illustrated by George Soper

Rifle Shooting [Pot-Hunters; Welsh Rifle Association] by Edward Leman

The Sporting Side of Motorcycling (2) by William McMinnies

Hockey and Hockey Players [Pavilion Thieves; The Elements of Hockey; Offside Rule Change] by Eustace White

Kennel Companions [Puppies; The Show Ring] by George Chesterton

The Young Man and His Future [Advertorial] by John MacLennan

The Turf [Breeding and Bloodstock Sales; Goodwood Meeting] by Norman Wentworth

Among the Golfers [Rye Golf Course; Short Holes] by Bernard Darwin

The Billiards Control Club and Union by Sydenham Dixon

With Rod and Gun [Letting of Moors; Shooting Party Court Case] by George Kelson; Illustrated by George Thorp

The Mechanics of Golf by Philip Vaile

In the Clubroom [Model Flying-Machines; Knitted Golf Coats; Food Preparation]

Issue 68 : November 1909 (p97-192 + 52)

Cover Design; Illustrated by Harry Rountree
Cableman's Sport; Illustrated by George Dabbs
The Master of Foxhounds; Illustrated by John Charlton
Gone to Ground; Illustrated by John Charlton
Hunting Pictures by Theodore Roberts; Illustrated by John Charlton
Some Reminiscences (1) by Harry Stevenson & James Bolton; Illustrated by Ada Lehany
Higginbotham's Bloomers by Horace Hutchinson; Illustrated by Henry Brock
The Way Out by Carter Platts
The Royal Sport of Cock Fighting by Alfred Cooper
Sport in Queensland [Game and Fishing] by John Hutcheon
The Loser by Rina Ramsay; Illustrated by Frederic Whiting
Men Who Fly [Wilbur Wright, Orville Wright, Henry Farman, Louis Bleriot, Hubert Latham, Alberto Santos-Dumont, Leon Delagrange, Roger Sommer, Robert Esnault-Pelterie, Glenn Curtiss, Samuel Cody, Paul Tissandier, Louis Paulhan, Lucien Lefebvre] by Richard Hearne
The Pheasant in New Zealand by Philip Vaile
Three Tigers by Arthur Mosse; Illustrated by Harry Rountree
The Self Reliant Sportsman; Illustrated by Frederick Buchanan
Trout Fishing in the Highlands by Lilian Bland
The First Class Cricket Season by Edward Sewell; Illustrated by John Mellor
Great Men and Golf (3) by Bertram Atkey; Illustrated by Charles Crombie
Racehorse and Trainer at Home: William Waugh (6) by Sidney Galtrey; Illustrated by George Thorp
The Fifth King by Digby Jephson; Illustrated by Caton Woodville
Visitor and Booking Clerk; Illustrated by Henry Bateman
In the Haunt of the Sea Trout by Arthur Sharp
Hockey and Hockey Players [Women's Hockey Association; Suggested Rule Amendments] by Eustace White
Among the Golfers: The Alphabet of Golf (1) by Bernard Darwin
Conger Fishing in Autumn by Henry Beck; Illustrated by George Soper
Rifle Shooting [Winter Ranges] by Edward Leman
Game and Game Preserving (4): The Red-Legged Partridge by George Malcolm; Illustrated by George Soper
Kennel Companions [Breeding; Cut of Coat; Show Entries] by George Chesterton
A Race With the Sun by Frederic Harrison
A Pigeon Book by Alfred Osman
The Turf [Doncaster Meeting; Rufford Abbey Plate] by Norman Wentworth
With Rod and Gun [Welsh Salmon Fishing; Driven Birds; Rough Shooting] by George Kelson; Illustrated by George Thorp
In the Clubhouse [Hunting Scarf; William Wyllie Painting]

Issue 69 : December 1909 (p193-288 + 64)

Cover Design; Illustrated by Septimus Scott
Winter Sports; Illustrated by Frank Norris

It Takes Some Time; Illustrated by Lionel Edwards
Reynard, Remus and Romulus by Lionel Edwards; Illustrated by himself
Some Reminiscences (2) by Harry Stevenson & James Bolton; Illustrated by Ada Lehany
The Finance and Golf of Tommy Cubitt by Horace Hutchinson & George Riddell; Illustrated by Wallis Mills
Saving a Blank Day by Denholm Armour; Illustrated by himself
The Sure Tip by Bart Kennedy; Illustrated by George Stampa
Punting in Concert by Philip Squire & Stanley Duncan
On the Floe by Archibald Sullivan; Illustrated by Harry Rountree
Bridge Stories by William Dalton
Skiing for Women by Carine Cadby
London and Its Golf by Bernard Darwin; Illustrated by Charles Ambrose
Ancestors by George Murdoch; Illustrated by Frederic Whiting
Boxing as a Profession by Frederick Thomas & James Bolton; Illustrated by George Thorp
Tis Folly to be Wise by Francis Marlowe; Illustrated by Edwin Shrader
Racehorse and Trainer at Home: Peter Gilpin (7) by Sidney Galtrey; Illustrated by George Thorp
A Practical Demonstration; Illustrated by Frederick Buchanan
Amazing Shots by Perry Robinson; Illustrated by George Soper
The Turf [Argentinian Yearlings; Newmarket Meeting; Middle Park Plate] by Norman Wentworth
Caution; Illustrated by Garth Jones
An Autumn Ride by William McMinnies
Kennel Companions [St.Bernard Dogs; Dog Thieves; British Bulldog Club] by George Chesterton
Three Dog Books [Reviews of *Sporting Dogs* by Frank Barton; *The Retriever* (also) by Frank Barton and *The Scottish Terrier* by Charles Davies]
Documents of Known Value [Advertorial] by John MacLennan; Illustrated by Percy Gossop
Billiard Notes by Harry Stevenson
Among the Golfers: The Alphabet of Golf (2) by Bernard Darwin
Not a Dry Page; Illustrated by George Soper
Game and Game Preserving (5): Wild Duck Rearing by George Malcolm; Illustrated by George Soper
Uncle by Carter Platts
Hockey and Hockey Players [Four Half-Backs System; Match Umpires; Staines Hockey Club] by Eustace White
An Elegant Chaffeur; Illustrated by Toby Hoyn
Rifle Shooting [North London and Havant Rifle Clubs; Territorial Army] by Edward Leman; Illustrated by George Thorp
An Hour With the Pollack by Bertram Atkey; Illustrated by Frederick Buchanan
In the Clubroom [Reviews of *Hockey* by Eric Green & Eustace White and *Rugby* by Harry Vassall & Arthur Budd; Bicycle Fittings; Rubber Heels; Golf Balls; Liquid Polish; Club Secretaries; Indian Polo Equipment; Billiard Tables; Motorcycle Distance Record; Alpine Outfits]
Naval Manoeuvres; Illustrated by Ernest Prater

Issue 70 : January 1910 (p289-382 + 44)

Cover Design; Illustrated by Harry Rountree
Eugene Corri; Illustrated by Charles Ambrose
The Quorn Hunt and Its Followers by Arthur Coaten; Illustrated by Thomas Somerfield
Golf in the Far East by Bernard Darwin; Illustrated by Thomas Browne
The Retort Practical by Mark Twain
Skiing in Norway and Sweden
Mr Jorrocks (1) by Robert Surtees; Illustrated by Frederic Whiting
New Games for the Billiard Table by Scipio Mussabini
The Force of Levity by Horace Hutchinson; Illustrated by Charles Crombie
A Rough Day's Shoot by Anthony Fane; Illustrated by George Soper
Weather and Winter Sports by Charles Diehl
A Little Beauty by Helena Bourne; Illustrated by Malcolm Patterson
My Reminiscences by Eugene Corri & James Bolton; Illustrated by Arthur Gough
Marylebone Cricket Club in South Africa by Edward Sewell; Illustrated by Charles Ambrose
The Black to Win by Warren Bell; Illustrated by Henry Brock
Concerning the Pike by Frank Bonnett
Racehorse and Trainer at Home: Robert Dewhurst (8) by Sidney Galtrey
At the End of the Game; Illustrated by Frederick Buchanan
A Woodcock Shoot by Edward Caswall; Illustrated by George Soper
Among the Golfers: The Alphabet of Golf (3) by Bernard Darwin
Billiard Notes by Harry Stevenson
The Moral of a Muddle [Advertorial] by John MacLennan; Illustrated by Percy Gossop
Hockey and Hockey Players [International Matches; Eric Green; Playing Tactics]
   by Eustace White
Kennel Companions [Airedale Terriers; Great Danes; Ladies' Kennel Association]
   by George Chesterton
The Coming of the Motorcycle by William McMinnies
The Turf [American Bred Horses; Hurst Park Meeting] by Norman Wentworth
In the Clubroom [Kodak Gallery; Cycle Rims; Review of *English Figure Skating*
   by Edward Benson]

Issue 71 : February 1910 (p385-480 + 56)

Cover Design; Illustrated by Charles Crombie
The Badminton Hunt by Arthur Coaten; Illustrated by George Thorp
Swimming the Worm for Grayling by Carter Platts
The Calling Golf Ball by Leigh Brownlee; Illustrated by Henry Brock
The Bull Terrier by Ralph Hodgson
A Four Cylinder White Elephant by George Fitch; Illustrated by Albert Levering
Some Racing Reminiscences by Arthur Birch & James Bolton; Illustrated by George Soper
Mr Jorrocks (2) by Robert Surtees; Illustrated by Frederic Whiting
The Three-Quarter of the Day: Edgar Mobbs by Edward Sewell; Illustrated by Charles Ambrose
Coursing: Record of a Meeting
Winter in Switzerland by Edward Lyttelton

The Right Length of Holes at Golf by Henry Leach; Illustrated by Charles Ambrose
The Cartridge by John Larus; Illustrated by George Stampa
Racehorse and Trainer at Home: Percy Peck (9) by Sidney Galtrey; Illustrated by George Thorp
The True Sporting Instinct; Illustrated by Frederick Buchanan
Lawn Tennis on Hard Courts by Wallis Myers
The Adoption of English Rugby in American Universities by Hugh Moran
The Lenses of Life by Eugen Sandow
The Turf [Tattersall's Sales; Steeplechasing] by Norman Wentworth
A Motoring Causerie [Thames Valley Frosts; Foglights] by Alexander Gray
Kennel Companions [Dutch Pug; Fox-Terriers] by George Chesterton
The Fragrant Weed [Advertorial] by John MacLennan
Among the Golfers: The Alphabet of Golf (4) by Bernard Darwin
Have You Got It; Illustrated by Howard Elcock
Billiard Notes by Harry Stevenson
Hockey and Hockey Players [Tactical Schemes; International Umpires] by Eustace White
The Lighter Side by Bertram Atkey
In the Clubroom [Never-Rust Golf Clubs; Roller Skating; Review of *Round Our Coasts* by Alan Wright]

Issue 72 : March 1910 (p481-576 + 52)

Cover Design; Illustrated by Charles Crombie
Reading in the Quiet; Illustrated by William Robinson
The Warwickshire Hunt and Its Followers by Arthur Coaten; Illustrated by George Thorp
Putting by Herbert Fowler; Illustrated by Charles Crombie
Mr Jorrocks (3) by Robert Surtees; Illustrated by Frederic Whiting
Poachers and Their Dogs by Owen Jones; Illustrated by George Soper
The Totalisator by Philip Vaile
Brock the Badger; Illustrated by George Thorp
The Flight by John Larus; Illustrated by Harry Rountree
Trapping Big Game in the Heart of Africa by Fritz Duquesne; Illustrated by Maynard Dixon
The Delights and Theories of Salmon Fishing by Anthony Fane; Illustrated by George Soper
The Romantic History of John Gully by Nicholas Waring
The Tale of a Baby Comet by Hal Ludlow; Illustrated by himself
On the Green; Illustrated by George Stampa
First Man Up by Frank Channon; Illustrated by Lionel Edwards
Racehorse and Trainer at Home: George Blackwell (10) by Sidney Galtrey; Illustrated by George Thorp
An All Round Sportsman: Ralph Payne-Gallwey by Frank Bonnett
Rugby Football: Colonial Improvements by Edward Sewell
Billiard Notes [Tones of Clashing Balls; Cue Delivery; Valentine Fleming] by Harry Stevenson
A Motoring Causerie [Grand Rapide Motorcycle; Heavy Machines; Minor Motors] by Alexander Gray
Many a Mickle Makes a Muckle [Advertorial] by John MacLennan; Illustrated by Percy Gossop
Among the Golfers: The Alphabet of Golf (5) by Bernard Darwin

Have You Got It; Illustrated by Howard Elcock
Cycle Camps in Wales by Percy Hill
Kennel Companions [Wolfhounds; Talking Sparrows; Water Finders] by George Chesterton
The Turf [Lincolnshire Handicap; Grand National Steeplechase] by Norman Wentworth
To the Fore; Illustrated by Alick Ritchie
In the Clubroom [Pipe Smoking; Ladies Billiards; Straker-Squire Motorcar)

Agnes Herbert

Aubrey Faulkner

Eric Green

Louis Jarrige

Reginald Graham

Thomas Hayward

Issue 73 : April 1910 (p1-96 + 64)

Cover Design; Illustrated by Charles Crombie
Pure Wool; Illustrated by Gladys Reid
Quickly Prepared; Illustrated by Henry Browne
The Queen as a Country Lady by Elizabeth Wolstenholme-Elmy
The Trapper Trapped by Horace Hutchinson & George Riddell; Illustrated by Henry Brock
The Art of Taking a Shoot by Owen Jones; Illustrated by George Soper
Amongst the Lions in British East Africa by Alfred Jordan; Illustrated by Lionel Edwards
Ole Skjarsen's First Touchdown by George Fitch; Illustrated by Gustavus Widney
The County Union Movement in Golf by Bernard Darwin
The Cottesmore Hunt and Its Followers by Arthur Coaten
On the Raft by Robert Vernede; Illustrated by Harry Rountree
The Palace Stables [Newmarket] by Sidney Galtrey
Mr Jorrocks (4) by Robert Surtees; Illustrated by Frederic Whiting
Bushcraft by John Mackie; Illustrated by Harry Rountree
The Genesis of the Aeroplane by Bernard Parsons
The Unfortunate Intervention of Thomas Bowles by George Wellings; Illustrated by Charles Crombie
The Grand National by Thomas Henry Browne; Illustrated by George Thorp
With the Anglers [Trout for Restocking; Grayling Tarradiddles] by James Bazley
My Queer Cycling Experience by Pollock Castors
Kennel Companions [Sanction Shows; Great Dane Clubs] by George Chesterton
The Lust of Speed: Isle of Man Racing by Harold Karslake
Among the Golfers [Portmarnock Tournament; Golfing Manners] by Bernard Darwin; Illustrated by George Thorp
Golfing Aphorisms [verses] by Walter Smyth
New Golden Kite; Illustrated by Howard Elcock
Billiard Notes [Amateur Championship] by Harry Stevenson
Billiards for Ladies by Archibald Williamson
Tennis Topics [Otto Froitzheim; William Larned] by Wallis Myers
A Motoring Causerie [Road Races; Vehicle Costs] by Alexander Gray
Motorcycle Waterproofs; Illustrated by Gladys Reid
Halley's Comet [Advertorial] by John MacLennan
In the Clubroom [Thomas Gradidge; Motorcycle Lamp; Monoplanes]
Dramatic Situations; Illustrated by Henry Brock

Issue 74 : May 1910 (p97-192 + 64)

Cover Design; Illustrated by Maud Earl
The House of Temperley by Bernard Parsons
A French Sportsman Caricaturist: Leonard de la Jarrige by Wallis Myers; Illustrated by the subject
The Ideal Caddie at Last; Illustrated by Frederick Buchanan
The Wheel by John Larus; Illustrated by Gordon Browne

Panther Spearing by George Hope; Illustrated by Lionel Edwards
A Bird's Eye View of English Agriculture (1) by James MacDonald; Illustrated by Frederick Babbage
The Hands of Florent by Gerald Rose; Illustrated by Septimus Scott
Club Law by James Atlay; Illustrated by William Mein
Mr Jorrocks (5) by Robert Surtees; Illustrated by Frederic Whiting
Philosophy From Jorrocks by Robert Surtees
The Art of Letting a Shoot by Owen Jones; Illustrated by George Soper
The Northern Mayfly by Carter Platts
A Very Close Thing by Armiger Barclay; Illustrated by Arthur Gough
James Jeffries the Fighter by James Corbett & James Bolton
The Rescue of Mr Gathercole by Bernard Darwin; Illustrated by Wilmot Lunt
A Famous Otter Pack by Ernest Holmes
The Turf [Lincoln Meeting] by Norman Wentworth
With the Anglers [Grayling; Coarse Fishing] by James Bazley
A Motoring Causerie [Engine Valve Mechanism] by Alexander Gray
Tennis Topics [Obituary of Carter Evelegh of *The Field*; Davis Cup; Review of *Lawn Tennis for Ladies* by Dorothea Lambert-Chambers] by Wallis Myers
Kennel Companions [West Highland White Terrier Club of England] by George Chesterton
The Motorcyclist [Light Machines; Variable Gears] by Harold Karslake
Out of Town [Norfolk Broads; Reviews of *Otters and Otterhunting* by Ludovick Cameron and *East Coast Holidays* by Percy Lindley] by Alfred Cooper
The Call of the Sea [Advertorial]
Among the Golfers [Douglas Rolland; Strange Courses] by Bernard Darwin
Have You Got It?; Illustrated by Howard Elcock
The Chairman; Illustrated by William Owen
Billiard Notes [Lady Champions] by Harry Stevenson
Cycle Camping in Devonshire by Percy Hill
Highways and Byways in Middlesex by Walter Jerrold
In the Clubroom [British Antarctic Expedition; Arthur Radclyffe-Dugmore; Shooting Boots]
Two Old Salts; Illustrated by Joseph Simpson

Issue 75 : June 1910 (p193-288 + 64)

Cover Design; Illustrated by Joseph Simpson
Theodore Roosevelt Sportsman by Hesketh Prichard; Illustrated by Harold Millar
First Up the Matterhorn by Martin Conway
Plumbing the Depths by Francis Atkins; Illustrated by Clifford Fleming-Williams
A Bird's Eye View of English Agriculture (2) by James MacDonald
A Run Across Channel by Charles Pears; Illustrated by himself
Bottle by Archibald Sullivan; Illustrated by Harry Rountree
The Morals of Sport by Frederick Aflalo; Illustrated by Lionel Edwards
Behind the Scenes of The Whip by Cecil Raleigh
Mr Jorrocks (6) by Robert Surtees; Illustrated by Frederic Whiting
The Good Gamekeeper by Owen Jones; Illustrated by George Soper

Providence and Mrs Urmy by Armiger Barclay; Illustrated by Clifford Fleming-Williams
Famous Matches of the Past by Thomas Henry Browne; Illustrated by George Thorp
The Women's Aerial League by [Miss] Beatrice Fry
The Humbug of County Cricket by Charles Fry
The Turf [Newbury Races; Craven Stakes] by Norman Wentworth
A Motoring Causerie [Car Tests; Rhodesian Roads] by Alexander Gray
Billiard Notes [Championship Match Stress] by Harry Stevenson
Securities That Never Depreciate [Advertorial] by John MacLennan
Travels With a Trailer (1) by Thomas Montague-Vesey; Illustrated by Frederick Bennett
Two Holiday [Golf] Courses [Woodhall Spa and West Runton] by Bernard Darwin
Good Value; Illustrated by Beatrice Spiller
Problems in Golfing Conduct by Bertram Atkey
Kennel Companions [Kennel Club; Repressive Legislation] by George Chesterton
Out of Town [Norway Fjords, Brussels Exhibition] by Alfred Cooper
Lawn Tennis Topics [American Volleyers; Roper Barrett] by Wallis Myers
The Motorcyclist [Chain Drive; Military Disinterest] by Harold Karslake
In the Clubroom [Review of *Camping Out* by Thomas Holding; Tennis Racket Stringer; Carriage Tyres]

Issue 76 : July 1910 (p289-384 + 56)

Cover Design; Illustrated by William Stott
The Zodiac; Illustrated by Horace Davis
Claude Grahame-White; Illustrated by Charles Ambrose
Barbarous Mexico (1) by John Turner
The Slaves of Yucatan by John Turner; Illustrated by George Varian
The Ribblesdale Buckhounds by Carter Platts; Illustrated by George Thorp
The Chaperon by John Larus; Illustrated by Joseph Skelton
The Great Thames Trout by Frank Bonnett; Illustrated by George Thorp
How and Where to Catch Thames Trout by Ratcliff Matthews
Black Fighters by Nicholas Waring
The Lost Man of the Lofodens by James Barr; Illustrated by Harry Rountree
The Racing Motorboat by Richard Hearne
Caribou Hunting in Timber and Brulee by Hesketh Prichard; Illustrated by Harry Rountree
The Straight Mile by David Ellis; Illustrated by Clifford Fleming-Williams
A Lady Horse Dealer: Josie Byron by John Bristow-Noble
Hobbs of Surrey by Jack Ingham; Illustrated by Charles Ambrose
Frank Wootton by Norman Wentworth; Illustrated by Charles Ambrose
A Certainty by Francis Marlowe; Illustrated by Frederic Whiting
Confidence and Nerve Control by Eugen Sandow
Travels With a Trailer (2) by Thomas Montague-Vesey; Illustrated by Frederick Bennett
The Royal Colours (1875-1910) by Norman Wentworth
Out of Town [Lake District Golf; Review of *Twixt Humber and Tweed* by Carter Platts; North Wales] by Alfred Cooper
Scrapped Putters by Bernard Darwin

On Staleness [Golf] by Bernard Darwin
Kennel Companions [Whippet Racing; Setters] by George Chesterton
With the Anglers [Gut Staining; Minnows] by James Bazley; Illustrated by George Thorp
Savage and Civilised [Advertorial] by John MacLennan; Illustrated by Percy Gossop
Review of *The Chance of a Lifetime* by Nat Gould
Some Famous Tennis Pairs by Wallis Myers
The Motorcyclist [Road Competitions; Tourist Trophy Race] by Harold Karslake
In the Clubroom [Photographic Lenses; Bell Tents; Golfing Coats]

Issue 77 : August 1910 (p385-480 + 48)

Cover Design; Illustrated by Maud Earl
Smoker's Throat; Illustrated by Frank Reynolds
So Near and Yet so Far; Illustrated by Thomas Browne
Barbarous Mexico (2) by John Turner; Illustrated by George Varian
How to Judge Distances by Harry Vardon; Illustrated by Edward Mitchell
Well Fielded; Illustrated by Frederick Buchanan
Jones of Arkshire by Alfred Tennyson; Illustrated by Joseph Skelton
British Flying Men by Richard Hearne
The Ever-Ever Bunny by Edward Sorenson; Illustrated by Harry Rountree
The Links That Failed by James Hurst-Hayes; Illustrated by Charles Crombie
The Foxhound's Summer by James Cooper
The Sport of Bullfighting by William Caird
Some Little Yachting Ports by Charles Pears; Illustrated by himself
The Conquest of Ben Craig by Ernest Punshon; Illustrated by Clifford Fleming-Williams
National Traits in Tennis by Wallis Myers; Illustrated by Charles Ambrose
The Man Who Knew by Bertram Atkey; Illustrated by Joseph Simpson
Epsom and Ascot by Norman Wentworth
A Motoring Causerie [Bad Cars] by Alexander Gray
When Betting is Not Gambling [Advertorial] by John MacLennan
Review of *Buckinghamshire* by Clement Shorter; Illustrated by Frederick Griggs
Lawn Tennis Topics [Cold Tea; Training; Doubles Players] by Wallis Myers
Out of Town [Sporting Cruises; Reviews of *Book of Travel* by Michael Hornsby, *Off the Beaten Track in Finland* by John Good, *Yachting List for Norfolk Broads* by Henry Blake, *From Dundee to London* by James Fleming; Ulverstone Golf] by Alfred Cooper
Some Reflections on Handicapping by Bernard Darwin
The Motorcyclist [Isle of Man Tourist Trophy Revised Rules; Tyre Strain] by Harold Karslake
Kennel Companions [Dog Shows; Review of *Our Dogs* by Frank Barton; Scottish Terriers] by George Chesterton
Travels With a Trailer (3) by Thomas Montague-Vesey; Illustrated by Frederick Bennett
In the Clubroom [Rifle Score Register; Review of *Lightweight Camping* by Owen Williams; Mustard Baths; *The Ladies' Field* magazine]

Issue 78 : September 1910 (p481-576 + 52)

Cover Design; Illustrated by Joseph Simpson

The King as a Game Shot by Cecil Hughes; Illustrated by George Thorp
How to Fly in Two Hours by Henry Farman
The Vigil of Adolph by James Dwyer; Illustrated by Leone Bracker
The Day After the Fair; Illustrated by Frederick Buchanan
Barbarous Mexico (3) by John Turner; Illustrated by George Varian
My Most Fateful Round [Tommy Burns, Sam Langford, James Corbett, John Sullivan,
   Frederick 'Welsh' Thomas, Jimmy Britt, Stanley Ketchell, Bob Fitzsimmons] by Cecil Hughes
The Visits of Ikey by Ralph Hodgson; Illustrated by Frederic Whiting
The Mind of the Thoroughbred by Thomas Henry Browne
International Yacht Racing by Ernest Hamilton
A Special Settlement by Herbert Shaw; Illustrated by Clifford Fleming-Williams
Some Long Drivers at the Championship by Bernard Darwin; Illustrated by Edward Mitchell
From a Far Country [verses] by Helen Lanyon
The Haunts of the Mountain Sheep by Charles Lane
The Syndicate's Jockey by Arthur Hales; Illustrated by Frederic Whiting
A Private Circus: Ernest Molier by Raoul de Frechencourt
The Wet Fly and Its Charms by Alan Haig-Brown
Advice to the First-Class Counties by Alan Miller
The Turf [Eclipse Stakes; Obituary of James Smith] by Norman Wentworth
Some Notes on the Niblick by Bernard Darwin
Travels With a Trailer (4) by Thomas Montague-Vesey; Illustrated by Frederick Bennett
Harvesting [Advertorial] by John MacLennan
An Experiment in Ocean Charting: Scientific Tests
The Motorcycle and the Sportsman by Harold Karslake
Out of Town [Chilterns; Reviews of *Far and Sure: Golf Links in Scotland* by George Bacon,
   Coarse Fishing by James Bazley, *Sea Fishing* by Frederick Aflalo, *Game Fishing* by
   Carter Platts, *East Anglia* by Harry Brittain, *Bonnie Scotland* by Robert Hope-Moncrieff,
   Twixt Thames and Tweed by Carter Platts, *Bude and Its Borderland* by Beatrix Cresswell and
   Through the English Lakeland by Ralph Graves] by Alfred Cooper
Kennel Companions [West Highland White Terriers; Review of *Our Dogs* by
   Barton William-Powlett; Canine Guardians] by George Chesterton
Lawn Tennis Topics [Beals Wright, Mixed Doubles] by Wallis Myers
With the Anglers [Coarse-Fish Angling; Rudd; Minnows] by James Bazley
In the Clubroom [Newbury Overcoat; Royal Academy; Golf Ball Marker; Obituary of
   Herbert Gradidge]
When You Picnic; Illustrated by Hal Ludlow

Volume 14

Issue 79 : October 1910 (p1-96 + 48)

Cover Design; Illustrated by Maud Earl
Across Unknown Labrador by Cecil Hughes; Illustrated by George Thorp
What I Hope to Do in Labrador by Hesketh Prichard
Fear by Hugh Clifford; Illustrated by Harry Rountree
Golfing With the President: William Taft
An Experiment in Gyro-Hats by Ellis Butler; Illustrated by Henry Raleigh
In the Ring by Henry Slowburn; Illustrated by George Soper
Barbarous Mexico by Herman Whitaker
Half the Town's Love Affair by Francis Marlowe; Illustrated by Frederic Whiting
Woodcock; Illustrated by Archibald Thorburn
Cock by Frank Bonnett
Kit by Rina Ramsay; Illustrated by Frank Taylor
By Canal and Canoe by Ladbroke Black; Illustrated by Frederick Dickinson
The Height of Politeness; Illustrated by Frederick Buchanan
Morocco by Lawrence Harris
The Man Who was Big Game by James Barr; Illustrated by Hamilton Williams
Health; Sandow Treatment [Advertorial]
Undesirables by Norman Wentworth; Illustrated by George Thorp
Travels With a Trailer (5) by Thomas Montague-Vesey; Illustrated by Frederick Bennett
Hockey and Hockey Players by Eustace White
A New Health Food [Advertorial]: Bacillus Bulgaricus
Kennel Companions [Expensive Pets; Cure of Chorea] by George Chesterton
Training for Golf Matches by Bernard Darwin
The Motorcyclist [Fifty Pound Cars; Military Uses] by Harold Karslake
Review of *Our Home Railways* by William Gordon
The Jump Shot in Billiards by Philip Vaile
In the Clubroom [Cascaes Royal Sporting Club; Brooklands; Review of *Cycling Spins in Beechy Bucks* by Thomas Smith]

Issue 80 : November 1910 (p97-192 + 40)

Cover Design; Illustrated by Joseph Simpson
Two Pairs of Trousers; Illustrated by Gladys Reid
Across Unknown Labrador (1): Its Interests by Hesketh Prichard; Illustrated by George Thorp
A French Sporting Centre: Bois de Boulogne by Raoul de Frechencourt
The Lady of the Leash by Cyril Doran; Illustrated by Henry Brock
Golf Clubhouses by Harry Colt
A Reverie of Indian Sport by Sidney Galtrey; Illustrated by Caton Woodville
The Double Fence by Joshua Trevethen; Illustrated by Frederic Whiting
Grouse Over Dogs in Ireland by Joseph Loughnan
The Scene Shifters by Herbert Shaw; Illustrated by Charles Crombie
The Genesis of the Balloon by Bernard Parsons

William Bass in War and Sport by Cecil Hughes
Hiram Maxim the Father of Flight by Cecil Hughes
Hard Cash; Illustrated by Frederick Buchanan
Swipe's Revenge by Robert Freeman; Illustrated by Wallis Mills
See How They Run; Illustrated by Charles Pears
With the Anglers [Gut versus Hair] by James Bazley
The Delights of a Winter Trip to Switzerland by Arthur Croome
The Motorcyclist [Secondhand Machines] by Harold Karslake
Some Winter Golf Courses by Bernard Darwin
Travels With a Trailer (6) by Thomas Montague-Vesey; Illustrated by Frederick Bennett
The Coloured Field Spaniel by Ralph Hodgson
Reviews of *North Devon and West Somerset* by Beatrice Home and *The Pilgrims' Road* by Frank Elliston-Erwood
Having and Hazarding [Advertorial] by John MacLennan; Illustrated by Percy Gossop
Billiard Notes [South African Players; Frederick Lindrum] by Harry Stevenson
Successful Technical Training [Advertorial]
The Evolution of the Hat by Robert Batho
In the Clubroom [Review of *The Book of Best Scotch Underwear* by Robert Turnbull; Herbert Dicksee Animal Artist; Leather Footballs

Issue 81 : December 1910 (p193-288 + 48)

Cover Design; Illustrated by Ivor Symes
Across Unknown Labrador (2): The Coast Folk by Hesketh Prichard; Illustrated by George Thorp
Misfits in the Hunting Field by Denholm Armour; Illustrated by himself
The Best Christmas Dinner [Auguste Escoffier, Sarah Bernhardt, Theodore Cook, Walter Winans, Charles Fry, Joseph Lyons, Hugh McIntosh, Robert Sievier, Eustace Miles, Jimmy Britt, John Mackie, Meredith Clease] by Cecil Hughes
When Kitchener Came Home by Hylton Cleaver; Illustrated by Henry Brock
The Perfect Garden by Walter Wright; Illustrated by George Thorp
The Punt Gunners Headquarters by Philip Squire
The Squire's Christmas Tale by Eyre Hussey; Illustrated by Frederic Whiting
The Art of Timing in the Golf Swing by Wallis Myers
My Reminiscences by Hugh McIntosh; Illustrated by George Soper
The Soup of Discord by Ellis Butler; Illustrated by Fletcher Thomas
Lewis Waller by Bertram Atkey; Illustrated by Charles Ambrose
Walter Winans by Cecil Hughes; Illustrated by Charles Ambrose
Particularly Exasperating; Illustrated by Frederick Buchanan
Number Thirteen in the Forest by Richard Hemingway; Illustrated by Hamilton Williams
A Great Rugby Half-Back: Adrian Stoop by Edward Sewell; Illustrated by Charles Ambrose
The Old Red Stag by Alexander Fisher; Illustrated by Harry Rountree
A Skating Tour in Holland by Stacey Blake; Illustrated by Frederick Dickinson
A Very Rough Shoot by Bertram Atkey; Illustrated by Ada Lehany
Reviews of *A Gamekeeper's Notebook* by Owen Jones and *The High Roads of the Alps* by Charles Freeston
Winter Golf at Home and Abroad by Horace Hutchinson

Hints on Tobogganing by Frederick Burlingham
Billiard Notes [George Gray; Edward Diggle; Melbourne Inman] by Harry Stevenson; Illustrated by Charles Grave
The Motorcyclist [Winter Riding; Variable Gears; Ladies' Machines] by Harold Karslake
The Irish Wolfhound by Ralph Hodgson
Travels With a Trailer (7) by Thomas Montague-Vesey; Illustrated by Frederick Bennett
The Happy Child; Illustrated by Olive Allen
In the Clubroom [Billiards; Golfing Tailors; Review of *The Queen of the Turf* by Nat Gould; Puttees]

Issue 82 : January 1911 (p289-384 + 24)

Cover Design; Illustrated by Frederic Whiting
The Muffler; Illustrated by Gladys Reid
An Opening Meet in the Days of Our Grandsires by Jack Fairfax-Blakeborough; Illustrated by Henry Brock
Charlie's Commission by Warren Bell; Illustrated by Henry Brock
Footprints in the Snow by Frank Bonnett
Across Unknown Labrador (3): On the Eve of Inland by Hesketh Prichard; Illustrated by George Thorp
Coursing Past and Present by Frank Bonnett
Physical Training in Relation to Golf by Cecil Hutchison
A Woman and a Horse by Emily Handasyde-Buchanan; Illustrated by Frederic Whiting
A Whale Hunt in the Faroes by Beresford Ryley; Illustrated by Edward Hodgson
The Heir and the Hound by Leslie Smith; Illustrated by George Stampa
The Lighter Side of Rugby Football by Sydney Boot; Illustrated by Stephen Dadd
A Triumph of Taxidermy by Harold Shepstone
Mrs Wrennie's Mistake by Perry Robinson; Illustrated by Gordon Browne
Prince's [Ice Rink] by Charles Thomas; Illustrated by Charles Ambrose
An Axiom of Sport; Illustrated by Frederick Buchanan
The Fancies of the Sporting Prophets by Michael Macdonagh; Illustrated by George Soper
Wildfowling for the Beginner by Arthur Conway; Illustrated by Harry Rountree
Among the Golfers: On Byes by Bernard Darwin
The Motorcyclist [Heavy Machines; Refinements] by Harold Karslake
Billiard Notes [Scoring Methods] by Harry Stevenson
Curling in Switzerland by Arthur Croome
On Buying a Puppy by Ralph Hodgson
Travels With a Trailer (8) by Thomas Montague-Vesey
In the Clubroom [Canadian Towns; Civil Service Examinations; Review of *More Tricks and Puzzles* by William Goldston]

Issue 83 : February 1911 (p385-480 + 20)

Cover Design; Illustrated by Frederic Whiting
A Chaser; Illustrated by Frederic Whiting
Stalking the Pinkfooted Goose by Percival Westell; Illustrated by Frank Southgate

The Intervention of Bunny by Robert Tarnacre; Illustrated by Henry Brock
The General Purpose Dog by Owen Jones
The Lion at Home by Arthur Radclyffe-Dugmore
Mr Varoline's Four-Legged Aeroplane by William McCartney; Illustrated by Charles Crombie
Across Unknown Labrador (4): Up to the Roof by Hesketh Prichard; Illustrated by George Thorp
Some Unconventional Fishing by John Bristow-Noble; Illustrated by George Soper
A Chaser in Training by Charles Coventry; Illustrated by Frederic Whiting
Rabbits Edinburgh by Stephen Moore; Illustrated by George Soper
The Last of the Lizards by James Barr; Illustrated by Harry Rountree
Old English Sport [published 1801] by Joseph Strutt
My Racing and Polo Reminiscences (1) by Geoffrey Phipps-Hornby
Sentenced to Death by George Chesterton; Illustrated by George Soper
Some Popular Fallacies Concerning Dogs by Ralph Hodgson
The Woes of a Golf Reporter by Bernard Darwin
Billiard Notes [House Parties] by Harry Stevenson
The Motorcyclist [Ease of Storage; Lubrication; Military Scouting] by Harold Karslake
Travels With a Trailer (9) by Thomas Montague-Vesey
Review of *The Perfect Garden* by Walter Wright

Issue 84 : March 1911 (p481-576 + 32)

Cover Design; Illustrated by Charles Crombie
A Herd of Black Buck; Illustrated by Lionel Edwards
Hunting in Northern India by Henry Lock; Illustrated by Lionel Edwards
The Bishop of Barchester by Philip Hichborn; Illustrated by Wallace Morgan
Across Unknown Labrador (5): Over the Great Plateau by Hesketh Prichard; Illustrated by George Thorp
My Racing and Polo Reminiscences (2) by Geoffrey Phipps-Hornby
Just Like a Cat by Ellis Butler; Illustrated by Henry Raleigh
The Other Lord by Courtenay Lacey; Illustrated by Wallis Mills
Anglers and Their Yarns by James Bazley; Illustrated by Frederick Reynolds
Adventure by Jack London; Illustrated by Charles Sparrow
Are Fishermen Selfish by Louis Rhead
The Precipitation of Diana by Elinor Maclachlan; Illustrated by Malcolm Patterson
Horsemanship Extraordinary by Frank Bonnett; Illustrated by Arthur Gough
At What Age Should a Man Give Up Games? [Eustace Miles, Neville Lyttelton, Edmond Warre, Arthur Cooper, Rudolf Lehmann, Richardson Moore, George Chesterton, John Edwards-Moss, Percy Longhurst, Arthur Russell, Henry Beresford, Thomas Browne, Samuel Waddington] by Valentia Steer
Health by Post by Eugen Sandow
Our Friend the Rabbit by William Molesworth
Routes and Branches in the Black Forest by Cecil Hughes
Tree Hazards by Bernard Darwin
The Motorcyclist [Cycle Cars; Jake de Rosier; Charles Collier; Glass Screens] by Harold Karslake

Issue 85 : April 1911 (p1-120)

Cover Design; Illustrated by Charles Crombie
Doggett's Coat and Badge by Aubrey Gentry
The Vogue of Games by Frederick Smith; Illustrated by Richard Mathews
Universal Military Training by Robert Blatchford; Illustrated by Cyrus Cuneo and Henry Sayen
Where is Sylvia?; Illustrated by Harry Rountree
The Last Straw [Review of *Gun, Rod and Rifle* by Frederick Chapman]
The Reform of County Cricket [Martin Hawke, George Hirst, Edward Dillon, Charles McGahey, Harry Foster, Levi Wright, Rowland Ryder] (1) by Wallis Myers
Horatio Bottomley: Sportsman by Charles Fry; Illustrated by Richard Mathews
England's Disappearing Dogs by Ralph Hodgson; Illustrated by Edwin Morrow
The God in the Golf Machine by Herbert Shaw; Illustrated by Charles Crombie
Angling Note; Illustrated by Harry Rountree
Can British Boxers Hold Their Own by Desmond Shaw
Tragedies of the Air by Richard Hearne; Illustrated by George Thorp
Nature Note; Illustrated by Frederick Buchanan
A Frenchman in the Pavilion by Edward Lucas; Illustrated by Edwin Morrow
Great Varsity Strokes [Douglas Stuart, Charles Pitman, William Fletcher, Harcourt Gold] by Guy Nickalls; Illustrated by Leslie Ward
The Man From the Monoplane by Bertram Atkey; Illustrated by Hamilton Williams
From Over the Hedge; Illustrated by Harry Rountree
The Qualities of the Compleat Angler by Edward Grey
My Heresies by Philip Vaile; Illustrated by Edwin Morrow
Who Shall Play Golf for England by Henry Leach
To My Mind [Cricket Interest; South African Cricketers; Boxing; Rugby; Old Boys Football Clubs; Obituary of William Murdoch] by Charles Fry
The Year of the Motorcycle by Horace Mann
In the Clubroom [Petrol Distillers; Dennis Bradley Tailoring]
Of More Than Passing Interest [Editorial]
Prominent People; Illustrated by Cecil Thomas

Issue 86 : May 1911 (p121-240)

Cover Design; Illustrated by Charles Crombie
The Connoisseur; Illustrated by Joseph Simpson
Winston Churchill: Adventurer by Charles Fry
A Golf Grumble; Illustrated by Harry Rountree
The Average Golfer by Henry Leach; Illustrated by Edwin Morrow
The Derby Horses of 1911 by Sidney Galtrey; Illustrated by Adam Horne
Anxious to Oblige; Illustrated by Harry Rountree
Night Fishing by Edward Grey
Sanders of the River by Edgar Wallace; Illustrated by Charles Sarka
Something Wanting by Bertram Atkey; Illustrated by Henry Sayen

Off the Ground [verses] by Walter De La Mare; Illustrated by Edwin Morrow
French Horsemanship by Raoul de Frechencourt
Boxer versus Fighter by Desmond Shaw
The Reform of County Cricket [Randall Johnson, Herbert Chaplin, Thomas Manning, William Burns, Leonard Braund, Francis Bacon, Gilbert Jessop, Albert Knight] (2) by Wallis Myers
A Wet Wicket; Illustrated by Charles Grave
The Sport of Sea-War by Frederick Jane
Marching by Hilaire Belloc; Illustrated by Henry Sayen
The Shambles of the Forest by James Buckland
Cup Finals I Have Seen by John Bentley
Cool; Illustrated by Cecil Aldin
To My Mind [Horse Racing; Richard Marsh; Herbert Jones; Joseph Bowker; Boxing; Manchester Dog Show; Motor Boats; Gymnastics; Otters; Olympic Cycling] by Charles Fry
Lawn Tennis Championship Prospects by Harry Scrivener
The Sport and Pastime of Motorcycling and Cycling by Vernon Woodhouse; Illustrated by Bohun Lynch
On the Nonpareil [verses] by John Hamilton-Reynolds
In the Clubroom [Small Disabilities; Tailoring; Moto Reve]
Of More Than Passing Interest [Editorial]

Issue 87 : June 1911 (p241-384)

Cover Design; Illustrated by Lionel Edwards
Edward Grey: Fisherman by Charles Fry; Illustrated by George Thorp
New Fashions and Needs in Golf Clubs by Henry Leach; Illustrated by George Thorp
Great Expectations; Illustrated by Harry Rountree
Animal Champions of Today by Arthur Horwood
Robert Loraine: Actor and Airman by Bernard Parsons; Illustrated by Adam Horne
The Mr Baker Champion Road Stakes by Bertram Atkey; Illustrated by Henry Brock
From Harwich to Dordrecht in a Three Tonner by Arthur Watts; Illustrated by himself
Taken by Surprise; Illustrated by Henry Sayen
Shabby Blood-Sports Worth Ending by Basil Tozer; Illustrated by Harry Rountree
Boxing as a Business by Bernard Parsons
The First-Class County Teams by Wallis Myers
Everything Comes to Him Who Waits; Illustrated by Charles Grave
The Birth of a Breed by Oliver Dunnesmyth
Ornithological; Illustrated by Harry Rountree
The Top of the Tree by Leo Munro; Illustrated by Adam Horne
Then and Now; Illustrated by Edwin Morrow
Speed and Sport on the Water by Richard Hearne; Illustrated by Adam Horne
Travel Notes [Norfolk Golf Links; Cornish Riviera Express; The Chilterns; Night Boat Services] by Arthur Anderson
The Charm of the Summer Cruise [Advertorial]
Lawn Tennis: England's Back Seat Accounted For by Harry Scrivener
A Holiday on the Broads by William Dutt

Review of *Yachting Lists* by Harry Blake

The World Awheel by Archibald Williams

Clothes and the Man [Knickerbockers; Riding Breeches; Leggings] by Basil Tozer; Illustrated by George Thorp

To My Mind [Men's Clothing; Cup Final Replays; Review of *The Book of Cricket* by Pelham Warner] by Charles Fry

In Clubland [Spare Tyres; Golf Balls; Motor Mascots]

To Our Readers [Editorial]

Issue 88 : July 1911 (p369-488)

Cover Design; Illustrated by Charles Crombie

And Here's a Hand; Illustrated by Edmund Sullivan

The Palace of Motoring: Royal Automobile Club by Richard Hearne

Game Fishes of Our Own Coasts by Frederick Aflalo

The Afrikander Sportsman by Wallis Myers

A Perfect Run; Illustrated by Harry Rountree

The Best Girl by Mary Howarth; Illustrated by George Thorp

The Smaller Ponies of the British Islands by George Miller

Beatrice Campbell [aka Mrs Patrick] *Alias Lady Patricia* by Bernard Parsons

In the Crowd at Goodwood by Edward Thomas; Illustrated by Arthur Watts

Oast Houses; Illustrated by Harry Rountree

Down the Thames in a Camping Boat by Charles Budden

Ancient and Modern; Illustrated by Edwin Morrow

The Clinch in Boxing by Philip Vaile

The Regatta: Henley Old and New by Arthur Austen-Leigh

Fallacies in Golf by Ernest Crawley

New Leaders in Lawn Tennis by Wallis Myers

Open the Other Gate; Illustrated by Henry Sayen

Mixed Bathing Abroad by Clive Holland

Real Summer Sport; Illustrated by Harry Rountree

Nature's Coronation by Frank Bonnett

Fishing on Sunday; Illustrated by Harry Low

Economy on a Small Cruiser by Arthur Watts; Illustrated by himself

Chick Evans of Chicago, Golfer by Henry Leach

Wild Australia at Crystal Palace by Philip Vaile

Travel Notes [River Sailing; Cotswolds; Wensleydale; Angling Rivers of Yorkshire] by Arthur Anderson

Woodland Counties by William Cobbett

Clothes and the Man [Soft Clothing; New Style Tie; Holiday Trunks] by Basil Tozer

The World Awheel [Motorcycle Air Pipes; Strange Records; Pottering Cyclists; Michelin Guides] by Archibald Williams

Lawn Tennis Topics by Edward Crawley

The Outdoor Man's Bookshelf [Reviews of *A Fisherman's Summer in Canada* by Frederick Aflalo and *The Danube With Pen and Pencil* by Bernard Granville-Baker]

In Clubland [Golf Balls; Review of *A Golf Guide* by James Braid; Water Filters]

Issue 89 : August 1911 (p489-600)

Health and Energy; Illustrated by Alick Ritchie
The Beginner on the Alps by George Abraham
Zoo-Logical; Illustrated by Alfred Leete
On Buying a Horse by Arthur Horwood; Illustrated by Lionel Edwards
The Sailing of the Glory [verses] by John Freeman
Amateur Gipsying by Clive Holland
Fallacies in Golf by Philip Vaile
A Record Flight [verses] by Frederick Buckley
Why He Signed the Pledge; Illustrated by Harry Rountree
The Pleasure and Sport of a Thames Season by Charles Thomas
Over the Grouse Moors by Aymer Maxwell
The Gentleman's Terrier by Freeman Lloyd
George Edwardes: The Gaiety Theatre and Musical Comedy by Bernard Parsons
A Sealed Handicap; Illustrated by Henry Sayen
Safeguarding the Aviator by Richard Hearne
Choosing An England Eleven by Charles Fry
Influences of International Polo by Sidney Galtrey
The Worm Turns; Illustrated by Fletcher Thomas
The Government of Golf by Philip Vaile
Tis a Pleasing; Illustrated by Cecil Aldin
Clothes and the Man [Home-Made Clothing; Duck Suits; Cubbing Coats; Hunting Boots; Motorcycling Kit] by Basil Tozer
My Needs [verses] by Digby Jephson
The World Awheel [American Motor Racing; Brooklands; Boulogne Meeting; Ivan Hart-Davies] by Archibald Williams
Travel Notes [English Homeland; Dutch Tour; Irish Channel] by Arthur Anderson
The Outdoor Man's Bookshelf [Reviews of *Scrambles in Storm and Sunshine* by John Ouseley and *Red Paint* by Arthur Johnson]

Issue 90 : September 1911 (p601-720)

In the Parlour; Illustrated by Arthur Watts
From London to Lowestoft in an Open Boat by Arthur Watts; Illustrated by himself
The British Boomerang: Billets by Carter Platts
Huskies: The Dogs of Labrador by Hesketh Prichard
The Sports; Illustrated by Edwin Morrow
In the Day's Work by John Lopez; Illustrated by David Hutchinson
A White Hope; Illustrated by Harry Rountree
Swimming and Diving for Girls and Women by Colin Hamilton
The Fellowship of Sport; Illustrated by Hope Read
The Shooting Outlook by Frank Bonnett
The Story of the Leger by Ernest Phillips

How to Catch Pike by Owen Jones
The Muscular Power of Wild Animals by Thomas Bridges
Harry Vardon and his Golfing Peculiarities by Henry Leach
Should the Holder Play Through by Anthony Wilding & James Bolton
Lawn Tennis as She is Spoke; Illustrated by Harry Rountree
The England Eleven for Australia by Charles Fry
Our Artist on the Links: A Silhouette Study by Oscar Larum
Cross Country Flying by Lucian Blin-Desbleds
Lost a Ball?; Illustrated by Harry Rountree
Sedan Chair; Illustrated by Cecil Aldin
How to Screw a Billiard Ball by Ernest Crawley
Travel Notes [Down-River Trips; Stonehenge; New Forest; Warwick Castle] by Arthur Anderson
The Outdoor Man's Bookshelf [Review of *Polar Exploration* by William Bruce]
First Aid for Dogs With Distemper by Freeman Lloyd
A Rural Ride by William Cobbett
The World of Wheels [Driving in Germany; Hooters; Friction Discs; Tourist Trophy Races; Brooklands Heats] by Archibald Williams
Clothes and the Man [Knickerbockers and Stockings; Moleskin Pockets] by Basil Tozer
In the Clubroon [Little Model Golf Balls; Mass Rackets; Chronometers; Motor Tyres]

Andrew Joyner

Horace Nicholls

Rubens Moore

Volume 16

Issue 91 : October 1911 (p1-120)

George Harris; Illustrated by Oscar Larum
The Australians We Shall Meet by Charles Fry
Thomas Pawley: England's Cricket Manager by James Slymn
Leading Actors and Actresses at Play [Gertrude Millar, Ellaline Terriss, Basil Foster, Ethel Irving, Oscar Asche, George Robey, Marie Studholme, Aubrey Smith] by Bernard Parsons
The Government of Golf by Arthur Croome
The Answer by Philip Vaile
The Watermen of the River Thames by Guy Nickalls
Hark! Italy's Music [verses] by John Hamilton-Reynolds
The Rugby Full Back by John Jackett
Wet and Dry Fly Fishing by Bertram Glossop
Alpine Sensations and Reminiscences by George Powell
You Smile Upon Your Friend [verses] by Alfred Housman
An Ingenious Device; Illustrated by Arthur Watts
The Car's Broken Down! by Richard Hearne
Jack Johnson on Feinting and Timing by James Bolton
A Promising Match; Illustrated by Harry Rountree
The Airdale by Vivian Hollender
Chalk Pits the Travellers' Rests by Edward Thomas; Illustrated by Bernard Gotch
Bridge Leads by Joseph Elwell
Hauling Out and Lying Up a Four Ton Cruiser by Charles Pears; Illustrated by himself
Golf and the New Town by Arthur Anderson
A Mistake Somewhere; Illustrated by Edwin Morrow
To Have Had; Illustrated by Cecil Aldin
Travel Notes [Fishing; False Advertising; Holiday Towns] by Arthur Anderson
Reviews of *Partridges and Partridge Manors* by Aymer Maxwell, *The Hampdenshire Warder* by John Beresford and *The Billiard Monthly* edited by Sydenham Dixon
The World of Wheels [Small Car Prices; Motorcycling Theory; Auto Cycle Union Yorkshire Trials] by Archibald Williams
Some Rugby Records by Sydney Boot
The Follow-Through in Billiards by Ernest Crawley
Clothes and the Man [Shooting Boots; Misfits; Moss Brothers Shop] by Basil Tozer
The Kennel [Valuable Tips; Areca Nuts] by Freeman Lloyd
Clubroom Notes [Reviews of *Motoring in the West of England* by Charles Harper and *Association Football Annual* by Alfred Davis; Golfing Shoes]

Issue 92 : November 1911 (p121-240)

County Cricketer; Illustrated by Edwin Morrow
The Morals of County Cricket (1) by Charles Fry; Illustrated by Edwin Morrow
How to Judge a Horse by Arthur Horwood; Illustrated by Lionel Edwards
The Coming of the Silent Small Car by Richard Hearne; Illustrated by Oscar Larum

Some Famous Guns; Illustrated by Oscar Larum
The New Scheme of Golf Government by Philip Vaile
Playing to the Gallery by Frederick Aflalo; Illustrated by Edwin Morrow
Thomas William Burgess: Master of the Channel by Montague Holbein
The Young Foxhound at School by Thomas Dale
Roughish Road; Illustrated by Harry Rountree
The Golf Ball: Present and Future by Henry Leach
A Country Ride by Arthur Watts; Illustrated by himself
The Raven in its Wild Home by Arthur Brook
The Soul of the Crowd by Desmond Shaw
Are Women Approaching Men in Sport by Hugh Chisholm; Illustrated by Oscar Larum
Horse Dealer; Illustrated by Alfred Leete
Some Famous Rugby Full-Backs by Sydney Boot
Clothes and the Man [Evening Wear; Fur Coats; Gauntlets] by Basil Tozer
Snooker and the Art of Potting by Ernest Crawley
The Kennel: On Exercising by Freeman Lloyd
The World of Wheels [Olympia Motor Show] by Archibald Williams
Travel Notes [English Woodlands; Cromer Field Paths; Penzance Footpaths] by Arthur Anderson
Indigestion?; Illustrated by George Soper
Golf at Home: Canons Park Golf Club (1) by Arthur Anderson
In the Clubroom [Handy Hobart Motorcycle; Billiard Tables]

Issue 93 : December 1911 (p241-384)

Incipient Influenza; Illustrated by Ralph Hodgson
The Irish Water Spaniel by Charles Wright
The Hockey Referee [verses] by Robert Kiff
Some Well-Known Hunting Men; Illustrated by Oscar Larum
Lawn Tennis: On Winter Play by Anthony Wilding
The Snow and Ice Sports of Switzerland by Walter Larden
A Memory of the Great Summer by Alan Haig-Brown
About Covert Shooting by Owen Jones
A Last Game of Billiards by John Alfred; Illustrated by Henry Brock
The Alpinisation of Inland Golf Courses (1) by Henry Leach
The Game of Hockey (1) by Philip Robson
In the Bay [verses] by Samuel Hunt
The Royal Motor Yacht Club by Charles Eldred; Illustrated by himself
The Football Association and the Amateur Football Association: A Plea for Reconciliation by Charles Fry
It's an Ill Fog; Illustrated by Alfred Leete
The Unbeliever; Illustrated by Edwin Morrow
Australia in International Sport (1) by Gordon Inglis
Open Ladies' Golf Championship by May Hezlet
The Morals of County Cricket (2) by Charles Fry; Illustrated by Edwin Morrow
My Funniest Sporting Story [Harry Tate, Phyllis Dare, Harry Lauder, Cicely Courtneidge, Huntley Wright, George Robey, Walter Passmore, Lily Elsie, Marie Studholme, Dan Rolyat,

Gabrielle Ray, Robert Evett, Florence Smithson, George Huntly] by Bernard Parsons
Folly [verses] by Robert Douty
Pleasant Habit; Illustrated by Cecil Alden
Putting for Pachyderms by Arthur Croome
Golf at Your Door: Canons Park Golf Club (2) by Arthur Anderson
Christmas Indoor Games by Cecil Hughes
The Gift; Illustrated by Charles Tresidder
Kennel Matters: The Untimely Swim by Freeman Lloyd
The Story of a Snooze; Illustrated by Alfred Leete
The Etiquette of the Billiard Room by Ernest Crawley
Last Minute Wins in Rugby Football by Sydney Boot; Illustrated by Horace Crowther-Smith
Christmas Travel and Sport by Basil Tozer
The World of Wheels [Olympia Cycle and Motorcycle Show] by Archibald Williams
Clothes and the Man [Bookstall Clerks; Panmure Gordon; Slumbering Suits; Motoring Waistcoats; Cranks] by Basil Tozer
In the Clubroom [International Hygiene Exhibition in Dresden; Waterproofs; Reviews of *Public Schools' Alpine Sports Club Yearbook* by Watkin Strang-Watkins and *The Care of the Teeth* by George Colburn; Turin International Exhibition]

Issue 94 : January 1912 (p385-504)

The Cock Pheasant [verses] by Alan Haig-Brown
John Bull's Own Dog: Walter Jefferies by Frederick Ward
The Only Survivor; Illustrated by Alfred Leete
The Alpinisation of Inland Golf Courses (2) by Henry Leach
Woodland Barbarities by Owen Jones
The Horse Dealer; Illustrated by Alfred Leete
Squash Rackets by Gerald Weigall
Quoits by Carter Platts
The Motorcycle Race [verses] by William Gordon
Luck in Sport by Archibald Maclaren
The Pessimistic View; Illustrated by Charles Grave
An Underground Ramble in London by Arthur Watts; Illustrated by himself
The Badger by Charles St.John
Skiing For the Man Who Doesn't Know by John Fulton
What Are You Doing?; Illustrated by Harry Rountree
Rugby Football in South Africa by Reginald Hands
Australia in International Sport (2) by Gordon Inglis
Happy Tyro Again; Illustrated by Hope Read
The Morals of County Cricket (3) by Charles Fry; Illustrated by Edwin Morrow
Apology to Gilbert Greenall by Walter Burton-Baldry
The Game of Hockey (2) by Philip Robson
Please Take Me Out [verses] by Alan Haig-Brown
Salmon Fishing From Coracles by Alfred Cutler
The Game of Morrice by William Batchelder

England and the Olympic Games by Richard Turner
Mainly About Putting by Philip Vaile
Golf at Your Door: Edgware Golf Club by Arthur Anderson
We Ought to Pick Up a Job?; Illustrated by George Soper
Billiard Pastimes by Ernest Crawley; Illustrated by Horace Crowther-Smith
Clothes and the Man [Public Schools; Fur Collarettes; American Shirts] by Basil Tozer
The Outdoor Man's Bookshelf [Reviews of *Through Trackless Labrador* by Hesketh Prichard; *With Ski in Norway and Lapland* by John Fulton; *The Sport of Shooting* by Owen Jones; *Sport on the Rivieras* by Eustace Reynolds-Ball; *Tee Shots and Others* by Bernard Darwin; *Notes on Bridge* by John Simpson; *A Winter Sport Book* by Reginald Cleaver]
Kennel Matters: On Grooming by Freeman Lloyd
The World of Wheels [Cost of Motoring; Cycle-Cars] by Archibald Williams
In the Clubroom [The Rest Home for Horses; Golf Balls; Scotch Knitted Collars]
As Others See Us [Reviews from various Newspapers and Magazines]

Issue 95 : February 1912 (p505-624)

The Amateur Vet by Arthur Horwood; Illustrated by Lionel Edwards
Flog; Illustrated by Horace Crowther-Smith
A Day at a Dog Show by Arthur Watts; Illustrated by himself
The Partridge [verses] by Alan Haig-Brown
Playing the Game; Illustrated by Harry Rountree
Charles Dickens: Tramp by Walter Dexter
The Buzzard by Arthur Brook
Badminton: A Game in Being by Ernest Crawley
Mixed Sports; Illustrated by Harry Rountree
Curling: The Roaring Game by Courtenay Vernon
The Post-Bound Net [verses] by Digby Jephson
North Country Kettle Shooting by Carter Platts
Why and How Birds Are Missed by Frank Bonnett; Illustrated by Christopher Strange
Lawn Tennis: Seeding the Draw by Anthony Wilding
The Origin of Golfing Expressions by Walter Tunbridge
The Mallard [verses] by Alan Haig-Brown
On Wild Duck and Ducklings by Charles St.John
Australia in International Sport (3) by Gordon Inglis
The Game of Hockey (3) by Philip Robson
The Rhode Island Red: A Rising Poultry Breed by Arthur Wheeler
Bruin: An Artist's Experience in Norway by Harold Gilman; Illustrated by himself
Description of Norway by Henrik Pontoppidan
Devonshire by George Smith
Somerset by Gerald Badcock
A Trout of Fame by William Houghton
The Serenity of Golf by Ernest Crawley
Golf, Tennis and Bowls (1) by Arthur Anderson
The World of Wheels by Archibald Williams

Billiards: How to Make Breaks by Ernest Crawley
The Outdoor Man's Bookshelf [Reviews of *Casuals in the Caucasus* by Agnes Herbert; *Sea Fishing* by Charles Minchin; *Stalks in the Himalayas* by Edward Stebbing; *Golf Guide* by James Braid; *Home Life of the Osprey* by Clinton Abbot]
Clothes and the Man [Fashion Modifications; Hunting Boots; Country Quality] by Basil Tozer
Kennel: Feeding by Vivian Hollender
In the Clubroom [Cocoa; Gentlemen's Corsets; Miniature Billiard Tables; Review of *The Fisherman's List* by William Ashford; Golf Grip Wax]
The Weather is Rough; Illustrated by Thomas Dale

Issue 96 : March 1912 (p625-748)

Dormack; Illustrated by William Shardlow
The Lady of the Stall; Illustrated by Arthur Watts
The [Caledonian] Cattle Market by Arthur Watts; Illustrated by himself
To Rory [verses] by Leslie Oyler
Ware Wire, Sir; Illustrated by Lionel Edwards
On His Majesty's Service by George Insh; Illustrated by Kingsley Howe
Some French Shooting Dogs by Henry Bryden; Illustrated by Paul Mahler
Volcano Climbing in Japan by Eustace Bruce-Mitford
On Applause in Play by Eustace Miles
The Playground of England: The New Forest by Rufus Carter
It Nods and Curtseys [verses] by Alfred Housman
A-Hunting We Will Go; Illustrated by Dorothy Hardy
Flying For You and Me by Lucian Blin-Desbleds
Golf: Lies Good and Bad by Arthur Croome
Cricket Suffragettes by William Holland; Illustrated by Arthur Watts
Cave Exploration as a Sport by Ernest Baker
The Stuff That Dreams are Made Of by Frederick White; Illustrated by Hamilton Williams
The Googly in Australia by John Hutcheon
The G-Ball by Charles Fry
Ware Wheat, Sir!; Illustrated by Lionel Edwards
Round the Saddle Room Fire by Jack Fairfax-Blakeborough; Illustrated by Dorothy Hardy
The Wary Wild Goose by Charles St.John
The New Billiard Handicapping Scheme by Bernard Parsons
The Coming of the Runabout by Charles Johnson
The Loose Head [Rugby] (1) by Edward Sewell
The Hoaxer Hoaxed by Arthur Watts; Illustrated by himself
Passing Notes [Olympic Games; Athletes Advisory Club; Amateur Rowing Association; British Olympic Council; Lingay Fen Skating Championships]
Pallone: National Game of Italy by Percy Longhurst; Illustrated by Ernest Prater
The Holder Does Not Play Through by Anthony Wilding
Pleasing; Illustrated by Cecil Aldin
The Royal and Ancient Game by Horace Hutchinson
Golf, Tennis and Bowls (2) by Arthur Anderson

Some Early Salmon and Trout Fishing in Ireland by Edgar Shrubsole
Clothes and the Man [*The Undertakers' Review*; Spats; Gum Shoes; High-Cut Waistcoats] by Basil Tozer
The World of Wheels by Archibald Williams
Cycling in Devonshire by William Curtis
Billiards: Cue-Tips by Ernest Crawley
Whelping and the Care of the Dam (1) by Morrell Mackenzie
Farming in British Columbia by Basil Tozer
In the Clubroom [Reviews of *Gamage's Hockey Annual* by Edward Thomson, *All About Tyres for Cycles and Motorcycles*, *The Birmingham Golfer*; Flask Drinks; Charles Lancaster]

Gladys Reid

Grantland Rice

Robert Nisbet

Volume 17

Issue 97 : April 1912 (p1-136)

My Most Thrilling British Climbs by George Abraham
A Good Catch; Illustrated by Alfred Leete
The Nineteenth Hole by Henry Leach
To a Favourite Hunter [verses] by Alan Haig-Brown
Broken Down Bus; Illustrated by Alfred Leete
Goh: The Oldest Known Game by Horace Cheshire
Cocks and Hens and Pigs and Goats by Arthur Horwood; Illustrated by Lionel Edwards
The Referee's Viewpoint by Eugene Corri
An Old Ball [verses] by Digby Jephson
Through Wild Galicia With a Flyrod by Walter Gallichan
Reporting Football Matches by Ernest Theobald
Riding Master; Illustrated by Harry Rountree
Scientific Fish Breeding by Rowland Kenney
Australia's Fast Bowlers by John Hutcheon
To Judy [verses] by Alan Haig-Brown
England versus Australia by Charles Fry
Partridges and Their Preservation by Owen Jones
The Loose Head [Rugby] (2) by Edward Sewell
The Sheldrake by Charles St.John
A Gamekeeper's Corner by Owen Jones
Gardening in a Nutshell by Howard Jenkins
A Bad Lie; Illustrated by Hugh Radcliffe-Wilson
Who's For the Animals by Basil Tozer
Passing Notes [British Olympic Council; Test Matches in Australia; Incogniti Cricket Club; Blackheath Rugby Club; University Sport; Lawn Tennis; Live Bait]
To Have Had; Illustrated by Cecil Aldin
Golf and the Weather by Ernest Worthing
Spring [verses] by Thomas Nash
The World of Wheels by Archibald Williams
A Nice Bit of Ham; Illustrated by Frederick Buchanan
Caring for the Clutch of the Automobile by Harold Slauson
Angling Gossip [Meteor Winch; Fourteen-Footers; Light Trout Rods] by Edgar Shrubsole; Illustrated by Henry Brock
The Highest Ambition; Illustrated by Charles Keene
Clothes and the Man [Dress Expert; Draughtless Sleeves; Cut-Away Coats; Billiard Players' Shirt] by Basil Tozer
Lawn Tennis: The Coming Style by Ernest Crawley
Whelping and the Care of the Dam (2) by Morell Mackenzie
In the Clubroom [Golf Balls; Goats; Reviews of *Goat Keeping* by Albert Sheppee; *Flying For You and Me* by Lucien Blin-Desbleds and *Fifty Golfing Resorts* by Archie Compston]
A News Item by Thomas O'Connor

Issue 98 : May 1912 (p137-280)

Summer Fabrics; Illustrated by Gladys Reid
The Triangular Tests (1); Illustrated by Ralph Hodgson
Dignity and Impudence; Illustrated by Arthur Watts
In Furrin Parts by Arthur Watts; Illustrated by himself
The Charter of the Wild by Arthur Brook
Outlaws of the Air by Arthur Brook
The Lifeline of the Mountaineer by Donald McLeish
The Pot-Egg System for Partridges and Pheasants by John Bristow-Noble
The Sheepdog in the Arena by Carter Platts
A Tour Round Brittany by Humphrey Joel
At the Beginning of the Season by Charles Fry
The Hospital at the Zoo (1) by Morell Mackenzie
Some Famous Tennis Players in Action; Illustrated by Oscar Larum
Five Ball Croquet by Horace Cheshire
Miniature Rifle Shooting by William Balshaw
The May Fly Up by Edgar Shrubsole
Albert Primrose; Illustrated by Oscar Larum
The Fillies of 1912 by Charles O'Hara
A Springtide Song [verses] by Thomas Heywood; [text] by Arthur Anderson
Australia's New Cricketers by John Hutcheon
Lawn Tennis: On Rackets by Anthony Wilding
Caravanning and Camping by Harvey Jarvis
Come Live With Me [verses] by Charles Marlowe
The Loose Head [Rugby] (3) by Edward Sewell
A Gamekeeper's Corner by Owen Jones
In the Stocks; Illustrated by Cecil Aldin
The Land of the Maple Leaf by Basil Tozer
Cruises to the West Highlands by John Langlands
The Buyer, The Dog and The Seller by Morell Mackenzie
Personality in Lawn Tennis by Ernest Crawley
In the Gun Room [William Horton; *The Field*; Lancaster's Under and Over Gun; John Robertson; Single Trigger System] by Edward Leman
Clothes and the Man [Serge Lounge Suits; Coloured Socks; Hunting Hats] by Basil Tozer
Angling Gossip [James Ogden; Halford's Patterns; *Fishing Gazette*; Folding Boats] by Edgar Shrubsole; Illustrated by Henry Brock
Golf in the Desert by Charles Mansford
So Little Harm; Illustrated by Charles Keene
Caravan Notes by Harvey Jarvis
Travel Notes [Coal Strike; Sea Trips] by Arthur Anderson
The World of Wheels [Small Cars] by Archibald Williams
In the Clubroom [Motorcycle Tyres; Racket Stringing; Reviews of *The Golf Book* for Samuel Benetfink, *The Magician's Annual* by William Goldston and *How to Go to Sea in the Merchant Service* by Frederick Stafford]

Issue 99 : June 1912 (p281-416)

What's Your Handicap?; Illustrated by Ralph Hodgson
Some Action Studies of Famous Cricketers; Illustrated by Oscar Larum
The Dipper by Arthur Brook
Motor Camping by Aldred Barker
The Long Trail by Julian Thunder; Illustrated by George Soper
The Life of the London Docks by Arthur Watts; Illustrated by himself
Spinning for Salmon, Trout and Other Fish by Arthur Hawley
The Superiority of Australian Swimmers by Frank Sachs
Life as a Lock-Keeper by Clive Holland
The Sapling by Frederick Ward
Native Sports in India by Nihal Singh
The Derivation of Sporting Terms by Percy Longhurst
Flying at Sea by Jean-Louis Conneau
The Craft of Croquet by Horace Crowther-Smith; Illustrated by himself
Manx; Illustrated by Alfred Leete
The Hospital at the Zoo (2) by Morell Mackenzie
The Summer Holiday of the Steeplechaser: Percy Whitaker
Fistiana by William Maas
The Sport of Swimming by Montague Holbein
Caravanning and Camping by Harvey Jarvis
Sea Fishing for the Beginner by Frederick Aflalo
Sport at the Royal Academy by Basil Tozer
To the True Motorist [verses] by Frederick Buchanan
A Gamekeeper's Corner by Owen Jones
Contentment; Illustrated by Cecil Aldin
Golf: The Genesis of the Open Championship (1) by Harold Macfarlane
Lawn Tennis [Review of *On the Court and Off* by Anthony Wilding] by Ernest Crawley
The World of Wheels by Archibald Williams
Caravan Notes by Harvey Jarvis
Kennel: On Judges and Judging (1) by Morell Mackenzie
Angling Gossip [Coarse Fish; Dace; Rudd; Hooked Fish] by Edgar Shrubsole; Illustrated by Henry Brock
Travel Notes [Dartmoor Valleys; Welsh Fishing; Wensleydale] by Arthur Anderson
The Entertaining Style; Illustrated by Charles Keene
Clothes and the Man [Wire Bootlaces; Roscut Riding Habits; Straw Hats; Frock Coats] by Basil Tozer
In the Clubroom [Caravan Tents; Vale of Aylesbury; Review of *C.B.Fry: The Man and His Methods* by Wallis Myers; British Columbia; Humber Motorcycles]

Issue 100 : July 1912 (p417-552)

The Triangular Tests (2); Illustrated by Ralph Hodgson
The Fascination of the Thames by Charles Thomas
Freshwater Swimming and Diving by Clive Holland

Lawn Tennis Champions and Their Methods by Bernard Parsons
A Woodland Tragedy by Charles Knight
Coracles and Things by Arthur Watts; Illustrated by himself
Old Friends [verses] by Digby Jephson
A Day on a Racing Yacht by Ernest Hamilton
The Sea Angler in Kent by Frederick Aflalo
Sporting Terms: Fishing by Edgar Shrubsole
Ferrets by Frank Bonnett
The Breeding of Big Dogs by Morell Mackenzie
Regattas by Guy Nickalls
The Pioneers of Golf (1) by Henry Leach
A Day on the Road by Humphrey Joel
A Fight With a Salmon by Edgar Shrubsole
Every Man and a Camera by Arthur Anderson
Golf at the Sea: Skegness and its Links by Henry Leach
A Gamekeeper's Corner by Owen Jones
Camping and Caravanning by Harvey Jarvis
There is None Better; Illustrated by Leo Cheney
Golf: The Genesis of the Open Championship (2) by Harold Macfarlane
Clothes and the Man [Laundresses; Thief-Proof Umbrellas; Cravenette Hats; Cut-Away Coats] by Basil Tozer
In the Gun Room [Automatic Pistols] by Edward Leman
Caravanning and Camping Notes by Harvey Jarvis
Lawn Tennis: What is Placing? (1) by Ernest Crawley
Angling Gossip [Greenheart Flyrod; *The Fishing Gazette*; Pollack Fishing; Weed Cutters] by Edgar Shrubsole; Illustrated by Henry Brock
For the Angler [Review of *The Salmon and Trout Magazine*] by Edgar Shrubsole
Travel Notes [North Wales Publicity; Railway Posters and Books] by Arthur Anderson
The World of Wheels by Archibald Williams
Kennel: On Judges and Judging (2) by Morell Mackenzie
In the Clubroom [Review of *Notes on Rifle Cleaning*; Small Cameras; Golf Ball Pattern; Chiltern Footpaths; Olympic Games Walking Contests]; Illustrated by George Thorp

Issue 101 : August 1912 (p553-688)

The Equipment of the Mountaineer by Donald McLeish
Poultry Craft by George Sweet
Rats and the Bar by Owen Jones
A Motorcycle Trip into the Broads Country by Humphrey Joel
Low Water Lures for Salmon by Hamish Stuart
Motor Boat Racing by Rendell Wilson
The Schooling of the Polo Pony (1) by John Knight-Bruce
The Spaniel's Holiday [verses] by Alan Haig-Brown
Walking by Thomas Hammond
A Ballyshannon Trout by Edgar Shrubsole

The Choice of Retriever by Stanley Duncan
The Pioneers of Golf (2) by Henry Leach
An English Carnival by Arthur Watts; Illustrated by himself
River Camping by Harvey Jarvis
Shooting Prospects of the Season by Frank Bonnett
A Gamekeeper's Corner by Owen Jones
Lawn Tennis: Retirement of Anthony Wilding
The British Sea-Anglers' Society by Edgar Shrubsole
Inexpensive Yachting by Ernest Pearce
The Scottie and Irish Terrier by William Haynes
Review of *Strolls in Beechy Bucks* by Thomas Smith
Contentment; Illustrated by Leo Cheney
Golf at Westward Ho! by Edmund Lacon-Watson
The World of Wheels by Archibald Williams
Travel Notes [Prestatyn] by Arthur Anderson
Angling Gossip [Coarse Fish; Groundbait; Hook Baits; Float-Leger; Fly Reels]
   by Edgar Shrubsole; Illustrated by Henry Brock
Clothes and the Man [Fancy-Dress Balls; Review of *A Chronicle of Friendships*
   by Luther Munday; Exotic Eccentricity; Town Boots] by Basil Tozer
In the Gun Room [Review of *Shots From A Lawyer's Gun* by Nicholas Everitt; Game Licences;
   Trespass] by Edward Leman
Caravan and Camping Notes by Harvey Jarvis
Kennel: The Buyer and the Breeder (1) by Morell Mackenzie
Lawn Tennis: What is Placing? (2) by Ernest Crawley
In the Clubroom [Ginger Ale; Golf Shoes; Singer Motorcycle; Postcard Cameras; Review of
   The Road Dust Problem]; Illustrated by William Houghton

Issue 102 : September 1912 (p689-820)

Sun and Air Bathing by Colin Hamilton
Wind and Petrol: Yachting and Boating by Ernest Hamilton
The Hound Trail by Mary Fair
The Premier Jockey: Frank Wootton by Bernard Parsons
The Setter [verses] by Alan Haig-Brown
On a Norwegian Salmon River by Mary Amherst
Walking Up Partridges by Owen Jones
The Schooling of the Polo Pony (2) by John Knight-Bruce
The Arcady of Derbyshire by Charles Moore
The Heron and its Haunts by Arthur Brook
Sport in the Canary Islands by Perry Robinson
The Polecat at Home by Alan Haig-Brown
Camp Life by Harvey Jarvis
Pigeons for the Country House by Alfred Osman
Are Sportswomen Unfeminine by Desmond Shaw
Successful Sea Angling by William Harrison

The Art of Catching Moles by John Bristow-Noble
A Gamekeeper's Corner by Owen Jones
Through the Middle Counties by Humphrey Joel
September Sea Trout by Edgar Shrubsole
The Editor's Chair [Extracts from Newspapers] by Walter Burton-Baldry
Fireside Repose; Illustrated by Leo Cheney
Clothes and the Man [Plate Smashing; Overseas Wardrobes; Hair Lotion; Rainproof Material] by Basil Tozer
Kennel: The Buyer and the Breeder (2) by Morell Mackenzie
The Dangers of Golf by Harold Macfarlane
Caravan and Camping Notes by Harvey Jarvis
Billiards: The Use of Side (1) by Ernest Crawley
Angling Gossip [Tench; Angling From a Punt] by Edgar Shrubsole; Illustrated by Henry Brock
Travel Notes [Minehead Harriers] by Arthur Anderson
In the Gun Room [Light Small Bore Guns; Wild Fowling in Donegal; Poor Partridge Shooting] by Edward Leman
The World of Wheels by Archibald Williams
In the Clubroom [Reviews of *Gray on Billiards* by George Gray and *How to Play Snooker Pool* by Wallace Ritchie; *Daily Express* Motorcycling Competition]

Alberto Santos-Dumont

Alfred Sheppard

Theodore Roosevelt

Volume 18

Issue 103 : October 1912 (p1-136)

Hints for the Golf Beginner by Edward Ray & James Bolton
Bridget's Shoes [verses] by Dorothy Dickinson
A Note on Pets by Ralph Hodgson
The Kennel Club: The Senate of the Canine World (1) by Morell Mackenzie
Rare and Refreshing by Owen Jones
Fell Racing by Percy Longhurst
An October Day by Frank Bonnett
The Valley of the Thames by Humphrey Joel
High and Fancy Diving by Clive Holland
The Sporting Muse by Percy Longhurst
The Art of Managing a Shoot by Owen Jones
The Kingfisher by Arthur Brook
What Does the Glass Say? by Frederick Aflalo; Illustrated by Edwin Morrow
James Driscoll: The Ideal Boxer by Eugene Corri
Lore, Legend and Tradition of An Old Racing Centre by Jack Fairfax-Blakeborough
The Meet of the Caravan Club at Stratford-on-Avon by Harvey Jarvis
Golf For the Man Who is Off His Game by Kenneth Kent
The Lieutenant by Brenda Spender; Illustrated by William Houghton
Badminton: New Players for a New Season by William Davies
A Gamekeeper's Corner by Owen Jones
Unsurpassed; Illustrated by Leo Cheney
Clothes and the Man [Silk Nightshirts; Hunting Stocks; Burlington Arcade; Beaters' Kilts] by Basil Tozer
The World Over; Illustrated by Arthur Michael
Motor Cycling by Archibald Williams
Some Legal Points Connected With the Dog by Morell Mackenzie
In the Gunroom [New Bore Gun; Handling a Game Gun; Cartridges] by Edward Leman
On the Motor Highway by Archibald Williams
Angling Gossip [Grayling; Red Tag Tip; Fly-Casting; London Club Anglers; Williams Tackle House] by Edgar Shrubsole; Illustrated by Henry Brock
Billiards: The Use of Side (2) by Ernest Crawley
Temperament in Golf by Endersly Howard
The World of Wheels: Cycling by Archibald Williams
Caravanning and Camping Notes by Harvey Jarvis
Home of Rest; Illustrated by Byam Shaw
Hockey Notes by Arthur Burrows
Lighting and Heating [Advertorial]
Punch; Illustrated by Charles Keene
In the Clubroom [Bed Sheets; Serge Patterns; Dog Shows Disinfectant; Billiard Cues]

Issue 104 : November 1912 (p137-272)

Practical Approaching by Harry Vardon & James Bolton
The Bowling Green by Seymour Cooper
The Kennel Club: The Senate of the Canine World (2) by Morell Mackenzie
How to Store Live Eggs by Owen Jones
The Heavy Horse of Scotland by Wodehouse Garland
The Woodcock [verses] by Alan Haig-Brown
Winter Sailing by Vernon Moore
How I Invented a New Game by James Lees
The Great Crested Grebe by Arthur Brook
Lines to the Otter [verses] by Alan Haig-Brown
A Brace of Beauties by Edgar Shrubsole
Picturesque Poultry by Frank Bonnett
Fish in Their Natural State (1) by Stanley Johnson
Mountaineering on Ski by Arnold Lunn
Our Short-Haired Cats by Frances Simpson
Through Picturesque Scotland by Humphrey Joel
The Trespasser by Frederick Aflalo; Illustrated by Henry Brock
Rabbit Shooting by William Balshaw
The Aftermath of Hounds by Owen Jones
The Springboks: Prospects of the Tour by Reginald Hands
The Power of the Rod by Edgar Shrubsole
Will the Aeroplane Ever Assist Us in Everyday Life [Hiram Maxim, Howard Wright, Henry de la Vauix, Francis Maclean, Horatio Barber, Victor Menard] by Bernard Parsons
A Gamekeeper's Corner by Owen Jones
Motoring by Archibald Williams
Caravan and Camping Notes by Harvey Jarvis
The Country House by Arthur Anderson
Hockey Notes by Arthur Burrows
For the Golfer's Library [Review of *The Book of the Links* by Martin Sutton]
The Peaceful Pause; Illustrated by Leo Cheney
The Making of a Golf Ball [Advertorial]
Dogs in Quarantine: Hackbridge Dogs' Home [Advertorial]
Companionable Dogs by Haigh Brown
Angling Gossip [Fishing Tackle; Silkworm Gut; Reel Lines; Wading Trousers] by Edgar Shrubsole; Illustrated by Henry Brock
The Poetry of Billiards (1) by Ernest Crawley
Motorcycling by Laurence Cade
In the Gunroom [Rabbit Shooting; Windsor Park; Sporting Shots; Driven Grouse] by Edward Leman
Cycling by Stanley Noble
Clothes and the Man [Taxi-Cabs; Clothing Insurance; *The Tailor and Cutter*; Newspaper Letters] by Basil Tozer
In the Clubroom [The London Scottish Societies Tournament; Army Orders; Dairy Produce; Jetton Cape]

Issue 105 : December 1912 (p273-416)

The Push Shot in Golf by George Duncan & James Bolton
Luckless Golf by Cecil Hughes
The Increasing Popularity of Curling by Bertram Smith
The Dog of the Day: West Highland White Terrier by Morell Mackenzie
A Salmon by Edgar Shrubsole
The Art of Driving Horses in Single Harness by Wodehouse Garland
Hornussen: The National Game of Switzerland by Violet Methley
Some Bridge Curiosities by Edwin Anthony
Playing the Game by Ralph Blumenfeld
The Holiday Angler by Ernest Phillips
The Opportunities of Timoleon Brass: The Ex-Viceroy by Bertram Atkey; Illustrated by Henry Brock
To a Faithful Dog [verses] by Mabel Richards
A Rat: Some Hints on Ferreting by Owen Jones
Some Simple Conjuring Tricks by William Goldston
The Clumber [verses] by Alan Haig-Brown
Testing a Motorcycle by Charles Johnson
Golfing Methods by Kenneth Kent
Concerning the Goose by Frank Bonnett
The Badminton Season by William Davies
The Grandeur of Dartmoor by Humphrey Joel
A Gamekeeper's Corner by Owen Jones
Hockey: League Competitions by Harold Allen
To the Last Shred; Illustrated by Leo Cheney
Christmas Hockey Notes by Arthur Burrows
The Poetry of Billiards (2) by Ernest Crawley
In the Gunroom [Burst Guns; English Gunpowder] by Edward Leman
Motoring [Olympia Motor Show] by Archibald Williams
Cycling by Stanley Noble
Motorcycling [Single Cylinder Machine; Parade Hogs; Cyclecars] by Laurence Cade
Caravan and Camping Notes by Harvey Jarvis
Clothes and the Man [Burberry's New Shop; Boots; Waterproofs; Seamless Trousers; Convertible Sheets] by Basil Tozer
Magicians of the Links by Endersly Howard
This is the Ball; Illustrated by Clement Flower
All About [Briar] Pipes
Angling Gossip [Injudicious Stock; Big Trout; Ruined River] by Edgar Shrubsole; Illustrated by Henry Brock
Kennel: Old British Breeds by Morell Mackenzie
In the Clubroom [Billiard Tables; Cherry Brandy; Health Books; Sidcup Golf Club; Mirrorscopes; Humberette Car]

Issue 106 : January 1913 (p417-528)

The Art of Putting by Thomas Ball & James Bolton
The [Indian] Christmas [Golf] Championship by Cecil Hughes
On a Grayling River by Horace Nicholls
When Turk Meets Greek by Frederick Aflalo; Illustrated by William Houghton
Park Cattle by Frank Bonnett
The Art of Driving: Pairs and Tandems by Wodehouse Garland
Life and Sport in the Duchy by Henry Stanton
Widgeon Shooting by Stanley Duncan
Wood Pigeons by Charles St.John
British Fish in Their Natural State (2) by Stanley Johnson
Parson Straight of Harkaway Cross by Clive Burlton; Illustrated by George Soper
Lawn Tennis Hard Courts by Ernest Crawley
The Trout Stream by Kenneth Dawson
The Social Side of Golf by Endersly Howard
A Weekend in Wintry Wales by Humphrey Joel
What is An Amateur by Basil Tozer
The Sport of Tobogganing by Bertram Smith
From Sussex to the Sahara (1) by Harvey Jarvis
A Gamekeeper's Corner by Owen Jones
In the Chair; Illustrated by Leo Cheney
Angling Gossip [Yare & Bure Preservation Society; Norfolk & Suffolk Fisheries Bill] by Edgar Shrubsole
Cuemanship in Billiards by Ernest Crawley
Cycling [Chain Driven Cycles] by Stanley Noble
Motoring [Value of Vehicles] by Laurence Cade
The Popularity of the Sidecar by Laurence Cade
Motorcycling: A Decade of Development by Laurence Cade
Before the [Dog] Show by Morell Mackenzie
Clothes and the Man [Norfolk Shooting Jacket] by Basil Tozer
The Golfer's Club-of-All-Work by Cecil Hughes
In the Clubroom [Model Railways; London Bus Routes; Golf Clubs; Gramophone Records]

Issue 107 : February 1913 (p529-648)

Don't Run Risks; Illustrated by Reginald Goodman
On Spoon and Iron Shots by Alexander Herd & James Bolton
Some Old English Rural Games and Sports by Paul Monckton
The Popularity of the Cocker Spaniel by Henry Lloyd
The Public Schools Alpine Sports Club by Arnold Lunn
Touts: Ancient and Modern by Bernard Parsons; Illustrated by Arthur Watts
Shooting Lunch Fairy Tales by Claude Scudamore [Jarvis]
Some Estuary Trout by Edgar Shrubsole
Frank Potter-Irwin; Illustrated by Horace Crowther-Smith
Hockey: The Game at the Universities by Henry Saunders

Modern Horsemanship by Thomas Walls & Basil Tozer
Rearing Trout for the Rod by Ernest Phillips
Billiards Sixty Years Ago by Bernard Darwin
The Badminton Season: The Game Abroad by William Davies
The Art of Pace-Making by Albert Frost
New Rules for the Golfer by Kenneth Kent
The Badger by Owen Jones
On Frost and Snow by Arthur Anderson
From Sussex to the Sahara (2) by Harvey Jarvis
Norway and Winter Sports by James Scott
A Gamekeeper's Corner by Owen Jones
The Heroic Side of Rugby Football by Sydney Boot
Caravan and Camping Notes by Harvey Jarvis
Motoring [Defective Cars] by Laurence Cade
Motorcycling [Cycle Cars] by Laurence Cade
Cycling [Richard Mecredy Presentation Dinner] by Stanley Noble
Billiards [Middle-Pocket Losers] by Ernest Crawley
Kennel: Puppy Growth by Morell Mackenzie
Angling Gossip [Loch Tay] by Edgar Shrubsole
Clothes and the Man [Knickerbockers; Ventilated Hats; Spurs] by Basil Tozer
Golf: The Golfer's Follow-Through by Henry Leach
In the Clubroom [Humber Motorcycle Catalogue; Dog's Homes; Tennis Hard Courts; Post Office Cycle Tyres; Review of *Croquet Alphabet* by Horace Crowther-Smith]; Illustrated by William Houghton
So Little Harm; Illustrated by Charles Keene

Issue 108 : March 1913 (p649-768)

The Road and the Sea; Illustrated by Sydney Cowell
Golf: Short Approaches by Jack White & James Bolton
The Social Side of Golf by Walter Burton-Baldry
The Sealyham Terrier by Morell Mackenzie
The Sportsman as a Preserver of Life by Alan Haig-Brown
Heroes of the Steeplechase by Norman Wentworth
Why Not Increase the Length of the Over by Ronald Graham
Fencing by Bargrave Deane
The Pangs of Putting by Henry Leach
Bird Studies in an English Thicket by Maud Haviland
The Pleasures of Cycling and Motorcycling by Richard Hearne
On a Highland Burn by Ernest Phillips
The Cyclecar Today by Charles Johnson
Deck Sports by Frederick Aflalo
Rugby Football 1913 by Sydney Talfourd-Padgett
The Fight by Rex Beach
The Art of Driving Four-in-Hand by Wodehouse Garland

The Briscoe Shield: Football by Robert Goodyear
A Gamekeeper's Corner by Owen Jones
Clothes and the Man [Newspaper Fashion Writers] by Basil Tozer
Kennel: Change of Type by Morell Mackenzie
Cycling [Rear Lights; Bicycle Training] by Richard Hearne
Motorcycling [Sidecars; Breakdowns] by Laurence Cade
Motoring [Talbot Cars; Benzol] by Laurence Cade
Golf [Overseas Players] by Henry Leach
Angling Gossip [Salmon Angler, Exceptional Rainfall] by Edgar Shrubsole
The Entertaining Style; Illustrated by Charles Keene
Billiards by Ernest Crawley
In the Clubroom [Tyres, Discarded Clothes; The Gamage Amateur Athletic Association; Floating Golf Balls]

Ernest Thompson-Seton

Harry Vardon

Vance Thompson

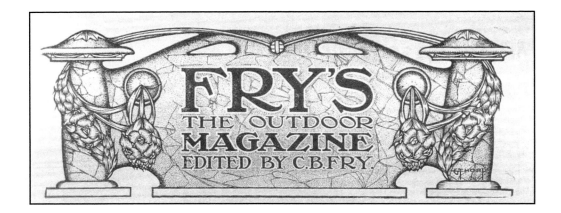

Volume 19

Issue 109 : April 1913 (p1-120)

Golf: The Art of Driving by Harry Vardon & James Bolton
The Social Side of Golf by Walter Burton-Baldry
The Dog of Mount St.Bernard by Harry Stocken
Badminton: Championship Impressions by William Davies
The Future of Cricket by Gerald Badcock
My Lady Wistaria [verses] by Mabel Richards
The Ancient and Royal Sport of Falconry by Gerald Lascelles
The Gentle Art of Fly-Tying by Charles Walker
The Frenchman in the Ring: Georges Carpentier by Desmond Shaw
What is Cricket by Digby Jephson
Big Fish in the North Minch by William Mackenzie
Lawn Tennis: The American Service by Gordon Scotter
Some Spring Flowers and Fruit Blossom by Arthur Anderson
How to Use a Revolver by Ernest Crawley
The Wind and the Spray [verses] by Vachell Philpot
The Hire of the Professional by Frederick Aflalo
The Long-Tailed Fowl of Japan by Walter Elkington
Phases of the Foursome by Walter Burton-Baldry
Stories From a Vet's Notebook by Herbert Shaw; Illustrated by Arthur Watts
The Science of the Googlie by Aubrey Faulkner
The Woodcock by Charles St.John
Point-to-Point Chasing by Basil Tozer
The Evolution of Golf Course Architecture by Kenneth Kent
Ancient Implements of British Sport by Elliott O'Donnell
Famous Double Events by Norman Wentworth
Kennel: Honour Cards by Morell Mackenzie
Clothes and the Man [Cashmere Dinner Suits; 'The Beloved Vagabonds'] by Basil Tozer
Thanks, Old Man; Illustrated by William Houghton
The Country House: Lighting by Arthur Anderson
The Light of His Life; Illustrated by Frank Gillett
Caravan and Camping Notes by Harvey Jarvis
Angling Gossip [Trout Fishing; Dry-Flies] by Edgar Shrubsole
Motoring [American Cars] by Laurence Cade
Motorcycling [Overloading Cycle Cars and Pillions] by Laurence Cade
Cycling [Territorial Army Cycles] by Richard Hearne
Lawn Tennis: A Great Year (1) by Wallis Myers
Golf [Straight-Faced Mashie] by Henry Leach
In the Clubroom [Fitness Drinks; *Built on Honour* Catalogue; Fife Boots]; Illustrated
    by William Houghton

Issue 110 : May 1913 (p121-240)

The Use of the Mashie by Wilfrid Reid & James Bolton
Extract from *The New Book of Golf* by Horace Hutchinson
On [Golf] Championships by Kenneth Kent
The Carp: Its Many Varieties by Stanley Johnson
Fencing With the Sabre (1) by Leonard Ross-Thomas
To the Trout [verses] by Alan Haig-Brown
From London to Sheerness by Humphrey Joel
Bowls and the Ancient Maori by Clarence Asper
The Ways of the Cuckoo by Arthur Brook
The Variety of Angling by Alan Haig-Brown
The Spirit of the Game [verses] by Digby Jephson
The Last Word in Lawn Tennis by Ernest Crawley
Tenants of Shooting by Alfred Burden
Golf: Team Matches by Bernard Darwin
Britain's Weak Spot in Athletics by Frederick Webster
How to Select a County Team by Home Gordon
The Salmon [verses] by Alan Haig-Brown
The Doormouse by Neville Aylesford
A Last Day Among the Pike by Edgar Shrubsole
The Briar Rose by William Coles-Finch
Beasts Without Bars by Frederick Aflalo
The Borzoi by Morell Mackenzie
Caravanning and Camping by Harvey Jarvis
The Photography of Wild Birds by Hugh Macpherson
Is Golf Getting Easier by William Cameron
The Social Side of Golf by Walter Burton-Baldry
Golf [Ages of Champions] by Henry Leach
Motoring [Abandonment of Races in Ireland and Isle of Man; Brooklands Race Track] by Laurence Cade
Motorcycling [New Devices] by Laurence Cade
Cycling [Cyclists Touring Club; Ill-Fitting Cycles] by Richard Hearne
Angling Gossip [May Trout; Irish Loughs] by Edgar Shrubsole
West Highlands Cruises by Arthur Anderson
Lawn Tennis: A Great Year (2) by Wallis Myers
Clothes and the Man [Tailoring Scams; Peg-Top Trousers; Cloth Uppers; Flea Powder] by Basil Tozer
Caravan and Camping Notes [Interior Fittings] by Harvey Jarvis
Kennel: The Education of a Dog by Morell Mackenzie
In the Clubroom [Suspender Socks; Playing Cards; Summer Canoes; Royal Serges]; Illustrated by William Houghton

Issue 111 : June 1913 (p241-368)

Cover Design: Illustrated by Alfred Leete

Happy Moments; Illustrated by Charles Crombie
Obituary of Raymond Etherington-Smith by Walter Burton-Baldry
Raymond Etherington-Smith; Illustrated by Alfred Leete
Leander by Guy Nickalls
The Truth About County Cricket by Charles Fry; Illustrated by Alfred Leete
Golf Recoveries: The Art of Bunker Play by Laurence Ayton & James Bolton
The Prospects of the English Polo Team in America by Sidney Church
Lawn Tennis: The Season's Prospects by Anthony Wilding
The Opening of the Ladies Golfing Season by May Hezlet
The Welsh Terrier by Morell Mackenzie
On Fishing a Strange River by Arthur Sharp
Up River Racing by James Maseley
Fencing With the Sabre (2) by Leonard Ross-Thomas
Saint Fluke by Brenda Spender
Cricket [verses] by Digby Jephson
Review of *A Few Overs* by Digby Jephson
Shooting and Mahseer Fishing in Assam by Stanley Beeman
The Tragedy by Christopher Sewell
The Nobbling of Bend-Or by James Muddock
The Derby [verses] by Frederick St.John
The New Mandalay [verses] by Bertram Atkey; Illustrated by Wilfrid Pippet
Cricket by Advertisement by Harry Smith-Turberville
A Vagabond's Notes by Harvey Jarvis
On a Southern Trout Stream by Alan Haig-Brown
The Sportsman's Library [Reviews of *The Confessions of a Tenderfoot* by Ralph Stock;
    Inland Golf by Edward Ray; *The Complete Horseman* by William Scarth-Dixon; *A Racing
    Story* by William Willmott-Dixon] by Laurence Southeby
Editorial [New Pictorial Front Covers; Ladies Golf; *Pearson's Magazine* Features; *Daily Mail*
    Article; County Cricket; Trout and Otters; Fry's Magazine Cups] by Walter Burton-Baldry
Kennel: The Curse of Anno Domini by Morell Mackenzie
Motoring [Motor Racing; High Speed] by Richard Hearne
Motorcycling [Hill Climbs] by Charles Messenger
Cycling [Pickwick Bicycle Club; Joseph Atto] by Charles Johnson
Golf: English County Associations in London by Endersly Howard
Caravan Notes [Review of *Camping with Motor and Camera* by Aldred Barker] by Harvey Jarvis
Footwork in Lawn Tennis by Ernest Crawley
Angling Gossip [Thames Trout Fishing; Molesey Lock; Norfolk Fishery Board]
    by Edgar Shrubsole
Clothes and the Man [Summer Attire; Tennis Sweaters] by Basil Tozer
Canada and the Panama Canal by Melvill Jamieson
In the Clubroom [Waterproof Coats; Kurnut Puncture Kit; Motors for Boats]; Illustrated
    by William Houghton
The Barrister; Illustrated by Lovent Brist

Issue 112 : July 1913 (p369-504)

Cover Design; Illustrated by Alfred Leete
The Road Hog by Bertram Atkey
The Modern First-Class Cricketer by Charles Fry
Fishing Lines [verses] by Ursula Pickering
Henley Past and Present by Guy Nickalls
The Best Mount I Ever Had [Frank Wootton, John Martin, William Higgs, Barrington Lynham, Mornington Cannon, Bernard Dillon, Otto Madden, Daniel Maher, Charles Wood, William Griggs] by Bernard Parsons
Golf for Everybody by Endersly Howard
Weekend Camps by Harvey Jarvis; Illustrated by George Thorp
The Great Dane by Morell Mackenzie
A Great Cricketer: Robert Poore by George Badcock
The Adventures of a Nonentity by Maud Haviland; Illustrated by Wilfrid Pippet
Styles in Boxing: English versus American by Norman Clark
Trout or Otter by Frederick Aflalo
A Motorcycle Tour Across Salisbury Plain by Humphrey Joel
Twenty-One Years of the Ladies Golf Union by May Hezlet
The Bowling Green by Seymour Cooper
The Sportsman's Library [Reviews of *Caravanning and Camping Out* by Harris Stone; *How to Make a Century* by Jack Hobbs & Jack Ingham; *The Rollings of a Mossless Stone* by Percy Naish] by Laurence Southeby
Editorial [Magazine Availability; Wiesbaden Tennis Tournament; Home Office Regulations; Rugby Football Union Annual General Meeting; Rowland Hill]
Mr Bigley's Cricket Match by Frederic Dale
Motoring [Congested Roads; Touring; Small Cars; New Cycle-Cars] by Richard Hearne
Motorcycling [Junior Tourist Trophy; Race Speeds; Hugh Mason] by Charles Messenger
The Smartest Cut; Illustrated by David Cottington-Taylor
Lawn Tennis: International Notes by Ernest Crawley
With Rod and Line [Izaak Walton; Andrew Lang; East India Cane Rod] by Hugh Sheringham; Illustrated by Wilfrid Pippet
The Social Side of Golf: Sundridge Park Golf Club by Endersly Howard
Anglo-American Golf by Endersly Howard
Clothes and the Man [Holiday Clothing; Dress Suit; Tailoring] by Basil Tozer
Kennel: Treatment of Old Age by Morell Mackenzie
Caravan and Camping Notes [Ipswich Caravan Club Meet] by Harvey Jarvis
With the Pleasure Fleet by Ernest Hamilton
In the Clubroom [Thames Canoe; Cycle-Car Repair Outfit; Reviews of *The Polo Annual* by Lester Simmonds and *The Rifle Score Register* by Arthur Fulton; Water Filters; Waterproof Coats]; Illustrated by William Houghton

Issue 113 : August 1913 (p505-640)

Cover Design; Illustrated by Alfred Leete
The Devil Fish; Illustrated by Leonard Brightwell

Hugh Lowther; Illustrated by Joseph Ginsbury
The Road to Improvement by Anthony Wilding
Some Other Aspects of First-Class Cricket by Charles Fry
Adventures in the Heart of the Dolomites by George Abraham
The Royal Cruising Club by Charles Eldred
An Exciting Moment; Illustrated by Lionel Edwards
Motor Polo by Walter Burton-Baldry
The Overturned Car; Illustrated by Lionel Edwards
Military Tactics by Hall Thorpe; Illustrated by himself
A Hat Trick [verses] by Bertram Atkey
Sea Fishing in the West Country by Frederick Aflalo
All's Fair by Ralph Stock; Illustrated by Joseph Ginsbury
Yells of Triumph; Illustrated by Alfred Leete
The Wrong Pocket; Illustrated by Alfred Leete
In the Land of the Grouse by Alan Haig-Brown
The Coloured Man in the Ring by Desmond Shaw
Sporting Camps by Harvey Jarvis
How to Improve at Golf by Harry Vardon & James Bolton
Minor Counties Cricket (1) by Edward Sewell
Side-Carring to the West Country by Humphrey Joel
The Sportsman's Diary by Clifford Leigh
The Defects of the Cycle-Car by Thomas Beacham; Illustrated by Wilfrid Pippet
Order, Order; Illustrated by Edward Reed
Kennel: Canine Ailments (1) Eczema by Morell Mackenzie
I Assure You; Illustrated by Thomas Wilkinson
With Rod and Line [Illingworth Reel; Roach Baits; Chub Fishing; Norfolk Broads] by Hugh Sheringham; Illustrated by Wilfrid Pippet
County Societies' Golf [Sandy Lodge Golf Club, Northwood] by Endersly Howard
Lawn Tennis: Wimbledon Reflections by Walter Burton-Baldry
Ballade of Lawn Tennis [verses] by Robert Davis
Caravan and Camping Notes by Harvey Jarvis
With the Pleasure Fleet by Ernest Hamilton
In the Clubroom [Brooklands Motorcycle Record; Life Saving Chair; Shooting Jackets; Wisden's Cricket Bats; Half Belts; Henley Regatta]; Illustrated by William Houghton

Issue 114 : September 1913 (641-776)

Cover Design; Illustrated by Alfred Leete
Alfred Lyttelton; Illustrated by Joseph Ginsbury
Socketing [Golf] by Raymond Needham
Physical Education: Physical and Educational Excellence by Charles Fry
Gathering Wood by George Wallace; Illustrated by Alfred Leete
The Last Hole [verses] by McDonnell Bodkin
The Tramp's Song [verses] by Frank Day; Illustrated by Adam Horne
Salmon or Trout by Frederick Aflalo

Ladies Championship Golf by May Hezlet
Golf Wisdom by Jerome Travers
The Sport of Pigeon Racing by Alfred Osman
Breaming in Broadland by Gordon Meggy
Narrow Escapes on the Heights by George Abraham
Partridge Shooting by Alan Haig-Brown
The Smooth Fox Terrier by Morell Mackenzie
The Meet of the Caravan Club [Ipswich] by Harvey Jarvis
Sidecarring From the West Counties to London by Humphrey Joel
Minor Counties Cricket (2) by Edward Sewell
Editorial [Eastbourne Tennis; Davis Cup; Australian Cricketers in America; Municipal Golf; Motor-Boating] by Walter Burton-Baldry
In the Days of the Vikings; Illustrated by Edward Reed
The Cycle and the Tourist by Charles Johnson
Kennel: Canine Ailments (2) Mange by Morell Mackenzie
Caravan and Camping Notes by Harvey Jarvis
Billiards [Losing Hazards] by Cecil Graves
With the Pleasure Fleet [Harve Regatta; Cape May Trophy; New York Yacht Club] by Ernest Hamilton
Brains and Golf by Endersly Howard
With Rod and Line [Thames Fishing; Punts; *The Field and Stream* Cup] by Hugh Sheringham; Illustrated by Wilfrid Pippet
In the Clubroom [Bridge Golf Grip; Golfing Picture Postcards; Fishing Tackle; Scottish Brogue Shoes; Portable Electric Company]; Illustrated by William Houghton

Leslie Ward   Lewis Waller   Patten Wilson

Issue 115 : October 1913 (p1-136)

Cover Design; Illustrated by Lionel Edwards
Arthur Kinnaird; Illustrated by Joseph Ginsbury
Edward Ray; Illustrated by Horace Crowther-Smith
Concentration in Golf by Edward Ray & James Bolton
Stag Driving Brocket; Illustrated by Lionel Edwards
The Wiles of the Hunted Red Deer by Henry Bryden; Illustrated by Lionel Edwards
Foiling the Line; Illustrated by Lionel Edwards
Physical Education: Systems Compared With Field Games by Charles Fry
The King of the Coverts by Alan Haig-Brown
The Coward by Ion Smeaton-Munro; Illustrated by Alfred Leete
The Cheat in Rugby Football by Edward Sewell
The Railway Dogs of England by Morell Mackenzie
Sprinting (1) by William Applegarth
Swear Not At All [verses] by McDonnell Bodkin
One Up on the Colonel by McDonnell Bodkin; Illustrated by Howard McCormick
Divers Methods of Play Through the Green by May Hezlet; Illustrated by Wilfrid Pippet
Too Killing for Words [verses] by McDonnell Bodkin
Lessons in Lacrosse (1): Stick Handling by John Hutcheon
Sidecarring From London to North Wales by Humphrey Joel
The Case for Hockey by Harold Saunders; Illustrated by Joseph Ginsbury
Tufts of Turf From Maoriland by John Wall
The Progress of Sport [Olympic Games Appeal; American Sporting Magazines; American Golf; County Cricket; Cricket Team for South Africa; Athletic Grounds; Boxing] by Walter Burton-Baldry
The Sportsman's Library [Reviews of *Motor Ways in Lakeland* by George Abraham; *Travers Golf Book* by Jerome Travers; *Quiet Roads and Sleepy Villages* by Allan Fea; *Olympian Field Events* by Frederick Webster; *Women in the Hunting Field* by Amy Menzies; *How to Play Golf* by Harry Vardon; *The Life of a Foxhound* by John Mills, Illustrated by James Shepherd] by Laurence Southeby
The Quest of Golfing Completeness by Endersly Howard
Rugby Notes [Combined Teams; Poor Fixture Arrangements; University Match at Queen's Club] by Sydney Boot
He Knew! [verses] by Millicent Hall
Billiards [Losing Hazards; Ten-Thousand Break; Thomas Reece] by Cecil Graves
Motor Retrospect and Prospect [New Fuels; Cadillac Engine Starters; *The Motor* Magazine] by Richard Hearne
With the Pleasure Fleet [British International Trophy; Owers Lightship] by Ernest Hamilton
Kennel: Canine Ailments (3) More on Mange by Morell Mackenzie
The Well-Dressed Man [Holiday Trousers; Trouser Press] by Basil Tozer; Illustrated by George Thorp
Proofing; Illustrated by David Cottington-Taylor
Caravan and Camping Notes by Clara Jarvis

In the Clubroom [Tyres; Physical Education; Autumn Clothes; Golfer's Boot Polish; Merchant Service; Golf Coats]; Illustrated by William Houghton

Issue 116 : November 1913 (p137-272)

Cover Design; Illustrated by Lionel Edwards
Thomas Bucknill; Illustrated by Joseph Ginsbury
Archibald Primrose; Illustrated by Oscar Larum
Why Britain Gets Beaten by Desmond Shaw
Pulling and Slicing at Golf by George Duncan & James Bolton
George Duncan; Illustrated by Oscar Larum
The Harlequins Rugby Football Club [Adrian Stoop, John Birkett, Geoffrey Roberts, Ronald Poulton] by Horace Crowther-Smith; Illustrated by himself
The Dogs is Gone!; Illustrated by Lionel Edwards
Michael Malony, Huntsman by Maud Haviland; Illustrated by Lionel Edwards
His Honour Himself; Illustrated by Lionel Edwards
The Wire-Haired Fox Terrier by Morell Mackenzie
The Joy of the Angle by Frederick Aflalo
Practical Approaching [Golf] by Kathleen Moore
Physical Education: The Swedish System by Charles Fry; Illustrated by William Robinson
Ancient Football: A Welsh Game of the Tudor Times; Illustrated by Lionel Edwards
The Case Against Professional Football by William Caldicott
Modern Football; Illustrated by Lionel Edwards
Sidecarring From Wales to London by Humphrey Joel
Lessons in Lacrosse (2): More On Stick Handling by John Hutcheon
Sporting Camps: Along the Kerry Shore by Harvey Jarvis
The Progress of Sport [Amateur Football Association; American Billiards Championship; Francis Ouimet; Canadian Ladies Golf; Hertfordshire Cricket; Review of *The Rugby Football Annual* by Charles Marriott; Dulwich Lawn Tennis] by Walter Burton-Baldry
Concerning County Hockey by Harold Saunders
Grit [verses] by McDonnell Bodkin
Rugby Notes [Crowd Behaviour; Rectory Field Blackheath; French Referees] by Sydney Boot
The Golfing Temperament [verses] by Reginald Arkell
The Sportsman's Library [Reviews of *My Game Book* by Alan Haig-Brown; *The Beaufort Hunting Diary* by Stuart Menzies; *How to Win at Auction Bridge* by Edwin Anthony; *Some Sporting Dogs* by Townend Barton, Illustrated by Vernon Stokes] by Laurence Southeby
With Rod and Line [Poole Harbour Bass; Highclere Water; Milford Lake] by Hugh Sheringham; Illustrated by Wilfrid Pippet
The Motor Shows by Richard Hearne
In Assyrian Times; Illustrated by Edward Reed
The Well-Dressed Man [Traveller Trouser Press; Bright Colours; Overcoats, Silk Hats] by Basil Tozer
Kennel: Canine Ailments (4) Distemper by Morell Mackenzie
With the Pleasure Fleet [Yacht Racing Association]; Illustrated by Gordon Browne
Why We Play Golf by Walter Burton-Baldry; Illustrated by Wilfrid Pippet
Billiards: The Question of the Amateur by Cecil Graves

Issue 117 : December 1913 (p273-408)

Cover Design; Illustrated by Alfred Leete
Aero Polo; Illustrated by Hugh Radcliffe-Wilson
George Coventry; Illustrated by Oscar Larum
South Africa and International Cricket by Charles Fry
Two Nursery Rhymes [verses] by Bertram Atkey
Winter Sports in Switzerland by William Cadby; Illustrated by William Robinson
Corncob Kelly's Benefit by Peter Kyne; Illustrated by John Woolrich
The Angler in Winter by Hugh Sheringham; Illustrated by Wilfrid Pippet
The Tribulations of a Golfing Cricketer by John Raphael; Illustrated by Alfred Leete
Golf Up-to-Date: The Post-Impressionist on the Golf Links; Illustrated by Oscar Larum
Some [Golf] Championship Recollections by May Hezlet; Illustrated by Wilfrid Pippet
Dog Stories and Reminiscences by Morell Mackenzie; Illustrated by Wilfrid Pippet
Tricks for the Smoking Room by Arthur Wrest; Illustrated by Wilfrid Pippet
The Sporting Parson by Lionel Edwards; Illustrated by himself
The Black Squire; Illustrated by Lionel Edwards
The Rectory Pool [with verses]; Illustrated by Lionel Edwards
Some Lawn Tennis Reminiscences by Charles Dixon
The Blackheath Rugby Club [Waldemar Craven, Harry Coverdale, Bernard Hartley,
   Charles Pillman] by Edward Sewell; Illustrated by Horace Crowther-Smith
Great Golfers On and Off the Links by Endersly Howard; Illustrated by Joseph Ginsbury
Review Essay of *The Game Fishes of the World* by Charles Holder; reviewed
   by Hugh Sheringham
The Progress of Sport [Billiards at Thurston's Hall; The *Daily Mail* Sports Pages; *Daily Chronicle*
   Review; International Boxing Union; Freak Golf Match] by Walter Burton-Baldry
In the Days of Queen Elizabeth; Illustrated by Edward Reed
The Complete [Golf] Foozler by Walter Burton-Baldry; Illustrated by Horace Crowther-Smith
The Fragrant Weed [Literature, Charles Kingsley, Francisco Fernandez; Cuban Plantations;
   Marie de la Ramee]
The Well-Dressed Man [Overcoat Pockets; Blue Frock Coats; Bow Ties] by Basil Tozer
Rugby Notes [Adrian Stoop; University Match; Queen's Club] by Sydney Boot
The Case for the Animals by George Ravenscroft
In the Clubroom [Reviews of *Hints to Dog Owners* by Alfred Sherley and *Blood Stock*
   by Hugh Clifford; Egyptian Cigarettes; Wood Milne Golf Ball; Motor Coats]
Winter Sports; Illustrated by James Shuffrey
Concerning Edward Aston by Walter Burton-Baldry

Issue 118 : January 1914 (p409-544)

Cover Design; Illustrated by Alfred Leete
Frederick Aflalo: A Wonderful Trip by Walter Burton-Baldry
The Timing of the Shot by Raymond Needham
Luging and Loafing in Switzerland by Frank Hart; Illustrated by himself
Hassayampa Jim by Peter Kyne; Illustrated by John Woolrich
The Queer Side of Boxing by Desmond Shaw; Illustrated by Henry Bateman

The Sport of Seeing the World by Frederick Aflalo
Trolling for Salmon off Vancouver Island by Stanley Rice
International Football and Rugger Crowds by Edward Sewell
The Game of Badminton by Stewart Massey
A Day's Snipe Shooting by Alfred McClelland
Bribery, Corruption and the Football Association by William Caldicott
The Art of Javelin Throwing by Frederick Webster
Sidecarring From London to Newcastle-upon-Tyne by Humphrey Joel
The Progress of Sport [County Cricket; Championship Rugby; Anthony Wilding; International Polo Cup; Frank Wootton; Athletics; Bias Newspaper Reporting] by Walter Burton-Baldry
The Sportsman's Library [Reviews of *A Vagabond in New York* by Oliver Hueffer; *The New Man* by Philip Gibbs; *The New Foresters* by William Caine; *A Tour in Touraine* by Raymond Needham; *A Year With a Whaler* by Walter Burns; *The Complete Amateur Boxer* by Bohun Lynch
A Duck Shoot on the Queensland Border by John Hutcheon
Rugby Notes [International Trial Matches; Dublin University Rugby] by Sydney Boot
The Laurel Crown; Illustrated by Edward Reed
Norway and Her Winter Sports by Harvey Jarvis
Golfing Problemania [The Rules of Golf Committee] by Endersly Howard
That Forty-Pounder Pike by Edgar Shrubsole
Billiards [Melbourne Inman; Matchplay Tournaments] by Cecil Graves
In the Clubroom [Billiard Tables; Rainproof Coats]; Illustrated by William Houghton

Issue 119 : February 1914 (p545-672)

Cover Design; Illustrated by Horace Crowther-Smith
Wake Up England; Illustrated by Christopher Clark
Flying: The New Sport by Claude Grahame-White
The Length of the [Golf] Upswing by Raymond Needham; Illustrated by Joseph Ginsbury
The Stalking Horse by Claude Scudamore-Jarvis; Illustrated by Alfred Leete
Concerning Winter Yachting by Ernest Hamilton; Illustrated by Edward Wigfull
Curling: A Game of Infinite Variety by Bertram Smith
The Deerhound by Morell Mackenzie
Figure Skating: English or International by Humphry Cobb
The Song of the Bobsleigh [verses]
Some Chinese Games and Sports by Leopold Katscher
The Possibilities of Drag Hunting by Basil Tozer
Hockey in Many Climes by Harold Saunders
Richmond Rugby Football Club [Robert Goodman, Lawrence Langton, Philip Lawless, Henry Oglethorpe] by Horace Crowther-Smith
Boxing: A Board of Control by Vivian Hollender
Hard Courts and Hard Court Play by Alfred Beamish
Bill Heenan Kidnapper by William McNutt; Illustrated by Alfred Leete
The Progress of Sport [Myth of Anglo-Saxon Superiority; Rhodes Scholars; Australian Cricket Board of Control; Golf in India]

Rugby Notes [Aggressive Play; England Selections; Irish Success] by Sydney Boot
Review of *Gardens for Small Country Houses* by Gertrude Jekyll and Laurence Weaver
Winter Sports in Sweden by Harvey Jarvis
Tempora Mutantur [verses] by Richard Keigwin
In the Clubroom [Charles Tuckey; Sporting Breeches; *Tailor and Cutter* Magazine; Golfer's Pen; Typewriters; Humber Car Company]; Illustrated by William Houghton

Issue 120 : March 1914 (p673-808)

Cover Design; Illustrated by Lionel Edwards
De Mortuis and So On [verses] by Walter Burton-Baldry
Touring by Air by Claude Grahame-White
I Had a Little Motor by Bertram Atkey
The 1916 Olympic Games by Walter Burton-Baldry; Illustrated by George Thorp
A Unique Family of [Lyttelton] Brothers by George Wade
The Billiards Championship [Melbourne Inman; Thomas Reece; George Gray, Harry Stevenson] by Cecil Graves
A Record Basket by Claude Scudamore-Jarvis; Illustrated by Alfred Leete
Laurels for Amateurs by Bohun Lynch
Blessed is He [Golf]; Illustrated by Inder Burns
The Lure of the Links by Alfred Swoyer; Illustrated by Rollin Kirby
James Sutherland: Ivory Hunter by George Ravenscroft
A Day's Beagling by Algernon Thompson; Illustrated by himself
The Greatest Steeplechase by Arthur Coaten; Illustrated by Wilfrid Pippet
The Bull-Terrier by Charles Adair-Dighton
Language Repeats Itself [verses] by McDonnell Bodkin
Sidecarring From Newcastle-upon-Tyne to Inverness by Humphrey Joel
Down the Belgian Coast and Across the Channel in a Seven-Ton Yacht (1) by Charles Pears; Illustrated by himself
Golf and Bad Sportsmanship by Bertram Atkey; Illustrated by Harry Rountree
The Progress of Sport [Patriotism; Amateur Football Association; *Washington Post* Article; Review of *Golf For the Late Beginner* by Henry Hughes; English Polo Team; Boxer Aaron Brown; Casper Whitney editor of *The Outdoor World*; National Sporting Club and Jack Johnson Letter]
Rugby Notes [*Football Evening News* article; Home International Matches; County Championship] by Sydney Boot
Quebec and Its Sports by Alexander Clements
Cars for Sportsmen: The Overland by Walter Burton-Baldry
Wonderful Flying; Illustrated by Cyrus Cuneo
Golf and the Weather (1) by Walter Burton-Baldry
Golfers' Gear; Illustrated by William Robinson
Outdoor Dress [Old Clothes; Country Wear; Breeches; Personality in Clothes] by George Armstrong
The Schlern by Clarence Elliott
Can Dog-Keeping be Made to Pay? by Morell Mackenzie

Travel Notes [St.Just-in-Roseland; Yachting Cruises; Trunks] by James Scott
Spring Cruises; Illustrated by Charles Harrison
Turf Topics [Rising Value of Bloodstock; Doncaster Sales; French Bred Horses] by Thomas Henry Browne
Science and Physical Fitness by Edward Aston
In the Clubroom [Safety Razors; Business Training; Dunlop Golf Ball]

Caspar Whitney

Herman Whitaker

William Wyllie

Volume 21

Issue 121 : April 1914 (p1-136)

Cover Design; Illustrated by Alfred Leete
The Making of the Golfer (1) by Henry Hughes & Henry Leach
Somerset: The Land of Sport by George Badcock
The Services [Rugby] by Edward Sewell
Dunkerque Harbour by Night; Illustrated by Charles Pears
Down the Belgian Coast and Across the Channel in a Seven-Ton Yacht (2) by Charles Pears; Illustrated by himself
In Mid-Channel at Midnight; Illustrated by Charles Pears
Review of *From the Thames to the Netherlands* by Charles Pears
Trout Fishing by Alan Haig-Brown
Joy Ranching by Jesse Williams
Slogging Around Burnham [Golf] by Hall Thorpe; Illustrated by himself
On Playing Lawn Tennis at Nice [verses] by Walter Burton-Baldry
Learning to Fly by Claude Grahame-White
The Boat Race by Charles Thomas
Baseball in England and America by George Ravenscroft
Lawn Tennis Tournaments by Alfred Beamish & Cecil Hartley
Sport in Kerry by Harvey Jarvis
Personalities of the Rugby Season [Jack Bancroft, Leonard Brown, Alban Davies, William Johnston, Richard Lloyd, Ronald Poulton, John Will] by Sydney Boot
The Progress of Sport [Readers Complaints About Excessive Golf Articles; Baseball; English Cricket Team in South Africa; Bad Sportsmanship; Billiards; All England Tennis Club Enquiry] by Charles Fry
An Episode of the Boat Race by Lechmere Worrall
The Australian Countryside and its Sport by Henry Gullett
Outdoor Dress [Lounge Suits; Sporting Overcoats; Flannels] by George Armstrong; Illustrated by Joseph Ginsbury
Turf Topics [Grand Military Meeting; Cheltenham National Hunt Races] by Thomas Henry Browne
Travel Notes [Guildhall Conference; James Glover; Yachting Centre; Hampshire Trout Streams; Ascot Racecourse] by Arthur Anderson
Motoring [Design and Construction] by Thomas Beacham
Golf and the Weather (2) by Walter Burton-Baldry; Illustrated by Wilfrid Pippet
Lawn Tennis [Poor Club Organisation; Tennis Leagues] by Cecil Graves
With Rod and Line [Stores' Tackle Departments; Spider Web Fishing Lines; Aerial Reel] by Edgar Shrubsole
Caravan and Camping Notes by Harvey Jarvis
In the Clubroom [Photography; Rain-Proof Coats; Silver Polish]; Illustrated by William Houghton

Issue 122 : May 1914 (p137-276)

Cover Design; Illustrated by Cyrus Cuneo
Johnny Douglas by Charles Fry
Cricket! [verses] by Digby Jephson
Fishing in Equatorial Africa (1): Sea Fishing at Mombasa by Frederick Aflalo
The Making of the Golfer (2) by Henry Hughes & Henry Leach
Sprinting (2) by William Applegarth
A Fisherman's Petition [verses]
Famous Derby Finishes by Arthur Coaten
Sanity and County Cricket by Charles Fry
Science in Lawn Tennis: The Backhand Stroke by Alfred Beamish
The Aerial Derby by Claude Grahame-White
Cyril Arthur Pearson by Charles Fry; Illustrated by William Robinson
Personalities in Golf: William McClure and Harold Gillies by John Bruce-Kerr
The Game [verses] by Digby Jephson
Cricket in South Africa [Further Comments on the English Cricket Team: Extracts from the *Bloemfontein Friend; Natal Advertiser* and *Transvaal Leader*]
Our Point of View [William Stead; Joseph McCormick; Monaco Aerial Rally; Sheffield Handicap Runners; International Boxing Union; Cecil Rhodes; Josiah Ritchie; French Rugby; Francis Lacey; Jack Shuter; Olympic Games] by Charles Fry
The Three Strengths; Illustrated by Leo Cheney
The Colour of Salmon and Trout Flies by Bertram Glossop
Motoring [Two-Stroke Lightweight Motorcycle; Electric Lighting for Cars; Edison Battery] by Thomas Beacham
Travel Notes [Early Holidays; French Riviera; West Highlands] by Arthur Anderson
Norman Brookes and the Davis Cup by Walter Burton-Baldry
Memories; Illustrated by Philip Ebbutt
Golf Notes [Review of *The Book of Golf* by Henry Leach] by Walter Burton-Baldry
Camping and Caravanning: Ways and Means by Harvey Jarvis
Turf Topics [Lincolnshire Handicap; Liverpool Spring Cup; Greenham Stakes] by Thomas Henry Browne
Clubroom Gossip [House of Lords Betting Bill; Graphophones; Golfing Footwear; The Tan Yard]
Guide to the Theatre [Twenty-Five Reviews] by Walter Burton-Baldry

Issue 123 : June 1914 (p277-412)

Cover Design; Illustrated by Alfred Leete
Martin Hawke; Illustrated by Thomas Browne
Martin Hawke: Marylebone Cricket Club President by Charles Fry
Hawke [verses] by Henry Newbolt
Anthony Wilding by Walter Burton-Baldry; Illustrated by Oscar Larum and Alfred Leete
The Last Hole [verses] by McDonnell Bodkin
There's A Cry [verses] by Robert Service
The Lure of Little Voices [verses] by Grantland Rice
The Making of the Golfer (3) by Henry Hughes & Henry Leach

Frederick Smith by Charles Fry; Illustrated by Henry Mather, Percy Fearon, Francis Carruthers-Gould & George Thorp
The Winning of the America's Cup by Charles Gaunt
Fishing in Equatorial Africa (2): Trout Fishing in the Aberdares by Frederick Aflalo
The Davis Cup: Australasia's Chances by Stanley Doust
Salting a Shoot by Claude Scudamore-Jarvis; Illustrated by Alfred Leete
Personalities in Golf: Francis Ouimet by John Bruce-Kerr
The Lured Trout by Sydney Smith
Science in Lawn Tennis: The Forehand Stroke by James Parke
International Polo by Edward Miller
Our Point of View [Obituary of Reginald Foster; Polo; River Dart Fishing; Montague Shearman; *The American Cricketer* Magazine; *Sydney Sportsman* Article; French Sport; Surbiton Tennis; Amateur Golf Championship; Football Association Finances] by Charles Fry
The Champion; Illustrated by Charles Gibson
Dogs Trained for Useful Purposes by Edwin Richardson
The Wisdom of the Unwise; Illustrated by Leo Cheney
Outdoor Dress [Review of *The Man of Today* by Dennis Bradley; Women's Dress Sense; Soft Collars] by George Armstrong; Illustrated by John Hassall
Fish versus Fishing by Edgar Shrubsole
The Social Side of Golf: English County Societies Tournament by George Ravenscroft
Motoring [Royal Automobile Club Light Car Trial; The Swift Cycle Car] by Thomas Beacham
Ante-Post Betting Returns Exposed: The Making of the Market
From Start to Finish; Illustrated by Frederick Pegram
The River [Skiffs; Thames Punting Club; Tamesis Club; Royal Canoe Club] by Charles Thomas
In the Clubroom [Nerve Tonic; Rainproof Materials; Thames Angling Preservation Society]; Illustrated by William Houghton
Guide to the Theatre by Walter Burton-Baldry

Issue 124 : July 1914 (p413-540)

Cover Design; Illustrated by Alfred Leete
The Lure of Photography by Clifford Leigh
A Lady Golfer; Illustrated by Frederick Pegram
Albert Henry Hornby by Charles Fry
The Jungfrau by Thomas Legard
A Lawn Tennis Theorist at Large [Review Essay of *The Book of the Ball* by Ernest Crawley] by Edward Sewell
Camping DeLuxe by Arthur Johnson
Henley From the Pressbox by Charles Thomas
The Heart of the Shadow by Roy Cohen; Illustrated by Sidney Pride
Gustav Hamel Aviator by Walter Burton-Baldry
The Making of the Golfer (4) by Henry Hughes & Henry Leach
Four Polo Studies by Herbert Haseltine
Stanley Doust; Illustrated by Horace Crowther-Smith
Science in Lawn Tennis: Volleying by Stanley Doust

Fishing in Equatorial Africa (3): A Safari to the Yala River by Frederick Aflalo
The Humours of Golf by George Warner; Illustrated by Alfred Leete
From Inverness to John O'Groats by Humphrey Joel
George Hillyard; Illustrated by Horace Crowther-Smith
Our Point of View [Polo; Review of *A Lawn Tennis Alphabet* by Horace Crowther-Smith; Boxing] by Charles Fry
Wallis Myers; Illustrated by Horace Crowther-Smith
Golf in China by Hobart Mills
Review of *Sport in Switzerland* by Edward Benson
Luring the Lively Lythe by Edgar Shrubsole
Lawn Tennis by Herbert McDonald
Clothes and the Man [Lounge Jackets; Rainproof Cloth; Bowler Hats; Seaside Fishing] by George Armstrong; Illustrated by William Houghton
Turf Topics: Carbine [Taken from *Land and Water*]
Motoring [Motor Advertising] by Charles Fry
In the Clubroom [Auto-Wheels; Trunks; Golf Coats]; Illustrated by William Houghton

Issue 125 : August 1914 (p541-668)

Cover Design; Illustrated by Alfred Leete
Golf Talk by Walter Burton-Baldry
Motorcycling: The Wall Auto-Wheel
An Innovation by William Irving-Hamilton
Angling; Illustrated by Frederick Pegram
Ernest Shackleton's Dogs by Morell Mackenzie
What Money Can't Buy; Illustrated by Raeburn van Buren
Fishing in Equatorial Africa (4): With a Seine Net in Victoria Nyanza by Frederick Aflalo
Walter Winans; Illustrated by Alfred Leete
The Skiff Racing Season by Charles Thomas
Difficulties With Golf by William Wright
Frederick 'Welsh' Thomas by Eugene Corri
Alderson's Easy Job by Frederick Bechdolt; Illustrated by Sidney Pride
Lawn Tennis: Some Reflections on Wimbledon by Charles Fry; Illustrated by George Thorp
With the Border Counties; Illustrated by Lionel Edwards
Otter Hunting in North Wales by Lioned Edwards; Illustrated by himself
A Typical Mountain Stream; Illustrated by Lionel Edwards
The Joy of Putting by Raymond Needham
Golfing Proverbs by Gerald Batchelor
From Coop to Covert by Leonard Willoughby
To the End of the Road: From Delhi to Peshawar by Stanley Rice
The Eden Course at St.Andrews by George Meiklejohn
Summer on the Ouse by Cuthbert Corbould-Ellis; Illustrated by George Thorp
From Beauly to Glencoe by Humphrey Joel
Traveller's Tales by Mark Perety
Some Salmon Hatcheries in the South of Ireland by Mary Grehan

Our Point of View [English Sport; Anthony Wilding; Joseph Chamberlain; Boxing Promoters; Edward Smith; Georges Carpentier; Alfred Gardiner editor *Daily News*] by Charles Fry
With Rod and Line: A Place Called Goring by Edgar Shrubsole
Concerning Golf Coats by George Armstrong
Clothes and the Man [Review of *Hints on Golf* by Harry Vardon; Cricket Trousers; Golf Suits; Irish Army Uniforms; *Tailor and Cutter* Report; *Valetry* Periodical] by George Armstrong; Illustrated by William Houghton
Rufford Jacket; Illustrated by Gladys Reid
Golf Stories by Gerald Batchelor reviewed by George Ravenscroft
Turf Topics: Two-Year-Olds [Taken From *Truth Weekly*]
Motoring: The Roads of Great Britain by Wilfred Aston [Taken From *The Autocar*]
Lawn Tennis: The Value of Volleying by Walter Burton-Baldry
Can Dog-Keeping Be Made to Pay? by Morell Mackenzie
Learning to Shoot by Henry Ford
In the Clubroom [Pipe-Smoking; Shirt Patterns; Ultra-Violet Rays; Tourist Trophy Races]

Issue 125 (Final Issue)

LEADING WRITERS

The following writers provided series, stories and essays for the magazine over its one hundred and twenty-five issues. A few became famous over time while others slipped into oblivion after their work had been published. Some of the fictional characters created by these authors are still referred to today, over a century later, with virtually no one being aware of their origin.

Although many reference sources have been used in the production of this book there are still a number of names for which no detail is available. Some may be their real names; others might be nom-de-plumes: who knows after so many years. However, they are listed here for information and reference purposes.

ABRAHAM, George Dixon (1870-1965; climber, author, photographer; wrote twelve books; also in *Badminton, Cassell's, Cosmopolitan, Cornhill, Graphic, Gunter's, Harmsworth's, McClure's, Pearson's, Pall Mall, Strand, Windsor* and *Wide World*): Vols.15,17,19,20

AFLALO, Frederick George (1870-1918; author and traveller; also in *Chamber's, London, Cornish, English Illustrated, Badminton, Sievier's, Captain, Land & Water, Baily's, Pall Mall, Windsor, Cornhill* and *Boy's Own Paper*): Vols.1-3,5-8,11,13,15-21

ALEXANDER, Henry (author, journalist and editor; also in *Novel, Royal, Pearson's* and *Pall Mall*): Vol.11

ALEXANDER, Miriam (b.1879; author of historical novels and stories with Irish settings; won literary awards; also in *Badminton, Grand, Strand* and *Pall Mall*): Vols.6,12

ALLISON, William (1851-1925; pen-name The Special Commissioner; sporting journalist, author and barrister; managing director of The International Horse Agency & Exchange; also in *The Sportsman* and *Badminton*): Vol.9

AMHERST, Mary Rothes Margaret (1857-1919; hereditary peer, author, archaeologist, ornithologist): Vol.17

ANDERSON, Arthur Henry (b.1867; writer, editor, author; editor of both the *Homeland Guides* and *Where to Live Round London*; wrote sixty books; also in *Royal*): Vols.15-19,21

ANTHONY, Edwyn (1843-1932; pen-name Cut Cavendish; author and barrister; founder Oxford University Chess Club; wrote four books; also in *Badminton*): Vols.18,20

ARKELL, Reginald (1881-1959; script-writer, comic novelist, journalist, poet, dramatist and author; composed musical plays for the theatre; wrote thirty-two books; contributor to *Daily Mail* and *Daily Express*; also in *Pall Mall, Strand, Men Only, Grand, Bystander, Cassell's, Pan, Captain, Argosy, London, Pearson's, Novel, Windsor* and *London Opinion*. Vol.20

ARMSTRONG, Francis Philip (1871-1944; General Manager of the Royal Automobile Club; barrister and journalist; son of a newspaper proprietor; chairman of Motor Yacht Club): Vols.1-3

ARNOLD, Edwin Lester Linden (1857-1935; traveller and journalist; also in *Atalanta, Boy's Own Paper, Chamber's, Cornhill, Leslie's, Collier's, Cavalier, Harper's, Captain, Fores's, Belgravia; Idler, London, Pall Mall, Nash's* and *Windsor*): Vol.2

ATHORPE, Marmaduke (1872-1921; writer and landowner; also in *Red, Pearson's, Grand* and *Novel*): Vol.8

ATKEY, Bertram (1879-1952; pen-names J.Bird and Judson Bolt; author, poet, book editor, magazine writer; twenty-eight books published; also in *Adventure, Blue, Collier's, Corner, Idler, Cassell's, Cavalier, Crampton's, Elk's, Happy Mag, Lloyd's, London, Green, Grand, New, Novel, Pearson's, Popular, Yellow, Windsor, Outing, Red, Top Notch, Strand, Tatler* and *Saturday Evening Post*): Vols.P,2-15,18-20

ATKINS, Francis Henry (1840-1927; pen-names Frank St.Mars, Fenton Ash, Fred Ashley and Frank Aubrey; always known as Frank; had fourteen books published; many serials and stories in *Boys' Realm, Union Jack, Novel, Fores's, Argosy, Pearson's, Boys' Friend, English Illustrated; Munsey's, London, Red, Pluck, Chums, Yes or No, Eureka* and *Captain*; was the film critic of a London Sunday newspaper. Vols.11,13

ATLAY, James Beresford (1860-1912; barrister and writer; nine books; editor of *Hall's International Law*; also in *Cornhill*): Vols.5,13

BACCHUS, George Reginald (1874-1945; author, journalist and playwright; also in *Society* and *Ludgate*): Vol.6

BAKER, Ernest Albert (1869-1941; librarian, author, journalist, book editor; books on caving; also in *Red, Temple Bar* and *English Illustrated*): Vol.16

BAKER, Ray Stannard (1870-1946; author and journalist; pen-name David Grayson; started on *Chicago News-Record* then to *McClure's*; founded *The American Magazine* in 1907; also in *Collier's, Idler, Cosmopolitan, Munsey's, Harper's, Pearson's, London, Windsor, Strand* and *English Illustrated*): Vol.4

BARCLAY, Armiger (1886-1964; real name Marguerite Florence Laura Jarvis; among many pen-names were Oliver Sandys and Helene Barcynska; author, screenwriter and actress; also in *Cassell's, Grand, Tale-Teller, Novel, London, Top Notch, Pearson's, Strand, Novel, Sievier's, Royal, Pall Mall* and *London Opinion*): Vol.13

BARNES-AUSTIN, Edgar Harold Spedding (1862-1962; author and artist; pen-name Wynton Locke; also in *Grand, Captain* and *Windsor*): Vols.4,5,8,9

BARR, James (1862-1923; pen-name Angus Evan Abbot; author and short story writer; also in *Ainslee's, Appleton's, Blue, Chicago Leger, Cassell's, Grand, Idler, Red, Pearson's, Yellow, Ludgate, London, Sovereign, New, Hampton's, Popular, Novel, Royal, Strand* and *Saturday Evening Post*): Vols.9-11,13,14

BARROW, Kathleen Marion (1870-1952; novelist and journalist; fashion writer on *The Times*; numerous books; also in *John O'London's, Lloyd's* and *Windsor*): Vol.4

BARTON, Frank Townsend (1869-1948; author, veterinary surgeon, journalist; numerous books on animals; also in *Baily's, The Field, Scottish Farmer, Home, Gamekeeper* and *Badminton*): Vols.8,11-13

BAZLEY, James Henry Royston (1872-1933; angler, specimen hunter, writer and angling administrator; wrote eight books; also in *Fishing Gazette, Anglers News* and *Yorkshire Evening Post*): Vols.8,9,13,14

BEACH, Rex Ellingwood (1877-1949; novelist, playwright, author, Olympic water polo medalist; had thirty-five books published; wrote thirty-seven film scripts; on *Boston Sunday Globe*; also in *Appleton's, American, Argosy, Britannia, Country Gentleman, Collier's, Cosompolitan, Everybody's, Esquire, Hutchinson's, Hampton's, Hearst's, Lippincott's, Liberty, Leslie's, McClure's, Nash's, Piccadilly, Popular, Red, Smart Set* and *Saturday Evening Post*): Vol.18

BEACH-THOMAS, William (1868-1957; author and journalist; wrote numerous books about the countryside; reported for *Daily Mail, The Observer, Spectator, Country Life, The Globe, Outlook, Saturday Review, Times Literary Supplement* and *Daily Mirror*; also in *Atlantic, Cornhill, London* and *Strand*): Vol.3

BECHDOLT, Frederick Ritchie (1874-1950; fiction writer; also in *Adventure, Argosy, Blue, Cosmopolitan, Cassell's, Everybody's, Esquire, Green, Grand, Harper's, Liberty, McClure's, Nash's, New, Pearson's, Popular, Pall Mall, Smith's, Sunset, Red, Watson's* and *Saturday Evening Post*): Vol.21

BEGBIE, Edward Harold (1871-1929; author and journalist; on *The Globe*; also in *Strand, London, Pall Mall, Quiver, Cornhill, Printers' Pie, Grand, Pearson's, Butterfly, Ludgate, Temple Bar, Cassell's, Nash's* and *Boy's Own Paper*): Vols.1-6,10

BELDAM, George William (1868-1937; photographer, cricketer, artist and author; pioneer of action photography; also in *Cassell's, Captain* and *Baily's*): Vols.1-5,10,11

BELFORT, Roland (stockbroker and author; also in *Grand, Ludgate, Strand* and *Windsor*): Vol.9

BELL, Robert Stanley Warren (1871-1921; pen-names Hawkesley Brett and W.W.Mayland; author, writer, journalist on *London Evening News*; contributor to *Daily Mail*; then first editor of *Captain*; in *Chums, Grand, Windsor, Novel, Cassell's, Boy's Own Paper, Strand, London* and *Tit-Bits*): Vols.P,1,3,5-7,11,12,14

BELLOC, Joseph Hilaire Pierre Rene (1870-1953; poet, author, writer, politician; wrote over one-hundred and fifty books; also in *Argosy, Bellman, Britannia, John Bull, John O'London's, Radio Times, London, Land & Water, Pearson's, Nash's, Men Only, Pall Mall, Temple Bar* and *Saturday Evening Post*): Vol.15

BENNION, Benjamin (1877-1952; author and journalist; on *The Field* and *Fishing Gazette*; also in *Pearson's, Badminton, Men Only* and *Britannia*): Vol.4

BENSON, Claude Ernest (1863-1932; mountaineer; also in *Cornhill, Yellow, Red, Novel, Pearson's, Royal, Lloyd's, Cassell's, Argosy, Strand, Nash's, Badminton, Idler, Hutchinson's, Temple Bar, London* and *Pall Mall*): Vols.1,6

BEST, George Alfred (also in *Strand, Harmsworth's, Cassell's, English Illustrated, Royal, Pearson's, Captain, London* and *Windsor*): Vol.2

BETTINSON, Arthur Frederick (1862-1926; pugilist, co-founder of the National Sporting Club, promoter, author of books on boxing): Vol.11

BLACK, Ladbroke Lionel Day (1877-1940; pen-names John Andrew, Lionel Day and Paul Urquhart; assistant editor of *The Phoenix*, then *Morning Herald, The Echo* and *Weekly Dispatch*; editor of *Today*; also in *Union Jack, English Illustrated, Cassell's, Novel, London, Magnet* and *Grand*): Vols.P,6,14

BLACKWOOD, Algernon Henry (1869-1951; journalist, short story writer, novelist, playwright, broadcasting narrator; on staff of *New York Evening Sun* and *New York Times*; contributed to *Westminster Gazette*, *London Evening Standard* and *Daily Express*; told stories on BBC radio and television; also in *Argosy, Canadian, Century, Cassell's, Country Life, Boy's Own Paper, Windsor, Lilliput, McBride's, Novel, Pall Mall, Nash's Harper's Bazar, Radio Times, McCall's, Outlook, Lloyd's, Pearson's, Land & Water, McClure's, Golden, London, Strand* and *Bystander*): Vol.11

BLAKE, Francis William Stacey (1873-1964; started as a black-and-white artist before moving to writing; worked for Newnes, Pearson, Cassell and Thomson magazines with many of his stories appearing in *Big Budget* and *London*; later he was mainly in *Penny Pictorial, Chums, Captain, Golden, Premier, Happy Mag, Union Jack, Pearson's* and *Boys' Friend*): Vols.6,14

BLAND, Lilian (1878-1971; sports journalist and press photographer; pioneer aviator; on *Daily Mail* and *Belfast Telegraph*; also in *Badminton, Country Life, Tatler* and *Fores's*): Vols.10,12

BLATCHFORD, Robert Peel Glanville (1851-1943; journalist, author, campaigner; on *The Yorkshireman, Bells Life in London, Sunday Chronicle, Fortnightly Review* and *Daily Mail*; contributed to *Manchester Sporting Chronicle*; founded and edited *The Clarion*; also in *Argosy, Idler, Land & Water, London* and *Grand*): Vols.P,9,15

BLATHWAYT, Raymond (1855-1935; author and journalist on *Daily News*; also in *Black and White, Cassell's, English Illustrated, Green, Idler, Sievier's, McClure's, Pearson's, Ludgate, Windsor, Royal, Pall Mall* and *Strand*): Vol.1

BLUMENFELD, Ralph David (1864-1948; author, journalist, writer, editor; on *Chicago Herald, New York Morning Journal* and *New York Herald*; editor of both *Daily Mail* and *Daily Express*; BBC radio broadcaster; also in *Munsey's, John O'London's; Pearson's, Nash's* and *Harper's*): Vol.18

BODKIN, Mattias McDonnell (1850-1933; pen-name Crom-a-Boo; author, journalist and editor of various Irish newspapers; a barrister and parliamentarian; also in *Royal, Novel, Pearson's, Pan, Harmworth's, Strand, London, Everybody's, Smart Set, Grand, Blue* and *Cornhill*): Vols.3,10,12,19-21

BOLTON, James Thomas (pen-names Derek Ash and John Grey; a prominent Fleet Street writer and agent who ghosted articles and stories which were reputed to have come from those in the world of sport; on staff *Bolton Evening News, Cassells, Associated Press*; editor of *Blighty*, the forces newspaper, as well as being chairman of the London Press Club; founded Football & All Sports Press Agency; wrote boys stories for *Magnet, Modern Boy, London, Captain, Boy's Own Paper* and *Chums*): Vols.1,3-9,11-13,15,16,18-20

BONNETT, Frank (pen-name East Sussex; author, naturalist and athletics writer; also in *Baily's, Badminton, Country Life* and *Fores's*): Vols.10-18

BOSANQUET, Bernard James Tindal (1877-1936; cricketer for Oxford University, Middlesex and England; businessman; also in *Cassell's* and *Pall Mall*): Vol.5

BRADY, Cyrus Townsend (1861-1920; pen-name Wainwright Evesson; journalist, historian and adventure writer; wrote sixty-eight books; also in *Cassell's, Collier's, Munsey's, Smith's, Pearson's, New, Lippincott's, Ainslee's, Scribner's, Metropolitan, Idler, Red, Cavalier, McClure's, Cosmopolitan, Argosy, Harper's Bazar, Century* and *Saturday Evening Post*): Vols.P,8,11

BRAID, James (1870-1950; golfer; open championship winner; golf course architect; also in *Badminton, Lloyd's, Pearson's* and *Strand*): Vols.6,7

BRANDON, David (writer and playwright; also in *Idler, Bystander, Vanity Fair, Novel* and *Grand*): Vols.8,10

BRANN, George (1865-1954; played cricket for Sussex; football for England, Corinthians and Slough Town; for many years secretary of Home Park Golf Club in Surbiton; also in *Chums*): Vols.1,3-6

BRIDGES, Thomas Charles (1868-1944; pen-names Martin Shaw, Christopher Beck and John Stanton; born in France and lived in America until residing in London from 1894; initially contributed to *The Field*, then *Answers* where he became a sub-editor; wrote serials for *Boys' Realm* then for *Boy's Own Paper, Boys' Life, Scout, Cassell's, Badminton, Strand, Chamber's, Crusoe, Novel, Red, Windsor, Yellow, Lloyd's, Captain, Golden, Grand, London, Union Jack* and *Magnet*): Vols.9,15

BRISTOW-NOBLE, John Charles (author; also in *Boy's Own Paper, Badminton, Chatterbox, Chums, Fores's, Detective* and *Pall Mall*): Vols.8-11,13,14,17

BROWN, Charles Hilton (1890-1961; author, novelist, poet; also in *Argosy, Blackwood's, Britannia, Cornhill, Hutchinson's, Punch, Grand, Printers' Pie* and *Strand*): Vol.11

BROWN, Frederick Walworth (1875-1959; fiction writer; also in *Appleton's, Argosy, Blue, Century, Everybody's, Top Notch, Red, Pearson's, Smith's, Harper's* and *Metropolitan*): Vol.11

BROWNLEE, Leigh Dunlop (1882-1955; cricketer, schoolmaster, author and journalist; cricket for Oxford University, Gloucestershire and Somerset; news editor then editor of *Daily Mirror*; partner in a News Agency): Vol.12

BRUCE-MITFORD, Eustace (b.1875; journalist, geographer, author, vulcanologist; in *Athenaeum* and various academic journals): Vol.16

BRYDEN, Henry Anderson (1854-1937; pen-name Rallywood; author, writer, book editor; rugby international, athlete, traveller, solicitor, naturalist; wrote eleven books; also in *Cornhill, Badminton, Chambers's, Cricketer, English Illustrated, Fores's, Holly Leaves, Lippincott's, Longman's, Pall Mall, Novel, Temple Bar, Strand* and *Windsor*): Vols.2,16,20

BUCKLAND, James Charles (author and writer; in *Journal of the Royal Society of Arts*; also in *English Illustrated, Longman's, Pall Mall* and *Strand*): Vol.15

BUCKMASTER, Walter Selby (1872-1942; double Polo Olympian; Master of Warwickshire Hounds; City of London banker; also in *Baily's*): Vol.1

BUTLER, Ellis Parker (1869-1937; pen-names Sage Vesey and Zenda Warde; bank manager, author, poet but mainly a fiction writer; wrote thirty-five books and over two-thousand two hundred stories for two-hundred and twenty-five magazines; main publications were *Boston Sunday Globe, Chicago Leger, Saturday Evening Post* and *New Yorker*; also in *Ainslee's, Argosy, Appleton's, Atlantic, Black Cat, American, Boys' Life, Cavalier, Century, Cosmopolitan, Collier's, Everybody's, Esquire, Grand, Girl's Own Paper, Gaiety, Harper's, Holland's, Hampton's, Idler, London, Leslie's, Liberty, Lippincott's, London Opinion, Metropolitan, McClure's, Maclean's, McBride's, McCall's, Munsey's, Novel, Pall Mall, Putman's, Royal, Pearson's, Popular, Pan, Red, Smart Set, Smith's, Strand, Sketch, Sovereign, Windsor* and many others): Vol.14

BURROW, Francis Russell (1866-1945; barrister, journalist and author; on *Observer* and *Times*; also in *Bystander, Pearson's, Pan, Strand, Passing Show, Badminton* and *Punch*): Vol.5

BURTON-BALDRY, Walter: (see Preliminary pages): Vols.P,1,16-21

BUSSY, George Francis Philip (1871-1933; reporter, sporting editor, war correspondent and literary editor of *Westminster Gazette* for over thirty-five years, then editor of *Civil & Military Gazette*; also in *Pearson's*): Vols.1,4

CADBY, Carine (1871-1957; real name Katharine Mary Simpson Stevenson; children's writer and photographer; also in *Graphic, Lady's Realm, Pall Mall* and *Royal*): Vol.12

CADBY, William (1866-1937; husband of Carine; photographer, writer, author; also in *Lady's Realm* and *Pall Mall*): Vol.20

CADE, Laurence Herbert (1889-1969; author and motoring journalist; on *The Star* for over forty years; also in *Motor Sport, Autocar, Automobile Engineer, Automobile Journal* and *Light Car & Cyclecar*) Vols.18,19

CAMERON, Ludovick Charles Richard (1866-1947; pen-name Charles Hewson; born Richard Duncombe Jewell, became Louis Charles Richard Duncombe-Jewell; books on otterhunting, angling and yachting; on *The Times, Pall Mall Gazette, Morning Post* and *Daily Mail*; also in *St.James's, Sketch, Globe, Black & White, Britannia, Baily's, Fores's* and *Badminton*): Vols.6,9,10,13

CAMERON, William Ernest (1881-1939; pen-name Mark Allerton; author and barrister; also in *Cavalier, Canadian, Captain, Grand, Top Notch, Pearson's, Sovereign, Baily's, Lloyd's, Pall Mall* and *Sketch*): Vol.19

CARLISLE, Richard (1865-1941; author and journalist; seven books, mainly on horse breeding; columnist on *The Field* and *Land & Water*; also in *Badminton* and *Baily's*): Vol.3

CARRUTHERS, Thomas (1840-1924; surgeon, golf club creator and golf course designer; books on golf clubs and urology): Vols.10,11

CHAFY, Ralph Evelyn Westwood (1884-1949; poet; British Consul in Morocco; also in *Grand, Novel, Pall Mall, Pearson's* and *Royal*): Vol.10

CHAMBERLAIN, Lucia (1882-1978; author; also in *Ainslee's, Appleton's, Century, Cosmopolitan, Everybody's, Putnam's, Red, Smart Set, Scribner's, Metropolitan* and *Saturday Evening Post*): Vol.5

CHANNON, Frank Ernest (1870-1920; fiction writer; on *Boston Globe*; also in *Chicago Leger, Popular* and *Century*): Vol.12

CHASE, Clifford Hoffman (1870-1935; poet and fiction writer; also in *Leslie's, Windsor* and *New England Magazine*): Vol.1

CHETWYND-TALBOT, Charles Henry John (1860-1921; formed the Staffordshire Polo Club; ran the Greyhound coach service; started the Noiseless Tyre Company; founded Talbot Car Company): Vol.1

CHISHOLM, Hugh (1866-1924; journalist, editor, literary critic; editor of *St.James's Gazette, The Times* and *London Evening Standard*; also in *English Illustrated*): Vol.16

CHRISTIAN, Edmund Brown Viney (1864-1938; solicitor and author; books on the law and cricket; also in *Cornhill, Fores's* and *Windsor*): Vol.7

CLEAVER, Hylton Reginald (1891-1961; pen-name Reginald Crunden; a prodigious writer from an early age, his first published work appeared in the *Ladies' Gazette* when he was only thirteen; also in *Captain, Chums, Windsor, New, Cassell's, Grand, Munsey's, London Opinion, Badminton, Strand, Boy's Own Paper, Hutchinson's, Pearson's, Sovereign* and *Blue*; although a noted sporting journalist he also wrote numerous schoolboy books. Vol.14

CLIFFORD, Hugh Charles (1866-1944; colonial administrator and fiction writer; also in *Atlantic, Argosy, Blackwood's, Cornhill, Golden, London* and *Temple Bar*): Vols.14,20

CLINCH, Douglas Wetmore (1884-1953; writer on shooting and hunting; also in *Field & Stream* and *Badminton*): Vols.11,12

COATEN, Arthur Wells (1879-1939; pen-name Watchman; profilic author on hunting, polo and racing; editor of *Polo Monthly* and various sporting annuals; journalist on *Morning Post* for twenty-eight years; chairman of Racecourse Press Committee; also in *Badminton, Baily's, Bystander* and *Pall Mall*): Vols.12,13,20,21

COHEN, Octavus Roy (1891-1959; actor, author, writer, engineer, playwright, lawyer, scriptwriter; on staff of *Bayonne Times, Birmingham Ledger, Charleston News & Courier, Newark Morning Star*; contributed to *Chicago Tribune*; wrote fifty-six books; also in *American, Adventure, Ainslee's, Argosy, Blue, Black Cat, Corner, Cosmopolitan, Collier's, Country Gentleman, Cavalier, Delineator, Elks, Esquire, Everybody's, Green, Hearst's, Liberty, Malcolm's, McCall's, Munsey's, Mystery, Nash's, Novel, Pearson's, Parisienne, Royal, Red, Shrine, Strand, Suspense, Top Notch, Young's* and *Saturday Evening Post*): Vol.21

COLES-FINCH, William (1864-1944; author, historian, writer; wrote ten books; expert on anything Kentish): Vol.19

COLLINS, George (pen-name Nimrod Junior; author of hunting books; started on *Hull Weekly News*; also in *Baily's, Badminton, Fores's* and *Sporting Mirror*): Vols.8,10,11

CONE, Joseph Andrews (1869-1919; writer, humourist, playwright, painter; on *Boston Courier* then *Connecticut Valley Advertiser*; also designed covers for *The Draftsman, Life, Puck* and *Judge*: Vol.P,1

CONNEAU, Jean-Louis (1880-1937; pen-name Andre Beaumont; aviator, flying-boat manufacturer, author, writer): Vol.17

CONYERS, Dorothea (1869-1949; Limerick based writer and novelist who became a Master of Foxhounds; wrote over forty works of fiction; also in *Grand, Hutchinson's, Baily's, Nash's, Novel, Sovereign, Badminton, Windsor, Strand, Royal* and *Saturday Evening Post*): Vols.3,10,11

COOPER, Alfred Benjamin (1863-1936; pen-names: Paul Preston, Preston Weir and Vagrant. Attended Westminster College then invited by George Newnes to join his company. Became editor of the *Sunday Strand*. Contributed articles, fiction and verse to *Windsor, Idler, Captain, Pearson's, Punch, Boy's Own Paper, Red, St.George's, Novel, Scout, Badminton, Nash's, Grand, Strand, Detective, Chums, Cassell's* and *John O'London's*; wrote many books. Vols.2,4-9,11-13

CORDLEY, Clifford (writer and journalist; on *Western Morning News*; also in *Badminton, Chambers's, Chums, Gentlemen's, Fores's* and *Cosmopolitan*): Vol.8

CORRI, Eugene (1857-1933; boxing referee; original member of National Sporting Club; wrote several books; also in *Baily's* and *Badminton*): Vols.12,17,18,21

CORLETT, John (1841-1915; known as The Master; contributed to *Bell's Life in London & Sporting Chronicle*; on staff of *The Sportsman*; purchased *The Sporting Times* [The Pink 'Un] which he made into a popular social journal and horse racing digest; also in *Baily's, Badminton, Sporting Mirror* and *Fores's*): Vol.P

COUSSELL, Ernest Edward (1879-1947; pen-names Ithuriel and Audax; journalist and horse-breeder; founder of The British Bloodstock Agency; one of the founders of *The Bloodstock Breeders' Review*; on the staff of *The Sportsman*, then *Sporting Life*): Vols.2-4

COX, Harding Edward de Fonglanque (1854-1944; sports writer and author; also in *Baily's, Badminton, Fores's, John O'London's* and *Hutchinson's*): Vol.7

CRAWLEY, Alfred Ernest (1867-1924; schoolmaster, author, sports journalist, tennis player, social anthropologist; an authority on skating, golf and lawn tennis; contributed to *The Observer* and *The Times*; also in *Badminton, Captain, Fores's* and *Pearson's*): Vols.15-19,21

CROOME, Arthur Capel Molyneux (1866-1930; cricketer, journalist, schoolmaster; golf writer on *London Evening Standard* and *Morning Post*; cricket on *The Times* and *Daily Telegraph*; books on sport; also in *Badminton*): Vols.7-10,14,16

DABBS, George Henry Roque (1846-1913; doctor, author and playwright; editor of *Vectis* and *My Journal*; contributor to *London Argus*; books of fiction and poetry): Vols.P,1-12

DALE, Henry William Johnstone Bonnycastle (1868-1936; writer, naturalist and photographer; correspondent for Canadian nature magazines; also in *Badminton, Outing* and *Wide World*): Vol.10

DALE, Thomas Francis (1848-1923; author of books on fox-hunting and polo; book editor; magazine writer; also in *Field, Sporting Mirror, Baily's, Fores's, Harper's, Captain* and *Badminton*): Vols.3,6,16

DALTON, William; expert on card games and crosswords; author of books on the subjects; also in *Pearson's, Strand* and *Grand*): Vols.10,11

DARWIN, Bernard Richard Meirion (1876-1961; journalist, author, editor and barrister; contributed to *The Times* and *Country Life* for over forty years; represented England at golf; also in *Atlantic, Badminton, Cornhill, Punch, Tatler, Grand, John O'London's, Men Only, London Opinion, Lilliput, Pearson's, London, Nash's* and *Strand*): Vols.9-14,16,18,19

DE LA MARE, Walter John (1873-1956; pen-name Walter Ramal; poet, short-story writer, novelist; in *Westminster Gazette*; also in *Argosy, Atlantic, Cornhill, Blue, English Review, London Mercury, Golden, John O'London's, Yale Review, Everybody's, McClure's, Bookman, Harper's, Nash's, Temple Bar, London, Century, Lilliput* and *Pall Mall*): Vol.15

DEMAIN-GRANGE, Archibald Manisty (writer, lyricist and author; also in *Blue, Gaiety, Grand, Cassell's, Royal, Idler, Novel, Everybody's, Yes or No, Pearson's, New, Lloyd's, Girl's Own Paper, Story-Teller, Red, Nash's, Sievier's* and *Boy's Own Paper*): Vols.2,4,8,9

DEXTER, Walter (1877-1944; started in business before turning his hand to writing; his work appeared in periodicals such as *Cassell's, Captain, English Illustrated, Royal, Boy's Own Paper* and *Pearson's* but it was his involvement with the Dickens' Fellowship where he really shone; created

Dickens themed crosswords for *The Times* and *The Listener*. Vol.16

DICKINSON, John Hutton (journalist and footballer; assistant editor *Rotherham Advertiser*; on *Yorkshire Post, Yorkshire Evening News, News Chronicle, Daily Express, Daily Mirror* and *Press Association*): Vol.6

DIEHL, Charles Vidal (1866-1912; board game designer; director of the weather bureau; also in *Tale-Teller* and *London*: Vol.12

DIXON, Henry Sydenham (1848-1931; son of [Henry Hall Dixon] The Druid; pen-names Vigilant and Hazard; journalist and author; on the staff of *The Sportsman*; editor of *World of Billiards*; also in *English Illustrated, Fores's, Badminton* and *Baily's*; president of Billiards Association): Vols.3,10,12,16

DODINGTON, John (travel and fiction writer; also in *Badminton, Blue, Country Life, Fores's, Pearson's, Illustrated Sporting & Dramatic News* and *Sphere*): Vols.8-10,12

DORRINGTON, Albert (1870-1953; pen-names Alba Dorian and Alba Dorrington; novelist and war correspondent; in Australia worked on *The Bulletin* and contributed to *Lone Hand*; also in *Argosy, Cavalier, Corner, Blue, Top Notch, Popular, Novel, Red, Royal, Holland's, Yellow, Nash's, Blackwood's, Chamber's, Sovereign, Green, Chicago Leger, Grand, Pall Mall, Strand* and *Sketch*): Vol.10

DRUMMOND, Maud (croquet player; author; in *Badminton* and *Girl's Own Paper*; her daughter illustrated many of her books): Vol.7

DUDENEY, Henry Ernest (1857-1930; pen-name Sphinx; also in *Royal, London, Captain, Cassell's, Strand* and *Pall Mall*): Vol.1

DUQUESNE, Frederick [Fritz] Joubert (1877-1956; soldier, big-game hunter, spy and journalist; on staff *New York Herald*; also in *Adventure, Everybody's* and *Hampton's*): Vol.12

DUFFEY, Arthur (1879-1955; track and field athlete; journalist on *Boston Globe*; also in *Top Notch*): Vol.P.2

DUTT, William Alfred (1870-1939; author and journalist; on *Eastern Daily Press* and *National Press Agency*; numerous books on East Anglia; also in *Argosy, Badminton, Cassell's, Fores's, Pearson's* and *Temple Bar*): Vol.15

DWYER, James Francis (1874-1952; mailman, convict, tram conductor, pigeon buyer, compositor, novelist, short-story writer, author; pen-names included Burglar Bill and Marat; on *The Bulletin, Sydney Truth* and *Sydney Sportsman*; also in *American, Argosy, Adventure, Ainslee's, Blue, Britannia, Black Cat, Bohemian, Cavalier, Canadian, Chicago Leger, Collier's, Cassell's, Delineator, Esquire, Green, Grand, Hutchinson's, Harper's, Holland's, Harper's Bazar, London, Liberty, McCall's, Munsey's, Novel, Popular, Pearson's, Red, Royal, Strand, Star* and *Wide World*): Vol.13

EDGAR, George (1877-1918; journalist on *Liverpool Gazette* and *Warrington Guardian*; editor of *Modern Business, Careers* and *Advertisers' Weekly*; books on journalism; also in *Grand, Top Notch, Novel, Nash's, Cassell's* and *Sievier's*): Vols.2,4

EDGE, Selwyn Francis (1868-1940; motor journalist and racing driver; also in *Grand, Badminton, Boys' Life* and *Pearson's*): Vols.1,11

EVERITT, Nicholas (real name Henry Reeve Everitt; 1867-1928; solicitor, secret agent, sportsman, traveller, author; also in *Baily's, Badminton* and *Fores's*): Vols.5,17

FAIR, Mary Cicely (1874-1955; pen-names Donald Deane, Silverpoint, Silverpen; writer, photographer, archaeologist, author, lecturer, broadcaster; also in *Badminton, Lady's Realm, Pearson's, Fores's* and *Wide World*): Vol.17

FAIRFAX-BLAKEBOROUGH, John Freeman (1883-1976; author and racing judge; started on *Middlesbrough Evening Telegraph* then writer on country sports and horse racing; author of one hundred and twelve books; contributed to the *Darlington & Stockton Times* for fifty-four years; also in *Badminton* and *Baily's*): Vols.11,14,16,18

FARMAR, Constance (b.1871; poet and short-story writer; contributor to *Madras Mail*; also in *Chambers's, The Lady, Yellow, Pall Mall* and *Smart Set*): Vols.1,5

FINLASON, Charles Edward (1860-1917; cricketer, golfer, author and journalist; editor of *Johannesburg Star*): Vols.5,6

FITCH, George (1877-1915; humorist, columnist, journalist and writer; on staff of *Galva News* [Illinois], *Council Bluffs* [Iowa], *Daily Nonpareil* [Illinois] and *Illinois Herald-Transcript*; became a nationalally syndicated columnist; also in *American, Smart Set, Red, Hampton's, Grand, Cosmopolitan, Century, Collier's* and *Saturday Evening Post*): Vols.P,12,13

FRASER, William Alexander (1859-1933; Canadian novelist; mining engineer then politician before taking to writing and broadcasting animal stories; numerous articles in *Scribner's, Strand, Pall Mall, Metropolitan, Badminton, Collier's, McClure's, Ainslee's, Black Cat, Popular, Pearson's, Maclean's, Temple Bar, Lippincott's, Argosy, Red, Windsor, Royal, Captain, Yellow, Appleton's, Cassell's, Bohemian, Cosmopolitan, Harper's, Munsey's, Canadian* and *Saturday Evening Post*): Vols.P,1,2

FRECHENCOURT, Raoul de (1863-1921; pen-names Adrien Varloy and Dancourt; journalist on *La Gazette de France* and *Le Soleil*; also in many French magazines): Vol.14

FREEMAN, John Frederick (1880-1929; poet, essayist; wrote twelve books; also in *Argosy, Golden, To-Day, Lloyd's, Land & Water, London Mercury* and *Pall Mall*): Vol.15

FREEMAN, Robert Massie (1866-1949; journalist, author, fiction writer; also in *Flynn's, Cassell's, Grand* and *Strand*): Vol.14

FRY, Charles Burgess: (see Preliminary pages): Vols.1-11,13-17,19-21

GALE, Zona (1874-1938; playwright; poet, novelist and short-story writer; Pulitzer Prize winner; also in *Milwaukee Evening Wisconsin, Milwaukee Journal, New York World, The Delineator, Appleton's, Argosy, Ainslee's, Century, Collier's, Cosmopolitan, Harper's, Liberty, Munsey's, Nash's, Novel, Smart Set, Scribner's* and *Saturday Evening Post*): Vol.1

GALLICHAN, Walter Matthew (1861-1946; pen-names Geoffrey Mortimer and M.Secundus; essayist, author, publishers' reader, novelist, angler; wrote fifty-six books, many on angling; assistant editor on *Free Press*; first intake of *Daily Mail* journalists becoming a leader writer; also in *Boy's Own Paper*): Vols.7,8,17

GALTREY, Albert Sidney (1878-1935; pen-name Hotspur; racing journalist; on *Leeds Daily News* and *Leeds Mercury*; editor *Indian Sporting Times* and *Times of India*; assistant editor *The Sportsman* then *Daily Telegraph*; also in *Sporting & Dramatic News, Badminton, Tatler* and *Country Life*): Vols.7-15

GILLILAN, Strickland (1869-1954; journalist, author, poet, humorist; on *Jackson Ohio Herald, Baltimore American* and *Washington Post*; also in *Life, Smart Set, Cavalier, Munsey's, Ainslee's, Smith's, Argosy, Girl's Own Paper* and *Saturday Evening Post*): Vol.3

GOLDSTON, William (1878-1948; author, publisher and magician; editor *Magician Annual*; wrote twenty-two books; also in *Captain, Passing Show, Pearson's* and *Chums*): Vols.14,17,18

GOODYEAR, Robert Arthur Hanson (1877-1948; author, dramatist, fiction and sports writer; wrote seventeen books for boys; also in *Boys' Friend, Captain, Lloyd's, Yes or No* and *Vanity Fair* as well as in most Yorkshire newspapers and North Country magazines): Vol.18

GRACE, William Gilbert (1848-1915; doctor and cricketer; founded English Bowls Association; his concept created international football; many books and articles [all ghosted]; also in *Boy's Own Paper, Badminton, Chums, Captain, Cricket, Fores's, Ludgate, English Illustrated, Idler, New, Sporting Mirror* and *Strand*): Vols.P,1,6,7,11

GRAHAM, Jocelyn Henry Clive (1874-1936; pen-names Colonel D. Streamer, Percy Biffin and Reginald Drake; journalist, lyricist, humorous verse; wrote seventy-two books; also in *Cosmopolitan, Cornhill, Golden, McClure's, Metropolitan, Printers' Pie, Pall Mall, Pearson's, Radio Times, Strand* and *Saturday Evening Post*): Vol.2

GRAHAME-WHITE, Claude (1879-1959; aviator, author, founder of Aerofilms, property developer; wrote fourteen books; also in *Captain, Chums, Grand, Nash's, Badminton, Top Notch, Outing, Pearson's, Royal, Strand* and *Windsor*): Vols.13,20,21

GRAVES, Frederick (1866-1945; journalist and author; also in *Pall Mall, Tale-Teller, Yes or No, Nash's* and *Boy's Own Paper*): Vol.9

GREENE, Harry Irving (b.1868; journalist, poet and author; on *Chicago Tribune* then *Editor & Publisher*; founding member Chicago Press Club; also in *Leslie's, Blue, Argosy, Black Cat, Red, Adventure, Black Cat, Popular, Argosy, McClure's* and *Pearson's*): Vol.1

GREY, Edward (1862-1933; politician, author and writer; books on Fly Fishing and Ornithology; also in *New Review, Pearson's, Pall Mall, Nash's, London* and *Strand*): Vols.P,2,4,15

GROGAN, Walter Ernest (1871-1933; fiction writer; created theatre programmes, art music and musical settings; wrote American 'Dime Novels'; also in *Argosy, Badminton, Blue, Red, Yellow, Cassell's, Corner, English Illustrated, Idler, Grand, Harmsworth's, London, Hutchinson's, Top Notch, Popular, Pan, Sovereign, Truth, Windsor, Ludgate, Temple Bar, Strand, New, Royal, Pall Mall* and *Sketch*): Vol.6

GUITERMAN, Arthur (1871-1943; writer and humorous poet; editor of both *Woman's Home Companion* and *Literary Digest*; founded Poetry Society of America; also in *American, Ainslee's, Red, Everybody's, Scribner's, McClure's, Harper's, Smith's, Smart Set, Collier's, Putnam's, Lippincott's, McBride's, Boys' Life, Life, Liberty, New Yorker* and *Saturday Evening Post*): Vol.4

HAIG-BROWN, Alan Roderick (1877-1918; at Cambridge University; became a Master at Lancing College where he wrote books and many articles for the more serious periodicals; played football for clubs including Tottenham Hotspur and Brighton & Hove Albion; also in *Baily's, Fores's, Captain* and *Badminton*): Vols.P,1,4,5,7,9,10,13,16-21

HALES, Alfred Arthur Greenwood (1860-1936; journalist, novelist, author and adventurer; in Australia founded three newspapers, *Adelaide Standard, Coolgardie Mining Review* and *Boulder Star*; then on *Broken Hill Barrier Miner* and *Broken Hill Silver Age*; athletics editor of *Sydney Referee*; in London war correspondent on *Daily News* and *Evening News*; wrote numerous novels; fiction in *English Illustrated, Pearson's, Red, London* and *Pall Mall*): Vol.8,13

HAMEL, Herbert Gustave de (1880-1965; fiction writer, playwright, Treasury solicitor; also in *Punch, Badminton, Royal, Bellman, Pearson's, Blue, Grand, Pall Mall, Hutchinson's* and *Red*): Vols.7,8,21

HAMMOND, Thomas Edgar (1878-1945; stockbroker, Olympian, athlete; Blackheath Harriers Surrey Walking Club, Amateur Athletic Association Committee): Vol.17

HANDASYDE-BUCHANAN, Emily (1872-1953; artist, author, journalist, broadcaster; fiction books on high-society; also in *Badminton*): Vol.14

HAVENS, Ruth Genevia Dowd (1845-1928; schoolteacher, journalist, author, writer, poet, editor and women's suffrage; started on *Boston Cultivator*, then *Meriden Literary Recorder*; literary editor *Daily Republican*, editor *Washington Daily Morning Chronicle*, associate editor of Riggs newspaper group in Connecticut; also in *Nineteenth Century* and *Metropolitan*): Vol.P,6

HAVILAND, Maud Doria (1889-1941; ornithologist, entomologist, explorer, lecturer, photographer, author, writer; numerous books on her travels, birds and insects; also in *Illustrated London News, Badminton* and various academic journals): Vols.18-20

HAWKE, Martin Bladen (1860-1938; cricket player and administrator; military officer; also in *Captain, London, Pearson's, Badminton, Cassell's* and *Strand*) Vols.P,1,8,15,21

HEARNE, Richard (aviation and motoring journalist and author; also in *Land & Water, Badminton, London, Strand* and *Pall Mall*): Vols.12,13,15,16,18-20

HELME, Eleanor Evelyn (1887-1967; writer on hockey and golf; on *Yorkshire Post, Daily Telegraph, Morning Post* and *Somerset Free Press*; broadcaster on *BBC*; secretary Ladies Golf Union; wrote eleven books; also in *Pearson's, Badminton, Eve, Bystander, Tatler* and *Sporting & Dramatic News*): Vol.7

HEZLET, Ma(r)y Elizabeth Linzee (1882-1978; golfer and sports writer; British Amateur Ladies Golf champion; also in *Lady's Realm*): Vols.1,3,6,11,16,19,20

HICHENS, Robert Smythe (1864-1950; studied at Royal College of Music and London School of Journalism; playwright, journalist, lyricist and novelist; music critic on *The World*; wrote over fifty novels; also in *Atalanta, Argosy, Ainslee's, Britannia, Century, Cassell's, Cosmopolitan, English Illustrated, Harper's Bazar, Hutchinson's, Liberty, London, McClure's, Metropolitan, Nash's, Pall Mall, Pearson's, Printer's Pie, Badminton, Red, Royal* and *Strand*): Vol.6

HILTON, Harold Horsfall (1869-1942; golf writer and English amateur golf champion; editor of *Golf Illustrated*; also in *Gaiety, Outing, Pearson's, Pall Mall, Badminton, Windsor* and *Metropolitan*): Vol.9

HICHBORN, Philip Simmons (1882-1912; lawyer and writer; also in *Cosmopolitan, Cavalier, Pearson's, New* and *Metropolitan*): Vol.14

HOBBS, John Berry (1882-1963; cricketer, sports goods proprietor, journalist; on *News Chronicle* and *The Star*; produced twelve books along with his ghostwriter Jack Ingham; also in *Cassell's, Chums, John Bull, Boy's Own Paper, Badminton, Hutchinson's, Pearson's, Captain, Windsor* and *Strand*): Vols.13,19

HODGSON, Ralph (1871-1962; pen-name Yorick; poet, publisher, boxer, billiard player, comic artist, author, the theatre; Art Editor of *Fry's*; created his own London publishing house *At The Sign Of The Flying Fame*; in Ohio founded *Flying Scroll* imprint; also in *Golden, Pearson's* and *Argosy*): Vols.P,6,11-15,18

HOLBEIN, Montague Alfred (1861-1944; cyclist and Channel swimmer; cotton industry agent; wrote two books; also in *Sphere, Graphic, Boys' Realm* and *Illustrated London News*): Vols.6,7,16,17

HOLDER, Charles Frederick (1851-1915; naturalist, conservationist author and writer; curator at New York's American Museum of Natural History; books on marine biology and big game fishing; also in *Argosy, Badminton, Century, Cosmopolitan, Gunter's, Golden, London, Harper's, Wide Awake, St.Nicholas, Outing, McClure's, Scribner's* and Windsor): Vols.11,12,20

HOLLAND, Clive (real name Charles James Hankinson, 1866-1959; travel editor on *Queen*; also in *Pall Mall, London, Novel, Royal, Ludgate, Windsor, Grand, Idler, Cassell's, English Illustrated, Tatler* and *Boy's Own Paper*): Vols.1,15,17,18

HOPE, George Anthony (1863-1933; real name Anthony Hope Hawkins; wrote many short stories set mainly in schools; his serials were issued in book form of which there were thirty-two; also in *Boy's Own Paper, Idler, Ludgate, Century, Harper's Bazar, Longman's, Cassell's, English Illustrated, Metropolitan, Nash's, Chapman's, McClure's, Scribner's, Pearson's, Munsey's, Strand, Captain, Collier's, Ainslee's, Pall Mall, Saturday Evening Post, Windsor, Westminster Gazette* and *Chums*. Vol.13

HOPE, Linton Chorley (1863-1920; canoe and yacht designer, Olympian; books on yacht construction; also in *Badminton* and numerous technical and boating magazines): Vols.10,11

HOPCROFT, George Edwin (1871-1941; wrote and illustrated on yachting and sailing; also in *Captain, Badminton, Baily's, Chums, Boys' Own Paper, Cassell's, Fores's, Chatterbox* and *Lloyd's*): Vols.3,9

HORSLEY, John William (1845-1921; poet, author, expert in conchology, canon of Southwark, social reformer; also in *Cassell's, New, Strand* and *Boy's Own Paper*): Vol.7

HOWARTH, Mary (b.1858; journalist, writer, newspaper editor; first editor *Daily Mirror*; women's editor *Daily Mail*; also in *Atalanta, Badminton, English Illustrated, Harmworth's, Ludgate, London, Yellow* and *Pall Mall*): Vol.15

HUGHES, Cecil Eldred (1875-1941; author, poet and painter; on staff of *Fry's*; also in *Red* and *Cassell's*): Vols.P,1-8,10,13,14,16,18

HURST-HAYES, James (b.1875; writer and author; also in *English Illustrated, Harmworth's, Pall Mall, Royal* and *Temple Bar*): Vol.13

HUTCHINSON, Horatio Gordon (1859-1932; known as Horace; golfer and author; numerous books; insurance executive; company director; also in *Badminton, Cornhill, English Illustrated, Argosy, Fores's, Minster, Longman's, Hutchinson's, Pearson's, Metropolitan* and *Windsor*): Vols.1,4,6,7,11-14,16,19

HYATT, Stanley Portal (1877-1914; an English explorer, engineer, hunter and author; as a teenager he worked on an Australian sheep station; then as a gold-mining engineer in Rhodesia; followed by owning a rubber plantation in Mozambique; returned to London and had success with his first novel; also in *Metropolitan, Idler, Cassell's, Grand, Captain, Boys' Life; Boy's Own Paper, New, Red, Tit-Bits, Pall Mall* and *Sketch*): Vol.11

JANE, John Frederick Thomas (1865-1916; author, illustrator, editor; founded *Jane's Fighting Ships*; also in *Cassell's, Pall Mall, Minster, Collier's, London, Munsey's, English Illustrated, Pearson's, Longman's, Ludgate* and *Windsor*): Vol.15

JARVIS, Edward Harvey (1877-1969; military and writer; books on caravans and caravanning; also in *Autocar* and *Country Life*): Vols.17-21

JESSOP, Gilbert Laird (1874-1955; cricketer; also in *Strand, Boy's Own Paper, Captain, Badminton, Lloyd's, Chums, Windsor, Cassell's* and *Pall Mall*): Vols.1,5,8-11,15

JOHNSON, Arthur Edward (novelist; also in *Captain, Strand, Royal, Badminton, Everybody's, American, Century, Smart Set, Harper's, Scribner's, Metropolitan, Idler, Novel, Longman's, London* and *Pall Mall*): Vols.5,15,21

JONES, Dora Mae (essayist and novelist; assistant editor of *Travel*; also in *Cassell's, English Illustrated, Longman's, Strand, Lady's Realm, Ladies' Home Journal, Temple Bar* and *Quiver*): Vol.8

JONES, Owen (studied at Oxford University; ten years as a gamekeeper; author and magazine writer; also in *Badminton, Fores's, Pearson's* and *Royal*): Vols.6-18

JONES, William Unite (journalist; editor *Athletic Star*, on *Birmingham Daily Mail* and *Birmingham Evening Despatch*; also in *Athletic News*): Vols.6,10

KELSON, George Mortimer (1835-1920; pen-name Red Herl; author, county cricketer, fisherman, horseman, pigeon racer; fishing editor *Land and Water*; also in *Baily's* and *Badminton*): Vols.11,12

KENNEDY, Bart (1861-1930; travelled the world as a sailor, labourer, gold prospector, Indian fighter, opera singer, actor and writer; numerous published novels; stories in *Idler, Cassell's, Sketch, Nash's, London, Captain, Crampton's, Grand, Pall Mall* and *Strand*. Vols.2,4-6,11,12

KENNEY, Rowland (1882-1961; journalist and government press officer; editor *Daily Herald*; publisher of *Vanity Fair*; on *Reuter's, The Times, Observer* and *English Review*; news department Foreign Office; books in English, German and Scandinavian languages; also in *Nash's* and *Pall Mall*): Vol.17

KNIGHT, Albert Ernest (1872-1946; cricket player and coach; wrote a coaching book in 1906 which is still in print; also in *Ludgate, Badminton, Cassell's, Pall Mall* and *Strand*): Vols.7,15

KNIGHT-HORSFIELD, Herbert (1856-1932; author and ornithologist; also in *Badminton, Baily's, The Field, Country Life, Royal* and *National Review*): Vol.10

KNOWLES, Lees (1857-1928; president Cambridge University Athletic Club; inter-university sports administrator; author and book editor; also in *English Illustrated*): Vols.2,4,9

KYNE, Peter Bernard (1880-1957; magazine and screen writer, author, novelist; over one hundred of his novels were filmed; on *Los Angeles Times*; also in *American, Adventure, Blue, Britannia, Cassell's, Collier's, Cosmopolitan, Delineator, Esquire, Golden, Grand, Hearst's, Liberty, Metropolitan, Nash's, Novel, Pearson's, Popular, Red, Sunset* and *Saturday Evening Post*): Vol.P,20

LACON-WATSON, Edmund Henry (1865-1948; schoolmaster, writer, author, poet, essayist; *Reuters* war correspondent; editor *Albany*; on staff of *Literature, The Field* and *Daily Graphic*; in *Westminster Review* and *London Evening Standard*; also in *Pall Mall, Lady's Realm, Windsor, Badminton, Cornhill, London Mercury, Argosy, Happy Mag, Blue* and *Idler*): Vols.11,17

LEACH, Henry (1874-1942; journalist and author; editor of *Nottingham Evening News* until joining the Harmsworth group; on *London Evening News, Daily Mail, Pall Mall Gazette, Evening Standard, Sketch* and *Observer*; noted for his golfing reports; editor of *Golf Illustrated*; also in *Captain, Badminton, Cassell's, Pall Mall, Strand, Harmsworth's, London* and *Chamber's*. Vols.6-12,15-17,19,21

LEBRETON-MARTIN, Edward (1874-1944; author of children's and fishing books; narrator of documentary films; also in *Captain, Royal, Pearson's, Chums, Novel, Scout* and *Cassell's*): Vols.10,11

LEECHMAN, George Douglas (1865-1923; solicitor, barrister, engineer, chartered patent agent; motorcycle designer; also in *Autocar* and *Car Illustrated*): Vol.11

LEHMANN, Rudolf Chambers (1856-1929; rower and president of the Leander Rowing Club; edited *Granta* and *Daily News*; on staff of *Punch* for thirty years; journalist, poet, lyricist, author; secretary of the Amateur Rowing Association; barrister and parliamentarian; also in *English Illustrated, Cornhill, New, Pall Mall, Chambers, Baily's* and *Cassell's*): Vols.3,14

LEVITT, Dorothy Elizabeth (1882-1922; journalist, author, racing driver and aviator; on staff of *Graphic*; also in *London, Penny Pictorial* and *Yorkshire Evening Post*): Vol.12

LEWIS, John (1848-1926; footballer and referee; founded Blackburn Rovers; established Lancashire Football Association; secretary Worcestershire Football Association; vice-president Football League; also in *Captain* and *London*): Vols.4,6

LONDON, John Griffith (1876-1916; known as Jack; studied at University of California; travelled widely while on *San Francisco Examiner*; first book published in 1900 with others selling in large numbers. Also in *Strand, Hearst's, Popular, Nation, Columbian, Blackwood's, Captain, Grand, Red, Hampton's, Collier's, Century, Overland, Atlantic, McClure's, Leslie's, Harper's Bazar, Cosmopolitan, Munsey's, Ainslee's, Metropolitan, Pearson's, London, Pall Mall, Badminton, Harper's, Cassell's, Saturday Evening Post, Idler* and *Illustrated London News*) Vols.4,5,14

LONGHURST, Percy William (1874-1959; pen-names: Hubert Spence, Brian Kingston and Lewis Hockley; was an official at every Olympic Games 1908-32; on *Daily Mail* and *Observer*; wrote numerous articles on sport especially boxing in *All Sports, Boys Friend Weekly, Boys Realm, Pluck, Cheer Boys Cheer, Red, Novel, Pall Mall, Chums, Boys' Herald, Tale-Teller, Windsor, Fores's, Captain, Badminton, Yes or No, Magnet, Marvel* and *Boy's Own Paper*): Vols.14,16-18

LOPEZ, John (writer, author, playwright, film director; also in *Appleton's, Blue, Columbian,*

Hampton's, Harper's, Top Notch, Red, Popular and *Metropolitan*): Vol.15

LUCAS, Edward Verrall (1868-1938; pen-name E.D.Ward; journalist, author, editor, biographer, essayist, playwright, publisher, poet, chairman of *Methuen*; on *Sussex Daily News*; also in *Punch, Atlantic, Cornhill, Idler, Overland, Pall Mall, Nash's, London, Harper's, Pearson's, Windsor, Land & Water, English Illustrated, Printers' Pie* and *Strand*): Vols.P,1,5,6,15

LUCKMAN, Andrew Richard (1859-1918; pen-names The Scout and Magistral; started on *Chicago Tribune* then *New York Herald, St.James' Gazette, London Evening Standard, Daily News, Launceston Examiner (Tasmania), The Referee* and *Daily Express*; assistant editor at *Cassell's*; racing journalist and tipster): Vols.2,3,5

LUNN, Arnold Henry Moore (1888-1974; pen-names Sutton Croft and Rubicon; skier, mountaineer, writer, author; invented slalom skiing; wrote seventy-four books; editor *British Ski Yearbook* 1919-71; contributed to *Encyclopedia Britannia, English Review, The Times*; also in *Badminton, Pearson's, Lilliput, Cornhill* and *Pall Mall*): Vol.18

LYNCH, John Gilbert Bohun (1884-1928; educated at University College, Oxford; first book published in 1908 which presaged his parallel careers as a writer and caricaturist illustrator; started *The Field* then *Sport*. Also in *London Mercury, Quarterly Review, Tale Teller, Boys' Friend, John O'London's, Hutchinson's, Yes or No, Badminton, Windsor, Novel, Captain, Idler, Red* and *Chums*. Vols.5,9,11,15,20

MacDONAGH, Michael (1862-1946; journalist and author; on staff at *The Times*; many books on Parliament; also in *Chambers's, Cornhill, Grand, Lilliput, Longman's, Temple Bar* and *Pall Mall*): Vol.14

McEVOY, Charles Alfred (1879-1929; playwright and writer on stage matters; also in *Captain, Gaiety, Green, Grand, London, Windsor, Pearson's, John O'London's, Pan* and *Royal*): Vol.11

McFARLANE, Harold (d.1919; prolific sports writer who wrote extensively on Public Schools cricket, especially in *Badminton*; also published in *Ludgate, Cassell's, Argosy, Cornhill, Pall Mall, Longman's, Cosmopolitan, Captain, Royal, Strand, Idler, Atalanta, English Illustrated, Saturday Evening Post* and *Boy's Own Paper*. Vols.2,17

McKENZIE, Frederick Arthur (1869-1931; journalist on *Pall Mall Gazette, Daily Mail, Chicago Daily News* and *Daily Express*; author; also in *English Illustrated, Windsor, Munsey's, London, Harper's, Cassell's* and *Royal*): Vols.3,9,12

MACKIE, John (1862-1939; an author who had almost as many adventures as those he wrote about; his boys fiction was mainly devoted to sagas of his colonial escapades; also in *Daily Mail* then *Chums, Boys' Life, Grand, Cassell's, Boy's Own Paper, Captain, Wide World* and *Pearson's*): Vols.13,14

MACLACHLAN, Elinor (1870-1949; short-story writer; also in *Pall Mall, Pearson's* and *Grand*): Vol.14

MACLAREN, Archibald Campbell (1871-1944; cricketer, writer, editor; also in *Chums, Pearson's, Cassell's, Pall Mall, Grand, London, Strand, Captain* and *Badminton*): Vols.1,3,5,16

MCLEISH, Donald (1879-1950; photographer and mountaineer; studied at Regent Street Polytechnic; books on mountaineering; also in *London, Nash's, Cassell's, Pall Mall, National*

Geographic and many other geographical journals): Vol.17

MCNUTT, William Slavens (1885-1938; author, screenwriter, war correspondent, novelist, journalist; wrote humerous racetrack stories; on staff of *Seattle Post Intelligencer*; freelance for *Boston Sunday Globe* and *New Yorker*; also in *Argosy, American, Ainslee's, Cosmopolitan, Collier's, Cassell's, Cavalier, Corner, Elks, Everybody's, Hearst's, Liberty, McClure's, Metropolitan, Munsey's, New, Novel, Smart Set, Top Notch, Royal, Popular, Red* and *Saturday Evening Post*): Vol.20

MANSFORD, Charles John Jodrell (1863-1943; author and teacher; also in *Chums, Osborne, Strand, Windsor, Boys' Friend, Ludgate* and *Pall Mall*): Vol.17

MARLOWE, Francis Joseph (1870-1944; pen-name Felix Marlowe; crime fiction writer; published a dozen books and various periodical stories; also in *London Evening Standard, Boys' Life, Blue, Detective, Captain, Grand, Pall Mall, Chums, Flynn's, Top Notch, Corner, Novel* and *Boy's Own Paper*. Vols.12-14

MARTIN, James Sackville (1874-1954; writer; also in *Cornhill, Cassell's, English Illustrated, Everybody's, Grand, London, New, Novel, Pearson's, Temple Bar, Smart Set, Royal, Pall Mall, Red, Strand* and *Sketch*): Vols.5,7,9

MATSON, Charles George (1859-1914; motoring; on *Daily Mail*; also in *Badminton* and *Tatler*; many books on cars): Vols.2,6

MATSON-DOLSON, Cora Adele (1859-1936; poet; also in *Cavalier, Smart Set, Outing, Munsey's, Sunset, National, People's, Breezy, Cassell's, Watson's, Putnam's, Lippincott's, Argosy, Harper's* and *Pearson's*): Vol.3

MAXIM, Hiram Stevens (1840-1916; involved in scientific matters concerning artificial flight; wrote on it in *Cosmopolitan, Strand, London, Munsey's, Century* and *Cassell's*; a court case found him to have been a bigamist): Vols.11,18

MAYO, Earl Williams (author and playwright; also in *Argosy, Ainslee's, Appleton's, Munsey's, McClure's, Leslie's, Royal, Pearson's, Metropolitan, Idler* and *Windsor*): Vols.1,3

MECREDY, Richard James (1861-1924; cyclist, journalist, author, writer; on *Irish Motor News*; editor of both *Irish Cyclist & Athlete* and *Dublin Motor News*; also in *London*): Vols.3-8

MEGGY, Gordon (b.1878; author and journalist; on *Essex Chronicle, Daily Mail, London Evening News* and *Daily Express*; editor *Sunday Dispatch*; also in *Punch, Strand, Tatler, Royal, Novel, Pearson's, London, Gunter's, Cassell's* and *Boy's Own Paper*; books on journalism; founded Premier School of Journalism): Vol.19

METHLEY, Violet Mary (1882-1953; author, novelist, short-story writer, playwright; contributed to *Gloucester Journal, Tamworth Herald, Gloucester Citizen, Truth, Weird Tales* and various Girls' Annuals; twenty-one known books; also in *Boy's Own Paper, Blue, Cassell's, Canadian, English Illustrated, Yes or No, Munsey's, Novel, New, Red, Quiver, Sovereign, Strand, Windsor, Wide World, Lloyd's* and *Sketch*): Vol.18

MILES, Eustace Hamilton (1868-1948; real tennis champion, publisher and owner of health shops; also in *Cassell's, London, Metropolitan, John O'London's, Badminton, Strand, Pearson's, Windsor* and *Saturday Evening Post*): Vols.P,1-4,6,14,16

MILLS, Arthur Frederick Hobart (1887-1955; writer, author of thirty-six books; also in *Ainslee's, Argosy, Britannia, Blue, Canadian, Collier's, Everybody's, Grand, Hutchinson's, London, Nash's, Novel, Pall Mall, Pearson's, Royal, Sovereign, Wide World* and *Windsor*): Vol.21

MONCREIFF-TENNENT, Henry (1879-1941; known as Harry Tennent; hockey Olympian; founded Oxford University Occasionals Hockey Club; secretary of Hockey Association; theatre owner, producer, impresario, songwriter): Vols.2,9,10

MONTGOMERY, Lucy Maud (1874-1942; Canadian; wrote for *Halifax Morning Chronicle, Halifax Daily Echo* and *Charlottetown Daily Patriot*; author and short story writer): Vol.3

MUDDOCK, James Edward Preston (1843-1934; pen-names Dick Donovan and Joyce Emmerson; journalist on *Daily News* and *Dundee Weekly News*; author of over twenty books; also in *Strand, Captain, Grand* and *New*): Vols.10,19

MUSSABINI, Scipio Africanus (1867-1927; journalist and athletics coach; on *Pall Mall Gazette*; assistant editor *World of Billiards*; also in *Badminton*): Vol.12

MYERS, Arthur Wallis (1878-1939; pen-name Paladin; journalist although his success at tennis took priority; on the sporting staff at the *Daily Telegraph*; tennis editor of *The Field* and correspondent on the *Illustrated London News*; founded the International Lawn Tennis Club; also in *Cassell's, Ludgate, Royal, Captain, Windsor, Strand, Grand, London, Badminton, Atlantic* and *Harmsworth*): Vols.P,1-4,6-9,11-15,17,19

NICKALLS, Guy (1866-1935; Olympic rower; London Rowing Club; stockbroker; on *Morning Post*; also in *Baily's, Badminton* and *Strand*): Vols.6-9,15-17,19

NOSSIG, Alfred (1864-1943; sculptor, writer, activist; became an art curator and wrote the libretto of an opera; correspondent for various Eastern European newspapers; executed in Warsaw): Vol.4

O'DONNELL, Elliott (1872-1965; author, actor, novelist, writer, lecturer, broadcaster, book editor; wrote forty-four books; contributed to *London Evening News, Sunday Dispatch, Daily Chronicle, Daily Express*; also in *Cassell's, Blue, Everybody's, Tale Teller, Sievier's, Royal, Premier, Mystic, Hutchinson's, Pearson's, Tatler, Novel, Pan, Lloyd's, Bystander, Idler* and *Lilliput*): Vol.19

OGILVIE, William Henry (1869-1963; pen-names Glenrowan, Swingle-Bar, Free Mate, Freebooter; poet, journalist; Professor of Agricultural Journalism at Iowa State College; in Australia in *Border Watch* and *Bulletin*; in Britain in *Baily's, Badminton, Boy's Own Paper, Cassell's, Chambers, English Illustrated, Field, Grand, Idler, Nash's, Novel, Punch, Pall Mall, Top Notch, Temple Bar* and *Windsor*): Vols.7,10

OLIVER, Owen (1863-1933; real name Joshua Albert Flynn; director-general of finance at Ministry of Pensions; early science-fiction writer; in over eighty magazines including *Adventure, Argosy, Appleton's, Ainslee's, Chamber's, Cassell's, Collier's, English Illustrated, Green, Grand, Gaiety, Harper's, Holland's, Hampton's, Idler, Lloyd's, Liberty, Lippincott's, London, New, Metropolitan, Munsey's, Nash's, Pall Mall, Pearson's, Regent, Royal, Red, Sketch, Smith's, Yellow, Strand* and *Windsor*): Vols.2,3,9

OSBORNE, William Hamilton (1873-1942; author and magazine writer; also in *Argosy, Black Cat, Collier's, Gunter's, Leslie's, Smart Set, Munsey's, Royal, Metropolitan, Pearson's, McClure's, Strand, Smith's, Harper's, Lippincott's, Cosmopolitan, Red* and *Saturday Evening Post*): Vol.3

OYLER, Leslie Kathleen Mary (1884-1971; author, poet; wrote numerous children's books; also in *Argosy, Cassall's, Captain, Corner, Grand, Hutchinson's, Happy Mag, Idler, London, Quiver, New, Novel, Pearson's, Sovereign, Royal, Top Notch, Yellow, Red, Crusoe, Nash's, Windsor* and *Boy's Own Paper*): Vols.11,16

PAINE, Ralph Delahaye (1871-1925; journalist on *Philadelphia Press* and *New York Herald*; editor of *New York Telegraph*; contributor to *Le Figaro*; author; also in *Collier's, Century, Cosmopolitan, Ainslee's, Bohemian, Nash's, Red, Cassell's, Boys' Life, Scribner's, McClure's, Outing, Munsey's, Captain, Popular, Metropolitan* and *Saturday Evening Post*): Vols.3,4

PALMER, Frederick (1873-1958; journalist and war correspondent; on *New York Press, New York World, New York Globe, New York Times* and for the *North American Newspaper Alliance*; between the two main wars he wrote thirty-one books; also in *Collier's* and *Everybody's* for whom he covered a number of regional wars; then *Munsey's, Hampton's, Pall Mall, McClure's, Cosmopolitan, Liberty, Scribner's, Century, Worlds Work, Red, Popular, Pearson's, Cassell's* and *Saturday Evening Post*): Vol.P,2

PAYNE, Elizabeth Stancy (1868-1944; novelist, poet, fashion writer; also in *Ainslee's, Black Cat, Blue, Cassell's, Smart Set, Everybody's* and *Country Gentleman*): Vol.4

PHILLIPS, Ernest Arnold (1870-1956; author, writer, angler; Angling Editor *Yorkshire Evening Post*; also in *Boy's Own Paper, Fishing Gazette, Fores's* and *Strand*): Vol.18

PHIPPS-HORNBY, Geoffrey Stanley (1856-1927; army officer; owner of Compton Stud; polo player winning Hurlingham Championship Cup; formed Blackmore Vale Polo Club; president Dorset County Polo Association): Vol.14

PIER, Arthur Stanwood (1874-1966; science fiction writer and novelist; wrote thirty-two books; also in *American, Atlantic, Ainslee's, Collier's, Leslie's, Harper's, McClure's, Scribner's* and *Metropolitan*): Vol.8

PLATTS, William Carter (1864-1944; writer of fiction; books on angling and fishing; woollen cloth manufacturer, then journalist on *Yorkshire Post*; also in *Badminton, Grand, London* and *Strand*): Vols.10-13,15-17

POCOCK, Henry Roger Ashwell (1865-1941; author and journalist; also in *Argosy, Adventure, Pearson's, Ludgate, Chapman's, Idler, London, Boys' Life, Pall Mall, Munsey's, Badminton, Boy's Own Paper, Cornhill, Sketch* and *Chums*): Vols.2,3

POLLOCK-HODSOLL, George Bertram (1875-1914; footballer; machinery merchant; also in *Badminton* and *Grand*): Vol.6

POWELL, George Herbert (1856-1924; author and writer; wrote thirteen books; also in *Argosy, Badminton, Cornhill, Nash's, Pall Mall, Strand, Temple Bar* and *Windsor*): Vol.16

PRICHARD, Vernon Hesketh (1876-1922; hunter, explorer, writer, cricketer, author, soldier; many books; also in *Badminton, Chamber's, Cornhill, Chapman's, Captain, English Illustrated, London, Popular, Truth, Royal, Top Notch, Red, Pall Mall, Pearson's* and *Strand*): Vols.1,2,6-8,13-16

PRICHARD, Katherine O'Brien (1851-1935; author, wrote as 'Kate' or pen-name E.Heron; also in *Badminton, Cornhill, Chapman's, Royal, Red, Strand, Windsor, Pearson's, Chamber's, London* and *Pall Mall*): Vols.1,6-8

PUGH, Edwin William (1874-1930; writer, novelist and literary critic; also in *Argosy, Chapman's, Cassell's, Grand, Ludgate, John O'London's, Lloyd's, Idler, Windsor, Novel, Young's, Nash's, Metropolitan, London, Strand, Sketch, Red* and *Pall Mall*): Vols.1,5,9

PUNSHON, Ernest Robertson (1872-1956; author, novelist, writer; literary critic for *The Guardian*; pen-name Robert Halkett; contributed to *London Evening Standard*; also in *Britannia, Grand, Crampton's, Chambers's, Black & White, Cassell's, Chapman's, Red, Cornhill, English Illustrated, Everybody's, Flynn's, Top Notch, Gaiety, Horner's, Hutchinson's, Holly Leaves, Idler, MacKill's, Yes or No, Royal, Smart Set, Novel, Tale Teller, Sovereign, New, Pearson's, London, Windsor, Strand, Nash's, Tit-Bits* and *Punch*): Vol.13

RAMSAY, Rina (1875-1950; real name Catherine Mary Ramsay; novelist and short story writer; also in *Ainslee's, Chambers's, English Illustrated, Lady's Realm, Holland's, Lloyd's, Nash's, London, Windsor, Strand* and *Sketch*): Vols.8-10,12,14

RANJITSINHJI, Kumar (1872-1933; cricketer, controversial businessman and politican; also in *Badminton, Captain, Cassell's, Strand, London* and *Longman's*): Vols.P,1,3,5,6

RICE, Henry Grantland (1880-1954; journalist, sportswriter, poet, broadcaster and author; on *Atlantic Journal, Cleveland News* and *New York Tribune*; also in *American, Black Cat, Collier's, Esquire, Liberty, McClure's, Metropolitan, Popular* and *Saturday Evening Post*): Vol.21

RIDDELL, George Allardice (1865-1934; solicitor and newspaper proprietor, chairman Newspaper Proprietors Association; president of Periodical Trade Press & Weekly Newspaper Proprietors' Association, Advertising Association, London Newspapers Golf Society and Newspaper Press Fund; patron Newsvendors' Benevolent Institution; president Press Club; chairman *News of the World, George Newnes Ltd, Arthur Pearson Ltd* and *Country Life Ltd*; contributed to Encyclopedia Britannica and Chambers' Encyclopedia; wrote ten books): Vols.P,10-13

RIDGE, William Pett (1859-1930; pen-name Warwick Simpson; author, charity worker, film scriptwriter; started on *St.James's Gazette* before becoming a fiction writer; successfully sued *English Illustrated Magazine* for falsely publishing works using his name; also in *Argosy, Ainslee's, Crampton's, Cassell's, Cosmopolitan, Graphic, Grand, Gaiety, Hutchinson's, Idler, John O'London's, Ludgate, McClure's, Novel, London, Pearson's, Printers' Pie, Strand, Sketch, Royal, Windsor, Tatler* and *Saturday Evening Post*): Vol.1

ROBERTS, Charles George Douglas (1860-1943; became one of the first Canadian authors and poets to be known internationally; had works on exploration, natural history, verse, travel and fiction published; editor of *Toronto Week*; also in *Argosy, Liberty, Maclean's, Yellow, Hampton's, Red, McClure's, Metropolitan, Lippincott's, Peterson's, St.Nicholas, Leslie's, Ainslee's, Atlantic, Appleton's, Century, Collier's, Idler, Cosmopolitan, Cassell's, Scribner's, Harper's, Munsey's, Windsor, Captain, London, Fores's, Longman's, Badminton, Pall Mall* and *Saturday Evening Post*): Vols.P,1,4,8

ROBERTS, George Edwards Theodore Goodridge (1877-1953; novelist and poet; author of thirty-four books and over one hundred published stories and poems; on staff of *New York Independent*; founded and edited *The Newfoundland Magazine*; edited *Kitbag, Acadie, Swizzles* and *Spotlight* journals; also in *St.John Telegraph-Journal, Ocean, Century, Appleton's, Argosy, Ainslee's, Blue, Blackwood's, Black Cat, Boys' Life, Country Gentleman, Canadian, Collier's, Captain, Cavalier, Chums, Everybody's, Esquire, Frontier, Grand, Gunter's, Hutchinson's, Leslie's, London, Munsey's, Maclean's, Massey's, Metropolitan, New, Popular, Pearson's, Pall Mall, Smart Set, Smith's, Scribner's, Sovereign, Windsor* and *Saturday Evening Post*): Vol.12

ROBERTS, William Harris Lloyd (1884-1966; writer, playwright, poet; on staff of *McClure's* magazine; assistant editor at *Outing*; also in *Argosy, Appleton's, Cavalier, Captain, Canadian, Everybody's, Hampton's, Harper's, Hutchinson's, Maclean's, Metropolitan, Munsey's, Popular, Novel, Smart Set, Red, Windsor* and *Boy's Own Paper*): Vol.10

ROBERTSON, Alexander James (1854-1912; founder of Tooting Bec Golf Club; editor of *Golf*; book editor; on staff of *The Times*): Vols.4,5

ROBERTSON-SCOTT, John William (1866-1962; started on *Birmingham Daily Gazette* then *Pall Mall Gazette, Westminster Gazette* and *Daily Chronicle*; editor *The Countryman*; also in *World's Work, Country Gentleman, Quarterly Review, Nineteenth Century, Badminton, Spectator, Nation, The Times, Captain* and *Baily's*): Vols.1,2,4

ROBINSON, Harry Perry (1859-1930; journalist, naturalist, author and photographer; on *The Times* and *Daily News*; wrote twenty books; also in *Atlantic, English Illustrated, Badminton, Harper's Bazar, McClure's, Putnam's* and *Scribner's*): Vols.2,4,6,7,9,10,12,14,17

ROLKER, August Winfried (1869-1956; fiction writer; also in *American, McClure's, Strand, Pearson's, Collier's, Appleton's, Cassell's* and *Saturday Evening Post*): Vol.4

SANDOW, Eugen (1867-1925; real name Friedrich Wilhelm Muller; strong-man; also in *Boys' Friend, London, Cosmopolitan, Harmsworth's, Captain, Chums, Ludgate* and *Strand*): Vols.P,2,4,9,11-14

SCRIVENER, Harry Stanley (1865-1937; tennis player and referee; author, journalist; founded Lawn Tennis Association, also in *Badminton* and *Bystander*): Vols.3,15

SELOUS, Frederick Courteney (1851-1917; explorer; also in *Baily's, Strand, Cornhill, Badminton, Captain* and *Windsor*): Vols.1,11

SETON-KARR, Henry Carba (1853-1914; explorer, hunter, barrister, politician, writer, amateur golfer; also in *Baily's, Badminton, Chums, London, Pall Mall, Strand* and *Windsor*): Vol.11

SEWELL, Edward Humphrey Dalrymple (1872-1947; educated at Bedford School; first-class cricket and rugby player; on *Sunday Graphic* and various other newspapers; books on both of his sports; editor of *New Badminton*, also in *Grand, Sievier's, Cassell's, Captain, Windsor, Strand* and *Boy's Own Paper*): Vols.1-3,6-12,14,16,17,19-21

SHARP, Evelyn Jane (1869-1955; journalist, suffragette and children's fiction writer; editor of *Votes for Women*; worked on *Daily Chronicle, Pall Mall Gazette, Daily Herald* and *Manchester Guardian*; also in *Atalanta, Chapman's, Idler, Lippincott's, Pall Mall, London, Yellow, Quarto, Temple Bar* and *Saturday Evening Post*): Vols.1,2,6

SHARP, Jack (1878-1938; played football for Everton & England, cricket for Lancashire & England, businessman; also in *Boys' Friend* and *Boy's Own Paper*): Vols.1,5

SHAW, Frederick George (1866-1918; veterinary surgeon; books on fly-fishing, physical health and boxing; also in *Boys' Realm* and *Badminton*): Vols.7,10,12

SHAW, Herbert (pen-name Anthony Armstrong; also in *Bellman, Britannia & Eve, Happy Mag, Everybody's, Novel, Grand, Tit-Bits, John O'London's, Pearson's, Century, Windsor, London, Pall Mall, Red, Captain, Royal, Men Only, Strand* and *Sketch*): Vols.8,11,13-15,19

SHAW, Percy Reeves (1886-1952; started with Pearson's publications; became second editor of *The Captain*; also in *Pearson's, Tale Teller, Humorist, Strand, Rapid, Grand, Red, Sunny Mag, Golden, London Opinion, Crusoe, Happy Mag* and *Yes or No*): Vols.10,11

SHEPPARD, Alfred Tresidder (1871-1947; author and critic; also in *Watson's, Argosy, Novel, Nash's* and *Pall Mall*): Vol.4

SHEPSTONE, Harold James (1874-1951; started as a commercial clerk but moved into journalism; his stories reflected a futuristic trend for humanity; also in *Captain, Ludgate, Cassell's, Windsor, Harmsworth's, Pall Mall, Pearson's, Royal, Boy's Own Paper, Penny Pictorial, Quiver, Britannia, Hutchinson's, English Illustrated, Wide World, London, Chums* and *Strand*. Vols.11,14

SHERINGHAM, Hugh Tempest (1876-1930; pen-name Blue Phantom; writer, author, journalist; angling editor *The Field*; books on angling; also in *Badminton, Baily's, Cornhill, Fores's, Pan, Temple Bar* and *Windsor*): Vols.3,10,19,20

SIMPSON, Elizabeth Frances Ann (1857-1926; author, journalist, writer, cat breeder; contributed to *Dundee Evening Post, Belfast Newsletter, Living London, Queen* and *The Field*; also in *Cassell's, Lady's Realm, Hutchinson's, Illustrated London News* and *Illustrated Sporting & Dramatic News*): Vol.18

SINGH, Saint Nihal (1884-1949; journalist, writer, orator, foreign correspondent, author; over twenty books; on *The Observer, New York Times, Hindustan Times, Baltimore Sun*; also in *Cosmopolitan, Windsor, Nash's, London, Strand, Pearson's, Penny Pictorial, Asiatic Review, The Lady, Vanity Fair, Review of Reviews* and numerous overseas journals): Vol.17

SLANEY, George Wilson (1884-1978; pen-names George Woden and George Wouil; schoolmaster, writer and playwright; also in *Cornhill, Gaiety, Grand* and *Novel*): Vol.8

SMILEY, Maurice (author, also in *Appleton's, Bohemian, Collier's, Gunter's, Leslie's, American, Watson's, Pearson's, Scribner's* and *Saturday Evening Post*): Vol.1

SMITH, Frederick Edwin (1872-1930; barrister, politician, author; also in *Cassell's, Century, Britannia, Smart Set, Hutchinson's, Premier, John O'London's, Nash's, Pearson's, London, Strand, Windsor* and *Saturday Evening Post*): Vols.P,15,21

SOMERVILLE, Edith Anna Oenone (1858-1949; novelist, illustrator and short story writer; pen-name Geilles Herring; studied at South Kensington School of Art, Royal Westminster School of Art, Academie Colarossi and Academie Delecluse; numerous books; also in *Badminton, Strand, Longman's, Cornhill, Grand, Argosy, Novel, Blackwood's, Fores's* and *Land & Water*; Master of West Carbery Foxhounds): Vols.4,6

SORENSON, Edward Sylvester (1869-1939; novelist, poet, writer; on *Sydney Morning Herald* and *Bulletin*; also in *Lone Hand* and *Argosy*): Vol.13

SPENDER, Brenda Elizabeth (1884-1967; journalist, novelist, playwright, reviewer, author; literary editor *Country Life*; fiction, humour, children's short stories; also in *Church Times, Homes & Gardens, John O'London's, Quiver, Lady's Realm, London, Cassell's, Black & White, Novel, Red, Grand, Idler, Pall Mall, Sketch* and *Punch*): Vols.18,19

SPRIGG, Stanhope William (1867-1932; editor of newspapers in Sheffield, Nottingham and Southampton; then to *Amalgamated Press; Ward Lock & Co.* publishers; editor of *Daily Mail; Daily*

Express; Pearson's; editor of both *Windsor* and *Cassell's* magazines; *London Evening Standard*; editor of *Athenaeum*; wrote novels under various pen-names; also in *Ludgate* and *Royal*): Vol.2

STAWELL, Maud Margaret (1865-1949; pen-names Maud Cooper-Key, Maud Key, Rodolph Stawell; writer and novelist; also in *Country Life, Gentlemen's, English Illustrated* and *Pall Mall*): Vol.9

STEAD, John William (1877-1958; international rugby player, coach and administrator; on *Southland Times* and *New Zealand Truth*; also in *Badminton*): Vols.6,21

STEAD, William Thomas (1849-1912; journalist, campaigner; editor of *Darlington Northern Echo, Pall Mall Gazette* and *Review of Reviews*; also in *Appleton's, Century, Cosmopolitan, English Illustrated, Cassell's, Badminton, London, Watson's, McClure's, Pearson's, Idler, Windsor* and *Saturday Evening Post*): Vol.P,4

STEER, Valentia (b.1880; journalist, foreign correspondent, author; on staff of *West London Press* and *Daily Mail*; editor *Madras Times*; staff writer on *Pearson's*; also in *Cassell's, Badminton* and *Royal*): Vol.14

STEP, Edward (1855-1931; author of books on botany, zoology and mycology; editor of *Boys* magazine; Natural History editor of the *Captain*; literary adviser to publishers; also in *Cornish, Pall Mall, Pearson's* and *Windsor*): Vols.1-5

STEPNEY-RAWSON, William (1854-1932; Oxford Blue; England football international; played in, and refereed, Football Association Cup Finals; initially a schoolmaster then managing director of family electrical engineering business; his wife, Maud, was a popular fiction writer; also in *Badminton*): Vol.2

STIMSON, Frederic Jesup (1855-1943; pen-name J.S.of Dale; writer, lawyer and diplomat; novelist; wrote law books; also in *Atlantic, Appleton's, Century, Harper's, McClure's* and *Scribner's*): Vol.2

STOCK, Ralph (1881-1962; son of publisher Elliot Stock; no formal education as his youth was spent travelling the world; became an author, playwright and scenario writer; wrote many short stories; also in *Boy's Own Paper, Pearson's, Sievier's, Windsor, Black & White, Metropolitan, Collier's, Ainslee's, Hutchinson's, Grand, Red, Captain, Badminton, Cavalier, Popular, Argosy, Ocean, Hearst's, Bellman, Munsey's, Pacific, Liberty, Saturday Evening Post* and *Sketch*. Vol.19

STUART, Hamish (1862-1910; journalist on *The Star*; books on angling; also in *Blackwood's* and *Cork Examiner*): Vols.1,17

SULLIVAN, Archibald Giberd (author; also in *Appleton's, Captain, Badminton, Chums, Idler, Fores's, Top Notch, Sovereign, Windsor, Smart Set, Sievier's, Pearson's, London* and *Royal*): Vols.8,9,11-13

SURREY, George (b.1885; real name Gordon Volk; pen-names George Sussex, Raymond Knotts; author; also in *Boys' Life, Boy's Own Paper, Cassell's, Captain, Cavalier, Novel, Yes or No, Top Notch, Pearson's, Pall Mall, London, New, Windsor* and *Sketch*): Vol.9

TALBOT, Ethel Mary (1880-1944; novelist and poet; wrote ninety-seven books; also in *Cornhill, Collier's, Red, Pearson's, Novel, Putnam's, Smart Set, McClure's, Boy's Own Paper, Royal, Windsor, Pall Mall* and *Chums*): Vol.7

TARNACRE, Robert (b.1877; real name Robert Cartmell; short story writer; also in *Grand, New, Top Notch, Ainslee's, Pearson's* and *Strand*): Vols.9,14

TENNYSON, Alfred Browning Stanley (1878-1952; author, writer, poet; also in *Pall Mall*): Vols.2,13

THEOBALD, Ernest Henry (1886-1938; journalist, editor and writer; sub-editor *Daily Herald, The People, Sunday Express, Sunday Dispatch, Daily Graphic*; magazine editor *Daily Dispatch*; contributed to magazines and works of reference; sports writer): Vol.17

THORNE, Guy (1876-1923; real name Cyril Arthur Edward Ranger-Gull; other pen-name Leonard Cresswell Ingleby; author and writer; on literary staff of *Saturday Review, Daily Mail* and *Daily Express*; wrote one hundred and twenty-five novels; editor *London Life*; also in *Bookman, Academy, Society, Cassell's, Yes or No, Premier, London, Blue, Red, Lloyd's, Novel, Nash's, Chapman's, Ludgate, Pall Mall* and *Sketch*): Vols.1-5

TOZER, Basil John Joseph (1872-1949; author, journalist, writer, publicity agent, trainer of steeplechase horses; on staff *Daily Mail* and *Daily Express*; contributor to *London Evening Standard*; also in *Badminton, Blue, Bohemian, Cassell's, English Illustrated, Fores's, London, Nineteenth Century, Fortnightly Review, Nash's, Quiver, Pearson's, Windsor, Strand, Tatler* and *Sketch*): Vols.10,15-20

TREVOR, Leo (1865-1927; dramatist, playwright, amateur actor; also in *Pearson's, Badminton* and *Pall Mall*): Vols.2-4

TREVOR, Philip Christian William (1863-1932; on *Daily Telegraph*; wrote sporting books; also in *Cassell's, Idler, Captain, Baily's, Strand, Badminton, Pearson's, Blue* and *Pall Mall*): Vols.2-4,8

TURNER, John Kenneth (1879-1948; publisher, journalist, magazine writer; on *Fresno Republican, Los Angeles Herald, Portland Journal, Mexico Herald* and *American* magazine; publisher of *Stockton Saturday Night*; also in *Everybody's, Green, Black Cat, Adventure* and *Metropolitan*): Vol.13

VAILE, Philip (d.1915; pen-names Keene Twittome and Viator; writer on cricket, golf and lawn tennis; various sporting and humorous books; on *Westminster Gazette, Daily Mail, Evening Standard, Daily News* and *Evening News*; also in *Badminton, Field, Country Life, Captain, London* and *Pearson's*): Vols.1,4-7,9,12,14-16

VERNEDE, Robert Ernest (1875-1917; novelist, poet and writer; also in *Leslie's, Strand, Captain, Pall Mall, Cornhill, Harper's, Pearson's, Nash's, Metropolitan, Temple Bar, Royal, Grand, Lippincott's, English Illustrated, Tatler, Novel, Red* and *London*): Vol.13

VIELE, Herman Knickerbocker (1856-1908; novelist, short-story writer, poet; also in *Cosmopolitan, Appleton's, McClure's, Golden, Ainslee's* and *Idler*): Vol.P,1

WALBRAN, Francis (1851-1909; author and writer on angling; also in *Fishing Gazette, Leeds Mercury, The Field* and *Country Life*): Vol.10

WALLACE, George (1884-1938; real name Stanley Gordon Shaw; other pen-name Stanley Gordon; writer and author; in *Greyfriars Annuals*; also in *Boys' Friend, Cheer Boys Cheer, Boys' Realm, Penny Pictorial, Smart Set, Tale Teller, Yes or No, London, New, Chums, Lloyd's, Smith's, Corner* and *Cassell's*) Vol.19

WALLACE, Richard Horatio Edgar (1875-1932; writer, author, war correspondent, broadcaster, journalist, editor, scriptwriter; wrote eighteen stage plays, nine-hundred and fifty-seven short stories, one-hundred and seventy novels; chairman of London Press Club; on staff at *Reuters, Daily Mail* and *London Evening News*; editor of *Sunday News* and *Rand Daily Mail*; in *Cape Times* and broadcaster for *BBC*; also in *American, Argosy, Ainslee's, Adventure, Badminton, Britannia, Chums, Cosmopolitan, Corner, Cavalier, Collier's, Cassell's, Canadian, Detective, Everybody's, Flynn's, Golden, Grand, Green, Happy Mag, Hampton's, Harper's, Holland's, Hutchinson's, John O'London's, John Bull, Lloyd's, London, McClure's, Maclean's, Metropolitan, Novel, New, Pearson's, Pall Mall, Printers' Pie, Popular, Pan, Red, Royal, Radio Times, Smith's, Strand, Tale Teller, Yes or No, Windsor* and *Saturday Evening Post*): Vol.15

WALWORTH, Frederick (1875-1959; real name Frederick Walworth Brown; fiction writer; also in *Ainslee's, Boys' Life, Cassell's, New, Metropolitan, McClure's, Captain, Leslie's, Munsey's, Windsor, Everybody's, Red, Pearson's, Cosmopolitan* and *Saturday Evening Post*): Vol.3

WARD, Frederick William Orde (1843-1922; pen-name F.Harald Williams; writer and poet; also in *Novel, Strand* and *Windsor*): Vol.1

WARNER, Pelham Francis (1873-1963; journalist, barrister, author, cricket player and administrator; editor of *The Cricketer*; on *Westminster Gazette*; also in *Baily's, Badminton, Cassell's, Captain, Fores's, Grand, Pall Mall, Pearson's, Strand* and *Windsor*): Vols.1,7,15

WATSON, Alfred Edward Thomas (1849-1922; pen-name Rapier; journalist on *London Evening Standard* and *The Times*; editor of *Illustrated Sporting & Dramatic News* and *Badminton* Magazine; also in *Idler, English Illustrated, Fores's, Grand, Lloyd's* and *Longman's*): Vol.1

WEBSTER, Frederick Annesley Michael (1886-1949; pen-names: Michael Annesley, Camox, An Old Boy; took up writing after military service; on *Daily Sketch, Times, Guardian, Field, Daily Mail* and *News Chronicle*; wrote forty-six books on athletics and twenty novels; also in *Boy's Own Paper, Cassell's, Captain, Pearson's, Sovereign, Hutchinson's, Badminton, Tit-Bits, Blue, Baily's, Lloyd's, Grand, Windsor, Regent, New, Strand* and *Chums*. Vols.19,20

WENTWORTH, Norman (1868-1945; pen-name Lydeus Brindle; racing and boxing writer; also in *Harmworth's*): Vols.7-9,11-14,18,19

WESTELL, William Percival (1874-1943; naturalist; curator Letchworth Garden City Museum for thirty years; wrote eighty-four books; gave one hundred and forty-five BBC radio talks; also in *Badminton, English Illustrated, Fores's* and *Royal*): Vol.14

WHEELER, Daniel Edwin (1880-1972; writer and playwright; also in *Top Notch, Smith's, Ainslee's, Liberty, Popular, Detective, New, Ludgate* and *Collier's*): Vol.8

WHITAKER, Herman (1867-1919; author and writer; also in *Argosy, Ainslee's, American, Blue, Century, Cosmopolitan, Everybody's, Harper's, Hutchinson's, Munsey's, Pacific, Popular, Sunset, Royal* and *Strand*): Vol.14

WHITE, Eustace Evans (1870-1922; author; editor of *Hockey Field*; also in *Strand* and *Badminton*): Vols.2,4,6,7,9,11,12,14

WHITE, Frederick Merrick (1859-1935; fiction writer; also in *Cassell's, Blue, Crampton's, Cornhill, Gunter's, Grand, Ludgate, London, Munsey's, Metropolitan, Nash's, New, Pearson's, Premier, Popular, Quiver, Scribner's, Strand, Sketch, Top Notch, Yellow, Red* and *Windsor*): Vol.16

WHITE, Percy (1852-1938; author and journalist; editor of *Public Opinion* and *London Evening News*; also in *English Illustrated, Cassell's, McCall's, Pearson's, Red, Grand, New, London, Pall Mall* and *Munsey's*): Vols.1,3

WHITE, Stewart Edward (1873-1946; fiction writer; also in *Boys' Life, Country Gentleman, Esquire, Liberty, McClure's, Harper's, Lippincott's, Munsey's, Top Notch, Everybody's, Century, Outing, Collier's, Red, Blue, Badminton, Strand* and *Saturday Evening Post*): Vol.1

WILLIAMS, Archibald (1871-1934; Fellow of the Royal Geographical Society; technical journalist; camera and cycling editor of the *Captain*; also in *Grand, Chums, Pearson's, Strand, Harmsworth's, Ludgate, Cassiers* and *Fielden's*): Vols.1-3,5-8,15-18

WILLIAMS, Jesse Lynch (1871-1929; journalist, novelist, author, playwright; on staff of *New York Sun, New York Commercial Advertiser, New York Globe* and *Scribner's*; also in *Appleton's, Argosy, American, Collier's, Cosmopolitan, Golden, Grand, Harper's, McClure's, Metropolitan, Nash's, New, Pearson's, Red, Smart Set* and *Saturday Evening Post*): Vol.21

WINANS, Walter William (1852-1920; author, marksman, horse breeder, sculptor and painter; won Olympic gold medals; wrote ten books; also in *Badminton*): Vols.2,5,10,14

WISHING, Stuart (short story writer; also in *Novel, London, Captain, Pearson's, Royal, Cassell's* and *Grand*): Vol.5

WOOD, Eugene (1860-1923; author; also in *Ainslee's, American, Boys' Life, Century, Collier's, Everybody's, Harper's Bazar, Hampton's, Harper's, McClure's, Munsey's, Pearson's, Watson's, Smith's, Red* and *Metropolitan*): Vol.7

WOODS, Samuel Moses James (1867-1931; cricket, rugby and hockey international player; also in *Cassell's, Badminton, Captain* and *Vanity Fair*): Vol.4

WYNDHAM, Horace Cowley (1875-1970; journalist and author; contributor to *Morning Post, News Chronicle, Sunday Times*; also in *Argosy, Boy's Own Paper, Cassell's, Captain, English Illustrated, Gaiety, Grand, Humorist, Hutchinson's, Harmsworth's, Idler, London, Ludgate, Munsey's, Pall Mall, Royal, Badminton, Sketch, Strand, Tatler, Windsor* and *Saturday Evening Post*): Vol.2

ADDITIONAL WRITERS

ABREY, William; (1858-1921; also in *Badminton*): Vol.1

ADAIR-DIGHTON, Charles Allen (1885-1953; author, journalist, surgeon; on *Sporting Chronicle, The Sportsman, Sporting Life*): Vol.20

ALEXANDER, Harry (1879-1915; England rugby international; also in *Captain*): Vols.2,4

ALFORD, Charles Earl (1881-1944; canine writer; also in *Pearson's*): Vol.10

APPLEGARTH, William Reuben (1890-1958; athlete): Vols.20,21

ARMSTRONG, George (1856-1940; writer; also in *English Illustrated, Cornhill* and *Pall Mall*): Vols.P,20,21

ARP, Philip (also in *Idler*): Vols.3,5,8,9

AUNGIER, Julia (d.1947; international golfer; Blackheath Golf Club Ladies president): Vol.6

AUSTIN, Cyril Frederick (1884-1915; journalist and author; on staff at *Reuter's*; also in *Windsor*): Vols.3,8

BADCOCK, Gerald Horace (writer and military): Vols.16,19

BAGGE, Henri (expert on French kickboxing and duelling): Vol.8

BARKER, Aldred Farrar (1868-1964; textiles, sheepdogs, motor cars, caravans; books on caravanning): Vols.17,19

BARNETT, Francis Robert (barrister; short story writer): Vol.9

BARRETT, Blundell (also in *Bellman* and *Grand*): Vols.5-7

BATCHELDER, William James (1880-1958; writer; in *Temple Bar* and *Cornhill*): Vol.16

BATHO, Robert (b.1856; journalist and writer; on *London Evening News* and *Toronto Star*): Vol.14

BEACHAM, Thomas Edward (1890-1964; engineer; 'the father of industrial hydraulics'): Vols.19,21

BEAL, Ridley (also in *Leslie's*): Vol.2

BEAMISH, Alfred Ernest (1879-1944; tennis player and coach): Vols.20,21

BEEMAN, Stanley Welch (b.1879; military, author and journalist; on staff *London Evening Standard* and *Daily Sketch*; contributed to *Morning Post* and *Daily Telegraph*; also in *Pall Mall*): Vol.19

BEGG, Frederick (Cox of the Cambridge Eight in 1894 and 95): Vol.1

BENTLEY, John James (1860-1918; President of the Football League and Vice-President of the Football Association): Vols.1,2,4,6,7,15

BERESFORD-RYLEY, Margaret (d.1917; writer; also in *London* and *Ludgate*): Vol.14

BIRCH, Arthur (1875-1911; jockey): Vol. 12

BLACK, George Gordon (1885-1954; county cricketer): Vol.11

BLIN-DESBLEDS, Lucian (lecturer in aeronautical engineering at Regent Street Polytechnic; also in *The Engineer*): Vols.15-17

BLAKE, Harry (publisher; books on yachting): Vols.13,15

BOOT, James Sydney (1874-1950; sports writer; also in *Captain, Grand* and *Strand*): Vols.14,16,18,20,21

BOURKE, Dermot Robert Wyndham (1851-1927, politician): Vol.5

BRODRIBB, George Williamson (1876-1946; water polo referee): Vol.7

BROOK, Arthur (1886-1957; author, artist and ornithologist; also in *Badminton*): Vols.16-19

BROWNE, Thomas Henry (horse breeding; author; also in *Badminton*): Vols.1,2,4,8,11,13,20,21

BUCKLEY, Frederick (d.1976; journalist and poet; on staff *New York Evening Mail* and *Birmingham (UK) Evening Despatch*; *BBC* radio presenter; also in *Black Cat, Collier's, Liberty, McClure's, Adventure, Argosy, Blue, Hutchinson's, Royal, Saturday Evening Post* and *Idler*): Vols.8,15

BUDDEN, Charles William (1878-1952; author): Vol.15

BURDEN, Alfred (angling writer; also in *Fishing Gazette, Fores's* and *Baily's*): Vols.2,19

BURLINGHAM, Frederick (winter sports; also in *Badminton*): Vol.14

BURNS, Tommy (1881-1955; real name Noah Brusso, professional boxer): Vols.9,13

CALHOUN-HAINES, Alice (fiction writer and poet; also in *Metropolitan*): Vol.4

CAMPBELL, Alexander Boswell (1877-1917; Master of Hailsham Harriers): Vol.6

CAMPBELL, Dorothy Iona (1883-1945; both British and American ladies golf champion; North Berwick Golf Club ladies chairman): Vol.6

CAMPBELL, John (president Scottish Quoits Association): Vol.7

CANNON, Herbert Mornington (1873-1962; successful jockey): Vols.1,19

CARRUTHERS, James (Muswell Hill Bowls Club; English National Champion): Vol.5

CARTER, Bernard (rowing, grouse, horse racing): Vols.7-9,11

CARTER, Rufus Seaman (1866-1932; writer, farmer and politician; also in *Windsor*): Vol.16

CASTORS, Pollock (motoring and cycling): Vols.5-7,9,11,13

CHESHIRE, Horace Fabian (1854-1922; books on chess and board games): Vol.17

CHESTERTON, George Lewis (1869-1956; author): Vols.9,11-14

CLARE, Claremont (believed to be a nom-de-plume of Edith Somerville; also in *Baily's*): Vol.9

CLARK, Norman (b.1892; boxer, referee, administrator, author, writer; books on boxing; secretary British Boxing Board of Control; also in *Badminton, Baily's, Cassell's* and *Chums*): Vol.19

COBB, Humphry Henry (1873-1949; author and skater): Vol.20

COLT, Harry (1869-1951; golf course architect): Vol.14

COOK, Edgar (editor of *The Garden*): Vols.4,6-8

COOPER, James (huntsman for Vale of White Horse [Cricklade]): Vol.13

CORBALLY, Cyril (1880-1946; croquet player and administrator; also in *Croquet Gazette*): Vol.11

COVENTRY, Charles John (1867-1929; soldier, Test cricketer, trainer and rider of steeplechase horses): Vol.10,14

CRAVEN, Francis (writer; also in *Lady's Realm*): Vol.8

CRISP, Bertram (also in *Novel* and *Royal*): Vols.8,9

CROFT, Frank William (1865-1940; croquet player, tournament manager and writer on the sport): Vol.3

CURTIS, William Henry (bicycle designer and aviation fuel scientist; also in *Badminton*): Vol.16

CUTLER, Alfred Edward William (1875-1935; fisherman, writer, author, artist, photographer; various books; also in *Girl's Own Paper*): Vol.16

DAY, Frank Parker (1881-1950; poet; also in *Harper's, Atlantic* and *Red*): Vol.19

DEANE, Henry Bargrave Finnelley (1848-1919; fencer and High Court judge; in *Vanity Fair*): Vol.18

DE BEAR, Archibald (1882-1959; football writer, playwright, author): Vol.3

DICKINSON, Dorothy (poet; also in *Cassell's, Happy Mag, Nash's, Pearson's* and *Windsor*): Vol.18

DIXON, Charles Percy (1873-1939; tennis player and coach): Vol.20

DONEY, May (poet and author; also in *Smith's*): Vols.2-6

DUNCAN, George (golfer; also in *Badminton*): Vols.P,18,20

DUNCAN, Stanley (pen-name Wildfowler; writer; also in *Badminton*): Vols.10,12,17,18

DWIGHT, Jonathan (1858-1929; ornithologist; author and editor): Vol.2

EDWARDS-MOSS, John (1850-1935; author; also in *Badminton*): Vols.1,3,14

EGERTON-GREEN, Francis (manager of Hurlingham Club; also in *Sphere*): Vol.11

ELDRED, Charles Edward (author and naval engineer; also in *Wide World, Badminton, Temple Bar* and *English Illustrated*): Vols.16,19

ELGOOD, Paul (author; also in *Badminton, English Illustrated* and *Strand*): Vol.9

ELKINGTON, William (1852-1931; writer and author; also in *Lady's Realm, Young England, Captain* and *Windsor*): Vol.19

ELLIS, David (writer; also in *Novel*): Vol.13

ELWELL, Joseph Bowne (1873-1920; writer on bridge; nine books): Vol.16

FANE, Anthony Mildmay Julian (1859-1922; also known as Earl of Westmorland; cricket for Northamptonshire; military career): Vol.12

FFRENCH, Cyril (Australian racing journalist): Vol.9

FISHER, Alexander (1864-1936; fiction writer; also in *Pan, Novel* and *Windsor*): Vol.14

FLEMMING, Leonard (1880-1946; author and humorist; also in *Grand, Novel* and *London*): Vols.3,6

FOSTER, Reginald Erskine (1878-1914; cricketer and businessman; in *Badminton*): Vols.P,2,21

FOWLER, William Herbert (1856-1941; cricketer, golf course designer and banker): Vol.12

FRECHENCOURT, Raoul de (French writer): Vols.13-15

FRY, [Miss] Beatrice (aviation): Vol.13

FRY, [Mrs] Beatrice Holme (1862-1946, wife of Charles Fry; harridan): Vol.P,8

FRY, Sidney Harold (1869-1961; billiards & snooker player; amateur golfer; book author: also in *Badminton*): Vol.11

FULTON, John Henry Westropp (author; Ski Club of Great Britain; also in *Badminton*): Vol.16

GARLAND, Wodehouse Raven Heath (1854-1944; author and journalist): Vol.18

GIFFORD, Mabel (poet and author; also in *London*): Vol.7

GLOSSOP, Bertram Robert Mitford (1870-1941; military officer, author and writer; also in *Badminton*): Vols.16,21

GLOVER, James (writer; also in *Grand* and *Pall Mall*): Vol.21

GOLDIE, Claude John Dashwood (1876-1956; rowed for Cambridge University in Boat Race of 1898 and 1899; woolbroker): Vol.1

GORDON, Home Seton Charles Montagu (1871-1956; journalist, author, writer, publisher; contributed to *Encyclopedia Britannica*; also in *Cricketer, Windsor, Grand, Printers' Pie, Fores's* and *Badminton*): Vols.P,8,19

GOULD, Arthur Joseph (1864-1919; rugby international player, referee and selector; also in *Cassell's* and *Chums*): Vol.6

GRAHAM, Douglas Beresford Malise Ronald (1852-1925; outdoor sportsman, soldier, hereditary peer; also in *Strand*): Vol.18

GRAY, Alexander (motoring author and journalist; also in *Autocar* and *Bystander*): Vols.12,13

GRESWELL, Charles (fiction writer; also in *Lady's Realm*): Vol.10

GROGAN, Evelyn (author of children's books; also in *Novel, Pearson's, Badminton* and *Royal*): Vol.11

GULLETT, Henry Somer (1878-1940; journalist and writer; on staff of *Geelong Advertiser* and *Daily Telegraph*; also in *Strand* and *Lone Hand* [Australia]): Vol.21

HALL, Lue (writer; also in *McClure's, Leslie's* and *Saturday Evening Post*): Vol.4

HALLETT, Stephen (also in *Grand* and *Strand*): Vol.2

HAMILTON, Charles Edward Archibald Watkin (1876-1939; baronet, military): Vols.2,6,8,11

HAMILTON, Colin (wrote five books on swimming; also in *Chums* and *Badminton*): Vols.15,17

HAMILTON, Ernest (editor of *The Yachtsman*): Vol.13,17,19,20

HAMPOL, Leonard (science fiction writer): Vol.8

HANDS, Reginald Harry Myburgh (1888-1918; cricket and rugby international; barrister): Vols.16,18

HARRIS, Lawrence (travel writer; in *Cosmopolitan*): Vol.P,14

HARRIS, Stanley Shute (1881-1926; international footballer, cricketer and headmaster; also in *Cassell's*): Vol.6

HAYNES, Nathan Gallup Williams (1886-1970; author,journalist, editor, publisher; on staff *New York Sun*; editor *Field & Fancy, Massachusetts Herald Field* and various trade journals): Vol.17

HEMINGWAY, Richard D'Oyly (1878-1961; writer): Vol.14

HENDERSON, Kenneth (writer, author of forty-two books; also in *Idler*): Vol.11

HERD, Alexander (1868-1944; golfer; also in *Lloyd's*): Vols.P,18

HILL, Basil Alexander (1880-1960; England rugby international; Army Major-General; president Rugby Football Union): Vol.6

HILL, Leonard Erskine (1866-1952; physiologist, watercolour artist and children's author; also in *Britannia*): Vol.10

HOLDING, Thomas Hiram (1844-1930; camping writer and author; compiled *The Camper's Handbook*; founded The Association of Cycle Campers): Vols.3,9,13

HOLLAND, William Thomas (writer, artist, cricketer; also in *Yes or No*): Vol.16

HOLLENDER, Vivian Cecil (1880-1953; writer; also in *Badminton*): Vols.16,20

HOLMES, Ernest (sporting writer; also in *Badminton*): Vol.13

HORSPOOL, Arthur (b.1875; poet; also in *Boy's Own Paper*): Vol.5

HORWOOD, Arthur Reginald (1879-1951; author and writer; also in *Chums, English Illustrated, Captain* and *Boy's Own Paper*): Vols.15-17

HOUGHTON, William (fishing writer; also in *Fishing Gazette*): Vol.16

HOUSMAN, Alfred Edward (1859-1936; poet; also in *Argosy, Golden, McClure's* and *Cornhill*): Vol.16

HUGHES, Henry (golfer and author; also in *Cassell's*): Vols.20,21

HUNT, Samuel Syrus (1873-1953, pen-name Bernard Moore for poetry; author and poet; wrote six books of poetry and seven on Cornwall; also in *Royal, To-Day, Grand, Pall Mall* and *Windsor*): Vol.16

HUSSEY, Eyre William (b.1840; writer, archer, clergyman; also in *Badminton* and *Fores's*): Vols.3,6,9,14

HUTCHEON, John Silvester (1882-1957; Australian sportsman and administrator; barrister): Vols.12,16,17,20

HUTCHISON, Cecil (writer and golfer; in *Badminton, World of Golf* and *Golf Illustrated*): Vol.14

INCH, Thomas (1881-1963; strongman; books on weightlifting; also in *Chums*): Vols.3,7

INGHAM, Jack (journalist on *News Chronicle*): Vols.13,19

INGLIS, Gordon (1885-1924; founding member of The Federation of International Lawn Tennis; Australian Olympic Games Delegate; wrote *Sport & Pastime in Australia*, the seminal work on the subject): Vol.16

INNES, Arthur Norman (1874-1953; writer; also in *Grand, Red, Nash's* and *Windsor*): Vol.4

INSH, George Pratt (1883-1956; schoolmaster, historian, essayist, author and fiction writer; numerous books; in *Glasgow Herald* and *Glasgow Evening News*; also in academic and historical journals): Vol.16

INSKIP-HARRISON, Frederic (1831-1923; also in *Cornhill, Harper's, Badminton, New* and *Fores's*): Vol.4

JACKETT, Edward John (1878-1935; rugby union international; Cornish cycling champion; Cape mounted policeman; theatre manager): Vol.16

JAMIESON, Melvill Allan (b.1881; journalist, Consul-General, foreign correspondent; on staff *Montreal Star* and associated newspapers then European Manager; also in *Journal of the Paris Oceanographic Institute*): P,19

JARDINE, Alfred (fishing writer; also in *Fishing Gazette*): Vol.10

JARROTT, Charles (1877-1944; racing-car driver and businessman; also in *Badminton*): Vols.1,5

JEFFRIES, John Richard (1848-1887; nature and health articles, novelist): Vol.6

JENKINS, Edmund Howard (1856-1921; gardening writer and author; also in *Country Life*): Vol.17

JEPHSON, Digby Loder Armeroid (1871-1926; cricketer, author, Stock Exchange; also in *Boy's Own Paper, Badminton* and *Captain*): Vols.1,7,9,12,16,17,19,21

JERROLD, Walter Copeland (1865-1929; author and journalist; sub-editor on *The Observer*; literary staff *Daily Telegraph*, Amalgamated Press and *Glasgow Evening News*; many books): Vol.13

JOHNES, Gwendoline (1878-1953; real name Gladys Jones; novelist and playwright): Vol.2

JOHNSON, Charles (motoring journalist; also in *Autocar*): Vol.16,18,19

JOSLING, Harold William Edwin (b.1879; novelist and author; also in *Novel*): Vol.9

KATSCHER, Leopold (1853-1939; writer and author; also in *Pearson's*): Vol.20

KIFF, DeLaRue Robert (1875-1945; poet; also in *Blue* and *Royal*): Vol.16

KNIGHT-BRUCE, John Horace Wyndham (1885-1951; writer; also in *Strand* and *Badminton*): Vol.17

KNOWLES, William Henry (1857-1943; sporting articles): Vol.9

LACEY, Courtenay (fiction writer; also in *Sievier's*): Vols.10,14

LAMBOURNE, Allan Sampson (fiction writer): Vol.7

LANE, Charles Frederick (Canadian writer and explorer; also in *Idler, Badminton* and *Cavalier*): Vol.11

LANYON, Helen (1882-1979; poet and author; also in *Ainslee's, American, Cassell's, Grand, Novel, Pearson's* and *Pall Mall*): Vol.13
LARCOMBE, Ethel Warneford Thomson (1879-1965; lawn tennis and badminton champion): Vol.6

LARDEN, Walter (climber and author): Vol.16

LARUS, John Ruse (1858-1920; fiction and short story writer; also in *Cosmopolitan*): Vols.12,13

LATTIMER, Robert Binney (1863-1929; schoolmaster; magazine editor; rugby referee; also in *Cornhill* and *Badminton*): Vols.6,7

LEGARD, Thomas Francis (1885-1933; also in *Badminton* and *Pall Mall*): Vol.21

LEIGH, Clifford (1865-1913; actor and writer): Vols.19,21

LEMAN, Edward Maurice (b.1854; rifle shooting; also in *Outing, English Illustrated* and *Harmworth's*): Vols.P,4,9-12,17,18

LIVINGSTONE, Robert (journalist; writer on Scottish football): Vol.2

LLEWELLYN, Owen John (1870-1943; pen-name Owen John; motor writer; on *Autocar*; autobiography 1927): Vols.7-10

LLOYD, Freeman (author of canine books): Vols.15,16

LOCK, Henry Osmond (1879-1962; writer): Vol.14

LODGE, Arthur (1858-1929; also in *Crampton's, English Illustrated, Grand, Idler, Novel, London, Red* and *Pall Mall*): Vols.2,3

LORING, Andrews (1858-1929; real name Lorin Lathop; other pen-name Kenyon Gambier; wrote serial stories for magazines): Vol.2

LOUGHNAN, Joseph Patrick (grouse shooting; also in *Captain*): Vol.14

MAAS, William Harold (1862-1937; writer; editor *London Daily Chronicle*; also in *Strand* and *London*): Vol.17

McCARTNEY, William (author and humorous writer; in *Cassell's* and *Captain*): Vols.2,14

McDONALD, Daniel Alexander (1858-1937; curling): Vol.6

MacDONALD, James (editor of *Farmer and Stockbreeder*): Vols.2,13

McGREGOR, William (1846-1911; founder of the Football League): Vol.2

MACKENZIE, Morell (writer on canine breeds, author): Vols.16-20

MACLENNAN, John (b.1871; author; many books on Scotland; wrote advertorials): Vols.9-14

MCMINNIES, William Gordon (1887-1982; editor of *Light Car and Cyclecar*): Vols.11,12

MACPHERSON, Hugh (writer, also in *Fores's* and *Badminton*): Vol.19

MAGUIRE, Florence (pen-name Conor Maguire; fiction and religious writer; also in *Ladies' Home Journal*): Vol.9

MALCOLM, George (b.1840; pen-name Gunsman; grouse shooting; also in *Badminton*): Vols.11,12

MARKS, Howard (gunsmith; secretary of Miniature Rifle Clubs): Vols.4,5

MARSHAL, Alan (1883-1915; cricketer for Queensland and Surrey): Vol.7

MARSTON, Robert Bright (1853-1927; angler, publisher and editor of *Fishing Gazette*; also in *Harmsworth*): Vol.1

MASFRAND, Andre de (1865-1944; journalist on *The Aerophile*; Aero Club of France): Vol.6

MASSEY, Stewart Marsden (1877-1934; badminton player, writer, author; editor of *Badminton Gazette*; also in *Badminton* magazine): Vol.20

MATTHEWS, Arthur Ratcliff (1866-1932; editor of *The Angler's News*; also in *Country Life*): Vol.13

MAXWELL, Aymer Edward (1977-1914; military officer; wrote books on game; also in *Badminton* and *Red*): Vols.15,16

MEAGHER, George Alfred (1866-1930; figure skater; three books on skating): Vol.4

MERWIN, Henry Childs (1853-1929; author; also in *Harper's, Atlantic* and *Century*): Vol.1

MICHELL, Edward Blair (1842-1926; rowing and hawking; also in *English Illustrated*): Vol.2

MILLER, Alan (cricketer, writer and journalist): Vol.13

MILLER, George Arthur (1867-1935; Olympic Polo Medalist; Assistant Manager Roehampton Club): Vol.15

MONCKTON, Oliver Paul (1879-1919; writer and author; also in *Boy's Own Paper*): Vol.18

MONTAGUE-VESEY, Thomas (b.1888; motoring writer; also in *Idler* and *Autocar*): Vols.13,14

MOORE, Stephen (fiction writer; also in *Ainslee's* and *Badminton*): Vols.10,11,14

MOSSE, Arthur Henry Eyre (1877-1943; military writer and author; also in *Badminton* and *Cornhill*): Vol.12

MULLETT, Cyril (b.1853, writer; also in *Idler, Chapman's, Pall Mall* and *Badminton*): Vol.1

MUNRO, Leo Crawford (sports journalist and artist): Vol.15

MURDOCH, George (fiction writer; also in *Red*): Vol.12

NEWGASS, Edgar Isaac (author, poet and lyricist): Vol.10

NEWITT, Edward (1866-1952; real name Edward James Dunn-Newitt; Southfields Rifle Club; books on rifles; invented rifle sights; also in *Shooting & Fishing* and *Country Life*): Vols.5,6,8

NOBLE, Stanley (secretary National Cyclists Union; also in *Royal*): Vols.3,4,6,18

OLLEY, George Anthony (1881-1955; Anerley Bicycle Club): Vols.2,3,5

ORMISTON-SMITH, Frank (b.1878; mountaineer and film-maker): Vols.2-4,6

OSMAN, Alfred Henry (1864-1930; editor of *Racing Pigeon*; also in *Strand* and *Captain*): Vols.1,10,12,17,19

PARKE, James Cecil (1881-1946; rugby international, tennis player, golfer, solicitor, writer; also in *Strand, London* and *Boy's Own Paper*): Vol.21

PARSONS, Bernard (also in *Cassell's, Badmintn, Pearson's, Royal* and *Strand*): Vols.5,6,9,10,13-19

PAWLEY, Thomas Edward (1859-1923; cricketer, ground manager and publican): Vols.1,16

PEARSON, Frances Issette (1861-1941; golfer; founding secretary Ladies' Golf Union): Vol.6

PEARSON, Robert (rifle shooting): Vols.4-8

PHILLIPS, Ernest (1870-1956; sports writer; also in *Boy's Own Paper* and *Strand*): Vols.15,18

PHILPOT, Hamlet Cunningham Vachell (1887-1968; writer and military; also in *Grand, Red, Pall Mall* and *Windsor*): Vol.19

PHIPPS, Sidney Arnold (1866-1921; also in *Captain, Fores's, London Society* and *Chums*): Vol.7

PONTOPPIDAN, Henrik (1857-1943; Norwegian writer): Vol.16

PORTER, John (1838-1922; founded Newbury Racecourse, horse trainer; also in *Badminton*): Vols.1,8

RAMSEY, Hubert Walter (1874-1968; Olympic lacrosse medalist; stockbroker): Vols.2,6

RAPHAEL, John Edward (1882-1917; rugby international; first-class cricketer; barrister, politican, author; also in *Cassell's* and *Windsor*): Vols.2,20

RAYMOND, George Lansing (1839-1929; author and poet; nominated for the Nobel Prize in Literature seven times; many books on art): Vol.4

RICHARDS, Mabel (poet; also in *Captain*): Vols.3,4,11,18,19

ROBBINS, William Henry (horse racing): Vol.12

ROBERTSON, George Stuart (1872-1967; athlete, Olympian, author, barrister; also in *Badminton*): Vol.9

ROBERTSON, John Tait (1877-1935; Scottish football international and manager in England and Hungary): Vols.3,4

ROBSON, Philip (hockey administrator; wrote books on the game): Vol.16

ROLLS, Charles Stewart (1877-1910; motoring and aviation pioneer; also in *Cassell's* and *London*): Vols.2,6,11

ROSS-THOMAS, Leonard (fencer and barrister; also in *Boy's Own Paper*): Vol.19

ROWAN, Hill (author; also in *Sketch*): Vol.6

ROWLEY, Peter (fiction writer; also in *Strand*): Vols.4,5,10

SABINE, Henry William (b.1855; writer): Vol.9

SANDON, Richard (president of the Amateur Swimming Club): Vol.5

SAUNDERS, Harold (writer on hockey): Vol.20

SCOTT, Frederick Newton (1860-1931; short story writer): Vol.1

SCOTT, James (writer; also in *Boy's Own Paper, Minster, Ludgate, Pearson's, Royal, Captain, English Illustrated* and *Strand*): Vols.18,20

SCUDAMORE-JARVIS, Claude (1879-1953; colonial administrator, writer and author; also in *Fores's* and *Badminton*): Vols.18,20,21

SECKER, Edward Walter (1861-1927; musician and composer; best known for the rugby song *On The Ball*): Vol.4

SHAW, Desmond (1877-1960; writer; founder of The Boxers' Union; also in *Pall Mall*): Vols.P,15-17,19,20

SHELLEY, Eugene (writer, also in *Strand*): Vols.5,8

SHOVELLER, Stanley Howard (1881-1959; dual Olympic hockey gold medalist; won Military Cross; stockbroker; also in *Captain*): Vol.6

SHRUBSOLE, Edgar (pen-names Ibis Tag and Practical; author and angling writer; also in *Badminton*): Vols.16-21

SLOWBURN, Harry (bookmaker): Vol.14

SLYMN, James Abel (b.1879; on *Kent & Sussex Press*): Vol.16

SMEATON-MUNRO, Ion (1887-1970; journalist, author, soldier; on staff of *Glasgow Herald, Morning Post, Daily Telegraph, Daily Mail*): Vol.20

SMITH, Bertram (1876-1918; author; also in *Outing, Royal* and *Strand*): Vols.1,9,18,20

SMITH, George Bernard (writer and military): Vol.16

SMITH, Gilbert Oswald (1872-1943; footballer, author and school master; also in *Cassell's, Pall Mall, Strand* and *Windsor*): Vol.6

SMITH, Leslie (writer; also in *Strand*): Vol.14

SMITH, Macdonald (fitness writer and author; on International Congress of Physical Education): Vol.3

SOMERVILE, William (1675-1742; poet): Vol.6

SPOFFORTH, Frederick Robert (1853-1926; cricketer and company director; also in *Badminton, New, Baily's* and *Captain*): Vol.3

SQUIRE, Philip (secretary of Thames Punting Club): Vols.5,12,14

STEVENSON, Harry (1874-1944; world billiards champion; also in *Badminton*): Vols.3,6,12-14,20

STEVENSON, Philip (1871-1920; novelist mainly writing about French history; also in *Grand*): Vol.1

STUART, Maud (international ladies' golfer; Portrush Golf Club ladies' chairman): Vol.6

SULZBACHER, Willy (1876-1908; athlete, fencer, writer): Vol.5

SURTEES, Robert Smith (1803-1864; editor, novelist, sporting writer; founded the *New Sporting Magazine*): Vols.P,6,11-13

SWEET, George (1852-1923; writer on animals): Vol.17

SWOYER, Alfred Edward (1884-1963; writer, county court judge; also in *American, Boys' Life, Black Cat, New* and *Outing*): Vol.20

SYERS, Edgar Morris Wood (1863-1946; figure skater and coach; Olympic medalist; also in *Badminton*): Vol.4

SYERS, Florence Madeline (1881-1917; figure skating champion, Olympic medalist; also in *Badminton*): Vol.6

SYMONDS, Frank Eugene (1868-1956; writer): Vol.11

TALFOURD-PADGETT, Sydney (1868-1935; writer): Vol.18

TAYLOR, Jesse Paul (d.1923; first secretary of Fly-Fishers' Club; fishing writer; also in *Fishing Gazette, Boy's Own Paper, Ludgate* and *Windsor*): Vol.9

TAYLOR, John Henry (1871-1963; professional golfer; golf course architect; also in *Boys' Life* and *Cornhill*): Vols.2-5

THOMAS, Charles Edward (sculling; also in *Badminton* and *Captain*): Vols.5,7,8,14,15,17,21

THOMAS, Edward (horse racing; also in *Badminton*): Vols.11,15,16

THOMAS, Frederick Hall (1886-1927; known as Freddie Welsh; boxing champion; also in *Strand*): Vols.13,21

THOMPSON, Algernon Alfred Cankerien (1880-1944; painter and author): Vol.20

THOMPSON, Bertha Mildred (1876-1953; Women's Amateur Golf Champion): Vols.3,4

THOMPSON, Charles Vance (1863-1925; author, editor, playwright; also in *Cassell's, Captain, Cosmopolitan, Everybody's, Munsey's, Nash's, Phoenix, Hearst's, Hampton's, Harper's, London, Smart Set, Flynn's, Outing, Hutchinson's, Idler, Lippincott's* and *Saturday Evening Post*): Vol.2

THOMPSON, George Stafford (1833-1916; coxswain, gentleman rider, landowner): Vol.7

THUNDER, Julian Adair (1883-1934; fiction writer): Vol.17

TIMMIS, Edgar William (1868-1945; tennis player and railway engineer): Vol.3

TOWNSEND, Charles Lucas (1876-1958; cricket for Gloucestershire & England; solicitor): Vols.1,5

TREGASKIS, Mervyn (stage coaching): Vol.8

TREVETHEN, Joshua (fiction writer): Vol.14

TRUMBLE, Hugh (1867-1938; cricketer; secretary of Melbourne Cricket Club; wrote on cricket for Australian newspapers): Vol.3

TRUMPER, Victor Thomas (1877-1915; cricketer; treasurer of Australian Rugby League): Vol.3

TUNBRIDGE, Walter William (1856-1943; writer, also in *Argosy, Novel* and *Pearson's*): Vol.16

TURNER, Richard Whitbourn (1867-1932; barrister then County Court Judge; Cambridge University Athletic Blue): Vol.16

VANIMAN, Melvyn (1866-1912; avaitor and photographer): Vol.12

VERNON, Courtenay Percy Robert (1857-1926; dramatist and military): Vol.16

WADE, George Alfred (1863-1938; author and writer; also in *Pearson's, Cassell's, Windsor, Captain, Ludgate, Idler, Pall Mall, Badminton, London, Royal* and *Boy's Own Paper*): Vol. 20

WALLIS-TAYLER, Alexander James (1854-1934; motor writer and refrigeration designer; books on motor vehicles; also in *Autocar*): Vol.7

WALLS, Thomas Kirby (1883-1949; actor, director, playwright, horse trainer; also in *Pall Mall*): Vol.18

WARD, Frederick William (canine specialist): Vols.16,17

WARNER, George Townsend (1865-1916; author, schoolmaster, cricketer; also in *Cornhill*): Vol.21

WATSON, James (d.1915; author of books on dog breeding; also in *Century* and *Badminton*): Vol.4

WEBB, William Edward (b.1862; Olympian; president of Amateur Diving Association): Vol.9

WEIGALL, Gerald John Villiers (1870-1944; cricketer, rackets, squash; also in *Boy's Own Paper, Cricketer* and *Badminton*): Vol.16

WEISS, Frederic Henry (1862-1924; Australian billiards player): Vol.8

WHEELER, Arthur Stanley (author and writer; also in *Cavalier, Smart Set, Collier's* and *Outing*): Vol.16

WHITSON, John Harvey (1854-1936; teacher and writer; also in *Argosy, Red, Blue* and *Cavalier*): Vol.3

WILDING, Anthony Frederick (1883-1915; barrister and tennis player; wrote an autobiography; also in *Pearson's* and *Pall Mall*): Vols.15-17,19-21

WILKE, Dorette (1867-1930; founder Chelsea College of Physical Education): Vol.1

WILLIAMS, Henry Justus (croquet): Vol.11

WILSON, John Rendell (1881-1918; writer; also in *Motor Boating*): Vol.17

WOLSTENHOLME-ELMY, Elizabeth Clarke : (1833-1918; pen-name Ignota; writer and author): Vol.13

WOODHOUSE, Vernon Kerslake (b.1890; journalist, author and playwright; on staff of *Sporting Life*, *The People* and *Passing Show*; also in *Hutchinson's, Pan, Pearson's, Strand* and *Pall Mall*): Vol.15

WOODS, Litchfield (author, poet, magazine writer): Vol.3

WORRALL, Lechmere (1875-1957; real-name L.W.Clark; playwright, author, doctor): Vol.21

WREST, Arthur (1876-1925; writer): Vol.20

ILLUSTRATORS

As with the writers many sources have been used to try and get as much correct detail as possible about the magazine's illustrators. These talented men (but very few women) created so much which remained in the minds of the readers. Quite a number of their original works now reside in the Victoria & Albert Museum.

ALDIN, Cecil Charles Windsor (1870-1935; studied at South Kensington School of Art; sporting artist and humorous illustrator; Master of the South Berkshire Foxhounds; also in *Pearson's, Graphic, Windsor, Cassell's, Pall Mall, Sketch, Sphere, Printers' Pie, Ludgate, Royal, Captain, Boy's Own Paper, Poster, Idler, Punch, English Illustrated, John Bull, Badminton, Illustrated Sporting & Dramatic News* and *Illustrated London News*. Vols.2,15-17

ALLEN, Olive (1879-1957; pen-name Olive Biller; studied at Liverpool, Lambeth and Slade Schools of Art; taught at British Columbia College of Art; artist and book illustrator; also in *Studio, Cassell's* and *Idler*): Vol.14

AMBROSE, Charles Napier (1876-1946; a prolific writer, caricaturist and illustrator on sporting matters which appeared regularly in magazines of the day; also in *Golf Illustrated, Field, Captain, Bystander, Country Life, Punch, Badminton, Tatler, Strand* and *Pearson's*): Vols.6-11,13,14

ARMOUR, George Denholm (1864-1949; studied at Edinburgh School of Art and Royal Scottish Academy; illustrator, painter and author; drawings mainly on sporting and country subjects; also in *Badminton, Country Life, Daily Graphic, Gaiety, Strand, Punch, Tatler, Fores's, Graphic, Pearson's, Pall Mall, Unicorn, Butterfly, Longbow, Windsor* and *Illustrated Sporting & Dramatic News*): Vols.10,12,14

ASHTON, George Rossi (1857-1942; studied at South Kensington School of Art; black & white artist and illustrator; worked in Australia on *Illustrated Australian News, Illustrated Sydney News* and *The Bulletin* with Phil May; specialised in advertising and commercial drawings; also in *Illustrated London News, Pearson's, Graphic, St.James's, Pall Mall* and *Sketch*): Vol.1

BABBAGE, Frederick George (1858-1914; illustrator; animal painter and wood engraver noted for his sporting works; senior artist at *Baily's*): Vol.13

BACON, Henry Lynch (1839-1912; studied at City of London School and Royal College of Art; portrait painter, illustrator and commercial artist; also in *Boy's Own Paper* and *Captain*): Vols.2,4

BATEMAN, Henry Mayo (1887-1970; studied at the Westminster and New Cross Schools of Art; from 1904 he worked for *Tatler* but supplied drawings to numerous periodicals including *Bystander, Badminton, Gaiety, Grand, Graphic, Golden, Hutchinson's, Humorist, London Opinion, Punch, Illustrated Sporting & Dramatic News, Printers' Pie, Pearson's, London, Cassell's, Red, Pall Mall, Pan, Captain, Lloyd's, Nash's, Magpie, Liberty, Life, Windsor, Royal, Scraps, Sketch, Strand* and *Radio Times*; designed theatre posters): Vols.12,20

BENNETT, Frederick Stanley (1876-1939; staff artist Amalgamated Press; drew initial covers of both *Champion* and *Puck*; on *Daily Mail*; also in *Union Jack, Marvel, Chums, Cheerio, Boys' Friend, Boys' Herald, Boy's Own Paper, Scout, Chips, Jester, Wild West, London, New, Red, Cassell's, Royal* and *Punch*): Vols.2,7-11,13,14

BERE, Stephen Baghot de la (1877-1927; studied at Leicester and Westminster Schools of Art; figure and landscape painter; also in *Bystander, Captain, Illustrated London News, London Opinion, Windsor* and *Pall Mall*; illustrated many *Pears Annuals*): Vol.5

BERNEKER, Louis Frederick (1876-1937; studied at St.Louis School of Fine Art and Academie Julian in Paris; painter, illustrator and graphic designer; also in *Pearson's* and *English Illustrated*): Vol.P,2

BEVERIDGE, Robert Victor (1878-1945; pen-name Corporal Victor; postcard artist, motoring illustrator and journalist; artwork for *Advertising World*; journalism for *The Motor* magazine; also in *Illustrated London News*; from 1919 worked on American newspapers): Vols.1,3

BLAIKLEY, Ernest (1885-1965; studied at Slade School of Fine Art; painter and graphic artist; an official war artist then the first Keeper of Pictures at the Imperial War Museum; also in *Idler, Captain, Studio* and *Boy's Own Paper*): Vol.8

BRACKER, Michael Leone (1885-1937; studied at Cleveland School of Art and Art Students League of New York; magazine and advertising illustrator; designed war posters; also in *Nash's, Adventure, American, Lloyd's, Scribner's, Red, Everybody's, Harper's, Smith's, McClure's; Collier's, Munsey's, Hearst's, Cosmopolitan* and *Saturday Evening Post*): Vol.P,13

BRIGHTWELL, Leonard Robert (1889-1962; studied at Lambeth School of Art; wrote nineteen books; also in *Boy's Own Paper, Bystander, Idler, Graphic, Sketch, Punch, Captain, Humorist, London Opinion, Royal, Pall Mall, Hutchinson's, Chums, Pearson's, London, Red, Tatler* and *Strand*): Vol.19

BROCK, Henry Matthew (1875-1960; studied at Cambridge School of Art; worked in advertising as well as providing magazine illustrations; his art appeared in over two thousand books and comics such as *Sparkler, Knockout* and *Princess*; illustrated thirteen school serials in *Captain* and also contributed to *Chums, Badminton, Nash's, New, Printers' Pie, Quiver, Strand, Graphic, Wide World, London, Sphere, Cassell's, Punch, Pearson's* and *Pall Mall*): Vols.1,3,5-18

BROWN, Cecil Hew (1868-1926; studied at Westminster School of Art and Academie Julian in Paris; Scottish painter and writer of hunting and equestrian scenes; also in *Badminton, Fores's* and *Illustrated London News*): Vols.9,11

BROWNE, Gordon Frederick (1858-1932; son of 'Phiz'; studied at Heatherley's School of Art;

worked in watercolour and pen & ink; from 1880 he was one of Britain's most prolific illustrators, his work appearing in many newspapers, magazines and children's books; also in *Punch, Black & White, Commercial Tribune, Boy's Own Paper, Royal, New, Yellow, Red, London, Sporting & Dramatic News, Longman's, Poster, Illustrated London News, Quiver, Graphic, Girl's Own Paper, Captain, Cassell's, Badminton, Strand* and *Chums* (for which he supplied the original cover picture): Vols.1,6-10,13,14,20

BROWNE, Thomas Arthur (1870-1910; started his career by designing cigar-box labels. Then became a strip cartoonist in *Scraps* moving to *Comic Cuts* in 1890. His work also appeared in *Badminton, Graphic, Captain, Idler, Cassell's, Punch, Chips, Tatler, London, Boy's Own Paper, Sketch, Chums, Pearson's, Union Jack, Tatler, Royal* and *Strand*; did a vast amount of comic drawing and produced his own annuals; founded the London Sketch Club): Vols.P,1-6,8,10,11,13,14,21

BUCHANAN, Frederick Charles (1879-1941; pen names Charles Friend and Buchanan Friend; self taught as an illustrator; cartoonist to *Pall Mall Gazette* then Assistant Art Editor of *The Captain* and other Newnes magazines such as *Strand* and *Wide World*; also in *Chums, Sketch, Graphic, Crusoe, Printers' Pie, Grand, Yellow, Cassell's, Red, Tatler, London* and *Pearson's*; in later times Art Editor of *London Opinion*): Vols.1,3-8,11-15,17

BULL, Charles Livingston (1874-1932; contributed to *New York Tribune* with his illustrations of wildlife; designed many American war recruiting posters; also in *Century, Cosmopolitan, Country Gentleman, Collier's, Leslie's, Outing, Metropolitan* and *Windsor*): Vols.P,2,9

BUREN, Raeburn Lamar van (1891-1987; book, magazine and comic strip illustrator; studied at Art Students League of New York; on staff of *Kansas City Star*; also in *Cosmopolitan, Collier's, Elks, Esquire, Green, Life, Liberty, Metropolitan, McCall's, Red, Photoplay, Nash's, Screenland, Smith's, Smart Set* and *Saturday Evening Post*): Vol.21

BURNS, John Inder (1886-1958; book and magazine illustrator; on staff at *Punch*; also in *Boy's Own Paper, Britannia, Cassell's, Chums, Detective, Gaiety, Novel, Red, Yellow, Royal, Motor, Tatler, Printers' Pie, Popular* and *Illustrated London News*): Vol.20

CARRUTHERS-GOULD, Francis (1844-1925; a caricaturist and political cartoonist who was on the London Stock Exchange; he sketched members with many drawings published; illustrated for *Truth* and *Vanity Fair* before moving on to the *Pall Mall Gazette* and then the *Westminster Gazette*, where he became assistant editor; also in *Strand, Captain, English Illustrated, Idler* and *Cassell's*. Vols.3,21

CHARLTON, John (1849-1917; painter and illustrator of historical scenes; studied at both Newcastle and South Kensington Schools of Art; also in *Fores's* and *Badminton*; regularly in *Graphic* for over twenty years): Vol.12

CHENEY, Leo (1878-1928; writer, cartoonist, caricaturist, artist, illustrator; on staff *Accrington Observer & Times* and *Manchester Evening News*; staff artist on *Passing Show*; created the iconic Johnnie Walker character; also in *Boy's Own Paper, Cassell's, Pearson's, Grand, Happy Mag, Royal, Bystander, Strand* and *Illustrated London News*): Vols.17,18,21

CLARK, Christopher (1875-1942; book, annual and magazine illustrator, poster artist, painter of historical and military subjects; also in *Sphere, Cassell's, Captain, Quiver, Strand, Pall Mall, Red, Pearson's, Windsor, London, Royal* and *Graphic*): Vol.20

CLEAVER, Dudley (1872-1957; sporting artist; illustrator for the books of Rudyard Kipling; also in *London, Baily's, Captain, Penny Illustrated, Badminton* and *Pall Mall*. Many of his original illustrations are held in the Victoria & Albert Museum): Vols.1,3

CLEAVER, Reginald Thomas (1862-1954; illustrator, cartoonist, artist; also in *Cassell's, Hutchinson's, Wide World, Pearson's, New, London, Strand, Ludgate, Windsor, Punch* and *Graphic*): Vol.16

CONDE, Joseph (book illustrator and comic strip artist; also in *McClure's, Cosmopolitan, Harper's* and *Metropolitan*): Vol.7

COTTINGTON-TAYLOR, David (commercial artist, illustrator; also in *English Illustrated, Printers' Pie, Pearson's, Red* and *Royal*): Vols.10,19,20

COWELL, George Henry Sydney (1862-1926; painter, sculptor, book and magazine illustrator; also in *English Illustrated, Quiver, Temple, Pearson's, St.James's, Cassell's, Minster, Girl's Own Paper, Illustrated Sporting & Dramatic News, Idler, Windsor, Illustrated London News* and *Pall Mall*): Vol.18

CROMBIE, Charles Exeter Devereux (1880-1967; editorial cartoonist; staff illustrator for *Captain* as well as providing for other Newnes publications especially in *Strand*. Also in *Graphic, New, Nash's, Red, Pall Mall, Hutchinson's, Illustrated London News, Bystander, Crusoe, Detective, London, Printers' Pie, Royal, Humorist, Pearson's, Gaiety, Cassell's, Sketch, Windsor* and the American *Vanity Fair*): Vols.4-6,8-15,19

CROWTHER-SMITH, Horace Francis (1873-1959; author and illustrator; editor of *Horse Magazine* and *Croquet Gazette*; seven books on croquet; also in *Strand, Sketch* and *Windsor*): Vols.16-18,20,21

CUNEO, Cyrus Cincinato (1879-1916; flyweight boxing champion of California; studied at Hopkins Institute of Art in San Francisco and Academie Colarossi in Paris; worked in oils and watercolour; on *San Francisco Examiner* then on staff of *Illustrated London News*; also in *Pearson's, Pall Mall, Cassell's, Royal, Windsor, London, Cosmopolitan, Strand, Sketch, New, American, Nash's, Chums, Quiver, Lloyd's* and *Wide World*): Vols.15,20,21

DADD, Stephen Thomas (1858-1917; figure painter and illustrator; also in *Illustrated Sporting & Dramatic News, Cassell's, Fores's, Badminton, Pearson's, Union Jack, Captain, Graphic, Quiver, Chums, Boy's Own Paper* and *Illustrated London News*): Vols.4,9,14

DAVIS, George Horace (1881-1963; author and marine illustrator; studied at Ealing School of Art; on staff of both *Graphic* and *Sphere* then chief staff artist on *Illustrated London News*; official war artist; also in *Cassell's, London, Windsor, Happy Mag, Graphic, Captain, Pearson's, Lloyd's, Chums* and *Nash's*): Vols.11,13

DEWAR, William Jesmond (1864-1919; mainly black and white artist; also in *Ludgate, Black & White, Temple Bar, Rambler* and *Pearson's*): Vols.4,6

DICKINSON, Frederick Charles (1877-1945; black & white artist and watercolourist; prominent in *Red* and *Yellow* magazines; also in *London, Cassell's, Captain, Badminton, Quarto, Graphic* and *Pall Mall*; illustrated an edition of a Hans Andersen book): Vol.14

DIXON, Lafayette Maynard (1875-1946; studied at California School of Design; artist; book and newspaper illustrator; also in *Sunset* and *Overland*): Vol.12

EARL, Maud Alice (1863-1943; studied at Royal Female School of Art and Central Art School; best known for her canine paintings; also in *Badminton, Boy's Own Paper, Metropolitan* and *Windsor*): Vols.10,13,14

EBBUTT, Philip Guy (1866-1926; figure, humorous, book and annual illustrator; studied at Croydon School of Art; seventeen books; on *Daily Graphic*; also in *Boy's Own Paper, Captain, Chums, Fun, Crusoe, Quiver, Lady's Pictorial, Lady's Realm, Red, Graphic, Strand* and *Sporting & Dramatic News*): Vol.21

EDWARDS, Lionel Dalhousie Robertson (1878-1966; studied art at London School of Animal Painting; an artist who specialised in horses, horse racing, shooting, fishing and aspects of country life; author of many books; contributed to *Country Life* for over thirty years as well as to *Sphere* (where he was on the staff for six years); also in *Graphic, Bystander, Field, Punch, Printers' Pie, Tatler, Fores's, Pall Mall, Captain, Strand, Badminton, Illustrated Sporting & Dramatic News, Holly Leaves, Pearson's, Royal* and *Windsor*): Vols.8,12-17,19-21

ELCOCK, Howard Keppie (1886-1952; prominent for illustrating many of Conan Doyle's books; designed posters for London Underground and railway companies; sporting artist; also in *Red, Pearson's, Illustrated London News, Yellow, London, Grand, New, Britannia, Autocar, Hutchinson's, Collier's, Nash's, Novel, Royal, Gaiety, Happy Mag, Lloyd's, Captain, Cassell's, Pan, Windsor, Tatler, Punch* and *Strand*. Vols.12,13

ELSLEY, Arthur John (1860-1952; studied at South Kensington School of Art; an exponent of art, as well as prints and posters depicting children, horses and dogs; also in *English Illustrated, London* and *Ludgate*) Vol.8

ENRIGHT, Walter Joseph (1875-1969; studied at Chicago Art Institute; cartoonist and comic strip artist for the *Miami Herald*; also in *Adventure, Collier's, Leslie's, Idler, Outing, Strand, McClure's, Scribner's, Red* and *Metropolitan*): Vol.P,3

FEARON, Percy Hutton (1874-1948; studied at Art Students League of New York, Chase School of Art New York and Herkomer's Art School in Hertfordshire; on staff of *Manchester Evening Chronicle, Sunday Chronicle, Daily Dispatch, London Evening News* and *Daily Mail*; also in *London*): Vol.21

FINCH-MASON, George (1850-1915; main pen-names Uncle Toby and Fusbos; author, illustrator, sporting painter, cartoonist; on *Sporting Times*; art editor of *Fores's* 1884-1912; also in *Punch* and *Badminton*): Vol.7

FINNEMORE, Joseph (1860-1939; studied at Birmingham School of Art and Academie des Beaux Arts in Antwerp; prolific book and magazine illustrator particularly in *Strand* and children's publications. Also in *Ludgate, Longman's, Graphic, Captain, Cassell's, Windsor, Boy's Own Paper, English Illustrated, Girl's Own Paper, Black & White, Harmsworth's, Quiver, Atalanta, Chums* and *Sphere*): Vol.2

FLEMING-WILLIAMS, Clifford Charles (1880-1940; pen-name Streamline Bill; black and white artist and illustrator; on *Graphic* but also did illustrations for *Cassell's, New, Royal, Illustrated London News, Captain, Gaiety, Badminton, Windsor* and *Strand*; also an aviator and an inventor): Vol.13

FLOWER, Clement Balmboro (b.1878; studied at Herkomer School of Art; portrait and figure painter; also in *Cassell's, Windsor, Pearson's, Red, Royal, Lady's Realm* and *Graphic*): Vol.18

FOGARTY, Thomas (1873-1938; studied at Art Student's League of New York, eventually teaching there 1905-22; also in *Strand, Idler, Pearson's, Boys' Life, London, Windsor, Harper's, Collier's, Scribner's, Century, Metropolitan* and *Saturday Evening Post*): Vol.P,1

FOLKARD, Charles James (1878-1963; studied at Goldsmith's College of Art and St.John's Wood School of Art; artist, illustrator, playwright and author of children's books; staff artist on *Daily Mail*; also in *Printers' Pie, Strand* and *Tatler*): Vols.8,9

GIBBS, George Fort (1870-1942; author and illustrator; studied at Corcoran School of Art in Washington; initially on *New York Sun* and *New York Times* then worked for *Vogue*; stories in *Blue* and *Lippincott's* with illustrations in *Scribner's, Cosmopolitan, Pall Mall, Metropolitan, Appleton's, Nash's, Red, Munsey's, Harper's, Idler* but the majority in *Saturday Evening Post*): Vol.8

GIBSON, Charles Dana (1867-1944; studied at Arts Students League of New York; magazine and book illustrator, painter; editor of *Life*, then its owner; also in *Boys' Life, Cosmopolitan, Century, Cassell's, Collier's, Everybody's, Harper's, Hearst's, McClure's, Nash's, Happy Mag, St.Nicholas, Printers' Pie, Pearson's, Scribner's* and *Pall Mall*): Vol.21

GILLETT, Edward Frank (1874-1927; an illustrator who worked in pen & ink, pastel, watercolour and oil; the first staff editorial artist for *The Captain* before leaving to join the *Daily Graphic*; also in *Ludgate, Idler, Royal, Cassell's, New, Strand, Red, Nash's, Pall Mall, Yellow, Graphic, Black & White, Daily Sketch* and *The Illustrated Sporting and Dramatic News*): Vols.1,10,19

GINSBURY, Joseph William (1886-1959; impressionist portrait artist; studied at Birkbeck School of Art; contributed mainly to *The Bookman*): Vols.19-21

GOBLE, Warwick Waterman (1862-1943; studied at Westminster School of Art; initially specialised in chromolithography for a printer; on staff of the *Pall Mall Gazette* than an artist on *Westminster Gazette*; influenced by Oriental art; also in *Wide World, Idler, Captain, Windsor, Wide World, Cosmopolitan, Strand, Illustrated London News, Pall Mall, Boy's Own Paper* and *Pearson's*; his watercolours were exhibited at the Royal Academy. Vol.10

GOODWIN, Philip Russell (1881-1935; studied art at the Rhode Island School of Design; also in *Windsor, Scribner's, Collier's* and *Saturday Evening Post*): Vol.P,1

GOSSOP, Reginald Percy (1876-1951; graphic designer and landscape artist who created posters for London Transport; in-house artist for *The Captain* before becoming the first Art Editor for *Vogue*; in *Royal* and *Strand*; in later years had his own advertising agency): Vols.1,5,10-14

GOUGH, Arthur James (1864-1953; landscape painter and illustrator; known for his work which went with Conan Doyle's poetry; also in *Ludgate, Strand, Pall Mall, Red, Boys' Friend, Royal, Cassell's, Captain, Nash's, Harmworth's, Rambler, New, London* and *Windsor*): Vols.8-13

GRAVE, Charles (1886-1944; artist and cartoonist who focused on the marine world and low life characters; wrote short stories; on the staff of *Sporting Life, Daily Chronicle* and *Daily Graphic*; also in *Punch, Grand, Strand, Tatler, Captain, Printers' Pie, Royal, Nash's, Windsor, Pall Mall, Bystander* and *Illustrated Sporting & Dramatic News*): Vols.14-16

GRIGGS, Frederick Landseer Maur (1876-1938; book artist for Macmillans; also in *Golden* and *London Mercury*): Vols.1,13

HARDY, David Paul Frederick (1862-1942; historical painter and illustrator; prominent in *Strand* where he illustrated some one hundred and sixty-two stories and serials; other magazines and publishers used his work especially *Boy's Own Paper, Cassell's, London, Captain, Strand, English Illustrated, Quiver, Black & White, St.Paul's, Rambler, Wide World, Girl's Own Paper, Ludgate, Pearson's, New, Illustrated Sporting & Dramatic News* and *Chums*): Vols.1-3

HARDY, Dudley (1865-1922; studied at Academie Julian in Paris, Dusseldorf School of Art and Academie des Beaux Arts in Antwerp; a noted painter and illustrator; his interest in illustrations led to French influence poster imagery; also in *Boy's Own Paper, Captain, Illustrated London News, Strand, Idler, Pearson's, London, Punch, Today, Pall Mall, English Illustrated, Longbow, Sketch, Graphic, Studio, Ludgate* and *Windsor*): Vol.1

HARDY, Mabel Dora [Dorothy] (1868-1937; book illustrator and artist; specialised in images of animals; also in *Sporting & Dramatic News, Penny Pictorial, Badminton, Fores's, Pearson's, Royal* and *Strand*): Vol.16

HARRISON, Charles William (1860-1943; self taught cartoonist and illustrator; worked for *Cassell's*, then on staff of *Pall Mall Gazette* and *Daily Express*; contributed to *Daily Mail* and *London Evening News*; illustrated many books; also in *Chums, Crusoe, Gaiety, Grand, Humorist, London Opinion, Printers' Pie, Strand, Pearson's, Badminton, Captain, Pall Mall, Punch* and *Sketch*): Vols.4,5,20

HART, Frank (1878-1959; artist, magazine and book illustrator, lecturer, writer; also in *Cassell's, English Illustrated, Grand, Idler, Graphic, Temple, Printers' Pie, Pan, Red, Windsor, Men Only* and *Punch*): Vol.20

HASSALL, John (1868-1948; studied at Antwerp Free Art School and Academie Julian in Paris; mainly known for his advertisement and poster designs; initially with *Graphic* and *Punch*, and then for *Strand, Pearson's, London, Sketch, Idler, Sphere, Illustrated London News, Nash's, Cassell's, Printers' Pie* and *Pall Mall*; between 1896-99 he produced over six hundred theatre poster drawings; designed the cover of *Captain*): Vols.4,6

HEMING, Arthur Henry Howard (1870-1940; also in *Metropolitan, Windsor, Captain, Cassell's, McClure's* and *Saturday Evening Post*): Vols.1,2

HICKLING, Percy Bell (1876-1951; studied at the National Art Training School; became an art teacher then an artist, with his first illustrated book published in 1892; in numerous periodicals including *Fun, Sphere, Boy's Own Paper, Black & White, Cassell's, Grand, Captain, Graphic, Punch, Humorist, Hutchinson's, Red, Pearson's, New, Royal, Tatler, Strand* and *Girl's Own Paper*; it was his penchant for portraying young women which gained him a monopoly of work on illustrating girls' school stories): Vols.1,2,6

HIGGINS, Reginald Edward (1877-1933; studied at St.John's Wood School of Art and Royal Academy School; magazine illustrator, portrait and poster artist; also in *Royal, Captain, Printers' Pie, Strand, Gaiety* and *Idler*): Vol.11

HILL, Roland Pretty (1866-1949; pen-name 'Rip.' studied at Bradford School of Art and Herkomer Art School; caricaturist and line artist whose ability to draw cricket and football players saw him illustrate many articles of the games; his early work appeared in the *London Evening News* and then *Windsor, Truth, Black & White, Daily Mail, Weekly Dispatch, Captain, Sketch, Strand* and *Cricketer*): Vols.1,3

HODGSON, Edward Smith (1866-1937; artist and illustrator, who worked in oil, watercolour and pastel; in 1900 he began a long association with *Cassell's* but also provided illustrations for *Wide World, Strand, Pall Mall, Sphere, Sketch, Illustrated London News, Windsor, Captain, Pearson's, Chums, Quiver* and *Girls' Realm*): Vols.2,8,14

HOGG, Harold Arthur (1872-1949; studied in Paris at the Academie Julian; a graphic artist and illustrator who was also a mezzotint engraver; also in *Strand, Fun, Punch, Captain, Idler, London* and *Cassell's*): Vol.6

HOGGARTH, Arthur Henry Graham (1882-1964; black & white artist, illustrator, landscape painter and watercolourist; also in *Punch*): Vols.9,11

HOLLOWAY, Edgar Alfred (1870-1941; trained at Bradford Art School; became a lithographic artist; specialised in military subjects; also in *Illustrated London News, Windsor, Captain, Boy's Own Paper* and *Chums*; moved to Australia and provided illustrations for book publishers and periodicals such as *The Australian Women's Mirror* and *Consolation*): Vol.6

HORNE, Adam Edmund Peter Maule (1884-1955; initially worked for Newnes then became a freelance illustrator; also on *Yes or No, Yellow, Boy's Own Paper, Captain, Printers' Pie, Nash's, Cassell's, London, Graphic, Punch* and *Red*; went bankrupt in 1927; only in *Chums* afterwards): Vols.2,15,19

HOUGHTON, William (1864-1935; illustrator; also in *Pearson's, Puck* [for whom he designed many covers], *Red* and *Royal*): Vols.17-21

HOWE, Charles Kingsley (1889-1916; studied at New Cross School of Art; artist, watercolourist and book illustrator; served in Artists' Rifles; also in *Nash's*): Vol.16

HUTCHISON, David Chapel (1869-1954; pen-names David Hutchinson and Donald Hutchison; magazine, book and motor illustrator, muralist, portrait artist; studied at Edinburgh College of Art; also in *Argosy, Appleton's, Boy's Life, Collier's, Harper's, Liberty, McClure's, Metropolitan, Nash's, Pearson's, Putnam's, Success* and *Saturday Evening Post*): Vol.15

JALLAND, George Herbert (1863-1911; black & white artist specialising in equestrian subjects; regular in *Punch* for twenty-three years; also in *Badminton, Illustrated London News, Fores's, Graphic, Pall Mall, Illustrated Sporting & Dramatic News* and *Windsor*): Vols.4,8,9

JONES, Alfred Garth (1872-1955; studied at Westminster and South Kensington Schools of Art, Slade School of Fine Art, Academie Julian in Paris; landscape painter, illustrator and poster artist; he was on *La Revue Illustree* in France before becoming a visiting Master of Design at Lambeth and Manchester Schools of Art; also in *Studio, Collier's, Century, London, Scribner's, Smart Set, Idler, Graphic, Quarto* and *Strand*): Vols.10,12

KEENE, Charles Samuel (1823-91; illustrator, cartoonist, painter, etcher, artist, wood-engraver; on *Punch* for forty years; book illustrator; also in *Illustrated London News, Strand, Pall Mall, Once A Week, Good Words, Badminton, London Society* and *Cornhill*): Vols.17,18

KING, William (1880-1927; studied at Art Students League of New York; best known for his first war Red Cross posters; also in *Nash's, Cosmopolitan, Saturday Evening Post, Metropolitan, Munsey's, Harper's, Scribner's* and *Collier's*): Vol.P,1

KIRBY, Rollin (1875-1952; studied at Art Students Institute of New York and Academie Julian in Paris; painter, illustrator, political cartoonist, poet, playwright, writer, editor, book reviewer;

Pulitzer Prize winner [three times]; on staff at *New York Mail, New York World, New York Post*; also in *American, Century, Collier's, Harper's, Lippincott's, Look, Leslie's, Metropolitan, McClure's, Pearson's, Red, St.Nicholas, Smart Set, Scribner's* and *Saturday Evening Post*): Vol.20

LARUM, Oscar (1853-1931; ink and watercolour artist, cartoonist; also in *Punch, Sketch* and *Bystander*): Vols.P,15-17,20,21

LEETE, Alfred Ambrose Chew (1882-1933; self taught artist; on *Daily Graphic* then *Pall Mall Gazette*; also in *Punch, Red, Pearson's, Gaiety, Grand, Strand, London Opinion, Captain, Sketch* and *Bystander*; produced posters for the Tank Corps, Rowntree confectionary, London Underground and Bovril. Best known for his Lord Kitchener poster design): Vols.P,5,15-17,19-21

LEHANY, Ada (1873-1956; married the painter and illustrator George Soper in 1897; contributed to various magazines but primarily in *Captain*. Vols.8,10-12,14

LEIST, Frederick William (1873-1945; studied at Julian Ashton Art School in Sydney; portrait painter and illustrator; on *The Bulletin* and *Sydney Mail*; moved to London; on *The Graphic*; also in *Cassell's, London, Pearson's, Pall Mall, Strand, Hutchinson's* and *Windsor*): Vol.3

LEVERING, Albert (1869-1929; studied at National Academy in Munich; architect, cartoonist, magazine and book illustrator; staff artist on *Minneapolis Journal, Chicago Tribune, New York Journal, New York Sunday Tribune* and *New York Herald-Tribune*; then on staff at *Puck, Collier's, Life* and *Cosmopolitan*; also in *American, Elks, Harper's, Idler, McClure's, Scribner's, Pearson's* and *Metropolitan*): Vol.12

LODGE, George Edward (1860-1954; studied at Lincoln College of Art; bird artist and an authority on falconry; illustrated thirty-two books; also in *English Illustrated, Badminton, Atalanta, Pall Mall* and *Pearson's*): Vol.8

LUCAS, Henry Frederick Lucas (1848-1943; sporting artist working only on commissions; also in *Badminton* and *Fores's*): Vol.1

LUDLOW, Henry Stephen (1861-1947; known as Hal; portrait painter, artist and illustrator; studied at both Heatherley's and Highgate Schools of Art; also in *Cassell's, Chums, Penny, Sketch, Rambler, Queen, Captain, Strand* and *Illustrated London News*): Vols.12,13

LUNT, Samuel Wilmot (1856-1939; studied at Lancashire School of Art, Royal College of Art, Ecole des Beaux-Arts in Antwerp and Academie Julian in Paris; cartoonist; book, advertising and magazine illustrator; also in *Idler, Strand, English Illustrated, Royal, Cassell's, Pearson's, Red, Printers' Pie, New, Wide World, Pan, Graphic, London, Quiver, Premier, Yellow, Gaiety, Happy Mag, Magpie, Tatler, Bystander, London Opinion* and for fifteen years on staff of *Punch*): Vol.13

McCORMICK, Howard (1875-1943; studied at Indianapolis School of Art, Art Students League of New York, Academie Julian in Paris; illustrator, muralist, etcher, painter, wood engraver; also in *American, Century, Everybody's, Collier's, Gunter's, Captain, Metropolitan, Wide World, Pearson's* and *Chums*): Vol.P,20

MATHEWS, Richard George (1870-1955; portrait and war artist; on staff of *Montreal Star*; also in *Idler, Cassell's, Pearson's, Windsor, Graphic, Tatler* and *Bystander*): Vol.15

MEIN, William Gordon (1868-1939; book illustrator, artist, art editor; also in *The Dome* and *Pearson's*): Vols.7,13

MELLOR, John Paget (1862-1929; pen-name Quiz; caricaturist, artist, solicitor, barrister; also in *Vanity Fair* and *Punch*): Vol.12

MICHAEL, Arthur Cadwgan (1881-1965; painter, book and magazine illustrator; in Paris contributed to *L'Assiette, Cocorico* and *Beurre*; artist for *Illustrated London News*; also in *Boys' Life, Black & White, Cassell's, Quiver, Pearson's, Nash's, London, Pall Mall, New, Strand, Windsor, Captain, Cosmopolitan* and *Chums*): Vol.18

MILLAR, Harold Robert (1869-1940; studied at Birmingham School of Art; painter, book and magazine illustrator; also in *Black & White, Cassell's, Chatterbox, Chums, Detective, English Illustrated, Fun, Gaiety, Girl's Own Paper, Idler, Lloyd's, London, Ludgate, Minster, Nash's, New, Pan, Pearson's, Piccadilly, Premier, Printers' Pie, Punch, Quiver, Red, Scraps, Sketch, Windsor, Yellow, Strand* and *Tatler*): Vol.13

MILLS, Arthur Wallis (1878-1940; studied at the South Kensington School of Art; illustrated most of Pelham Wodehouse's magazine stories; worked for *Punch* 1905-39; also in *Black & White Budget, Ludgate, Royal, Humourist, Cassell's, Pall Mall, Windsor, Strand, London, Pearson's, Printers' Pie, Badminton, Gaiety, London Opinion, Graphic, Magpie, Hutchinson's, Nash's, New, Red* and *The Wanganui Chronicle* in New Zealand): Vols.1,3,5,6,9,10,12,14

MITCHELL, Edward Ernest Wise (1861-1917; book illustrator; also in *Captain, Idler* and *Ludgate*): Vols.8-10,12,13

MORGAN, Wallace (1873-1948; studied at National Academy Art School in New York; artist, author and illustrator; on *New York Sun* and *New York Herald*; also in *Life, Cosmopolitan, Delineator, Collier's, Pearson's, Gunter's, Everybody's, Red, Metropolitan, American, Scribner's, McClure's, Hearst's, Liberty, Shrine, Harper's, Nash's, New Yorker* and *Saturday Evening Post*): Vol.P,14

MORROW, Edwin Arthur (1877-1952; studied at Schools of Art in Belfast and South Kensington where he learned fresco; became a joke cartoonist as well as a portrait and landscape painter; had 299 cartoons in *Punch*; also in *Strand, Captain, Grand, Gaiety, Cassell's, New, Bystander* and *London Opinion*. Vols.15,16,18

MORROW, George (1869-1955; studied at Academie Julian in Paris; comic artist and illustrator; in *Punch* from 1906, joined staff in 1924, Art Editor 1932-37, contributed until his death; also in *Bystander, London Mercury, Golden, Printers' Pie, Pall Mall, Captain, Pearson's, Nash's, Sphere, Tatler, Radio Times, Strand, Badminton, Idler* and *Windsor*): Vol.6

MUNNINGS, Alfred James (1878-1959; painter, sculptor and poet; studied at Norwich School of Art; became part of the Newlyn School of Artists; known mainly for his equine paintings; president of Royal Academy of Arts; also in *Lilliput, John Bull, Windsor, Badminton, Pearson's* and *Strand*): Vol.5

NICHOLLS, Horace Walter (1867-1941; book and magazine illustrator; also in *Captain, Black & White, Lady's Realm, Quiver, Lloyd's, London, Nash's, Tatler* and *Illustrated London News*): Vol.18

NOBLE, John Edwin (1876-1961; studied at Slade School of Fine Art, Lambeth School of Art and Royal Academy Schools; animal painter, poster designer, book and magazine illustrator; instructor at Calderon's School of Animal Painting; lecturer at both Central and Camberwell Schools of Arts; official war artist; also in *Studio, Red, Cassell's* and *Yellow*): Vol.9

OAKLEY, Thornton (1881-1953; studied at the Howard Pyle Art School eventually becoming an illustrator for major periodicals *Century, Collier's, Harper's* and *Scribner's*; became a lecturer in art at a number of universities; created war effort pictures for *National Geographic Magazine*; also in *Appleton's, Leslie's* and *Metropolitan*): Vol.P,2

O'MALLEY, Power (1877-1946; real name Michael Augustine Power; studied at the Dublin Metropolitan School of Art; moved to New York and illustrated covers for *Life, Literary Digest, Harper's* and *Puck* as well as painting film sets for Cecil B. DeMille, also in *Irish Review, McClure's, Pearson's, Smith's* and *Hampton's*): Vols.1,4

OSBORNE, Rex (studied at Manchester School of Art; from a family all of whom were artists and illustrators; drew for many editions of the *Young England Annuals*; also in *Strand, Quiver, Royal, Captain, English Illustrated* and *Idler*): Vols.1,3,4

OWEN, William (1869-1957; studied at Lambeth School of Art; book illustrator, caricaturist, poster artist and cartoonist best known for his iconic images of the Bisto Kids, Bovril, Lux and Lifebuoy; a journalist on the *East Kent Mercury*; also in *Strand, Illustrated Sporting and Dramatic News, Bystander, Captain, Sketch, Pearson's, Windsor, London, Printers' Pie, Gaiety, Pall Mall, Cassell's, Metropolitan, Grand, Magpie, Yellow, New* and *Graphic*): Vols.5-7,9-11,13

PATTERSON, George Malcolm (1873-1941; watercolourist, cartoonist and illustrator; worked in pencil and chalk; school art teacher; also in *Cassell's, English Illustrated, Quiver, Windsor, Royal, Red, New, Idler, Strand* and *Punch*): Vols.11,12,14

PEARS, Charles (1873-1958; marine painter, illustrator, poster artist, lithographer; first president of the Royal Society of Marine Artists; prolific for London Underground, Empire Marketing Board and British Railway posters; wrote extensively on sailing and yachting; also in *Punch, Graphic, Yellow, Badminton, Royal, Britannia, Strand, Idler, Ludgate, London, Pearson's, Wide World, Pall Mall, Illustrated London News; Printers' Pie, Cassell's, Nash's, Fun, Sketch, Dome, Red, Longbow* and *Windsor*): Vols.2,4,5,7,11,13,14,16,20,21

PEARSE, Alfred William (1855-1933; cartoonist, illustrator, editor and vigorous campaigner for women's equality; started on the *Boy's Own Paper* for whom he worked for over fifty years; also provided drawings for *Pictorial World*, then to *Sphere* and *Illustrated London News*, with his artwork also appearing in *Girl's Own Paper, Wide World, Strand, London, Cassell's, Royal, Captain, Red, Ludgate, Punch, Pearson's* and *Yellow*; designed campaign posters advocating women's suffrage and composed a weekly cartoon for *Votes for Women*): Vols.1,3,4

PEARSE, Dennis Colbron (1883-1971; son of Alfred who generally sketched for Newnes publications and was in *Strand, Captain, Royal* and *Pearson's*. Moved to Australia and illustrated books before becoming an arts administrator): Vol.2

PEGRAM, Frederick (1870-1937; studied at Westminster School of Art and Academie Julian in Paris; magazine and book illustrator, painter, etcher, cartoonist; theatrical sketches in *Pall Mall Gazette*; on staff of *Punch* for forty-three years; on *Daily Chronicle*; also in *Black & White, Cassell's, Fun, Harmsworth's, Holly Leaves, Idler, Judy, Lady's Pictorial, Ludgate, Chums, Pall Mall, Strand, Windsor, New, Scribner's, Magpie, Minster, Harper's, Printers' Pie, Queen, Quiver, Tatler, Illustrated Sporting & Dramatic News* and *Illustrated London News*): Vol.21

PRATER, Ernest (1864-1950; artist and illustrator; a Boer War correspondent for *Sphere* then *Black & White Budget* and *Graphic*; specialised in illustrating boys' adventure stories; also in *Pall Mall, Pearson's, Red, Wide World, Strand, Yellow, Idler, Windsor, Ludgate, Badminton, Holly Leaves, Cassell's, Chums, Novel, Royal, Captain, Boy's Own Paper* and *Girl's Own Paper*. Vols.12,16

RADCLIFFE-WILSON, Hugh (d.1979; magazine and book illustrator and cartoonist, motoring artist; also in *Pearson's, Strand, Pall Mall, Red, Boys' Friend, Rocket, Crusoe, Detective, Captain, Royal, Yellow* and *Windsor*): Vols.17,20

RALEIGH, Henry Patrick (1880-1944; studied at Hopkins Academy of Art in San Francisco; on *San Francisco Bulletin, San Francisco Examiner, New York Journal* and *New York World*; also in *American, Appleton's, Cosmopolitan, Collier's, Century, Everybody's, Red, Hampton's, Harper's, Pearson's, Metropolitan, McCall's, Nash's, Shrine, Scribner's, Pall Mall, Harper's Bazar, Hearst's, Vanity Fair* and *Saturday Evening Post*): Vol.P,14

RANKIN, George James (1864-1937; animal, bird and equestrian painter; also in *Boy's Own Paper, Badminton, English Illustrated, Captain* and *Strand*): Vol.8

RAVEN-HILL, Leonard (1867-1942; artist, illustrator, cartoonist; studied at Lambeth School of Art and Academie Julian in Paris; Art Editor of *Pick-Me-Up*; founded both *The Unicorn* and *The Butterfly*; on staff at *Punch* for thirty years and also on *Daily Mail, Daily Graphic, Daily Chronicle* and *Pall Mall Gazette*; also in *Strand, Sketch, Windsor, Idler, Butterfly, John O'London's, Pearson's, Scribner's, Ludgate, Pall Mall, Captain, London, Printers' Pie* and *Illustrated London News*): Vols.7-9

READ, Harold Hope (1881-1959; studied at the South Kensington School of Art; pen & ink and watercolour artist; lived an unorthodox and Bohemian lifestyle in Tunbridge Wells where he painted the people and properties for various Galleries; contributed numerous political cartoons to *Punch*: also in *Cassell's, Captain, London, Red, Printers' Pie* and *Idler*. Vols.15,16

REED, Edward Tennyson (1860-1933; author, caricaturist, political cartoonist, book illustrator, lecturer; studied at Calderon's Art School; on *Punch* staff for forty-four years; also in *Cassell's, English Illustrated, Idler, Bystander, Sketch, Graphic, Studio, Pall Mall, Printers' Pie, Badminton, London* and *Strand*): Vols.19,20

REYNOLDS, Frank (1876-1953; studied at Heatherley's School of Art; black and white artist, illustrator; on *Sketch* and *Illustrated London News*; art editor *Punch*; also in *Longbow, Judy, Flag, Playgoer, Pick-Me-Up, Sketchy Bits, Cassell's, Grand, Graphic, London, New, Printers' Pie, Quiver, Pearson's, Windsor, Pall Mall* and *Strand*): Vols.4,8,13

RHEAD, Louis John (1857-1926; poster and book illustrator; studied at South Kensington School of Art; on staff at *Cassell*; also in *Cosmopolitan, Gunter's, Bohemian, Harper's, Appleton's, Harper's Bazar, Badminton, Scribner's* and *Century*): Vols.12,14

RITCHIE, Alexander Penrose Forbes (1868-1938; studied at Academie des Beaux Arts in Antwerp before settling in London as an artist, illustrator, designer and caricaturist; became known for both his theatrical and London Underground posters; also in *Sketch, Bystander, Strand, Captain, Grand, Pall Mall* and *Ludgate*; produced ninety-nine satirising portraits of celebrities for *Vanity Fair*): Vols.12,15

ROBINSON, William (1838-1935; architectural draughtsman and illustrator; specialised in industrial subjects; also in *English Illustrated, Pall Mall, Illustrated London News, Pearson's* and *Strand*): Vols.1-3,8-10,12,20,21

ROLLER, George Conrad (1856-1941; portrait painter, designer, illustrator; studied at Lambeth School of Art and Academie Julian in Paris; founding member of Cornwall's St.Ives Arts Club; on staff of *Pall Mall* for five years; restored paintings for Royal Academy; sporting advertising designer for Burberry's for forty years; also in *Pick Me Up* and *Black & White*): Vol.11

ROUNTREE, Harry (1878-1950; born in Auckland and moved to London in 1901; studied art at Regent Street Polytechnic; first published in *Humorist, Playtime* and *Punch*, then joined staff of *Little Folks*; illustrated comic annuals, children's books and designed posters; also in *Red, London, Captain, Strand, Printers' Pie, Boy's Own Paper, Chums, Pearson's, Sketch, Illustrated London News, Pall Mall, Punch* and in later years *Radio Times*): Vols.3-17,20

SARGENT, Louis Augustus (1881-1965; studied at South Kensington School of Art and Royal Academy School; painter, illustrator and sculptor; illustrated many boys annuals; also in *Captain*): Vols.10,11

SARKA, Charles Nicolas (1879-1960; studied at Art Institute of Chicago; muralist, painter, printmaker, illustrator; staff artist on *Chicago Record, New York World* and *New York Herald*; also in *American, Blue, Collier's, Cosmopolitan, Columbian, Everybody's, Hearst's, Harper's, Hampton's, Leslie's, Munsey's, Metropolitan, McClure's, New, Scribner's, Red* and *Strand*): Vol.P,15

SAYEN, Henry Lyman (1875-1918; studied at Pennsylvania Academy of Fine Arts; scientific inventor, landscape artist, catalogue and poster designer; regular exhibitions at Philadelphia Sketch Club; also in *Saturday Evening Post*): Vol.15

SCHOU, Carl Sigurd (1875-1929; painter and illustrator; on *Chicago Tribune* and *Washington Post*; also in *Gunter's, Pearson's, Smith's, Bohemian, Popular, New* and *Captain*): Vol.10

SCOTT, Septimus Edwin (1879-1965; studied at Royal College of Art; landscape and portrait painter, railway company poster and adverting illustrator, comic strips for Amalgamated Press; also in *Strand, London, Windsor, Pearson's, Royal, Graphic, Red* and *Punch*): Vols.12,13

SHAW, John Byam Liston (1872-1919; studied at both St.John's Wood and Royal Academy Art Schools; black and white artist, magazine and book illustrator; founded Campden Hill School of Art; on *Daily Mail*; also in *Graphic, Dome, Connoisseur, Studio, Punch, Strand, Black & White, Comic Cuts, Country Life, The Field, The Flag, Idler, Printers' Pie; Bellman; Pall Mall* and *Sphere*): Vol.18

SHRADER, Edwin Roscoe (1878-1960; painter, magazine illustrator and art instructor; studied at Chicago Art Institute School and School of Illustrative Art in Wilmington; president of California Art Club; also in *Harper's, Red, Scribner's, Century, Popular, New* and *Saturday Evening Post*): Vol.12

SIMPSON, Joseph (1879-1939; studied at Glasgow School of Art; then London where he designed posters and painted in oils; taught at London School of Art; a war artist with the Royal Air Force; illustrated many books and in *Nash's, London, Strand, Pall Mall, Yellow, Captain, Wide World, Land & Water* and *London Opinion*): Vols.13-15

SKELTON, Joseph Ratcliffe (1865-1927; originally a watercolour artist but later an illustrator contributing to *Bystander, Graphic, Strand, Royal, Pearson's, Idler, Captain, Nash's, London, Windsor, Red, Pall Mall, Yellow, Hutchinson's, Sketch* and *Illustrated London News*; his books included those written by Warren Bell who had regularly commissioned him for Newnes magazines): Vols.2,3,11,13

SKINNER, Edward Frederick (1865-1924; started his periodical work for *Pall Mall* then *Windsor, Idler, Black & White, Captain, Cassell's, Royal, London* and *Pearson's*; during the first war he painted numerous pictures of female munitions factory workers): Vols.1,2

SMALE, Bertram Haylock (1879-1963; illustrator and postcard artist; in wartime Ministry of Munitions; also in *Studio*): Vols.1,9

SMITH, Alfred Talbot (1877-1971; studied at Croydon School of Art; became a professional artist; illustrated books before turning to cartoons for *Punch, London, Cassell's, Red, Cheer Boys Cheer, Bystander, Humorist, Sketch, Captain, London Opinion* and *Strand* amongst many others; in later years worked as a journalist on *The Times*): Vols.1,10

SOMERFIELD, Thomas (1876-1937; started with contributions to *Sheffield Weekly Telegraph* and *Boys' Friend*; moved to London and was soon in *Cassell's* and then on staff at *Chums*; also in *Red, New, Yellow, Captain, Wide World* and *Strand* as well as becoming a book illustrator): Vols.8,10,12

SOPER, George (1870-1942; his first painting was exhibited at the Royal Academy when he was nineteen; had a talent for drawing people in action which was put to use illustrating books, book jackets, magazines and journals; he drew images for dashing tales of the British Empire in *Chums, Boy's Own Paper, Captain, Cassell's, Country Life, Graphic, Badminton, Strand, Windsor, Idler, Red, Illustrated London News* and *Wide World*): Vols.2,6,7-14,16-18

SOUTHGATE, Edward Frank (1872-1916; studied at Bideford Art School and Cambridge School of Art; book illustrator; country and hunting painter; also in *Pearson's* and *Royal*): Vol.14

STAMPA, George Loraine (1875-1951; pen-name Harris Brooks; studied at Royal Academy and Heatherley's Art Schools where his cartoons and illustrations showed a preference for the London streets, urchins and their mongrel dogs; a major contributor to *Punch* for over fifty years; also in *Cassell's, Idler, Graphic, Bystander, Humorist, London Opinion, Strand, Captain, Sketch, Tatler, Pall Mall* and *Windsor*; he designed posters for London Transport): Vols.9-12,14

STANNARD, Henry John (1844-1920; studied at South Kensington School of Art; founded Bedford Academy of Arts; watercolour artist; also in *Illustrated London News, Baily's, Badminton, Pearson's* and *Sporting & Dramatic News*): Vol.8

STOTT, William Robertson Smith (1878-1939; portrait and landscape painter, illustrator; on the staff of *Graphic*; also in *Strand, Wide World, London, Cassell's, Hutchinson's, Printers' Pie, Magpie, Windsor, Pearson's* and *Illustrated London News*): Vol.13

STROTHMANN, Frederick (1872-1958; illustrator of magazines and books who also drew political cartoons and posters; studied at the Carl Hecker School of Art in New York as well as in Berlin and Academie Julian in Paris; for fifty years he was a regular contributor to *The Saturday Evening Post*; also in *Collier's, Harper's, Nash's, Life, Smith's* and *Metropolitan*): Vol.P,2,9

STUDDY, George Ernest (1878-1948; pen-name Cheero; studied at Heatherley's and Calderon's Art Schools; cartoonist, illustrator and animator; on *Sketch, Tatler, Bystander, Graphic* and *Illustrated London News*; also in *Punch, Strand, Printers' Pie, Pall Mall, Captain, Chums, New, Cassell's, Red, Yellow, Magpie, Novel, Pearson's, Grand, Field, Tit-Bits, Fores's, London, Windsor* and *Humorist*): Vol.6

STURGESS, John (1839-1903; sporting painter, lithographer and artist; prolific book illustrator; principal hunting and racing artist for *The Illustrated London News*; moved into advertising with his hunting sketches; also in *English Illustrated* and *The Illustrated Sporting & Dramatic News*): Vols 4,5

SULLIVAN, Edmund Joseph (1869-1933; painter, watercolourist, illustrator; on staff of *Daily Graphic*; lecturer on book illustration and lithography at Goldsmith's College of Art; also in *English Illustrated, Pall Mall, Yellow, New, London, Graphic, Black & White, Ludgate, Windsor, Pearson's* and *Punch*): Vol.15

SVOBODA, Alexander Richard (1877-1961; landscape painter; also in *Boys' Life, Ainslee's, Leslie's* and *Harper's*): Vol.4

SYMES, Ivor Isaac John (1875-1941; studied at Herkomer Art School; painter and illustrator; also in *Pearson's, Graphic* and *Royal*): Vol.14

TAFFS, Charles Harold (1876-1964; studied at South Kensington School of Art; magazine and book illustrator; portrait painter; also in *English Illustrated, Graphic, St.Pauls, Quiver, Strand, Royal, London, Cassell's, Pearson's, American, Red, Harper's, Nash's, McCall's, Metropolitan, Argosy, Everybody's, Collier's, Saturday Evening Post* and *Illustrated London News*): Vol.5

TAYLOR, Frank Walter (1874-1921; studied at Pennsylvania Academy of the Fine Arts and Academie Julian in Paris; also in *Harper's, Scribner's, McClure's, Collier's* and *Saturday Evening Post*): Vol.14

THOMAS, William Fletcher (1863-1938; pen-name Didymus; started as a calico print designer; studied in Paris with early drawings appearing in the comic *Random Readings* and the Leeds journal *Toby: The Yorkshire Tyke*; became the cartoonist for *Ally Sloper's Half-Holiday*; designed many *Captain* front covers; also in *Cassell's, Crusoe, Punch, Red* and *Strand*): Vols.14,15

THORBURN, Archibald (1860-1935; became a celebrated painter and illustrator of birds and mammals; many of his lavishly produced books were published by *Longmans*; also in *Pall Mall, Badminton, London, English Illustrated, Young England, Captain, Illustrated London News* and *Sporting & Dramatic News*. Vols.7,14

THORP, George (in-house illustrator; appeared in many of Newnes publications; also in *Captain* and *Pearson's*): Vols.2,4-15,17,19-21

THORPE, James Hall (1876-1949, pen-name Thorp; studied at Lambeth School of Art, Heatherley's School of Art; illustrator, painter, woodcutter; on the *Morning Leader*; *Punch* cartoonist 1909-38, on *Graphic* 1908-15; designer for *London Press Exchange* advertising 1902-22; also in *Cassell's, Captain, Bystander, Sketch, Tatler, Gaiety, Grand, Windsor, Strand, Yellow, Pearson's, Printers' Pie, Red, London* and *Idler*): Vols.1,19,21

TRUE, Allen Tupper (1881-1955; illustrator, easel painter and muralist; studied at the Corcoran School of Art and Howard Pyle School of Art; his muralist assignments included painting eight panels for the Wyoming State Capitol; also in *Outing, Collier's, Scribner's, Art & Progress, Leslie's* and *Saturday Evening Post*): Vol.P,2

VARIAN, George Edmund (1865-1923; artist and illustrator; also in *Strand, Century, McClure's, Idler, Pearson's, St.Nicholas, American, Hampton's* and *Windsor*): Vol.13

WALKER, Henry George (1876-1932; studied at Birmingham School of Art; etcher; at London Faculty of Arts; on staff of *Boy's Own Paper*; also in *Lady's Realm* and *Pall Mall*): Vol.8

WALTON, John Ambrose de (1874-1963; specialised in military subjects; lived for many years in Cornwall; illustrated books for Percy Westerman and wrote for *Punch*; also in *Cassell's, Badminton,*

Chums, Boy's Own Paper, Captain, Pearson's, Windsor, Strand, Royal and *Wide World*. Vols.10,11

WARD, Leslie Matthew (1851-1922; pen-names: Spy and Drawl; artist and caricaturist; entered Royal Academy Schools in 1871; two years later he sent some of his work to *Vanity Fair* who immediately hired him; spent forty years with the magazine drawing one thousand three hundred and twenty-five cartoons; also in *Mayfair, Graphic, Cassell's, Captain, Strand* and *Idler*): Vols.P,14,15

WATTS, Arthur George (1883-1935; studied at New Cross School of Art, Slade School of Fine Art, Antwerp Free Art School, Academie Julian in Paris, Moscow School of Painting and Academia de San Fernando de Bellas Artes in Madrid; taught at Regent Street Polytechnic; illustrator, painter and cartoonist; on staff at *Punch* 1912-35; also in *Boy's Champion, Bystander, Humorist, London Opinion, Radio Times, Nash's, London, Pearson's, Tatler, Pall Mall, Life, Sketch* and *Strand*): Vols.1,15-19

WESTOVER, Russell Channing (1886-1966; studied at the San Francisco Art Institute; became a sports cartoonist on the *San Francisco Bulletin* also contributing to the *Chronicle, Post* and *Oakland Herald*; then went to the *New York Herald* and also worked for *Life*; also in *Captain*; his syndicated cartoons were carried by over six hundred newspapers): Vol.12

WHITE, Dyke (1885-1933; real name Charles Gordon McClure; also in *Red, Captain, Gaiety, Yellow* and *Happy Mag*): Vol.10

WHITING, Frederic (1874-1962; studied at St.John's Wood School of Art and Academie Julian in Paris; portrait and figure painter; covered the Chinese and Russo-Japanese wars for *Graphic*; also in *Boy's Own Paper, London, Captain, Cassell's, New* and *Red*): Vols.7-14

WHITWELL, Thomas Montague Radcliff (1868-1928; a lithographic artist before becoming a book illustrator; was the main artist on *The Captain* providing most of the magazine's front covers as well as pictures for many Wodehouse's stories; also designed covers for *Yes or No* and *Chums*. In *Boys' Life* and *Strand*): Vols.2,5-7,11

WIDNEY, Gustavus Chafee (1871-1955; studied at Chicago School of Art and Academie Julian in Paris; advertising artist, painter and illustrator; also in *Scribner's, Red, Smith's, Circle, Collier's, Outlook* and *Saturday Evening Post*): Vol.13

WIGFULL, William Edward (1874-1944; studied at Sheffield School of Art; become a magazine and book illustrator specialising in adventure stories and the sea; also in *Bystander, Pall Mall, Poster, Cassell's, Red, Sphere, Yellow, New, Golden, Scout, Quiver, Girls' Realm, Captain, Longbow, Royal, New, English Illustrated, Idler, London, Chums, Strand* and *Wide World*; known widely as Handy Billy): Vols.5,10,12,20

WILCOX, David Urquhart (1876-1941; studied at both New York and Buffalo Art Students Leagues; magazine illustrator; also in *Scribner's, Idler, Century, McClure's, Windsor* and *Metropolitan*): Vol.P,3

WILKINSON, Thomas William (1875-1950; black & white artist, painter and illustrator; studied at both Bradford and Ipswich Schools of Art; also in *Illustrated Bits, Printers' Pie, Judy, Fun, Punch, London* and *Strand*): Vol.19

WILLIAMS, Hamilton (author, figure artist and illustrator; also in *Munsey's, Cassell's, Red, Captain, Pall Mall, Punch, London Opinion, Royal* and *Saturday Evening Post*): Vols.14-16

WILLIAMSON, Harry Grant (1866-1937; studied at Cincinnati Art Students League; magazine illustrator and landscape painter; also in *Ainslee's, Harper's, Pearson's, Munsey's, Smith's, Scribner's* and *Saturday Evening Post*): Vol.P,3,8

WILSON, Patten (1869-1934; studied at both Kidderminster and Westminster Schools of Art; book and magazine illustrator; also in *Yellow* and *Pall Mall*): Vol.7

WIRGMAN, Hannah Frances Georgiana Augusta (1888-1976; portrait and landscape painter, pastel artist; art teacher; studied at Southport School of Art, London School of Art and Stratford Studios): Vol.11

WOOD, Clarence Lawson (1878-1957; studied at the Slade School of Fine Art and Heatherley's School of Art; black and white artist and illustrator; worked, as head artist, on Pearson's various periodicals; from 1902 he pursued a successful freelance career being published in *Grand, Collier's, Humorist, Graphic, Strand, Metropolitan, Pearson's, Royal, Cassell's, Printers' Pie, London, Nash's, Sketch, New, Punch, Captain, London Opinion, Illustrated London News* and *Boy's Own Paper*): Vols.6-8

WOOD, Stanley Llewellyn (1866-1928; a third generation artist; military painter and illustrator; started at publishers *Chatto & Windus* as an in-house artist; *Harper's* and *Illustrated London News* took many of his cowboys' and indians' drawings; also in *Pearson's, Bystander, Captain, Idler, Windsor, Cassell's, London, New, Wide World, Graphic, London Opinion, Chums, Boy's Own Paper, Royal, Illustrated Sporting & Dramatic News; Strand; Sketch* and *Black & White*): Vols.1-3,10,11

WOODVILLE, Richard Caton (1856-1927; painted battle scenes in oil; spent most of his career working for *The Illustrated London News* having previously studied at Dusseldorf School of Art, Academie Julian in Paris and in Russia; his illustrations also appeared in the *Strand, Boy's Own Paper, English Illustrated, Captain, Sketch, Pearson's, Windsor, Harper's, Cornhill* and *Tatler*; for all his success he went bankrupt in 1905 and died destitute, having committed suicide by using his military revolver): Vols.3-5,10,11,12,14

WOOLRICH, John Frederick (1878-1954; illustrator; also in *Lady's Realm, English Illustrated* and *Strand*): Vol.P,20

OTHER ILLUSTRATORS

BRIST, Lovent (commercial artist): Vol.19

BROWNE, Henry (commercial illustrator; also in *Windsor* and *Ludgate*): Vol.13

CHRISTIE, William (illustrator; also in *Lady's Realm*): Vol.1

CLARKE, Richard Edward (1878-1954; studied at Scarborough School of Art; mainly a commercial illustrator; also in *Captain*): Vol.2

DALE, Richard Thomas (commercial illustrator): Vol.16

DAWSON, Charles Edwin (1873-1924; illustrator; also in *English Illustrated, Harmworth's, London* and *Sphere*): Vol.2

DENSLOW, William Wallace (1856-1915; studied at National Academy of Design New York; artist and illustrator; also in *Lippincott's, Life* and *St.Nicholas*): Vol.11

DICKSEE, Herbert Thomas (1862-1942; mezzotint artist and book illustrator; studied at Slade School of Fine Art; taught art at City of London School; painted mainly for Christian Klackner Gallery): Vol.14

FISCHER, Edgar Hugh (1880-1943; pen-name Dormy; animal painter): Vol.1

GILMAN, Harold John Wilde (1876-1919; studied at Hastings and Slade Schools of Art; artist and illustrator): Vol.16

GOODMAN, Reginald Moon (1889-1915; served in Artist's Rifles; also in *Chums, Pearson's, Cheer Boys Cheer* and *Royal*): Vol.18

GOTCH, Bernard Cecil (1876-1963; studied at Winchester School of Art; watercolourist and book illustrator for Methuens): Vol.16

HALPIN, James (commercial artist): Vol.10

HELMER, Anthony (illustrator; also in *Captain* and *Strand*): Vols.1,2

HEWERDINE, Matthew Bede (1868-1909; cartoonist and book illustrator; also in *Vanity Fair*; murdered on a train in Northamptonshire): Vol.2

HOME, Percy (illustrator; also in *Lloyd's*): Vol.6

HOYN, Toby (chief artist when *The Merry Mag* commenced publication; also in *Happy Mag, Captain, Grand* and *New*): Vol.12

JARRIGE, Leonard Marie Louis de Leynia de la (1873-1933; cartoonist): Vol.13

JOEL, Humphrey (illustrator and photographer): Vols.P,17-21

LOW, Henry Charles (book and magazine illustrator; also in *Red, Cassell's, Windsor, Pearson's, Yellow, Printers' Pie, New* and *Grand*): Vol.15

MAHLER, Paul (1864-1923; French artist and watercolourist; specialised in drawing animals): Vol.16

MATHER, Henry (illustrator): Vol.21

MOONY, William (1877-1956; artist and illustrator; also in *Idler, Pearson's* and *Chums*): Vol.7

MOORE, Rubens Arthur (1860-1933; artist and illustrator): Vol.7

NISBET, Robert Hogg (1879-1961; artist and illustrator): Vol.7

NORRIS, Frank (illustrator; also in *Captain*): Vol.21

PIPPET, Wilfrid (1873-1958; of the Pippet family of artists; book illustrator, poster designer, painter): Vols.19-21

PRIDE, Sidney (1873-1942; artist and illustrator; on staff of *London Evening News* then Amalgamated Press; also in *Lady's Realm, Union Jack, Butterfly, Punch, Boy's Realm, Yes or No, Golden* and *Strand*): Vol.21

RANSOM, Fletcher Charles (1870-1943; painter and illustrator; also in *American, Appleton's, Captain, Collier's, Harper's, Idler, Leslie's* and *Scribner's*): Vol.7

REID, Gladys (fashion illustrator; also in *Badminton, Country Life* and *The Lady*): Vols.13,14,17,21

REYNOLDS, Frederick William (b.1879; journalist and illustrator; on *Wolverhampton Express & Star*): Vol.14

SEXTIE, William (animal painter; also in *Badminton*): Vol.1

SHARDLOW, William (commercial artist): Vol.16

SHARP, Felix (commercial artist): Vol.8

SPARROW, Charles (Canadian painter; also in *Captain*): Vol.14

SPILLER, Beatrice (fashion illustrator; also in *Badminton, Vogue, Tatler* and *Country Life*): Vols.5,7,13

STEWART, John (painted American hunting scenes): Vol.4

STRANGE, Christopher William (1878-1963; landscape and still-life artist): Vol.16

SWAINE, Frank Arthur (d.1952; illustrator and photographer; also in *Captain*): Vol.7

THOMAS, Cecil (1885-1967; studied at Slade and Heatherley Schools of Fine Art; sculptor, poster and commercial artist): Vols.2,10,11,15

THOMSON, Ernest (d.1925; painter, watercolourist and commercial artist): Vol.1

THOMSON, Robert Percy (1885-1961; studied at Glasgow School of Art; solicitor and military artist): Vol.2

TRESIDDER, Charles (illustrator; also in *Captain*): Vol.2,16

WUTHRICH, Ernst Arnold (studied at Institut Artistique Zurich): Vol.5

NAME INDEX

ABBOT, Clinton : Vol.16
ABBOTT, Eleanor : Vol.4
ABEL, Robert : Vol.1
ABSOLON, Charles : Vol.9
ADEMOLA, Ladapo : Vol.2
ADOLPH, Gustaf : Vol.1
ALCOCK, Charles : Vol.5
ALDERSON, Joseph : Vol.3
ALEXANDER, Frederick : Vol.11
ALEXANDER, George : Vol.1
ALFONSO, Dom : Vol.2
ALFRED, John : Vol.16
ALGER, John : Vol.9
ALKEN, Henry : Vol.1
ALLAN, Francis : Vol.10
ALLEN, Harold : Vol.18
ALLPORT, Douglas : Vol.3
ANSTEY, Thomas : Vol.5
ANTON, Edward : Vol.4
APTED, Samuel : Vol.11
ARCHER, William : Vol.5
ARNOLD, Edward : Vol.1
ARNOLD, Thomas : Vol.8
ARNOTT, Walter : Vol.3
AROUET, Francois : Vol.10
ASCHE, Oscar : Vol.16
ASHCROFT, Maynard : Vol.1
ASHFORD, William : Vol.16
ASPER, Clarence : Vol.19
ASQUITH, Herbert : Vols.3,4
ASSHETON-SMITH, Thomas : Vol.8
ASTLEY, John : Vols.6,7
ASTON, Edward : Vol.20
ASTON, Wilfred : Vol.21
ATKINS, John : Vol.2
ATTO, Joseph : Vol.19
AUNGIER, Julia : Vol.6
AUSTEN-LEIGH, Arthur : Vol.15
AXEL, Charles : Vol.2
AXEL, Christian : Vol.2
AYLESFORD, Neville : Vol.19
AYTON, Laurence : Vol.P,19

BACHE, Joseph : Vol.1
BACHELLER, Irving : Vol.6
BACON, Francis : Vol.15
BACON, George : Vol.13
BADCOCK, Gerald : Vol.19
BADDELEY, Thomas : Vol.1
BADEN-POWELL, Baden : Vol.11

BADEN-POWELL, Robert : Vol.7
BALFOUR, Arthur : Vols.1,3
BALFOUR, Gerald : Vol.1
BALFOUR-MELVILLE, Leslie : Vol.3
BALL, Thomas : Vol.P,18
BALSHAW, William : Vols.17,18
BANCROFT, Jack : Vol.21
BANKS, Alfred : Vol.8
BARBER, Horatio : Vol.18
BARING-GOULD, Sabine : Vol.6
BARKER, William : Vol.2
BARNES, George : Vols.7,9
BARNES, Sydney : Vol.P
BARRETT, Roper : Vol.13
BARRIE, James : Vol.3
BARSON, Robert : Vol.4
BARTHOLOMEW, John : Vols.5,8
BARTON, Townend : Vol.20
BASS, William : Vol.14
BATCHELOR, Gerald : Vol.21
BAZETT, Annesley : Vol.11
BEADLE, William : Vol.P
BEARD, Daniel : Vol.3
BECK, Henry : Vol.12
BEDELL-SIVWRIGHT, David : Vol.4
BEERBOHM-TREE, Herbert : Vol.3
BELL, Keble : Vol.P
BENETFINK, Samuel : Vol.17
BENNETT, Arnold : Vol.8
BENSON, Edward : Vols.12,21
BENSUSAN, Samuel : Vols.5,8
BERESFORD, Charles : Vol.2
BERESFORD, Henry : Vol.14
BERESFORD, John : Vol.16
BERNHARDT, Sarah : Vols.2,14
BETHAM, John : Vol.3
BEVINGTON, David : Vol.8
BIRCH, Arthur : Vol.12
BIRCH, Noel : Vol.7
BIRCH-REYNARDSON, Charles : Vol.8
BIRKETT, John : Vol.20
BLACKWELL, George : Vol.12
BLERIOT, Louis : Vol.12
BLOOMER, Stephen : Vol.4
BLYTHE, Colin : Vol.1
BOARD, Jack : Vol.1
BOILEAU, Etienne : Vol.8
BOTTOMLEY, Horatio : Vol.P,15
BOULTON, William : Vol.9
BOURCHIER, Arthur : Vol.2

BOURNE, Helena : Vol.12
BOWKER, Joseph : Vol.15
BOWMAN, Larrey : Vol.3
BRABAZON, Reginald : Vol.6
BRADLEY, Dennis : Vols.15,21
BRADSHAW, Annie : Vol.5
BRAID, James : Vols.3,4,15,16
BRASIER, Henri : Vol.11
BRAUND, Leonard : Vol.15
BRAWN, William : Vol.1
BREARLEY, Walter : Vol.P
BRITT, James : Vols.13,14
BRITTAIN, Harry : Vol.13
BRITTEN, Thomas : Vol.9
BRODRICK, Arthur : Vol.2
BROOKE, Leslie : Vol.4
BROOKES, Norman : Vol.21
BROOKS, Frederick : Vol.6
BROWN, Aaron : Vol.20
BROWN, Haigh : Vol 18
BROWN, Leonard : Vol.21
BROWNELL, Leverett : Vol.2
BROWN-POTTER, Cora : Vol.1
BRUCE, Alexander : Vol.2
BRUCE, William : Vol.15
BRUCE-KERR, John : Vol.21
BRYCE, James : Vol.4
BUCKNILL, Thomas : Vol.20
BUDD, Arthur : Vol.12
BUICK, Albert : Vol.1
BULLER, Redvers : Vol.9
BURGESS, Thomas : Vol.16
BURLTON, Clive : Vol.18
BURNABY, Samuel : Vol.11
BURNAND, Francis : Vol.4
BURNS, James : Vol.4
BURNS, John : Vol.4
BURNS, Walter : Vol.20
BURNS, William : Vol.15
BURROWS, Arthur : Vol.18
BURROWS, Thomas : Vol.8
BURT, Richard : Vol.5
BUSBEY, Hamilton : Vols.2,4
BUSH, Percy : Vol.10
BUTLER, Elisabeth : Vol.1
BUTLER, George : Vol.3
BUTLER, William : Vol.9
BUTT, Harry : Vols.1,3
BYRON, Josie : Vol.13

CAINE, Hall : Vols.1,6
CAINE, William : Vol.20

CAIRD, William : Vol.13
CALDICOTT, William : Vol.20
CAMBRIDGE, George : Vol.1
CAMPBELL, Alma : Vol.4
CAMPBELL, Beatrice : Vol.15
CAMPBELL, Colin : Vol.3
CAMPBELL, Francis : Vol.3
CAMPBELL, Gertrude : Vol.5
CAMPBELL, Reginald : Vol.2
CAMPBELL-BANNERMAN, Henry : Vol.4
CANE, Claude : Vol.1
CANFIELD, Henry : Vol.3
CANNON, Thomas : Vol.1
CANTLIE, James : Vol.5
CAREY, Alfred : Vol.11
CAREY, Jeanette : Vol.4
CARINGTON, Rupert : Vol.4
CARLOS, Dom : Vol.2
CARNE, Leslie : Vol.8
CARNEGIE, Andrew : Vol.4
CARNEGIE, William : Vol.11
CARPENTIER, Georges : Vols.19,21
CARTER, Samuel : Vol.8
CASTLE, Edward : Vol.7
CASTLE, Lewis : Vol.6
CASWALL, Edward : Vols.10,12
CATTON, Jimmy : Vol.P
CAVE-BROWNE-CAVE, Genille : Vol.10
CAVENDISH, Victor : Vol.2
CAXTON, Alfred : Vol.5
CHAMBERLAIN, Joseph : Vol.21
CHANDLER, Joseph : Vol.3
CHAPLIN, Herbert : Vol.15
CHAPMAN, Frederick : Vols.8,15
CHAWORTH-MUSTERS, John : Vol.8
CHARRON, Ferdinand : Vol.11
CHESTERTON, Gilbert : Vol.7
CHETWYND, George : Vol.12
CHILD-BAYLEY, Roger : Vols.7,8
CHURCH, Sidney : Vol.19
CHURCHILL, Winston : Vols.3,4,15
CLARRY, William : Vol.P
CLEASE, Meredith : Vol.14
CLEMENT, Adolphe : Vol.11
CLEMENCEAU, Georges : Vol.P
CLEMENTS, Alexander : Vol.20
COBBETT, William : Vol.15
CODY, Samuel : Vol.12
COKE, Henry : Vol.3
COLBURN, George : Vol.16
COLES, Percy : Vol.2
COLL, Ernest : Vol.4

COLLETT, Anthony : Vol.6
COLLIER, Charles : Vol.14
COLVILLE, Henry : Vol.8
COMMON, Alfred : Vol.1
COMPSTON, Archie : Vol.17
COMPTON, Herbert : Vol.1
CONNELL, William : Vol.6
CONWAY, Arthur : Vols.10,14
CONWAY, Martin : Vol.13
COOK, Charles : Vol.11
COOK, Theodore : Vols.9,14
COOPER, Arthur : Vols.6,14
COOPER, Seymour : Vols.18,19
COOTE, Nina : Vol.3
CORBETT, Bertie : Vols.6,10
CORBETT, James : Vol.13
CORBOULD-ELLIS, Cuthbert : Vol.P,21
CORBOULD-ELLIS, Eveline : Vol.P
CORELLI, Marie : Vol.2
CORNWALLIS, Kinahan : Vol.2
CORNWALLIS-WEST, Jeanette : Vol.11
COUPIN, Henri : Vol.6
COURTNEIDGE, Cicely : Vol.16
COVERDALE, Harry : Vol.20
COX, Jack : Vol.1
CRAIG, Albert : Vol.1
CRAVEN, Waldemar : Vol.20
CRAWFORD, Jack : Vol.P,5
CRAWFURD, Oswald : Vol.6
CRAWSHAW, Thomas : Vol.1
CRESSWELL, Beatrix : Vol.13
CREWE-MILNES, Robert : Vol.4
CRIBB, Thomas : Vol.9
CRICHTON, Madge : Vol.1
CROSSING, William : Vol.6
CUBITT, Thomas : Vol.12
CUMMING, Roualeyn : Vol.1
CUMMINGS, Gordon : Vol.8
CUNNINGHAM, John : Vol.9
CURTIS, Edward : Vol.7
CURTISS, Glenn : Vol.12
CUSTANCE, Harry : Vol.8

DALE, Frederic : Vol.19
DALMENY, Harry : Vol.8
DALZIEL, Hugh : Vol.11
DARE, Phyllis : Vol.16
DARLING, Samuel : Vol.11
DARRACQ, Alexandre : Vol.11
DAVEY, Fitzner : Vol.P
DAVIES, Alban : Vol.21
DAVIES, Charles : Vol.12

DAVIES, William : Vols.18,19
DAVIS, Alfred : Vol.16
DAVIS, Robert : Vol.19
DAWSON, Daniel : Vol.6
DAWSON, Kenneth : Vol.18
DAY, Samuel : Vol.1
DELAGRANGE, Leon : Vols.11,12
DENTON, David : Vol.1
DEROSIER, Jake : Vol.14
DEWAR, Thomas : Vol.3
DEWHURST, Robert : Vol.12
DICKENS, Charles : Vols.2,7,16
DICKINSON, Francis : Vol.8
DIGGLE, Edward : Vol.14
DILKE, Charles : Vol.2
DILLON, Bernard : Vol.19
DILLON, Edward : Vol.15
DISRAELI, Benjamin : Vol.8
DONOVAN, Henry : Vol.12
DORAN, Cyril : Vol.14
DOUGLAS, Johnny : Vol.P,21
DOUST, Stanley : Vol.21
DOUTY, Robert : Vol.16
DRISCOLL, James : Vol.18
DUKE, Joshua : Vol.11
DUNN, Archibald : Vol.11
DUNN, Arthur : Vol.3
DUNNE, John : Vols.8,11
DUNNESMYTH, Oliver : Vol.15
DWIGHT, Jonathan : Vol.2
DYER, Edward : Vol.4
DYKE, Henry van : Vol.5

EAST, William : Vol.2
EATON, Herbert : Vol.9
EATON-FEARN, James : Vol.11
EDWARDES, George : Vol.15
EGERTON, Granville : Vol.10
ELEY, William : Vol.4
ELLIOTT, Clarence : Vol.20
ELLIS, Beth : Vol.8
ELLISTON-ERWOOD, Frank : Vol.14
ELSIE, Lily : Vol.16
ESCOFFIER, Auguste : Vol.14
ESMOND, Henry : Vol.1
ESNAULT-PELTERIE, Robert : Vol.12
ETHERINGTON-SMITH, Raymond : Vols.9,19
EVANS, Charles : Vol.15
EVANS, Herbert : Vol.4
EVELEGH, Carter : Vol.13
EVETT, Robert : Vol.16
EWART, Henry : Vol.1

EYRE-TODD, George : Vol.6

FALLON, Walter : Vol.10
FANE, Frederick : Vol.1
FARMAN, Henry : Vols.12,13
FARRANDS, Frank : Vol.5
FAULKNER, Aubrey : Vol.19
FEA, Allan : Vol.20
FERNANDEZ, Francisco : Vol.20
FINDLAY, Frederick : Vol.1
FIRTH-SCOTT, George : Vol.7
FISHER, John : Vol.1
FITZPATRICK, Percy : Vol.8
FITZSIMMONS, Robert : Vol.13
FLAMMARION, Camille : Vol.5
FLEMING, James : Vol.13
FLEMING, Paul : Vol.11
FLEMING, Valentine : Vol.12
FLETCHER, William : Vol.15
FORD, Henry : Vol.21
FORD, Lionel : Vol.2
FORDHAM, George : Vols.7,8
FORREST, Archibald : Vol.5
FOSTER, Basil : Vol.16
FOSTER, Ciceley : Vol.3
FOSTER, Harry : Vol.15
FOSTER, Michael : Vol.1
FREESTON, Charles : Vol.14
FRICKER, Edgar : Vol.1
FROITZHEIM, Otto : Vol.13
FROST, Albert : Vol.18
FRY, Joseph : Vol.10
FULTON, Arthur : Vol.19

GAGE, Henry : Vols.5-8
GAME, Francis : Vol.P
GARDINER, Alfred : Vol.21
GARNETT, Harold : Vol.1
GAST, Camille du : Vol.5
GAUNT, Charles : Vol.21
GENTRY, Aubrey : Vol.P,15
GEORGE, Walter : Vol.7
GEORGE, William : Vol.10
GERARD, Montague : Vol.2
GIBBS, Philip : Vol.20
GIBSON, Alfred : Vols.5,6
GILBEY, Walter : Vols.1,3
GILLIES, Harold : Vol.21
GILPIN, Peter : Vol.12
GINISTRELLI, Eduardo : Vol.9
GLADSTONE, Herbert : Vol.4
GLASFURD, Alexander : Vol.3

GODWIN, George : Vol.9
GOLD, Harcourt : Vol.15
GOLWALLA, Dady : Vol.5
GOLWALLA, Framroze : Vol.5
GOOD, John : Vol.13
GOODMAN, Robert : Vol.20
GORDON, Armyne : Vol.1
GORDON, Panmure : Vol.16
GORDON, William : Vols.14,16
GORDON-BENNETT, James : Vol.1
GORELL-BARNES, Frederic : Vol.1
GOULD, Nathaniel : Vols.9,10,13,14
GOWER, Lily : Vol.1
GRACE, Edward : Vol.3
GRADIDGE, Herbert : Vol.13
GRADIDGE, Thomas : Vol.13
GRADIDGE, Timothy : Vols.3,9
GRANVILLE-BAKER, Bernard : Vol.15
GRAVES, Cecil : Vols.19-21
GRAVES, Ralph : Vol.13
GRAY, George : Vols.14,17,20
GRECIA, Emmanuel : Vol.3
GREEN, Eric : Vol.12
GREEN, John : Vol.8
GREENALL, Gilbert : Vol.P,16
GREENE, Evie : Vol.1
GREENER, William : Vol.9
GREHAN, Mary : Vol.21
GRENFELL, William : Vols.3,5,9
GREVILLE, Frances : Vol.1
GREY, Vivian : Vol.6
GRIGGS, Walter : Vol.7
GRIGGS, William : Vol.19
GROSSMITH, George : Vol.1
GROSVENOR, Hugh : Vol.1
GRUHN, Ferdinand : Vol.1
GUEST, Montague : Vol.9
GULLY, John : Vol.12
GUNN, George senior : Vol.1
GUSTON, George : Vol.6
GWYNN, Stephen : Vol.7

HAIG, Alexander : Vol.2
HAIG-BROWN, William : Vol.3
HALL, Marshall : Vol.3
HALL, Millicent : Vols.7,20
HAMILTON, Edward : Vol.19
HAMILTON, Ian : Vol.7
HAMILTON-REYNOLDS, John : Vols.15,16
HAMMOND, Charles : Vol.5
HANCOCK, Irving : Vol.3
HANDS, Reginald : Vol.18

HANLAN, Edward : Vol.8
HARBY, Harry : Vols.10,11
HARDING, Arthur : Vol.6
HARGREAVE, Samuel : Vol.1
HARLEY, Henry : Vol.10
HARNETT, George : Vol.2
HARPER, Charles : Vols.6,16
HARPER, Claude : Vol.P,20
HARRIS, George : Vol.16
HARRISON, Frederic : Vols.10-12
HARRISON, William : Vol.17
HART-DAVIES, Ivan : Vol.15
HARTING, James : Vol.5
HARTLEY, Bernard : Vol.20
HARTLEY, Cecil : Vol.21
HARWAR, Ernest : Vol.3
HASELTINE, Herbert : Vol.21
HATT, Doris : Vol.4
HAWKER, Peter : Vol.10
HAWKINS, Henry : Vols.1,8
HAWLEY, Arthur : Vol.17
HAWLEY, Joseph : Vol.1
HAYES, Ernest : Vol.1
HAYWARD, Thomas : Vols.5,6
HEALY, Christopher : Vol.2
HEARNE, Jack : Vol.1
HEATH, Sidney : Vol.5
HEBERT, Alan : Vol.11
HEDGES-BUTLER, Frank : Vol.11
HENDERSON, Charles : Vol.2
HENHAM, Ernest : Vol.6
HENRY, William : Vol.9
HERBERT, Agnes : Vols.8,10,16
HERBERT, Alan : Vol.11
HERBERT, Charles : Vol.3
HEYWOOD, Thomas : Vol.17
HICKS, Seymour : Vol.1
HIGGS, William : Vol.19
HILL, Percy : Vols.12,13
HILL, Rowland : Vol.19
HIRST, George : Vols.1,5,15
HODGSON, Earl : Vol.3
HODGSON, William : Vol.2
HOHENZOLLERN, Wilhelm : Vol.1
HOLE, Reynolds : Vol.7
HOLLAND, Sydney : Vol.3
HOLMES, Robert : Vol.1
HOLT, Arden : Vol.3
HOME, Beatrice : Vol.14
HOOKER, Joseph : Vol.8
HOPE-MONCRIEFF, Robert : Vol.13
HORNADAY, William : Vol.11

HORNBY, Albert Henry : Vol.21
HORNBY, James : Vol.3
HORNE, Silvester : Vol.3
HORNSBY, Michael : Vol.13
HORTON, Robert : Vol.2
HORTON, William : Vol.17
HOWARD, Endersly : Vols.P,18-20
HUDSON, Frank : Vols.9,11
HUEFFER, Ford : Vol.5
HUEFFER, Oliver : Vol.20
HUMPHRIES, Joseph : Vol.1
HUNTLEY, George : Vol.16
HUTTON, William : Vol.1
HYNE, Cutcliffe : Vol.8

INKSON-MCCONNOCHIE, Alexander : Vol.10
INMAN, Melbourne : Vols.14,20
INNES, Frederick : Vol.11
IREDALE, Frank : Vol.8
IRVING, Ethel : Vol.16
IRVING-HAMILTON, William : Vol.P,21

JACKSON, Stanley : Vol.3
JARVIS, Clara : Vol.20
JEFFERIES, Walter : Vol.16
JEFFRIES, James : Vol.13
JEFFRIES, Richard : Vol.6
JEKYLL, Gertrude : Vol.20
JENATZY, Camille : Vol.1
JEROME, Jerome : Vol.2
JEUNE, Francis : Vol.1
JOHNSON, Jack : Vols.9,16,20
JOHNSON, Randall : Vol.15
JOHNSON, Stanley : Vols.18,19
JOHNSTON, John : Vol.9
JOHNSTON, William : Vol.21
JOHNSTONE, William : Vol.4
JONES, Arthur : Vols.1,10
JONES, Edison : Vol.6
JONES, Herbert : Vol.15
JONES, Kennedy : Vol.P
JORDAN, Alfred : Vol.13
JOY, Lilian : Vol.7
JOYNER, Andrew : Vol.11
JUPP, Claude : Vol.2

KARSLAKE, Harold : Vols.13,14
KEIRAN, Bernard : Vol.3
KEIGWIN, Richard : Vol.20
KENEALY, Arabella : Vol.2
KENT, Kenneth : Vols.18,19
KERNAHAN, Coulson : Vol.10

KERR, John : Vol.2
KERRIDGE, Albert : Vol.5
KETCHELL, Stanley : Vol.13
KINGSLEY, Charles : Vols.2,20
KINNAIRD, Arthur : Vol.20
KIPLING, Rudyard : Vols.6,7
KNIGHT, Charles : Vol.17
KNIGHT, John : Vols.10,11
KNOX, Neville : Vol.P
KYLE, Robert : Vol.4

LACEY, Francis : Vol.21
LAIDLAY, John : Vol.3
LAMBERT-CHAMBERS, Dorothea : Vol.13
LAMBTON, George : Vol.12
LANCASTER, Charles : Vols.4,16
LANG, Andrew : Vol.19
LANG, Mervyn : Vol.11
LANGFORD, Samuel : Vols.11,13
LANGLANDS, John : Vol.17
LANGTON, Lawrence : Vol.20
LARNED, William : Vol.13
LARNER, George : Vol.2
LASCELLES, Gerald : Vol.19
LASSEN, Edward : Vol.10
LATHAM, Hubert : Vol.12
LATHAM, Peter : Vol.4
LAUDER, Harry : Vol.16
LAVER, Frank : Vol.3
LAWLESS, Philip : Vol.20
LEAKE, Alec : Vol.1
LEBLOND, Elizabeth : Vol.8
LEES, James : Vol.18
LEES, Peter : Vol.4
LEFEBVRE, Lucien : Vol.12
LENO, Dan : Vol.4
LESTER, Kate : Vol.6
LEWIS, Alfred : Vol.8
LILLEY, Arthur : Vol.4
LINCOLN, Abraham : Vol.9
LINDLEY, Percy : Vols.5,13
LINDLEY, Tinsley : Vol.3
LINDRUM, Frederick : Vol.14
LIPTON, Thomas : Vol.10
LITTLE, May : Vol.10
LLOYD, Henry : Vol.18
LLOYD, Richard : Vol.21
LLOYD-GEORGE, David : Vol.3
LOCKWOOD, William : Vol.1
LODGE, Oliver : Vol.1
LOHMANN, George : Vol.2
LONG, Mabel : Vol.10

LONG, Walter : Vol.3
LONG, William : Vol.4
LORAINE, Arthur : Vol.15
LOWE, Bruce : Vol.7
LOWTHER, Hugh : Vols.2,19
LYNCH, Jeremiah : Vol.1
LYNHAM, Barrington : Vol.19
LYONS, Albert : Vol.6
LYONS, Joseph : Vol.14
LYTTELTON, Alfred : Vols.1,3,19,20
LYTTELTON, Edward : Vols.3,12,20
LYTTELTON, Neville : Vols.14,20

MCCELLAND, Alexander : Vol.20
MCCLELLAND, Alfred : Vols.20,21
MCCLURE, William : Vol.21
MCCONNELL, Dunbar : P
MCCONNELL, Primrose : Vol.7
MCCORMICK, Joseph : Vols.5,21
MACDONALD, Alexander : Vol.8
MCDONALD, Herbert : Vol.21
MCDONNELL, Percy : Vol.3
MCDOWALL, John : Vol.4
MACDUFF, Alexander : Vol.2
MCEWAN, James : Vol.1
MCGAHEY, Charles : Vols.1,15
MACGREGOR, Gregor : Vol.1
MCGOUGH, John : Vol.4
MCINTOSH, Hugh : Vol.14
MCKENNA, Reginald : Vol.3
MACKENZIE, William : Vol.19
MACLEAN, Francis : Vol.18
MACLEAR, Basil : Vol.8
MCMAHON, Alexander : Vol.3
MACNAGHTEN, Edward : Vol.3
MACNAMARA, Thomas : Vol.1
MACPHERSON, William : Vol.6
MADDEN, Dodgson : Vol.9
MADDEN, Otto : Vol.19
MADELEY, James : Vol.19
MAETERLINCK, Maurice : Vol.7
MAHER, Daniel : Vols.11,19
MAHONY, Harold : Vol.3
MALFIANCE, Albert : Vol.11
MANN, Horace : Vol.15
MANNING, Thomas : Vol.15
MANNOCK, John : Vol.2
MARLOWE, Charles : Vol.17
MARRIOTT, Charles : Vol.20
MARSH, Charles : Vol.5
MARSH, Richard : Vols.11,15
MARSHALL, Percival : Vol.4

MARSHAM, Cloudesley : Vol.1
MARSON, Charles : Vol.2
MARTIN, John : Vol.19
MASELEY, James : Vol.19
MASON, Hugh : Vol.19
MAUDE, Cyril : Vol.2
MAXTEE, John : Vol.11
MAXWELL, Herbert : Vol.8
MAXWELL, Patrick : Vol.9
MAXWELL, William : Vol.6
MAY, John : Vol.4
MAY, Walter : Vol.1
MEIKLEJOHN, George : Vol.21
MELVILLE, John : Vol.4
MENARD, Victor : Vol.18
MENZIES, Amy : Vol.20
MENZIES, Stuart : Vol.20
MERCEDES, Jelineck : Vol.11
MEREDITH, Billy : Vol.4
MEREDITH, George : Vol.2
MEREDITH, Leon : Vol.2
MERRIMAN, Henry : Vol.6
MESSENGER, Charles : Vol.19
METHUEN, Algernon : Vol.P
MEYER, Olga de : Vol.1
MEYNELL, Esther : Vols.4-6
MEYSEY-THOMPSON, Richard : Vol.8
MILLAIS, John E. : Vol.1
MILLAIS, John G. : Vol.1
MILLAR, Gertrude : Vol.16
MILLER, Edward : Vol.21
MILLER, Peat : Vol.4
MILLS, John : Vol.20
MILTOUN, Francis : Vol.5
MINCHIN, Charles : Vol.16
MITCHELL, Horace : P
MITTON, Geraldine : Vol.2
MIYAKE, Taro : Vol.5
MOBBS, Edgar : Vol.12
MOLES, Thomas : Vol.P,20
MOLESWORTH, William : Vol.14
MOLIER, Ernest : Vols.13,14
MONET, Claude : Vol.P
MONEY, Albert : Vol.3
MONTAGU, William : Vol.2
MOORE, Decima : Vol.1
MOORE, Frederick : Vol.5
MOORE, Charles : Vol.17
MOORE, Kathleen : Vol.20
MOORE, Richardson : Vol.14
MOORE, Vernon : Vol.18
MORAN, Hugh : Vol.12

MORGAN, Edward : Vol.6
MORRIS, Malcolm : Vol.3
MORRISON-BELL, Arthur : Vol.7
MORRISON-BELL, Clive : Vol.6
MORTIMER, Francis : Vol.6
MOSS, William : Vol.4
MOTT, Lawrence : Vols.4,8
MUIR-MACKENZIE, Susan : Vol.3
MUNDAY, Luther : Vol.17
MURDOCH, William : Vol.15
MYNN, Alfred : Vol.7
MYTTON, Jack : Vol.9

NAISH, Percy : Vol.19
NASH, Thomas : Vol.17
NAZZARO, Felice : Vol.7
NEEDHAM Ernest : Vol.3
NEEDHAM, Raymond : Vols.19-21
NELSON, Horatio : Vol.4
NETHERSOLE, Olga : Vol.1
NEVILL, Dorothy : Vol.8
NEVILL, Ralph : Vol.8
NEWBOLT, Henry : Vol.21
NEWNES, George : Vol.P
NEWTON, Isaac : Vol.5
NEWTON-ROBINSON, Charles : Vol.9
NICHOLL, Vera : Vol.2
NICHOLLS, Gwyn : Vol.6
NIGHTINGALL, Arthur : Vol.9
NOEL, Evan : Vol.5
NORMAN, Francis : Vol.4
NORRIS, John : Vol.11
NORTHCOTE, Henry : Vol.6
NYREN, John : Vol.5

OATES, Coape : Vol.3
O'CONNOR, Thomas : Vol.17
OGDEN, James : Vol.17
OGLETHORPE, Henry : Vol.20
O'GORMAN, Mervyn : Vol.10
O'HARA, Charles : Vol.17
O'SULLIVAN, Charles : Vol.11
OUIMET, Francis : Vol.20
OUSELEY, John : Vol.15

PADLEY, Arthur : Vols.9,10
PAPE, William : Vol.11
PARKER, Harry : Vol.11
PARMLY-PARET, Jahial : Vol.2
PARTMAN, Lionel : Vol.8
PASSMORE, Walter : Vol.16
PATTERSON, Arthur : Vols.8,11

PATTERSON, John : Vol.8
PATTERSON, William : Vol.11
PAULHAN, Louis : Vol.12
PAYN, Frederick : Vol.4
PAYNE-GALLWEY, Ralph : Vols.11,12
PEARCE, Ernest : Vol.17
PEARSON, Arthur : Vol.21
PECK, Percy : Vol.12
PEMBERTON, Max : Vols.1,3,4
PERCY, James : Vol.6
PERETY, Mark : Vol.21
PERKS, Robert : Vol.4
PETHICK, Thomas : Vol.4
PHILLPOTTS, Eden : Vols.5,6
PHIPPS, William : Vol.8
PICKERING, Ursula : Vol.19
PICKFORD, Anutot : Vol.7
PICKFORD, William : Vols.5,6
PILLMAN, Charles : Vol.20
PITMAN, Charles : Vol.15
POLLARD, James : Vol.2
PONSONBY, Vera : Vol.3
POORE, Robert : Vol.19
POTTER-IRWIN, Frank : Vol.18
POULTON, Ronald : Vols.20,21
PRATT, Anne : Vol.3
PRIMROSE, Archibald : Vol.20

QUILLER-COUCH, Arthur : Vol.5

RADCLYFFE-DUGMORE, Arthur : Vols.13,14
RALEIGH, Cecil : Vol.13
RAMEE, Marie de la : Vol.20
RANKIN, Margaret : Vol.5
RAVENSCROFT, George : Vols.20,21
RAY, Edward : Vols.18-20
RAY, Gabrielle : Vol.16
READ, Stanford : Vol.6
REECE, Thomas : Vol.20
REES, Powell : Vol.10
REEVE, John : Vol.6
REID, Jack : Vol.4
REID, Robert : Vol.4
REID, Wilfrid : Vol.P,19
RENAULT, Louis : Vol.11
RENSHAW, William : Vol.2
REY, Guido : Vol.8
REYNOLDS-BALL, Eustace : Vols.2,16
RHODES, Cecil : Vols.11,21
RICE, Samuel : Vol.20
RICE, Stanley : Vols.20,21
RICHARDSON, Edwin : Vol.21

RICHARDSON, Ryder : Vol.9
RICHARDSON, Thomas : Vol.1
RITCHIE, Josiah : Vols.3,21
RITCHIE, Wallace : Vol.17
RIXON, Guy : Vol.2
ROBERTS, Charles [Billiards]: Vol.4
ROBERTS, Francis : Vol.9
ROBERTS, Frederick : Vols.P,1,4,9
ROBERTS, Geoffrey : Vol.20
ROBERTS, John : Vol.3
ROBERTSON, Forbes : Vol.1
ROBERTSON, Jack : Vols.1,17
ROBEY, George : Vols.8,16
ROBINSON, Frederick : Vol.2
ROLLAND, Douglas : Vol.13
ROLYAT, Dan : Vol.16
ROMANOV, Nicholas : Vol.2
ROOSEVELT, Archibald : Vol.1
ROOSEVELT, Theodore : Vols.1,2,4,5,13
ROSE, Gerald : Vol.13
ROSE, Ralph : Vol.1
ROSS, Margaret : Vol.5
ROTHSCHILD, Walter : Vol.1
RUDMOSE-BROWN, Robert : Vol.7
RUMFORD, Kennerley : Vol.1
RUMNEY, Abraham : Vol.9
RUSSELL, Arthur : Vols.3,14
RUSSELL, Charles : Vol.5
RUTZEN, Albert de : Vol.3
RYDALL, Edward : Vol.10
RYDER, Rowland : Vol.15
RYE, Walter : Vol.11

ST.JOHN, Charles : Vols.11,16-19
ST.JOHN, Frederick : Vol.19
SACHS, Frank : Vol.17
SALOMONS, David : Vol.3
SALVESEN, Edward : Vol.4
SAMUEL, Marcus : Vol.9
SAUNDERS, Henry : Vol.18
SANTOS-DUMONT, Alberto : Vols.1,6,12
SCARTH-DIXON, William : Vol.19
SCHILLINGS, Carl : Vol.7
SCOTT-MONTAGU, John : Vols.1,4-6,9
SCOTTER, Gordon : Vol.19
SCROPE, Christopher : Vols.4,8,10
SCUDAMORE, Frank : Vol.8
SENIOR, William : Vol.1
SERVICE, Robert : Vol.21
SETON, Grace : Vols.8,10
SEWELL, Christopher : Vol.19
SHACKLETON, Ernest : Vol.21

SHAKESPEARE, John : Vol.1
SHARP, Arthur : Vols.12,19
SHAW, Alfred : Vol.3
SHAW, Lewis : Vol.4
SHAW, Vero : Vol.7
SHAYER, Joseph : Vol.2
SHEARMAN, Montague : Vol.21
SHEPHERD, Edward : Vol.9
SHEPHERD, James : Vol.20
SHEPPEE, Albert : Vol.17
SHERLEY, Alfred : Vol.20
SHERWELL, Percy : Vol.7
SHIPTON, Ernest : Vol.3
SHOLTO-DOUGLAS, John : Vol.8
SHORTER, Clement : Vol.13
SHRUBB, Alfred : Vols.1,2
SHUFFREY, James : Vol.20
SHUTER, Jack : Vol.21
SIEVIER, Robert : Vols.6,14
SIMMONDS, Lester : Vol.19
SIMPSON, John : Vol.16
SIMS, George : Vol.1
SINCLAIR, Upton : Vol.5
SKIPTON, Ernest : Vol.3
SLAUSON, Harold : Vol.17
SLOSS, Robert : Vol.5
SMITH, Aubrey : Vol.16
SMITH, Edward : Vol.21
SMITH, James : Vol.13
SMITH, Sydney : Vols.6,21
SMITH, Thomas : Vols.14,17
SMITH, William : Vol.2
SMITH-TURBERVILLE, Harry : Vol.19
SMITHSON, Florence : Vol.16
SMYTH, Walter : Vol.13
SNAITH, John : Vol.6
SOMMER, Roger : Vol.12
SOUTAR, Daniel : Vol.8
SOUTH, Richard : Vol.5
SOUTHEBY, Laurence : Vols.19,20
SPENDER, Percival : Vol.11
SPIKSLEY, Frederick : Vol.3
STAFFORD, Frederick : Vol.17
STANER, Herbert : Vol.5
STANHOPE, Charles : Vol.1
STANNARD, Henrietta : Vol.2
STANTON, Henry : Vol.18
STEAD, Alfred : Vol.5
STEBBING, Edward : Vol.16
STEENSON, Martin : Vol.4
STEFAN, Carl : Vol.1
STEINMANN, Maurice : Vol.11

STEPHENS, Davy : Vol.1
STEPHENS, William : Vol.1
STEVENS, Frederick : Vol.4
STEVENSON, Alexander : Vol.3
STEVENSON, Robert : Vol.4
STEWART, William : Vol.4
STEWART-RICHARDSON, Constance : Vols.2,6
STIVENS, John : Vol.1
STOCKEN, Harry : Vol.19
STODDART, Andrew : Vol.9
STOKES, Charles : Vol.10
STOKES, Vernon : Vol.20
STONE, Geoffrey : Vol.1
STONE, Harris : Vols.6,19
STOOP, Adrian : Vols.6,14,20
STOREY, Harry : Vol.7
STRANG-WATKINS, Watkin : Vol.16
STRUTT, Joseph : Vol.14
STUART, Douglas : Vol.15
STUART, Leslie : Vol.3
STUART, Maud : Vol.6
STUDHOLME, Marie : Vol.16
SULLIVAN, John : Vol.13
SUTHERLAND, James : Vol.20
SUTTON, Martin : Vol 18
SWEENEY, John : Vol.2

TAFT, William : Vols.9,14
TATE, Harry : Vol.16
TAYLOR, Alec : Vol.11
TERRISS, Ellaline : Vols.1,16
TERRY, Ellen : Vol.5
THOMAS, Ralph : Vol.2
THOMAS, William : Vol.8
THOMPSON, Alfred : Vol.1
THOMPSON, Francis : Vol.6
THOMPSON, Hugh : Vol.2
THOMPSON-SETON, Ernest : Vol.6
THOMSON, Edward : Vol.16
TISSANDIER, Paul : Vol.12
TOD, Ewen : Vol.10
TOMPKINS, Herbert : Vol.6
TRAVERS, Jerome : Vols.11,19,20
TRELOAR, William : Vol.2
TREVES, Frederick : Vol.6
TREVOR, Roy : Vol.11
TUCKEY, Charles : Vol.20
TURNBULL, Robert : Vol.14
TWAIN, Mark : Vol.12
TWEDDELL, Ethel : Vol.10
TYLDESLEY, John : Vol.5

UNDERHILL, George : Vol.2
UNGER, Frederick : Vol.7
UPWARD, Allen : Vol.1

VARDON, Harry : Vols.P,13,15,18-21
VASSALL, Harry : Vol.12
VAUIX, Henry de la : Vols.11,18
VAY, Adelina : Vol.1
VINCENT, Howard : Vol.9
VINE, Joseph : Vol.1
VOGLER, Ernest : Vol.3

WADDINGTON, Samuel : Vol.14
WALKER, Charles : Vol.19
WALL, Frederick : Vol.9
WALL, John : Vol.20
WALLER, Lewis : Vol.14
WALTON, Izaak : Vol.19
WALTON, James : Vol.4
WANOSTROCHT, Nicholas : Vol.7
WARD, Joseph : Vol.7
WARING, Nicholas : Vols.12,13
WARRE, Edmond : Vols.1,3,14
WASHINGTON, George : Vol.9
WAUGH, William : Vol.12
WEAVER, Laurence : Vol.20
WEBB, Matthew : Vol.7
WEBBE, Alexander : Vol.1
WEBSTER, Richard : Vol.3
WELHAM, Frederick : Vol.11
WELLINGS, George : Vol.13
WELLS, Herbert : Vol.6
WETHERED, Frank : Vol.2
WHITAKER, Percy : Vol.17
WHITE, Arthur : Vol.7
WHITE, Jack : Vols.P,3,18
WHITNEY, Caspar : Vols.7,20
WIEHE, Charlotte : Vol.1
WILBAR, Lincoln : Vol.11
WILL, John : Vol.21
WILL, William : Vol.P

WILLIAM-POWLETT, Barton : Vol.13
WILLIAMS, Owen : Vol.13
WILLIAMS-BENN, John : Vol.2
WILLIAMSON, Archibald : Vol.13
WILLMOTT-DIXON, William : Vol.19
WILLOUGHBY, Leonard : Vol.21
WILSON, Constance : Vol.1
WILSON, George : Vols.1,4
WINDHAM, Walter : Vol.11
WINDISCHGRATZ, Hugo : Vol.1
WINDT, Harry de : Vol.9
WINNINGTON-INGRAM, Arthur : Vol.1
WODEHOUSE, Pelham : Vols.2,11
WOLSELEY, Frances : Vol.3
WOOD, Charles : Vol.19
WOOD, Hickory : Vol.4
WOODWARD, Vivian : Vol.1
WOON, Harry : Vol.11
WOOTTON, Frank : Vols.13,17,19,20
WORKMAN, William : Vol.2
WORTHING, Ernest : Vol.17
WRAGGE, Clement : Vol.5
WRIGHT, Alan : Vol.12
WRIGHT, Charles : Vol.16
WRIGHT, Howard : Vol.18
WRIGHT, Huntley : Vol.16
WRIGHT, Levi : Vol.15
WRIGHT, Orville : Vols.9,12
WRIGHT, Thomas : Vol.11
WRIGHT, Walter : Vols.7,14
WRIGHT, Wilbur : Vols.9,12
WRIGHT, William : Vol.21
WYLLIE, William : Vol.12
WYNTER, Maud : Vol.8

YEO, Burney : Vol.3
YOUNG, Filson : Vol.2

ZOLA, Emile : Vol.P
ZUYLER, Etienne de : Vol.11

Fry's Heritage Plaque